RINGO

RINGO
WITH A LITTLE HELP

Michael Seth Starr

Backbeat
Books

AN IMPRINT OF HAL LEONARD CORPORATION

Published in 2015 by Backbeat Books
An Imprint of Hal Leonard Corporation
7777 West Bluemound Road
Milwaukee, WI 53213

Trade Book Division Editorial Offices
33 Plymouth St., Montclair, NJ 07042

Every reasonable effort has been made to contact copyright holders and secure permissions. Omissions can be remedied in future editions.

Printed in the United States of America

Book design by Michael Kellner.

Library of Congress Cataloging-in-Publication Data is available upon request.

ISBN 978-1-61713-120-2

www.backbeatbooks.com

Contents

Introduction

Let's get it out of the way so we can move on.

No, we're not related. I was born with that last name. He wasn't. It's just a happy coincidence.

Why *not*? He's The World's Most Famous Drummer.

It's not a book about Them. So don't expect a year-by-year, blow-by-blow account of the band's internal life and/or minutiae regarding their recording sessions, etc. It's all been documented exhaustively elsewhere.

They do, of course, "loom large in his legend," to steal a line from George Harrison referring to his band's drummer in *A Hard Day's Night*. This book would likely have been non-existent had not John Lennon, Paul McCartney, and Harrison fired Pete Best in August 1962 and invited Ringo Starr to join them in The Beatles.

No one knows how Ringo Starr's life would have turned out if he had said "No thanks" to Messrs. Lennon, McCartney, and Harrison and stayed loyal to Rory Storm and the Hurricanes, with whom he'd spent the previous four years thwacking away on his drums.

Ringo likely would have taken the spotlight with Rory and the Hurricanes for his mid-set "Starr Time" turn, singing "Boys" in his flat, nasal baritone and basking in the adulation of the hometown fans. Maybe he'd get his photo, and perhaps even a mention or two, in the *Liverpool Echo* or *Mersey Beat* magazine.

And then, like so many other Liverpool musical favorites from that era relegated to yellowed scrapbook clippings, he would likely have been swept into the dustbin of history— watching in awe and envy as The Beatles (and a drummer not named Pete Best) changed the world within a year.

But he didn't say "No thanks." And that's why this book exists.

"I'm here because it happened," Ringo once said, several years after The Beatles were, well, *The Beatles*. "But I didn't do anything to make it happen apart from saying 'Yes.'"

Classic, understated Ringo. He was already considered the best drummer in Liverpool—indeed, in the entire northern part of England—when John, Paul, and George offered him the job. He almost didn't take it—there was another local band who wanted his services—but The Beatles were offering more money. It was a no-brainer.

So Ringo Starr said yes, and The Beatles have defined his life, for better or worse, for the past fifty-three years. He was the oldest Beatle in age but was the last to join the group, and the ride lasted just eight short years, although it seems like a lifetime in history's rear-view mirror.

But The Beatles made Ringo Starr wealthy beyond his wildest dreams and vaulted him into the firmament of one-named icons alongside Marilyn, Cher, Madonna, Frank, Elvis, et al.

So, yes, John, Paul, and George, along with other Beatle insiders (Neil Aspinall, Mal Evans, George Martin, Brian Epstein, et al.), figure prominently into Ringo Starr's life story from 1962 to 1970, when it all began with so much giddiness and hope—and ended with such acrimony and finger-pointing.

But my goal in writing *Ringo: With a Little Help* is to walk the reader through the entire narrative arc of Ringo Starr's life, from his birth as Richard Starkey in Liverpool through the present-day—and all the important and remarkable milestones in-between.

John, Paul, and George did not, as you will see, disappear from Ringo Starr's life after The Beatles broke up. Like him, they all pursued solo careers with varying degrees of success and got on with their lives. Each of them traveled very different roads. But they continued to flit in and out of Ringo's orbit, and he theirs.

Paul McCartney continues to guest-star in Ringo's life; John and George, if they were still alive, probably would, too. After all, good old "Ring" was always the amiable peacemaker. His "brothers" never stopped loving him, or he them. So you'll read about John, Paul, and George every now and then in the narrative following Ringo's life after 1970.

But you will also read about much more, starting with Richy Starkey's sickly childhood growing up in the Dingle, one of Liverpool's toughest areas, where he was raised by a single mother who worked several jobs to keep a roof over her beloved son's head and food on the table. (And, yes, he spelled "Richy" without the "e.")

You will also read about young Richy's emergence as a locally renowned drummer, while he was working as an apprentice joiner, and the influence of fellow Liverpudlian Rory Storm on his early career. You will also read about the years following the breakup of The Beatles, when Ringo started strongly out of the gate as a top-selling solo recording artist—which eventually gave way to the dissolution of his marriage to hometown girl Maureen Cox, the mother of his three children.

Once he was in the wilderness—a celebrity lost at sea, searching for some meaning in his life—Ringo had a tough time finding his way out. There were two booze-soaked, jet-setting decades carousing with Harry Nilsson, Keith Moon, et al., a music and acting career on life support, and, ultimately, his inevitable spiral into alcoholism.

You will also read about Ringo Starr's eventual triumphs, spurred by his marriage to Barbara Bach, the couple's lifesaving stint in rehab and Ringo's rebirth as a clean-living children's television star and elder statesman of rock—delighting a generation of kids as Mr. Conductor on *Shining Time Station*, touring with his family-friendly All-Starr Band, raising money for charities, writing books, and selling various products.

And, yes, still (grudgingly) answering endless questions about The Beatles.

What you won't find in *Ringo: With a Little Help*, are any overt judgments, from this author, on Ringo Starr's technical skills as a drummer vis-à-vis The Beatles. That's one of those endless arguments among Beatles fans best waged in barrooms and on the Internet. It could be a book in itself, and maybe one day will be. I'm not a musician—I played the drums, badly, for a spell in my teen years—but, for the record, I think Ringo's steady backbeat and unflashy style was perfectly suited to The Beatles and their sound.

And, let's face it: you can't change history. That's Ringo Starr's drumming you hear on all of the group's immortal hits, from their first number-one single ("Please Please Me") to their last number-one hit ("The Long and Winding Road") and nearly everything in-between. It speaks for itself. Get over it.

I have, in the following pages, noted some instances where Ringo's drumming was criticized—and even some instances where Ringo himself mentioned the criticism. So it can't be completely glossed over. It's there. But I have also included sections in the book's narrative where his skills as a drummer were praised—in one instance by D. J. Fontana, Elvis Presley's drummer who worked with Ringo in Memphis in the mid-'80s, on the ill-fated Chips Moman sessions. "He had the greatest conception of tempo I've ever heard in my life," Fontana said.

And I don't think anyone who lived through Beatlemania can doubt the influence Ringo Starr had on the world of rock and roll drumming, particularly for kids in America seeing The Beatles for the first time on *The Ed Sullivan Show* in February 1964.

I do question, though, why some music fans continue to focus on Ringo's skills as The Beatles' timekeeper, and never seem to argue the merits of George Harrison's chops as a lead guitarist or John Lennon's skills as a rhythm guitarist. (Paul McCartney's bass-playing is beyond reproach. I think everyone can agree on that.)

"More than any other drummer, Ringo Starr changed my life," Max Weinberg, the longtime drummer for Bruce Springsteen's E-Street Band—and for Conan O'Brien on NBC's *Late Night* and *The Tonight Show*—wrote in his 1984 book, *The Big Beat*. "Ringo's beat was heard around the world and he drew the spotlight toward rock & roll drumming. From his matched grip style to his pioneering use of staggered tom-tom fills, his influence in rock drumming was as important and widespread as Gene Krupa's had been in jazz."

(Weinberg is one of four drummers—along with Phil Collins, Kenny Aronoff, and John Densmore—who talk about Ringo's drumming in the book's epilogue.)

A biography does not magically write itself. It's a combination of research, interviews, and queries that go nowhere, queries that pay off in spades, and many, many people who help, in one way or another, along the long and winding road (sorry, but it's apropos).

Toward that end, I would like to thank the following people for assisting me while I was working on this book. Some of them agreed to be interviewed about Ringo Starr, others lent me guidance and/or moral support throughout this long process, and still others just listened to me complain. A lot.

John Cerullo, Bernadette Malavarca, and Wes Seeley at Hal Leonard (Backbeat Books), for their patience and belief in this project; Keith Allison; Kenny Aronoff; Randy Bachman; Tony Barrow; David Bedford, for his hospitality in showing me around Liverpool and his expert knowledge of all-things Beatles; Peter Brown; Clem Cattini; Ray Connolly; Joe Connolly; Phil Collins; Robert Coulthard; Mick Coyle, Liverpool Talk Radio Station 105.9; Marilyn Crescenzo; John Densmore; Ken Ehrlich; David Essex; Mark Farner; Julie Farin ("Lady Macca"); David Fishof; Simon Flavin; Carl Gottlieb; Doug Hoefer; Lawrence

Hollis; Dr. John; Catherine Jones from the *Liverpool Echo*; Harold Jones; Larry Kane; Sarah Kestelman; Ian La Frenais; Stephanie La Motta; Sam Leach; Ken Mansfield; Jeff Margolis; Steve Marinucci; Chris O'Dell; Sean O'Mahony; Terry O'Neill; Dave Patterson, for sharing his childhood memories of Richy Starkey, and for the use of those two terrific photographs; Marius Penczner; John Romain; Dora Rotondella; Reba Russell; Keith Seppanen; John Scheinfeld; Sam Shoup; Rick Siggelkow; Barry Sinkow; Phyllis Smith; Doreen Speight; Sean Styles at BBC Radio Merseyside, for having me on his show, twice, to talk about the book; Seth Swirsky; the late Sir John Tavener; Isaac Tigrett; Larry Turman; Tim Van Rellim; Enid Williams; Trina Yannicos.

Last but not least, a huge thank you to my daughter, Rachel, and especially to my wife, Gail, for her patience and understanding while I worked on this book. I love you both very much.

Any biographer whose subject is still alive and well, is required, by some unwritten literary law, to approach his or her subject in order to let them know the author is writing a book about them. I was no different.

Shortly after I signed my deal to write this book in the spring of 2012, I approached Ringo Starr's publicist, to let her know my intentions. She, in turn, informed me that all-things-Ringo had to go through his attorney in Los Angeles. Fair enough. I sent Ringo's attorney several e-mails, informing him of my book and asking if Ringo might be available for an interview to talk about his life and career. I never heard back.

Then, in September of 2012, I finally had my answer, when Ringo posted the following message on his Facebook page and on his website, ringostarr.com:

> There is an unauthorized biography being written by Michael Starr and I want my friends & fans to know it has nothing to do with me. I'm not participating with it at all.
>
> Peace & Love,
> Ringo

Here's his story.

RINGO

1

LITTLE RICHY

The remarkable story of The World's Most Famous Drummer begins, rather unremarkably, in July 1940.

The weather that month was unseasonably warm in Northern England, a welcome respite from the drums of war beating loudly as the country braced for its inevitable showdown with Germany. For now, though, there was no hint of Hermann Goering's Luftwaffe planes. In late August they would swoop down over the River Mersey in nighttime bombing raids, unleashing horrific death and destruction in what was called "The Liverpool Blitz."

By the end of the war in 1945, nearly four thousand Liverpudlians were among the dead killed by Hitler's bombs. The city, fifteen miles from Wales and an important Nazi target—its ports were vital to the British naval effort vis-à-vis supplies—laid claim to a sad distinction: save for London, it incurred the greatest number of casualties and architectural devastation of any British city.

For now, though, all was relatively quiet at 9 Madryn Street, Liverpool 8, save for the wailing of Richard Starkey, who entered the world kicking and screaming, eyes wide open, a little after midnight on July 7, 1940, a week later than expected.

The baby, who weighed a healthy ten pounds, was born at home and not in the hospital—not an uncommon occurrence in the Dingle, the gritty, working-class district where Richard and Elsie Starkey conceived their first and only child. It was obviously cheaper to have the baby at home; a hospital stay, however short, would further diminish the family's already precarious financial condition.

Richard Starkey was a baker who specialized in making cakes, a profession that put just enough money in the coffers to keep food on the table. Elsie Gleave had met and fallen in love with Richard at Cooper's Bakery in Liverpool while they were both working there. She now brought in extra money toiling as a domestic, cleaning other people's houses, and working as a barmaid.

Richard and Elsie had married in 1936 and lived a life not much different from their neighbors in the Dingle, which the future Ringo Starr would describe as drab and dreary. The district, located in the southern part of Liverpool, was close to the docks bustling with hard-living sailors and workers loading and unloading supply ships.

The Dingle had a hardscrabble reputation as one the toughest areas in Liverpool. But its reputation belied its reality; for all the talk, everyone knew everyone else—"It was like a village," recalls a Starkey family friend—and everyone kept an eye out for friends and family. That wasn't hard to do, since the row houses were stacked nearly on top of each other, neighbor upon neighbor. Privacy was a scarce commodity.

The house at 9 Madryn Street was typical of its era, with the downstairs consisting of a front room, which most people (including the Starkeys) used as a parlor area, and a tiny kitchen. Upstairs were three small rooms. There was indoor plumbing, to a point; the house had only cold running water and no bathtub. Washing was done in what Liverpudlians called a "tin bath," which was what it sounded like—a tin tub filled with hot water boiled on the gas stove.

"Your mother would boil the water on the boiler and throw it into the bath and once a week you'd get into the bath," recalled Davy Patterson, who would become one of young Richard Starkey's best friends. The toilet, located outside in the tiny back yard, was a four-sided wooden structure with thin walls and a hole inside. A flimsy door provided a modest bit of valued privacy. The structure had no heat, which wasn't much fun in the freezing English winters. Toilet paper, or lack thereof, was often an issue. "Nine times out of ten you had no toilet paper," Patterson recalled. "You used to use the local newspaper, which hung on a nail. You would cut it up into squares. That's how primitive it was."

Both Richard and Elsie Starkey were native Liverpudlians, although Richard, who was born in 1913, took his Starkey surname via paperwork and not bloodline. His father, Ringo Starr's grandfather, was born John Parkin, but legally changed his name to John Starkey when his mother remarried a man with that last name. It was a family fact which Ringo Starr uncovered only when he had his family tree traced in the 1960s—and learned the truth from his family, who wanted to keep it a secret from the probing press.

Elsie was born Elizabeth Gleave in 1914 into a very large family, being one of fourteen siblings. She was content to have only one child to care for, especially on such a frugal budget in the Dingle.

Everyone called the new baby Richy. He had big, blue, puppy-dog eyes and his father's nose, later to be famously immortalized by Paul's "clean" grandfather (Wilfrid Brambell) in *A Hard Day's Night* as Ringo's "enormous hooter." Richy was a good-natured baby and Elsie doted on him. Richard, for his part, was mostly an absentee father. There was trouble in the marriage, and as the arguments between Richard and Elsie became more frequent, so, too, did the new father's absences.

He was around the Madryn Street house enough so that the neighbors began referring to father and son as "Big Richy" and "Little Richy." But by the time little Richy turned three years old, his father had had enough, and, in 1943, walked out on Elsie and his young son. He would have little-to-no contact with either of them for the rest of his life.

Ringo would later say that he had no tangible memories of his father and thought badly of Richard Sr. after being "brainwashed" by Elsie's stories about her ex-husband.

But Richard Starkey's abandonment of his family had a silver lining, of sorts. His parents, little Richy's Starkey grandparents, lived just a few doors down at 59 Madryn Street with their dog, Blackie, and Rich's aunt Annie, and John Starkey embraced their grandson wholeheartedly, helping Elsie out when they could, perhaps out of a sense of guilt due to their son's abandonment.

But family was family, and the Starkey grandparents loved their little Richy. Elsie welcomed the support and harbored no ill will toward her in-laws. Little Richy spent a lot of time over at 59 Madryn Street—which was strange, he thought, since they were his paternal grandparents (whose son had abandoned his wife and small child). He held a warm place in his heart for them.

John Starkey loved to bet on the horses, or "the gee-gees," as he called them. Ringo Starr would fondly remember his grandfather's favorite chair, on which he sat all through the war, even while the bombs dropped on Madryn Street. That chair was the only thing young Richy wanted at such a young age. Grandma Annie, meanwhile, was a large woman who towered over her husband and coddled her grandson.

Ringo remembered that when he got sick, his mother would wrap him in a blanket and bring him over to Grandma Starkey—whose cures for any ills were a bread poultice and a hot toddy. Richy enjoyed the attention and everyone fussing over him. There were Starkey cousins in Liverpool, but Elsie and little Richy didn't have much interaction with that branch of the family.

Elsie's mother, who Richy called "Grandmother Gleave," lived alone in another part of Liverpool. She had a friend named Mr. Lester, who would come over to her house and play the mouth organ for her—eliciting a sly nod and wink from family members who knew what he was after. But Grandma Gleave refused to marry Mr. Lester, who eventually met and married someone else.

Richard Starkey's departure from Madryn Street, and from Elsie and Richy's lives, meant one less paycheck in the weekly kitty, and Elsie eventually found herself having a tough time keeping up with the rent at 9 Madryn Street. "I was just able to manage," she said. "There was a lot of work to be done in bars, with the war on." (The majority of houses in the Dingle were rentals; it was rare to find a family who owned their own place.) Besides, with only two people in the house now, Elsie didn't need the three bedrooms and she didn't want to take in any boarders. Downsizing to a smaller house became a priority.

"My father sort of decided to leave when I was three so it was just my mother and I," Ringo said. "It was six rooms and it was very big and the rent was expensive." As for Elsie, he averred, "She did everything. Scrub steps. She was a barmaid. She worked in a food shop. She had to earn a living."

The dilemma was solved shortly thereafter. Elsie had become good friends with Muriel Patterson, who was married to Jack Patterson and lived a few blocks away on Admiral Grove, a street adjacent to the Empress Pub (which Ringo Starr would later immortalize on the cover of his 1970 album, *Sentimental Journey*).

The Patterson house at 10 Admiral Grove was a "two up, two down" structure (a parlor and kitchen downstairs, two small rooms upstairs, the toilet outside). Elsie and Muriel met while cleaning pubs together and hit it off. Muriel's son, Davy, was five months older than Richy and they, too, soon became inseparable—a bond made even stronger when Elsie and the Pattersons decided to switch houses.

In 1945, Elsie and five-year-old Richy packed up and moved what little they had to Number 10 Admiral Grove. The Pattersons, meanwhile, relocated to 9 Madryn Street. "We swapped houses with them," Davy Patterson recalled nearly seventy years later. "Richy's mom and my mom were good friends, so we exchanged houses 'cause we were five people living in a two-bedroom and they were two people living in a three-bedroom house."

"We moved into a great house," Ringo said, "which was condemned ten years before we moved in!"

Davy Patterson remembers the Dingle as being "a reasonably tough" neighborhood. "The war had finished and there wasn't a lot to do," he said. "Everybody was in the same boat, really. No one in that district was rich. The first car that came onto our street must have been when I was twelve. The first person to own a car was a fellow called Mr. Kraft, and he was a builder, so he had a van. You were lucky if you saw a taxi coming down the street. That was the type of district it was."

For the next seven-plus years, Davy would walk to school with Richy nearly every day, and would sit next to his best mate in the classroom. It was Elsie, though, who walked Richy to St. Silas Primary, close by on Pengwern Street, on his very first day of school.

Years later, Ringo Starr was unable to say whether he actually remembered his first day at school—or only recalled the stories Elsie told him about walking him up to the gate of what seemed to the youngster to be an enormous building, with kids running around the playground. The St. Silas students who lived close to the school were allowed to walk home for lunch, and Richy soon settled into a routine, which also calmed his nerves.

Ringo Starr's first teacher, Enid Williams, could still recall Richy Starkey, nearly seventy years later (although his later fame might have a lot to do with coloring the details of those memories). It's debatable, and highly unlikely, that Enid Williams ignited the spark that fired Richy Stark's inner drummer. But at the age of ninety-two she still had a sharp and vivid memory of her kindergarten pupil. "I think I gave him his first drum," she said. "We had what we called a percussion band, and the children played things like triangles and bells, and if they had a good sense of rhythm, I would have given him his first drum. He would have been only five or so at the time.

"He was very quiet and rather delicate," she recalled. "He was an only child and he was rather coddled. He was kept out of school quite a lot . . . he had lots of colds and things. I remember there was a family of cousins, quite a big family of them. I remember them better—Ronnie and Maureen—and they were always nice and jolly. They were healthy, you know, having these rosy cheeks and round faces."

Richy's time at St. Silas was abruptly cut short a year later after feeling what he later described as "an awful stab of pain" which left the six-and-a-half-year-old child sweating, shaking, and quite frightened. His appendix had burst, and his worried family closed ranks and tried to comfort him. He was taken to the Royal Children's Infirmary, also called Myrtle Street Children's Hospital, where he was diagnosed with peritonitis and rushed into surgery to have his appendix removed (he remembered asking for a cup of tea before he was put under anesthesia). The doctors told Elsie that Richy might not make it. The surgery, which is routine today, was much more complicated and risky in 1947.

Elsie was told by the doctors three times that Richy wouldn't make it through the night. But, by morning, Richy had pulled through. It would not be an easy recovery. He was barely conscious at times and was nearly comatose for ten weeks. He was lucky to survive—and he knew it.

Elsie and grandparents John and Annie visited Richy when they could, but it was a long, boring, and tedious stretch for Richy, and not without its medical complications.

Initially, his condition was serious enough to warrant a surprise hospital visit from his estranged father who had been out of his son's life for over three years. Richard Sr. stood in Richy's hospital room with a notebook and asked Richy what he wanted for his birthday, which was just a few days away. He jotted something down in his notebook but never bought anything for his son. Richard Starkey Sr. scarcely came around thereafter.

"I remember [Richard] coming back to Liverpool and Richy knocking on my door and saying, 'Do you want to go see my dad?'" said Davy Patterson. "It was a Sunday morning and his dad was a confectioner—he made cakes and sweets—and I remember he was making sweets in the small kitchen at Richy's grandma's and he gave us a chocolate each. That was sort of a treat, because in those days, it was very rare you got chocolates, you know, after the war. That's probably when we were around six."

During his long hospital stay Richy got to know the nursing and medical staffs, and his fellow patients, very well. Lying in his cot for long periods of time, and killing time however he could, he became very adept at retrieving small items—including pennies—with his feet. Richy's doctors were confident that he could be sent home imminently, but that plan was foiled when Richy leaned over to show another patient his new toy bus and fell out of bed—tearing out his stitches and re-opening his surgical wound. He spent another six months in the hospital before he was finally discharged and sent back to 10 Admiral Grove. He'd been away from home for nearly a year.

It was great to be home, but all that time away from St. Silas Primary meant that Richy, who turned seven while in the hospital, had a lot of catching up to do with his school work. It wouldn't be easy. Although he was home now, he needed more time to recuperate, and it was to be another twelve months before he would return to St. Silas. Having missed two entire school years, he didn't know how to read and was behind in all the other subjects, including mathematics.

"After that, I think that's when I really started to hate it," he said of school. "I know I didn't like it before I went to hospital, but then because . . . you're never caught up with class, you know. There was no teacher gonna take special care of me. And you had to try to get yourself up there. And I always found it very hard. So it was easier to stay off."

Elsie, meanwhile, was determined to help Richy catch up, but she had to work every day and couldn't take the time to tutor her son. But her good friend Annie Maguire had a daughter, Marie, who was four years older than Richy. The Maguires had lived across the street from the Starkeys on Madryn Street, and it was Annie Maguire who sat in the hospital through the night with Elsie two years before when Richy was lingering near death—despite the fact that Annie's husband had died earlier that day.

Marie often babysat for Richy, occasionally taking him to the movies and often retrieving the sleeping child from his grandparents' house. "He was so much a part of our family that people used to come and knock at our door and say, 'Your Richy's doing so and so,'" Marie told Beatles biographer Hunter Davies. "When he had meals with us and we were having scouse [beef stew] I always had to pick the onions out for him. He hates onions. I was always cursing him."

Marie was enlisted by Elsie to teach nine-year-old Richy how to read, a pursuit in which she was ultimately successful. "I started teaching him to read and write when he came out of hospital. He wasn't stupid," she said. "He'd just missed a lot. We had it properly organized. Twice a week I used to give him lessons and his mother would give me pocket money for doing it. I bought Chambers Primary Readers and we used to sit up at his kitchen table and read them."

Ringo Starr remembered Marie using a book called *Dobbin the Horse* to teach him how to read. He always had trouble spelling and would spell words out phonetically.

Having finally recovered from the burst appendix and all the proceeding trauma (both physical and emotional), Richy returned to St. Silas, where he was given the nickname "Lazarus" by some of the kids, for having risen from the dead. He was shorter than most of his classmates, but he was wiry and spunky and didn't let bigger boys push him around. And he was already flashing the sharp wit that would define him as a Beatle; that, more often than not, helped him win friends and remain reasonably popular among his classmates.

In those days, there was no catching up on lost school time, and Richy was always at least a year behind. He used his sense of humor as a shield and always tried to make friends with the biggest kid in the class, who would protect him. His dislike of school intensified, and it became easier to cut classes and walk around the park with a few friends. They would write "excuse" notes—but were always busted, because none of them could spell.

"We were always in contests with each other: who was the tallest, who was the brownest in the summer, who was the most clever, things like that," recalled Davy Patterson. "We had a friendly rivalry. He wasn't a sickly kid at all, really. He wasn't the sporty type. I was more sporty. I played basketball and football and things like that. Richy didn't play sports. But he was a tough little bugger. He wouldn't take no nonsense. He was no sissy."

Richy, Davy Patterson, and another friend, Brian Briscoe (who was a year younger and lived nearby), formed "The Black Hand Gang" and "The Skull Gang" and did what boys of that age do—they horsed around, went to the movies, walked to the park in Speke (approximately eight miles away), and rode their bicycles, sometimes pedaling all the way to Wales and back (a thirty-five-mile round trip).

Ringo remembered he was so sore after that trip that he lost interest in his bicycle. They joined the Life Boys, the Boys Brigade, the Sea Brigade, and even joined the church choir "because you got paid," Davy Patterson recalled. "We would come out of the movies and we'd be the cowboys and Indians, or we would be Zorro with our swords and different things. We loved Gene Autry and Roy Rogers and all that. We'd be riding along on our 'horses' . . . of course we didn't have horses, but we pretended. Generally we did what most kids did. We went to see the first 3D movie together. I think it was Abbott and Costello and you had to wear the glasses, one blue side and one red side."

Richy took a keen interest in Gene Autry, especially after hearing Autry's rendition of "South of the Border"—his first musical memory. He recalled that hearing Autry sing the song gave him the shivers. Autry would remain one of Ringo Starr's biggest heroes.

At night, they rushed home to listen to their favorite radio program, the BBC's *Dick Barton: Special Agent*, which aired weekdays at 6:45 p.m. and recounted the exploits of ex-commando Dick Barton, who solved crimes and saved England from disaster, assisted by his trusty mates Jock Anderson and Snowy White. Television had yet to infiltrate Liverpool and, besides, no one could have afforded a television set anyway. (Patterson remembers his and

Richy's first experience with the small screen watching Queen Elizabeth's coronation in 1953 from the window of a local electronics store.)

When they weren't hiking in the woods outside of town or walking to Speke, the boys played on the "bombie," the cratered-out bomb sites on Madryn Street. "That was our playground on Madryn Street," Patterson said. "There were about five houses which had been blown up during the war. We used to play football there and everything. And we were only about maybe a ten-minute walk from the park. But we sort of played on the bomb site, mostly. We used to have a bonfire on Guy Fawkes Night, November 5, and when the fire died down we would throw potatoes in and roast them in the embers of the fire."

Ringo Starr fondly remembered those times with Davy Patterson and Brian Briscoe—and how they vowed to do everything together. They were detectives and cowboys and spent countless hours playing in the "bombie," letting loose with their vivid imaginations.

Richy's paternal grandfather, John Starkey, became a confederate of sorts. "His grandfather was a boiler maker in Cammell Laird Shipyard [in nearby Birkenhead] and he made this big, steel locomotive," Patterson recalled. "You could light a fire in it. It had steel wheels and you could actually sit on it—it was that heavy. You could hardly move it. We used to play with that a lot. It was always in the yard." Richy decided he would charge admission to the kids in the neighborhood if they wanted to sit in the locomotive. "That was probably the most fabulous toy I ever had," he said.

Davy also remembered that "We made our own go-carts, things like that. And then we got bicycles. There was a guy who had a bicycle shop and he would make them up, bits and pieces of different bikes. You never had a proper bike. Just bits and pieces, different wheels off one, a different seat off another."

With the Liverpool docks playing such a huge role in the city's economic and cultural life, it was no surprise that young Richy dreamed of a life at sea. He had his heart set on being a merchant seaman and recalled the camel saddles sitting in the corner of Liverpool houses, brought back by men who had been at sea—along with records and different styles of clothes.

When he wasn't planning for his life as a merchant seaman, Richy followed more mundane pursuits. One of Richy and Davey's boyhood adventures in the park involved a plan to catch rabbits, just for the fun of it. "He always liked drums," Patterson said. "The first drum he got was a wooden tom-tom from West Africa. And we came up with this idea. There was place called Jericho Farm and it was all green fields and there were rabbits there, so he said, 'We'll get a sack and take the tom-tom. I'll bang the tom-tom down one hole and you'll hold the sack over the other hole. And the rabbits will run into the sack.' Of course they didn't. But those are the types of things we did."

Richy also had the brilliant idea, one day, to "borrow" some money from Elsie and put it to good use. "We had been on school holiday, and Richy came to me and said, 'Look, me mum has a pound note in a little silver tea pot on the mantelpiece and it's been there for about a month and I think she's forgotten about it,'" Davey said. "Now, in those days you didn't forget about a pound note, and the rent was like six shillings a week. So Richy said, 'We'll exchange it for two tenshilling notes and fold it back and then we'll have ten shillings.' And ten shillings, in those days, was like a small fortune. So myself, Richy, and Brian Briscoe go into town, into a big store called Lewis's, and they had an escalator. We had never seen an escalator, so up and down on the escalator we went and up to the cafe on top and had sausage, eggs, and chips, twice. This is all for ten shillings."

Their bellies full but their minds still at work, the boys then went into the store's basement, which housed cutlery and ironware. "We tried to buy big knives and the woman wouldn't sell us a knife but sold us an axe!" Davey remembers. "Off we went to the park with the axe and tried to cut trees down. Anyway, that night we still had money left, so we hid it under the lino under Richy's front door and about an hour later Richy is knocking on my door and saying, 'My mum wants to see you.' She had come home and noticed the pound note was changed into ten shilling notes. So we got into trouble for that one."

When Richy Starkey later morphed into the world-famous Beatle Ringo Starr, the portrait that usually emerged of his childhood was one of hardscrabble deprivation and poverty in the gritty slums of Liverpool. But the myth is different from the reality. While Elsie and Richy Starkey were by no means middle-class, they were, by Dingle standards, no worse off than any of their neighbors. The house at 10 Admiral Grove was clean and tidy and there was always food on the table. Richy's clothes weren't always second-hand, and he was not lacking for love. As far as material possessions, what else did he need except a tatty bicycle by day and the family radio by night? He made do with what he had.

Elsie and his aunts and uncles lavished gifts on him when they could afford it, sometimes just some sweets or a toy. Richy collected stamps and Dinky cars for a while but always ended up swapping these for something else.

"As a kid you didn't care," he said of his modest surroundings. "That's what we knew. Every woman in our street was a mother if mine wasn't there. If you fell over they'd pick you up. If you had a cough they'd be putting cough mixture in you. I had a great childhood, besides being a little ill."

A photograph of Richy and Davy Patterson, taken when the boys were around thirteen years old, is snapshot-proof that life in the Dingle was not so bad, all things considered. (It also illustrates how enterprising the friends could be.) Both boys are dressed in smart suits and ties, and their hair is carefully combed.

"That was taken at a place called Jerome's, which was a proper photographer," Patterson recalls. "We paid for that photograph ourselves. In them days, people didn't have cameras. You would be lucky to know anybody who had a camera." Another professionally taken photograph, snapped on the day of their prom, shows the two pals smiling while walking on the boardwalk at New Brighton. They're both sporting rakish, oversized homburg hats. "We paid for that photograph, too, probably from choir money," Patterson said. "We were always scheming to make money. We used to have yard sales and things like that . . . sell off our comics and books and things."

Elsie toiled hard and often held down several jobs—cleaning houses, working as a bar maid—but she made ends meet, and Richy was not a neglected child. He had his mother's unconditional love and support and a very close relationship with grandparents John and Annie Starkey. Richy Starkey was a typical product of the Dingle—tough, resilient, not a complainer. He "got on with it," as Liverpudlians would say. He didn't bemoan his lack of proper schooling and, besides, he was only an average student.

But for most of the boys and girls in the Dingle, school was simply a timepasser required by law. Most of them could look forward to lives lived much like their parents before them—for the boys, leaving school at the age of fifteen or sixteen and entering the labor force as an apprentice, eventually working as a metal worker, dock hand, or perhaps on the British railway—good, dependable jobs that would put food on their families' tables. For the girls, it usually meant leaving school at the same age, getting married, and raising a family. Their futures weren't so much filled with exciting new opportunities as they were with predictability. And that was just fine.

If Richy Starkey resented his parents' divorce, and his father's absence from his life at a very young age, he didn't let it show; even years later, at least publicly, he would gloss over his parents' breakup and defer from criticizing Richard Starkey, who became merely a footnote in his famous son's life. "Sometimes he used to wish there was more than just the two of us," Elsie said. "When it was raining he used to look out of the window and say, 'I wish I had brothers and sisters. There's nobody to talk to when it's raining.'"

Elsie had been alone since her divorce from Richard but had recently started seeing Harry Graves, a good-natured painter and decorator from "down South" (London's Romford area) who had relocated to Liverpool for health reasons he could never quite remember. They were fixed up by Elsie's friend Annie Maguire, but Harry wasn't a total stranger; he'd dated Richy's widowed aunt, Edie Starkey.

Harry was working at Burtonwood, a military base in Warrington, Cheshire, located about thirty miles outside of the Liverpool city limits. Burtonwood was originally used as a World War II production facility—where planes for the RAF were built and serviced—and was one of the largest military bases in Europe. By the time Harry arrived there, it was a maintenance and supply base for the United States Air Force.

He loved music, particularly the Big Band sound and American jazz vocalist Sarah Vaughan. He was gentle, was fond of children and animals, and quickly fell in love with Elsie. He also took a shine to eleven-year-old Richy. "You couldn't help but like Harry," recalled Davy Patterson. "Everybody liked Harry. He was really nice. He was a dapper little man. He used to sing 'That Old Black Magic.' That was his party song."

Working at an American military base gave Harry access to American entertainment, including comic books, which he would bring to Richy when he came to call on Elsie. He made Richy laugh, and he loved music, a passion he tried to share with the young boy. Harry would always ask Richy "Have you heard this?" when referring to a song, which amused Richy to no end.

"He was great," Ringo continues. "In fact I used to take his side if he and me mum had any rows. I just thought she was being bossy and felt sorry for Harry. I learned gentleness from Harry. There's never any need for violence."

"With Harry working on the American base, he used to get all the classic comics, you know, like Superman and things like that, which we didn't have in England then," said Davy Patterson. "Richy had a suitcase full of them. I used to sleep at his house when Elsie and Harry would go out and have a drink and we used to sit in the bedroom and read all these classic comics from America. He was a popular lad with those comics."

Elsie's burgeoning relationship with Harry dovetailed with Richy's entrance, at the age of eleven, into a new school, Dingle Vale Secondary Modern. The school was nearly a thirty-minute walk from 10 Admiral Grove and was intended—under Britain's Secondary Modern education system established the previous decade—to prepare students with lesser academic skills for life in the work force. "So you'd be an engineer or a joiner, if you were lucky," Ringo explained.

Richy's attendance record at Dingle Vale wasn't much better than it had been at St. Silas, and his absentee rate was notable; at one point, he missed thirty-four days of school over the course of only half the year. He did, though, receive an "A" for punctuality (so at least he was on time when he *did* show up for class). He also earned "A's" for his "general appearance" and "conduct," but was given "D's" in arithmetic and English. He fared much better in Drama class. "Takes a real interest and has done very well," his Dingle Vale drama teacher noted on Richy's report card next to his "A."

The long walk from Admiral Grove to Dingle Vale would have repercussions of a different sort since his path took Richy past a music store on Park Road. Other than beating a tom-tom and trying to catch rabbits with Davy Patterson—and enjoying listening to Harry's Big Band numbers—Richy had shown little interest in music as he entered his early teen years. He had seen legendary jazz drummer Gene Krupa in the movies and was a fan, but didn't rush out and buy Krupa's records. His grandparents played the mandolin and banjo, but Richy's only musical interludes would be singing "Nobody's Child" to Elsie as the expected Saturday-night party piece ("Little Drummer Boy" was Elsie's parlor song).

But every time he walked past that little shop, something caught his eye. He was taken with the instruments in the window—guitars, banjos, accordions—and, in particular, a tom-tom that he just had to have. But at £26, it was a small fortune.

By this time, Elsie had been seeing Harry for two years, and the relationship took a serious turn when Harry asked Elsie to marry him. Richy genuinely loved Harry, but was not keen on having his mother's attentions taken away from him. As an only child, he was used to being the center of attention. A stepfather could ruin the Starkey family dynamic. He reacted predictably when Elsie broke the news and asked Richy what he thought of Harry's proposition. He was angry, but knew that if he objected to Elsie's marrying Harry, she wouldn't get married. It was a tough dilemma for a thirteen-year-old kid, but Richy wanted his mother to be happy, and he liked Harry. The marriage was a go.

Elsie's version differs slightly. "I told Richy that Harry wanted to marry me. If he'd said no, I wouldn't have done it," she said. "But he said, 'You get mar-

ried, Mum. I won't always be little. You don't want to end up like me grandma.'"
Harry and Elsie were married on April 17, 1953, and Harry moved into the
house at 10 Admiral Grove. Their marriage meant that Elsie didn't need to
work anymore, since Harry's income from his job at Burtonwood was enough
to support them both. She could finally relax.

But not for long.

Shortly after Richy turned thirteen, he was hospitalized again. Most
accounts of Ringo Starr's life mark this hospital stay down to pleurisy, an
inflammation of the lining surrounding the lungs. Ringo himself claimed
that it started as pleurisy and "turned into tuberculosis. Liverpool was a
breeding ground for tuberculosis." Family friend Marie Maguire, who had
taught Richy to read several years before, recalls the incident more bluntly.
"Richy contracted tuberculosis which of course was serious," she told Beatles
historian David Bedford. "At the time, there was a terrible stigma attached to
having TB, and so the family said it was pleurisy." Whatever the case, it was a
serious health risk which could potentially turn deadly. Richy was taken first
to Myrtle Street Children's Hospital—the site of his previous hospital stay six
years earlier—and spent ten weeks recuperating. "There used to be balconies,
so when it was a fine day they'd wheel your bed out so you could get some
fresh air and could watch the traffic—that was the big news," he said. Davy
Patterson remembers the balcony, too. "They used to push him out on the
veranda for some fresh air and we used to go down and wave to him, you know,
the gang of kids," he said.

After ten weeks at Myrtle Street, Richy was moved to Heswall Children's
Hospital, located on the Wirral, about a twenty-minute drive from the center
of Liverpool. He would spend the next two years of his life there and never
returned to school.

But it was also at Heswall that Richy Starkey discovered the drums.

2

"IT WAS IN MY SOUL"

The exact date when The World's Most Famous Drummer first noticed his unique gift is lost to history. Ringo Starr remembered it only as "1954." But it's safe to say that, by all accounts, the two years Richy Starkey spent recuperating at Heswall Children's Hospital set him on a path that would change the course of music history. Several people might lay claim to spurring Richy's interest in the drums, including his kindergarten teacher Enid Williams or (more credibly) Marie Maguire, who visited Richy in Heswall and brought him Eric Delaney's rendition of Alyn Ainsworth's "Bedtime for Drums," "which he loved."

But it's more likely that Richy's preoccupation with the drums began organically. Sometimes, history be damned, there's just no simple explanation—no particular day or incident on which to pin a life-changing event. So it was with Richy Starkey.

But fate was on his side.

The boy whose interest in music had, up to now, been negligible at best was once again confined to his bed for long periods of time. There was little else to do at Heswall save for teasing the nurses and hoping to cop a goodnight kiss from one of their younger charges. Richy was now a teenager with raging teenage hormones, and very little opportunity to channel those feelings. His entire world was confined to the TB ward at Heswall.

Forty years later, he could still recall the names of Sister Clark and nurse Edgington. He was hitting puberty at thirteen, with raging hormones, and would get frisky with the nurses when they kissed him good night. He remembered later how young the nurses were—and how many kisses he was able to steal. Richy was in the boy's ward, which was separated by a partition from the girls on the other side. Teenage passion, or at least an attempt at teenage passion, was the norm—tuberculosis be damned. At night, the boys would sneak into the girls' ward, trying to awkwardly cop a feel.

The hospital tried, in its own way, to provide some rudimentary education for its young patients. Many of them, including Richy, were missing entire school years because they were so seriously ill. In addition to classes in mathematics, English, etc., the hospital provided recreational outlets; Richy learned how to knit, and dabbled in papier-mâché creations. There were also music classes. He remembered how a teacher would come in with an easel containing symbols for all the different musical instruments and hand out triangles, tambourines, and drums. Richy would only participate if she gave him a drum. Before long, Richy had joined the hospital band, using "cotton bobbins" to bang on the cabinet next to his bed. He remembered that as the time he really started to play music—and, from that point on, he never wanted to do anything else.

Consumed by his new passion, Richy was constantly banging on anything within his reach. A drum set, for now, was out of the question—his TB kept him confined to his bed for long hours at a stretch and he was weak. Besides, Heswall didn't have that kind of musical equipment.

It's possible that the distance of forty years played some chronological tricks with Ringo Starr's memory when he talked about discovering his passion for the drums at Heswall. Robert Coulthard, who was admitted to Myrtle Street Children's Hospital in February 1954 with rheumatic fever, vividly remembers spending around eight weeks in the same ward as Richy Starkey. Robert was four months younger than Richy, and had been the oldest kid in his "massive" ward until Richy's arrival. The two boys, both from Liverpool—Robert lived several miles away from Admiral Grove—hit it off and became fast pals. They got up to lots of hijinks.

"We used to make general nuisances of ourselves," he recalled. "We used to have metal lockers, and we used to make drums. I was in the Boy's Brigade, where I played drums. We used to make the drum sticks from a cardboard bobbin used to keep bandages on. They were conical. And we used to put them together to make drum sticks. We played on the metal lockers and they made a hell of a noise. It used to drive the nurses round and round."

Robert's mother and Elsie got along well, and when Elsie couldn't make it to the hospital "she used to give my mum things to bring in for Richy," he said. "So we got on pretty well together." Their short friendship ended when Richy was transferred to Heswall.

By the time he was finally well enough to be discharged from Heswall, it was 1955. Richy was fifteen, and though he had missed two more years of school he had no intention of ever returning to a classroom. Years later, the famous

Beatle would repeat the story of how, as fifteen-year-old Richy Starkey—about to enter the workforce—he returned to Dingle Vale Secondary Modern. He needed certain papers to prove that he had attended the school, but was told in no uncertain terms that they had no record of any student named Richy Starkey. They ended up finding his student's records but had no recollection of Richy ever attending the school. The kicker to the story: When The Beatles became world-famous around eight years later, Dingle Vale school officials held a garden party, where they charged admission to sit at "Ringo's Desk."

Leaving Liverpool to find a job wasn't much of an option. Richy never had traveled much farther than New Brighton or the 180 miles south to London, where he spent a few days with Elsie and Harry, visiting Harry's relatives in Romford and seeing the sights of the city. There were trips to Seaforth and to New Brighton—and to Sunderland to visit his Aunt Evie and Uncle Jim—but nothing too fancy.

But if he needed to find a job now, his options were limited. Besides his newly acquired passion for playing the drums, Richy had no discernible skills. He didn't have a proper drum kit yet—he hadn't even taken any lessons—so getting a job thwacking the skins in a band was out of the question, at least for now.

When he was around fifteen, Richy saw the American crooner Johnny Ray, who was playing The Empire, out on the balcony of his room at the Adelphia Hotel "throwing photographs to the girls in the crowd. I thought, 'That's the job for me.'" Richy and a friend (probably Davey Patterson) followed Ray when he went for dinner at a Chinese restaurant called The Golden Dragon. "I remember looking in the window and thinking 'He's eating like a real person.'"

But following in Johnny Ray's footsteps was just a childish fantasy. Richy continued to rest at home under the watchful eyes of Elsie and Harry—whom Richy had nicknamed his "stepladder." When he felt well enough, Richy registered with the local Youth Employment Office in Liverpool, which found him his first job, that of a messenger boy for British Railways. The job paid fifty bob a week, and came with a uniform—or so he thought. "I went to the railways really so I could get a suit," he said. "All they gave me was a hat, so I was very disappointed." That job lasted five weeks. "It wasn't just not getting the uniform," he said. "You have to pass a medical exam, and I failed."

From there, Richy got a job tending bar on the St Tudno, a pleasure steamer operated by the Liverpool and North Wales Steamship Company which ferried passengers back and forth between the Liverpool docks and the Menai straits in

North Wales. "One night a week we all had to stay on board so we all felt like real sailors," he remembered. "I wanted, in the end, to be in the real merchant navy. It was great for picking up girls—well, it wasn't actually great, but it helped. You'd go into a pub; 'What do you do?' 'I'm in the navy.' 'Oh, yeah? When did you get back?' 'I just got back.' 'When did you leave?' 'Ten o'clock this morning.'"

That job lasted around six weeks; it ended the day Richy showed up at work, drunk, after an all-night party, and mouthed-off to his boss.

His next stop was Henry Hunt and Son, an engineering and manufacturing firm located on Windsor Street in Liverpool. His "stepladder," Harry, had a connection there who helped Richy get hired on as an apprentice joiner. It was also a way to avoid being called into active military service, since apprentices were exempt from serving in the army (which was one of Richy's big fears at the time). He considered it his best alternative to the dreaded military service.

Hunt and Son manufactured equipment for schools—chairs, desks, even gymnastics gear—and Richy was consigned to the company's training program. But he wasn't getting much training early on. "I was on the bike delivering parcels for six weeks and I was fed up and I said, 'When can I start my apprenticeship as a joiner?' and they said, 'There's no room for you.'" Richy was offered a spot as an apprentice fitter, which he accepted without complaint. It was a job he would keep for the next four years. One of his close friends at Hunt and Son was Harold Jones, who was a year older than Richy and had grown up on Aberdeen Street, not far from Admiral Grove in Liverpool 8.

"Richy and I were apprentice bench fitters," Jones confirms. "We used to make gymnasium equipment. You made horses for the gyms and they were wood, and our other friend was a lad called Roy Trafford. He was a joiner. And the three of us were quite close. We used to have our breaks together and we used to go out on the weekend to the Liverpool City Center to a place called the Lisbon. Now it's a gay bar, but I assure you it wasn't when we went. Richy used to walk about with bits of wood and that and bang on everything. We just all used to laugh. But at lunchtime, in the winter, when it was cold out, we used to get around in a group at lunch and there used to be another lad there, Eddie Myles. He could play guitar and sing—and he was good."

"It was a great gang of people," Trafford told Beatles historian Bob Spitz. "Eventually, we were taught to finish the wooden parts—all the balancing beams for the gymnasium bars. There was only thirty-eight and six in our pay packets—no more than a handout—but at the time the money was secondary.

We were learning a trade, which was more than most guys in our situation, and as we well knew, it was considered a job for life."

Richy's apprenticeship at Henry Hunt dovetailed with the emergence of the "skiffle" craze in England, which followed closely on the heels of Elvis Presley's breakthrough in America. Skiffle groups used homemade instruments to create their sound, which was based on American blues music. In England, that sound was created by "instruments" including a tea chest, which was used as a bass, usually with an attached string that could be manipulated to create the desired pitch (American skiffle groups used a washtub bass). A washboard, tapped on or scraped with the fingers, was used as percussion to keep the back beat (as a substitute for the drums). Jugs and acoustic guitars usually rounded out the musical lineup.

"When I started playing I started gradually moving out of 'walking with the lads,' as it was called," Ringo Starr would say about that time. "In England in '58 this big craze came up called 'Skiffle,' which was based on American bottle parties . . . like blues bottle parties, where you take a washboard into the house and a bottle of beer. . . . It'd be like made-up instruments, you know. So that's how I started, in one of those. But, I mean, I had the drums."

Skiffle's first superstar in the UK was Scottish-born Lonnie Donegan, whose 1954 cover of Lead Belly's "Rock Island Line" exploded on the British charts two years later. It would eventually earn the distinction as the becoming the first debut record in the UK to go gold. Donegan, who was twenty-five at the time, was called "The King of Skiffle" and would go on to have a string of best-selling hits, including "Wabash Cannonball" and "Gamblin' Man." His catchy, mellifluous, upbeat sound—showcased on his many British television and radio appearances—appealed to nascent musicians who were yet to be proficient on their chosen instruments and/or couldn't afford out-of-reach electric guitars, amplifiers, and drum kits.

Unlike Elvis Presley, who was also very popular in England, but really only used his guitar as a prop, Donegan played his own guitar and was an ordinary-looking bloke. As Donegan's popularity soared and the skiffle craze swept across England, many British teenagers were inspired to form their own skiffle groups. Among them was a fledgling sixteen-year-old guitarist named John Lennon, who formed The Quarrymen in 1957. The group's members would eventually include Paul McCartney and George Harrison. "Rock 'n' roll was beyond our imagination," said Lennon's friend Eric Griffiths. "But skiffle was music we could play and sound okay [doing] right away."

Richy also caught the skiffle bug and, when he was eighteen, even considered moving to America with his friend Bob Hardy to live the dream and to be closer to American blues music, which he loved. Their plan was to move to Texas to be closer to their hero, Lightnin' Hopkins. He and Hardy went to the United States consul in Liverpool, telling officials there they wanted to move to Houston. Richy and Bob got the forms and started to fill them out, but it proved to be too daunting of a task. They even went as far as getting a list of possible factory jobs in Houston before throwing in the towel.

Richy was enamored of the drums, but could only dream of a "proper" drum kit. Several years earlier, after his discharge from Heswall, he had bought a big one-sided bass drum for thirty shillings, but couldn't do much except thwack on it during family gatherings, using firewood as drum sticks. After that he fashioned his own homemade kit from biscuit tins and firewood, but it was rudimentary at best and didn't have the sound or the feel of a real drum kit. "Flat tins were cymbals, and a big biscuit tin with some depth in it was the tom, and a shallow biscuit tin was the snare drum, and so forth," he recalled.

That changed in late 1957 when Harry left for London to attend a family member's funeral. He returned by train, schlepping a drum kit he had brought for Richy for £12. Richy received the kit on Boxing Day, and was amazed at its size: a snare drum, bass drum, hi-hat, tom-tom, cymbal, and bass-drum pedal. It was his first real drum kit.

"It was a sort of mixture of different parts, about twenty-five years old. I was really proud," he said. "Every time I got behind it, it used to hide me, what with me being little and the drum being a fantastic size. I wouldn't be surprised if you told me it was ten feet across.

"I couldn't play a note at the time," he said. "I just used to bash around in the house until I got some idea." One night, Elsie came into Richy's room. A neighbor's husband was in a band. She thought they played jazz, but she wasn't sure. Why didn't Richy go along and see what it was all about—and maybe join in? "Anyway, I went to rehearsals and there was this crowd of blokes playing in a silver band! They were all working out the numbers they were going to do in the park that Sunday. It wasn't for me. I left the same night."

He thought he would take lessons to learn how to play properly—and "went to the house of a little man who played drums"—but that only lasted around three weeks. The "little man" who gave Richy Starkey his first drum lessons has never been positively identified, though Beatles historian David Bedford believes it could have been Red Carter, who would have been around thirty-six years old at the time. Carter had a studio in Tempest Hey, Liverpool, and had backed some of the biggest acts—including Lonnie Donegan. But being tutored on how to play the drums by a professional entailed learning how to read music—and Richy was having none of that. He didn't want to be bothered and couldn't stand the monotonous routine.

Instead, he set up his new drum kit in his bedroom and began banging away, with Elsie and Harry constantly having to yell at him to keep the noise down because the neighbors were complaining. It was obvious that practicing in his room at 10 Admiral Grove wasn't going to work in the long run. If he wanted to continue playing the drums on a regular basis, Richy would need to join a band.

His neighbor Eddie Myles also worked at Henry Hunt. Eddie sister, Cathy, remembers her mother banging her shoe on the wall in irritation when Richy was pounding away on his drums. It was rumored that Eddie's father was an American GI who had abandoned Eddie's mother after the end of the war. Regardless of who Eddie's real father was, he left behind an extremely talented musician who could not only play a mean guitar, but was quite good on several other instruments, including the violin.

"He could play anything," said Richy's co-worker and friend Roy Trafford. Eddie was a lathe operator at Henry Hunt, and was the guitarist who, according to Harold Jones (another of Richy's co-workers and friends) used to entertain the Hunt workers during lunchtime on cold winter days.

Roy Trafford also played guitar, and when he and Richy discovered their shared passion for skiffle music, the two boys began, very gingerly, to put together a band, of sorts. "I played guitar, and [Richy] just made a noise on a box," Trafford said. "Sometimes, he just slapped a biscuit tin with some keys, or banged on the backs of chairs." Before too long, after Richy and Roy worked on a few songs in the Hunt and Son basement, Richy invited Eddie Myles to join them.

Richy, Roy, and Eddie began calling themselves The Eddie Myles Band, which shortly thereafter morphed into The Eddie Clayton Skiffle Group. (It is widely believed that Clayton was the surname of Eddie's American GI father.)

Ringo Starr recalled getting the drum kit on Boxing Day and joining a group by February. He couldn't play, but no one else could, either, except for Eddie Myles, who knew a few chords. No one had any sense of time, and Richy was forced to borrow different drum kits. But he taught himself to play—and later admitted it was the best learning experience he could have had.

Richy's friendship with Roy, meanwhile, blossomed. Davy Patterson, Richy's childhood friend—whose family had swapped houses with the Starkeys and who sat next to his pal in school all the way through to St. Silas—had joined the navy when he turned fifteen. He was off seeing the world and would spend the next ten years at sea, followed by a thirty-three-year career in the Liverpool Pilot Service. He would have little contact with Richy Starkey thereafter. The younger Brian Briscoe, too, had faded from the picture.

Richy and Roy shared a passion for music, movies, and girls (and not necessarily in that order). They also loved to dance at places like the Winter Garden, the Rialto, and Wilson Hall, and Trafford claims he even dragged Richy to nearby Skellen's Dance School for a few lessons. "We used to visit the Rialto for dances, and being good dancers, we got the girls," Trafford said. "One night, there was a gang who started beating up a couple of lads, and then they looked at us and said, 'You're next!' We just turned and ran home."

It was also with Roy that Richy made his first visit to the Cavern Club on Mathew Street in Liverpool, which would eventually play a significant role in his young life. And, like many other Liverpool teens, Richy and Roy often tuned in to Radio Luxembourg to hear the latest rock 'n' roll records (which were deemed unworthy for broadcast by the staid suits at BBC Radio). Radio Luxembourg's signal was faint, but Richy and Roy loved to listen to Alan Freed's Saturday night show and were thrilled to discover new sounds from American artists.

Richy's apprenticeship at Henry Hunt and Son was working out, which was a relief to Elsie and Harry. Elsie never pressured her beloved Richy into choosing a particular line of work—and good-natured Harry didn't cause any waves with his stepson—but they knew that, with Richy's limited education, his prospects were limited. The apprenticeship promised a reliable future if Richy could stick with the program, which included a three-month stint at Riversdale Technical College to improve his engineering skills.

"That's where I met him," said Joe Connolly, who was in Richy's class for their session at Riversdale, which was taught by a Mr. Paris. "He was pretty quiet. He wasn't sort of a loud character. One day when a group of us were trying to do our homework during the lunch hour Starkey was there and was strumming on a guitar and we told him, in no polite manner, to pack it in as it was really annoying us. He was always interested in music and used to go to the recording studios to listen to other artists."

Nearing his eighteenth birthday, Richy was still living at 10 Admiral Grove, which was just fine with Elsie and Harry, who welcomed his company (as long as Richy, Roy, and Eddie practiced elsewhere).

Richy continued to bang away on the drum kit Harry had brought back from London, and as The Eddie Clayton Skiffle Group progressed, they added John Dougherty on the washboard and Frank Walsh as a second guitarist. The guys even began to pick up paying gigs here and there. In 1957 (the exact dates are lost to history), The Eddie Clayton Skiffle Group debuted at the Peel Street Labour Club in Liverpool, with Richy Starkey on the drums. They also played at Wilson Hall, Garston, at the Florence Institute (for Boys' Clubs meetings), and debuted at the Cavern Club on Mathew Street at the end of July. They would appear at the Cavern several more times, including a gig the following December and several dates in early 1958.

The band's real draw, to those who remember the lineup, was Richy's next-door-neighbor and co-worker, Eddie Myles, who "with his bird's-eye maple Hofner cutaway and its homemade pickups, was something of a guitar dynamo in Liverpool."

"Eddie used to take his guitar to work every day," Elsie would recall. "He was a smashing fellow—if ever a lad should have got somewhere, *he* should have."

"The Eddie Clayton Skiffle Group was the best skiffle group in Liverpool at the time—I don't know why," said Roy Trafford. "But we just kept winning the cups. I think a lot of it was down to Eddie Myles. He filed down the frets on our guitars to lower the action and even made the pickups. He then made his own steel guitar, too. Eddie didn't have the greatest singing voice, but, without blowing my own trumpet, I used to sing harmony and together we sounded pretty good."

At one of the group's gigs at Wilson Hall, Trafford claims it was he who showed Richy how to use the brushes on his snare drum to imitate the sound of a train while the group was launching into a railroad or folk song. When he wasn't playing his drums, Richy would pick up the washboard for skiffle standards like "Rock Island Line." He and the group played all the free gigs they could find—clubs, weddings, etc. If someone they knew was getting married, they would get their gear and play for a few hours. The experience was priceless.

In the summer of 1958, Richy borrowed £46 from his paternal grandfather, John Starkey, to use as a deposit on a new £100 drum kit, an Ajax set he'd seen in the store window. "If his granddad even refused him a shilling he'd do a war dance," Elsie said of Richy. "This time his granddad came to see me. 'Hey do you know what that bloody noddler of yours wants?' He always called him the 'noddler.' But he gave him the money. Richy paid it back faithfully, a pound a week out of wages."

"It was in my soul, I just wanted to be a drummer," Richy said. "I didn't want to be a guitarist; I didn't want to play bass. I wanted to be a drummer, and that's how it is. My grandparents played mandolin and guitar and they gave me their instruments—and I just broke them. I had a harmonica; I dumped it. We had a piano; I walked on it. I just was not into any other instrument."

The new drum kit also lent a more professional appearance to the band. Richy bought the kit from Hessy's Music Centre, *the* go-to shop for local musicians, which also counted fledgling musicians Paul McCartney, John Lennon, and George Harrison among its patrons.

Richy also needed a new identity to go along with his part-time career as a musician. He and Roy began dressing like Teddy Boys for their nights out at the Cavern Club or the Lisbon Pub, usually wearing matching outfits: black-and-gray-striped jackets, crepe trousers with red stripes, a red-and-black-striped shirt, studded belts, and string ties they'd bought at Woolworth's. (The subculture of "Teddy Boys," or "Teds," was prevalent in England in the 1950s and referred to the Edwardian dress worn by these youths.) Richy, who had a streak of premature gray in his hair—which gave him an older, different appearance—greased his thick black locks down with goop. "We thought we were the bee's knees," Trafford said.

Their newly adopted look was a necessary contrivance to survive in the rough-and-tumble world of Liverpool, especially for Richy, who lived near the docks. Gangs were common, and many young men joined a particular gang for self-preservation, both to survive in their own neighborhoods and to have allies when traveling through someone else's turf. Richy joined the Dingle gang, whose main activities were walking up and down the street, looking tough, and getting into fights (with varying degrees of success). Fights were started for any number of reasons, the most prevalent being a perceived dirty look, which inevitably led to a fistfight. So the rough Teddy Boy look helped, if just a bit.

Richy's Teddy Boy suit was a hand-me-down from one of his Starkey cousins, who'd been to sea. But since his cousin was much taller—and the Teddy Boy suit didn't quite fit—Richy had to use a heavy belt, to which he'd attached washers, to hold up his tight trousers. He filed both the washers and belt buckle into razor-sharp weapons, which could be used in the event of a gang fight. But he never went as far as some other Teddy Boys, who would hide actual razors in the lapels of their jackets (so the other guy grabbing the lapels in anger would have his fingers maimed—or worse).

Richy wasn't a great fighter, but he was quick on his feet and was a good sprinter. He said later that he never knifed or killed anyone but was beaten up a few times, even by the guys he was running with. He saw people lose eyes and get stabbed or beaten with hammers. It was not for the faint of heart.

While Richy's Teddy Boy phase was a necessary means of survival, he was growing bored with the gang routine, particularly since The Eddie Clayton Skiffle Group was becoming more popular. While his days were spent at Henry Hunt and Son, training as a joiner, his nights were increasingly filled with music. The gang life began to take a back seat to Richy's preoccupation with the drums. And when he wasn't playing with Eddie Clayton, he was off playing with other local groups in other neighborhoods, sitting in for a night here or there. It helped everyone to get to know one another; if someone got sick before a gig, or didn't show up, another guy would sit for him. Ringo remembered practicing with virtually every group in Liverpool.

He was either unable or unwilling to read music, but that didn't really matter; he was honing his timekeeping skills behind the drum kit and reaping the side benefits of being recognized as an up-and-coming rocker. The girls would always be looking at the musicians, angering their dates and the other guys in the audience—which sometimes led to fights when the band played in a strange neighborhood.

Richy had several steady girlfriends around this time, including Patricia Davis, a blonde who attended St. Anthony of Padua Secondary School, located in Mossley Hill. Pat wanted to be a hairdresser, and along with her best friend, Priscilla White (later to become British pop star Cilla Black), would often work on Elsie's hair.

"Neither of our mums would let us near their hair," Pat said. "The only woman we ever met who didn't mind us doing the practical work on her was Ringo's mother, Elsie Starkey. On Wednesday nights we went round to her house, and she was the soul of patience. She let us bleach her hair and do terrible things to it, but she never once complained. She also gave us our tea—either boiled ham or spam and homemade cakes. Mrs. Starkey was a fantastic lady."

After Pat, Richy had a more serious relationship with Geraldine McGovern, who worked in a Liverpool upholstery factory. Geraldine and Richy met in 1957 at Litherland Town Hall—The Beatles would later perform there many times—and soon thereafter the pair became inseparable. Richy called her "Gerry," and he liked the fact that she and her parents lived on Kent Gardens, not too far from 10 Admiral Grove. "Richy used to call 'round a lot in those days," Gerry's father recalled. "He and Geraldine were very close to each other."

A grainy photo from that time shows Richy and Geraldine on the dance floor at a Henry Hunt and Son holiday party—Richy wearing a vest and bolero tie, and Gerry wearing a white shirt, dark skirt, and dark shoes. "Richy was shy in a way, but he was determined to be famous," she remembered. "He wasn't at all flamboyant—his humor was quiet and witty without being offensive or cynical."

Richy's prowess behind the drum kit, meanwhile, began to earn him something of a local reputation. He wasn't a flashy player but he looked great behind his drum kit, and that was half the battle. He had grown a wispy beard, which was an unusual look for someone his age in late-1950s England. The beard was accentuated by his long, slicked-back black hair with the gray stripe running through it, giving him an exotic look that caught people's attention as he pounded away behind his Eddie Clayton band mates.

Shortly after he turned eighteen, Richy also bought his first car, a red-and-white Standard Vanguard, from a fellow drummer named Johnny Hutch. That meant he no longer had to travel to gigs by hitching a ride with someone—or, worse yet, getting there by bus and having to carry a snare drum, cymbal, and his drumsticks, using the rest of someone else's drum kit when he got to the venue. He would recall one particularly shitty night when, after a gig, he took the bus home carrying four cases filled with his drum equipment. After being dropped off by the bus, he had to run back and forth retrieving the cases left behind on the side of the road, hoping they wouldn't be stolen. The Standard Vanguard would come in handy.

"It was very difficult for a drummer in those days," Ringo said. "I'd take the snare drums to the gigs, and I begged a drummer who drove his whole kit there, 'Let's use your kit, man.' I'd use my snare and his kit. Sometimes he said, 'Yes,' and sometimes he said, 'No.' And then, when I did get a car and would be able to take my kit to the venues, other drummers would ask me, 'Can I use your kit, man?' and I said, 'Sure.'"

Love eventually drove a wedge into The Eddie Clayton Skiffle Group. In 1958, Eddie Myles got married and the group disbanded. It wasn't exactly a tragedy for Richy, as he'd been sitting in with a number of other local bands and was a hot commodity with his fancy drum kit. He claims to have had a short stint with a band called The Cadillacs, though very little is known about this group.

Years later, Ringo Starr told music journalist Chris Hutchins that he joined The Cadillacs in November 1958, and that the group's unnamed leader "had a car and used to pick me up, so for the first time I was able to take out the full kit." But Richy, by this time, already had bought his first car, so we'll take his succinct account of The Cadillacs with the proverbial grain of salt.

Richy's next band, though, did exist and is fondly remembered by locals. The Darktown Skiffle Group, which Richy joined briefly in early 1959, was considered one of Liverpool's best skiffle groups and even boasted a rare female lead singer, Gladys Jill Martin. But as well known as the band was, its members had no ambitions to further their musical careers, and were content to keep their day jobs. And while Richy was still working at Henry Hunt and Sons, he was dreaming of bigger and better things. He wanted to make music his livelihood; the other guys didn't think it would last and played it safe, working as engineers and joiners, getting married and settling down. Trivia buffs might be interested to note that Beatles historian Bill Harry, who founded *Mersey Beat* magazine, notes in his *Ringo Starr Encyclopedia* that The Darktown Skiffle Group eventually moved to a rock 'n' roll sound—and changed its name to The Cadillacs.

3

RINGO STARRTIME

The skiffle craze was already ebbing by 1958, and by the following year more and more skiffle groups were dropping the "home-made" sound and turning to pure rock 'n' roll—using amplifiers, electric guitars, and full drum kits now that they had perfected (at least to a point) their chosen instruments.

One of the local Liverpool groups trending away from skiffle was Al Caldwell's Texans, which went through a laundry list of names, including The Raving Texans, Al Storm and the Hurricanes, and Jett Storm and the Hurricanes, before finally settling on Rory Storm and the Hurricanes in late 1959. The band was started by Alan Caldwell, who was born in Stoneycroft, Liverpool, in January 1938.

The son of a window cleaner and part-time porter, Alan had a younger sister, Iris. He was tall (six feet two inches) blond, handsome, athletic, and charismatic, and loved to run and play football. He was also quite proficient at swimming and ice skating. "He could walk on water," recalled Alan's band mate Johnny Byrne. "He was athletic, he looked the part, he could put the songs over."

If Alan had a handicap, it was his stutter; his friends never let him tell a joke or order a drink, since it took too long. But he overcame the stutter and, after completing his school education, began a career as a cotton salesman. Bitten by the skiffle bug, he decided to form a group called Dracula & the Werewolves, which evolved into Al Caldwell's Texans and, in March 1958, he opened the Morgue Skiffle Club in the basement of an old Victorian house in the Broadgreen section of Liverpool (the building once housed retired nurses). The Quarrymen, fronted by John Lennon and Paul McCartney, was one of the many bands to play at the Morgue Skiffle Club, and the band would audition guitarist George Harrison there.

Alan Caldwell was a showman at heart and a show business hustler with moxie. He worked hard to get his band recognized and, by mid-1958, he and The Raving Texans had already appeared on Radio Luxembourg's *Amateur*

Skiffle Club show. (He never stuttered when he sang—a huge plus.) By 1959, Alan Caldwell had changed his stage name to Rory Storm (borrowing the first name from British rocker Rory Blackwell) and his group's name to Rory Storm and the Hurricanes. The band's lineup fluctuated, but as it moved into a rock 'n' roll sound and away from skiffle its regulars would eventually include guitarists Johnny Byrne and Charles O'Brien, Wally Eymond on bass, and the flashy Rory handling vocals.

Rory Storm was enamored of American Westerns, so Byrne became "Johnny Guitar" (after the 1954 movie starring Joan Crawford) and O'Brien became Ty O'Brien, named after the star of ABC's late-'50s TV series, *Bronco* and its star, Ty Hardin. Rory thought that Wally Eymond was too pedestrian a name for a rocker, so he rechristened his bass player Lu Walters.

Rory wasn't setting any trends by renaming both himself and his band mates, but was following in the footsteps of other British musicians of that era, including Liverpool's Ronald Wycherley, who, like Richy, was born in the Dingle in 1940 and was (briefly) one of Richy's schoolmates at St. Silas. He was now the rock 'n' roll star Billy Fury, complete with a hit single, "Maybe Tomorrow."

So Rory Storm and the Hurricanes were on their way. Now all the band needed was a reliable drummer.

And they were keenly aware of Richy Starkey.

"We knew him pretty well. He'd gotten a snare drum, a hi-hat and a cymbal by then," Byrne said. "When we told him we were going into rock 'n' roll full-tilt, he said he was interested." Richy, of course, was aware of the band and knew Rory in passing, having met him at a talent show called *6.5 Special*. "They were the first ones in Liverpool who really wanted to get into rock 'n' roll," Richy said. "We were all playing skiffle before that, but they had a rock 'n' roll blond-hair attitude—Rory liked being the big cheese, to be Mr. Rock 'n' Roll, and Johnny 'Guitar' Byrne was Liverpool's Jimi Hendrix."

Storm sent word that he wanted to audition Richy as his drummer. Was he interested? Yes, definitely. He knew the band's entire repertoire—almost every group's set list was the same, including standards like Chuck Berry's "Roll Over, Beethoven" and Ray Charles's "Boys"—though he figured he might have to change his look if he passed the audition. He admitted later that he looked rough in his black drape jacket, his hair slicked back in a Teddy Boy coif style. He figured he intimidated Rory, but he passed the audition. He was in.

Richy made his first appearance as Rory Storm's new drummer at the end of March 1959, when the band played at the Mardi Gras Club on Mount Pleasant Street in Liverpool's City Centre. The band was still known as either Al Caldwell's Texans or the Raving Texans—accounts differ—and would not become Rory Storm and the Hurricanes until later that year. By that time, Richy, confident enough in both his growing abilities as a drummer and in his new band's future, decided to turn professional and leave Henry Hunt and Sons— and a promising career as a joiner—behind.

His decision coincided with a recent ruling by the British army, which announced that anyone born after 1939 would not be called up for active duty. Richy Starkey, born in July 1940, could now pursue his new music career full-time, without interruption. The decision was made less painful by the fact that Henry Hunt had moved elsewhere in Liverpool, meaning that Richy—not a morning person by any means—had to get up a half hour earlier.

He asked to go with Rory and the band to Butlin's for the princely sum of £16 a week, which resulted in a family meeting. Richy stated his case: It was steady work, not just at night or the random afternoon. Elsie and Harry were not thrilled with Richy's decision, but, supportive as always, they didn't stop him from chasing his dream. Richy would have been the first engineer in the family had he remained at Henry Hunt. His aunts and uncles, and even his boss at Henry Hunt, all told him he'd be back in three months and would regret not finishing his apprenticeship. But it was all to no avail. Richy had made his decision.

"I was an apprentice engineer, which was very big news in our family," he said. "But I was also playing with Rory and the Hurricanes, and we got the offer of a three-month gig in Butlin's at Skegness and Pwllheli, so we had to give up our jobs. All my uncles and aunties came over to try and tell me that drumming was OK as a hobby. I had to stand there and defend myself. I said, 'No, I'm a drummer, I'm off.' That's a Sliding Doors moment. Some decisions are good."

Rory had scored a major coup in lining up a summer-long gig for his Hurricanes at Butlin's in Pwlhelli (in northwestern Wales). The holiday camp chain, founded in 1936 by Billy Butlin, was a popular and affordable summer destination, with locations all over England. Entertainment was a big part of its appeal—both for its patrons and for its hired performers. "We were probably the first rock 'n' roll group, I think, in Liverpool at that time, so we wrote to Butlin's, they auditioned us, thought we were good enough and offered us a job at Butlin's holiday camp Pwlhelli," recalled Hurricanes guitarist "Johnny Guitar"

Byrne. "Now that was a big thing in 1960 to get a contract to play a holiday camp, because the money was good, probably about £25 a week, £30 a week, which back in 1960 was a lot of money.

"I think Ringo was a bit hesitant because he was serving an apprenticeship and it meant that if he did pack up . . . his job would be gone. So anyway we persuaded him that it's a good opportunity for him. I think Rory said, 'We'll club together, we'll buy the kit' because I think he didn't have a good kit of drums at that particular time. We got a kit of drums together and went to Pwlhelli and from then on we never looked back."

Richy didn't need much more persuading when Johnny informed him what else that "good opportunity" implied. "We told him of all the women that would be 'available,'" he said.

"I just felt I wanted to," Ringo later said. "I was getting by then £6 at Hunt's and about £8 by playing at nights. Butlin's was offering me £20 a week in all, £16 when they took off the money for the chalet."

By the end of 1959, Rory Storm and the Hurricanes were the hottest group in Liverpool, and not only for their onstage sound. Storm, ever the showman, dressed his guys in matching shoes and suits—their outfits were comprised of black-and-white shoes, red suits with matching red ties, and handkerchiefs tucked into their jacket breast pockets. Rory, sometimes dressed in a pink suit, would jump around the stage.

"Everyone was doing covers of the same records, but Rory's group would be throwing in high-kicking steps, dance routines, and really putting on a show," said Rory's sister, Iris Caldwell, who eventually dated both George Harrison and Paul McCartney. "I went to the Broadgreen School of Dancing and Rory would come with me. He couldn't dance, but he would sing and do the songs for the shows. He learned all about the art of performing onstage, entertaining an audience and putting on a show. He learned about the importance of dressing up in costume and working the audience."

Sam Leach, a Liverpool promoter who organized shows at The Cavern Club, among other local venues, worked with just about all the Liverpool bands, including Rory and the Hurricanes.

"When you see Rod Stewart today, that was Rory Storm all those years ago," he said. "They were a very good show band. They had six different-colored suits, you know, and they went to Butlin's a lot. They did all the bandstands, partly because of me, I think.

"Ringo and I used to go out regularly. We were the two studs of Liverpool in those days! I got the better-looking ones, though. Ringo was no trouble at all. He did his job and he had a good personality. Never turned up late. Never got drunk. He did his business. Very professional."

In late 1959, Rory and the Hurricanes appeared at the Carroll Levis Discoveries contest at the Empire Theatre in Liverpool. "Visually, as well as instrumentally, they were stunning," recalled an eye-witness fan. "Each one was a showman and at the back was a showman drummer: Ringo Starr! At the front, writhing ecstatically like a golden snake was the greatest showman ever to step onto a Liverpool stage—Rory Storm!"

Once, at one open-air gig in New Brighton, where the band performed often, his athleticism and flamboyant style combined for the perfect episode of (Rory) Storm showmanship. With the other band members set up on the side of the big pool, Rory climbed to the top of the pool's highest diving board and stripped off his clothes. "He had a pair of gold lamé shorts underneath . . . he would do a triple somersault perfectly into the swimming pool, [retrieve a] microphone at the bottom of the diving board, come out and finish 'Whole Lotta Shakin'.' You can't follow that."

When the band was playing in clubs, Rory would also end "Whole Lotta Shakin'" by climbing on top of a piano and jumping over Richy's head—or, dressed in a pink suit with matching pink tie, he would saunter over to the piano, take out a comb and comb his hair. "He was very fit and quite often he used to run home from gigs," said Liverpool emcee Ron Appleby. "One day a porter at Bootle station caught a chap writing 'I love Rory' all over the walls. He was asked for his name and it turned out to be Rory himself."

Rory's flair for the dramatic also extended to his band mates. Richy had begun sporting several rings on his fingers, courtesy of Elsie, who bought him three cut-glass "gems." Having already renamed Byrne, O'Brien, and Eymond, Rory decided it was time to change his drummer's stage name to fit the other band members' catchy monikers.

Richy, who had already earned the nickname "Rings" for his bejeweled digits, now became "Ringo." He usually wore four rings, two on each hand, including his grandfather's wedding ring. Other rings came from female admirers. He assured everyone he was "no sissy! I just happen to like trinkets." "Starr" was a natural substitute for Starkey. And Rory had to love the fact that "Ringo Starr" sounded a lot like the real-life Wild West outlaw Johnny Ringo, whose name was also the title of an American television show that aired on CBS and premiered in 1959. Created by Aaron Spelling, it starred Don Durant in the title role. (On TV,

Johnny was no longer an outlaw but the sheriff of an Arizona town.) And then there was John Wayne's roguish character, The Ringo Kid, who was featured in John Ford's classic 1939 Western, *Stagecoach*. It was perfect.

Ringo Starr was born.

And there was more. Rory noticed that his new drummer captured the attention of the crowds with his energetic style and the way he shook his head while playing, almost like he was mesmerized by the beat. Always quick to capitalize on a gimmick, Rory's showman instincts kicked in and, before too long, Ringo had his chance to share in the band's ever-brightening limelight with his own set called "Ringo Starrtime," during which the drummer would take the mike to sing a few songs, usually "Boys" and "Alley Oop!," while bashing away at his drums. Ringo also used strips of black adhesive tape to spell out "Ringo Starr" on his bass drum to emphasize his new stage name.

"Ringo Starr always seemed to be the quiet one, to me, of the Hurricanes," Bill Booker told Beatles chronicler Bill Harry. "He used to just sit there and tap out drum breaks on his knees. He was the only one out of the Hurricanes who couldn't swim when they went to Butlin's."

There were other perks to playing the drums in Liverpool's most popular band. While Ringo was singing "Boys" every night, it was the girls who held his interest. The gaggle of (mostly) young females who came to see Rory Storm and the Hurricanes was plentiful—and willing. Offstage, Richy Starkey was still serious with Gerry McGovern, his girlfriend of three years. But the onstage Ringo Starr was also nineteen years old and catching up on lost time. And that didn't stop him from enjoying the romantic opportunities available to him as the newly minted drummer of Liverpool's top rock 'n' roll group.

Each week a new coachload of young girls would arrive at Butlin's, enamored of the guys in the band, a time Ringo Starr described as "paradise." He ended up living for a time that summer with a hairdresser in a caravan.

Whether or not Gerry knew of her Richy's amorous adventures is anyone's guess, but the couple became engaged in 1960, with an eye toward a March 1961 wedding date. A hall was booked. Plans were afoot. Richy's paternal grandfather, John Starkey, even gave Richy his gold wedding ring. But there were problems in the relationship. Gerry didn't approve of Richy's turning professional and joining Rory Storm on a full-time basis. To her, rock 'n' roll was just a phase. Richy's training at Henry Hunt and Son ensured him a solid (if drab, in his mind) future and a steady paycheck.

Geraldine began pressuring Richy to make a choice: it was either her or the drums. One night, Richy left Geraldine at the bus, thinking about what would happen if he never returned. Playing the drums was too important to him, but he also wanted to honor his commitment to Geraldine. They began preparing for marriage.

"His music always came first," Gerry told a writer for a fan magazine. "He was playing most nights, and if I wanted to see him I had to trail along with him to a dance. We were never able to have much time together." When Ringo decided to join Rory's band full-time and go to Butlin's for the summer, it was officially over. "He went and I said that was it. Well, we both agreed really that we couldn't go on." She returned the engagement ring to Ringo who, in turn, gave it to Elsie for safe keeping. He would eventually wear the ring again; it can be seen in photographs of The Beatles as late as 1965.

As Rory Storm and the Hurricanes caught on, their bookings increased, and the band was now a full-time vocation for all of its members. In early January 1960 the Hurricanes, with Ringo on the drums, appeared at the Cavern Club for the first of several appearances that month.

The Cavern, at that time, was strictly a venue for jazz—the club's management "banned" rock 'n' rollers—so the Hurricanes toed the line in their first two appearances there, first with The Cy Laurie Jazz Band and then the following week, supporting The Saints Jazz Band and Terry Lightfoot's New Orleans Jazz Band. But when the Liverpool Jazz Festival began on January 10, Rory and the Hurricanes decided to switch it up a bit a week later, when they shared a Cavern bill with Micky Ashman's Jazz Band and The Swingin' Bluejeans. According to *Mersey Beat* founder Bill Harry:

> They began their set with "Cumberland Gap." Then they decided to switch to a rock 'n' roll set and played "Whole Lotta Shakin' Goin' On." The jazz fans became furious and started pelting the group with copper coins. The Hurricanes continued the show but were drowned out by a booing audience. When they came offstage, a furious McFall fined them 6 (shillings) for daring to play rock 'n' roll music. The group were able to collect all the coins off the stage, which more than compensated for the fine.

In May, the Hurricanes appeared at Liverpool Stadium on the same bill as Gene Vincent, with Ringo still bashing away on his Ajax drum kit. That summer, the Hurricanes spent three months as the house band at Butlin's, playing sixteen hours each week. By that time, Ringo had bought a new drum kit, a four-piece Premier (bass drum, rack-tom, floor tom, and snare), with two cymbals (ride and crash) and a high-hat. The mahogany-colored kit cost him around £125; on the front of the bass drum, Ringo stenciled an "R-S." "It could stand for 'Rory Storm' or 'Ringo Starr' so he was killing two birds with one stone," noted Johnny Guitar. "Later, when we became more well-known, he put his full name on the head."

At Butlin's that first summer, "Ringo was the lazy one of the group," Hurricanes bassist Lu Walters remembered. "In the morning he used to sleep late, and if woken would be very bad-tempered. The first signs of him waking took the form of one open eye, which was staring round the chalet. Then it would be between one hour and one-and-a-half hours before he'd stir properly. Then he wouldn't speak for an hour or so. After that he'd refer to his normal self. He was the life and soul of any party we went to and was well-liked because of his sense of humor."

Ringo used part of his summer experience at Butlin's learning to swim from Hurricanes guitarist Ty O'Brien—and, at one point, went in too deep and had to be pulled out by O'Brien and several other Hurricanes.

Ringo was now earning £25 a week for his Butlin's gig, around four times as much as he'd been paid at Henry Hunt and Son. He sold his first car, the Standard Vanguard, and bought a more expensive Zephyr Zodiac—eliciting admiration and envy for his fancy set of wheels.

He was also the King among local drummers, and he honed his singular style and time-keeping skills as the Hurricanes worked steadily and grew into a cohesive unit. Unlike other drummers who used a traditional grip in holding their drum sticks—the right hand gripping one stick in an overhand style with the left hand gripping the other stick in an underhand style—Ringo used an more unorthodox "match-stick" style approach, gripping both of his drum sticks in an overhand style, curling his index and middle fingers around the bottom of the drum stick, with his thumbs on top of the sticks.

(A new generation of drummers would adopt Ringo's technique after seeing The Beatles for the first time—particularly American drummers, mostly teenagers, who saw Ringo on *The Ed Sullivan Show*.)

Ringo was also left-handed, but played his drum kit as he would if he were right-handed, which gave his drum fills a unique, unorthodox, distinctive sound. "I can't go around the kit. . . . I can't go snare drum, top tom, middle tom, floor tom," he said in describing his approach. "I can go the other way. So all these things made up these so-called 'funny fills,' but it was the only way I could play. Mine might be strange in its way, but it was my style."

In October 1960, after finishing their summer run at Butlin's, Rory and the Hurricanes flew to Hamburg, Germany, to replace Derry and the Seniors as the headliners at Bruno Koschmider's Kaiserkeller nightclub, located in the city's red-light St. Pauli district near the Reeperbahn.

Koschmider had a working relationship with British promoter Allan Williams, who ran the Jacaranda club in Liverpool. Williams booked Derry and the Seniors into Koschmider's Kaiserkeller in the summer of 1960 and they became the first Liverpool band to play in the rough-and-tumble German city. As the Seniors' popularity grew in Hamburg, Koschmider wanted more Liverpool acts for his club.

Williams's first choice was Rory and the Hurricanes, but they were already booked into Butlin's for the summer and had to turn him down. Williams then turned to Gerry & the Pacemakers, led by Gerry Marsden, but they, too, declined the invitation. So Williams considered his third option, The Beatles, who'd been making some noise in Liverpool and seemed to be going places.

Band members John Lennon, Paul McCartney, George Harrison, Stuart Sutcliffe, and drummer Pete Best jumped at the chance and were driven to Hamburg by Williams himself to begin a month-long run at Koschmider's other club, the Indra. Instead of the expected hotel, they were relegated to dingy rooms situated in the back of a movie theater, the Bambi Kino, which Koschmider owned. Beatles drummer Pete Best described the band's accommodations as being "like the black hole of Calcutta."

In October, German authorities sent Derry and the Seniors back to England after discovering that the band did not have the proper work permits. That, in turn, opened the door for Rory and the Hurricanes, who were now free to accept the gig. They packed their bags for their first trip to Germany—and for their first time working outside of England.

Unlike the more pedestrian Beatles, Rory and the Hurricanes wore suits and traveled by plane, but, once they arrived in Hamburg, that didn't matter. Koschmider wanted them to sleep in the back of the Kaiserkeller, since The Beatles were staying in the back of the cinema. Union Jack flags were to be used as sheets. No dice. Rory and his band were too good for that, so they decamped for a room in the German Seaman's Mission. The height of luxury.

In the meantime, Koschmider had closed the Indra and moved The Beatles to the Kaiserkeller. They arrived there just as Derry and the Seniors were on their way out—and Rory and the Hurricanes were arriving as the club's head-line act. To John Lennon, Rory and the Hurricanes were "professionals" who'd worked at Butlin's and knew how to put on a show; The Beatles, he thought, were "amateurs" compared to these polished guys.

The members of both bands knew one another in passing. The Beatles' lead guitarist, George Harrison, had, at one point, even considered joining the Hurricanes after meeting Johnny Guitar—but more for lustful reasons than professional ones. "I was trying to knock off Johnny Guitar's little sister at the time," he said.

But while The Beatles admired Rory and the Hurricanes for their profes-sionalism, matching suits and a polished stage act ("Out of all the amateur bands in Liverpool, they were most professional," Harrison recalled), they were initially wary of the band's drummer. Ringo was still dressing like a tough-guy Teddy Boy, and when Rory and the guys weren't playing, he often sat in the back of the Kaiserkeller, drunkenly yelling at The Beatles, who had the last set, to play some slow songs.

Harrison recalled that he and his fellow Beatles were wary of Ringo, who'd sit in the back watching the group—looking slightly sinister, the gray streak in his hair offset by half a gray eyebrow. A real tough guy.

Paul McCartney remembered Ringo coming into the club late at night, pre-ferring the "bluesy" sessions when the audience was sparse and The Beatles would play "Three-Thirty Blues." Ringo would settle in, order a drink, and re-quest that particular song.

Ringo's first encounter with The Beatles, back in Liverpool, was quick and unmemorable. He'd been at the Jacaranda Club (founded by Beatles' first man-ager, Allan Williams) one afternoon with Rory and Johnny Guitar. It was short-ly before the Hurricanes were headed to Butlin's for their summer season, and the three band members wandered downstairs to see what was going on. They found John Lennon and Paul McCartney teaching Stuart Sutcliffe to play his bass. The difference between the two bands was distinct: Rory and his "profes-sional" guys and The Beatles, struggling to make a name for themselves with a guy who couldn't play his instrument. Ringo remembered them as a group of "scruffs."

Bruno Koschmider was a tough taskmaster, and he expected the bands playing in his club to be up onstage for most of the night, playing one set after another. They would play up to twelve hours each night—six hours for each band, Rory and the Hurricanes switching off every hour with The Beatles.

And Koschmider was there to constantly demand, in German, that they "mach shau!" ("make a show!") before a rowdy, drunken crowd that included gangsters among its numbers.

It was survival of the fittest, with Rory and the Hurricanes and The Beatles adhering to Koschmider's grueling "mach shau!" schedule by popping copious amounts of uppers, usually Preludin, supplied to them by the Kaiserkeller waiters (who had a seemingly never-ending supply of the stuff). Ringo said that was the only way the band could continue to play for so long—that and the crates of beer the Germans would send to the band if they liked what they heard. Out-of-towners or monied people would sometimes send the band champagne. The guys drank anything and popped anything, usually Preludin, that came with their reach.

The impossible hours also forged a close bond between the two bands transplanted to the Kaiserkeller from Liverpool. While they competed to see who could put on a better show, it was all in good fun. Photos from the time show Rory posing with John Lennon, Paul McCartney, and Pete Best, and a bearded Ringo clowning around with George Harrison and McCartney—camaraderie among young men, none older than twenty-two, sharing a common experience fueled by drink, drugs, and plenty of available women.

They hit all the strip clubs in town; previously, Ringo's only experience to that was back in Liverpool watching "Nudes on Ice," the naked women standing stock-still. Now, it was there for the taking—and he and everyone else indulged freely and often.

(Harrison lost his virginity in Hamburg while McCartney, Lennon. and Pete Best were in the same room in adjoining bunk beds—they applauded him when he was finished. Obviously, privacy was a rare commodity in Hamburg.)

It was during that time that Harrison, writing a long letter to his pal Arthur Kelly back in Liverpool, first mentioned Ringo (but not by name). In the letter, Harrison described Rory Storm and the Hurricanes as "crummy," but had some nice things to say about the guy behind the drum kit. "The only person who is any good in the group is the drummer," he wrote.

Ringo also learned his first few words in German from Beatles bassist Stuart Sutcliffe. The two men ran into each other, early one morning, shortly after Ringo's arrival in Hamburg with Rory and the Hurricanes. As Ringo recounted the story, he was wandering around the streets, bumped into Sutcliffe in Grosse Freiheit, and they went to a cafe that sold pancakes. Everyone would hang around in the Reeperbahn, eating cornflakes and pancakes—and picking up a few words from the locals. (Ringo learned how to say "pancakes" and "eggs and potatoes" in German.)

Beatles drummer Pete Best was the one member of either band who often did not participate in the offstage hijinks. Harrison said Best never hung out with his fellow Beatles, preferring to go off on his own after a gig. Ringo would often join Harrison, John Lennon, and Paul McCartney—and Harrison said it felt "rocking" when the four of them were together.

Ringo would occasionally join The Beatles on the Kaiserkeller stage for a jam session if Pete wasn't around, or if Pete just didn't show up, which wasn't unusual. "It's no offense, but I never felt he was a good drummer," Ringo said of Best. "He had sort of one style, which was very good for them in those years, I suppose, but I think they felt that they wanted to move out of it more."

Ringo got his chance to play with John, Paul, and George in a more "official" capacity in mid-October. Allan Williams, back in Liverpool, had been impressed with Lu Walters's voice, and he now arranged for Rory's bass player to record three ballads—"Fever," "September Song," and "Summertime"—in Hamburg's Akoustik Studio. As recounted by Bill Harry in *Mersey Beat* magazine:

> Due to their ability on vocal harmony, Williams asked John, Paul and George to back Lu. Ringo remained on drums because he was familiar with the numbers and Pete Best had gone into Hamburg centre to buy some drumsticks. This was the first time the four who were to become internationally famous as the Beatles, performed together.

And then, just like that, it was over. After eight weeks in Hamburg, Rory, Ringo, and the Hurricanes headed home. Back in England, they found that the gigs, once plentiful, were harder to come by. The competition among local bands was fiercer now, and they weren't making a lot of money. The Beatles, too, had returned to Liverpool in November. They'd been poached by Koschmider's rival, Peter Eckhorn, and had moved on to Eckhorn's Top Ten Club without Harrison who, at seventeen, wasn't old enough to work in Hamburg and was deported back to England.

One day in November, McCartney and Best returned to Koschmider's Bambi Kino to retrieve their belongings, only to find that the place had been shut down. Pissed off, they nailed a condom to the cement wall and lit it on fire. Koschmider reported them to the cops, and McCartney and Best, after cooling their heels for a few hours in jail, were deported back to England. Lennon followed shortly thereafter while Sutcliffe stayed in Hamburg with his new girlfriend, Astrid Kirchherr.

After regrouping back in Liverpool and taking a short break, The Beatles began playing again in early 1961—often crossing paths with the Hurricanes, playing gigs at the same venue. Ringo would go and watch The Beatles; he loved the way they played, loved their song selection and their attitude. All their practice had paid off; Ringo knew The Beatles were better than Rory and the Hurricanes.

In April, The Beatles returned to Hamburg, and to the Top Ten, this time with an eighteen-year-old (and legal) George Harrison.

Rory and the Hurricanes soldiered on, playing gigs where they could find them. The band was still popular enough to earn another summer season at Butlin's, this time at the Butlin's camp in Pwhelli, located about a hundred miles from Liverpool. During that summer, Ringo started a romance with Doreen Walker, a sixteen-year-old on vacation with her family. Doreen and a friend came to see Rory and the Hurricanes perform one night, met the band, and hit it off. "We'd gone on holiday there and we walked into the ballroom and my friend went up to Rory Storm to ask him to play a certain tune," Doreen recalled. "Rory said to her, 'Do you want to go to a beach party when we're finished? And bring your friend for Ringo.' That's how it all started.

"Obviously I knew he was the drummer but nobody special," she said. "He was just sort of Richard Starkey, and then people said they called him 'Ringo.'"

Doreen remembered going to the Butlin's staff beach party that night. "We went in Rory's car. Ringo didn't have a car and it was lovely weather. Ringo brought the drinks. He was nice . . . when I say 'drinks' I don't mean alcohol, I mean like Coca-Cola and things like that. Even Rory Storm was a perfect gentleman and he was good fun because he used to play football and volleyball outside. And then we spent most of the week with them, playing tennis or different things."

Rory offered to get Doreen and her friend a job at Butlin's for the rest of the summer. But, according to Doreen, this was not to be: "My friend phoned her parents and they said, 'No way, you come back on that coach, and if you're not on that coach, we will be there to collect you.'"

Was there any romance between Doreen and Ringo? "Well, I was only sixteen, so it was only like holding hands and kisses on the cheek and things like that," she said. "I think he respected the fact that I was sixteen, because I didn't know how much older than me he was at the time. Obviously there was money at Butlin's, so he would buy the drinks and Rory would pay for the petrol for the car, so as far as I'm concerned he was a perfect gentleman—and he was really nice."

Ringo and Doreen kept in touch after the summer season at Butlin's was over. Since neither of them had a phone, they corresponded by mail. Ringo often sent his letters to Doreen from 10 Admiral Grove. He always signed off with "Lots of love and luck, Ringo xxx." Doreen even sent him some stamps so he could mail his letters back to her. (Over fifty years later, after she'd married and become Doreen Speight, she found several of the letters stashed away in a box in her garage.)

But despite the good times with Rory and the Hurricanes at Butlin's, Ringo was getting restless. He was considered by most Liverpool music insiders, and by many of the city's music fans, as Liverpool's best drummer. When Ringo turned twenty-one, Elsie threw a party for him at the little house at 10 Admiral Grove. Guests included Gerry & the Pacemakers, Cilla Black, and The Big Three. But Ringo was starting to feel more and more that Rory and the Hurricanes were growing stagnant.

The Beatles, meanwhile, were playing bigger and better venues and were starting to generate the lion's share of local press with their stage act, even after erstwhile bass player Stuart Sutcliffe decided to stay in Hamburg and settle down with Astrid Kirchherr to pursue his interest in art (and Astrid). Stuart never really did learn how to play his bass, though he looked damn good onstage doing his best James Dean impersonation (which was enough reason to keep him in the band). Paul McCartney, who was left-handed like Ringo, switched over from guitar to the bass as Sutcliffe's replacement.

"We were making . . . not great money, but enough to live on," Ringo said. "And The Beatles were making a bit more—they were coming up real fast. But I loved the band so much. . . . And I liked the boys as well as the music. And I thought I had done everything our band could do at the time. We were just repeating ourselves." Around that time, Ringo was considering an offer to join Derry and the Seniors. After giving it some serious thought, he passed.

There wasn't "lots of love" when Ringo had a chance meeting with his father around that time. Elsie and Harry had been married for nearly ten years now, and Ringo, for all intents and purposes, considered Harry his father. Richard Starkey, Sr., absent from his son's life for twenty years, had moved about fifty miles away from Liverpool to Crewe, where he re-married and got a job as a confectioner in a bakery while also working part-time as a window cleaner.

They met again, by chance, when Ringo went to visit his grandparents in 1962. "He happened to be at the Starkeys one day when I called," Ringo said. "I wasn't so childish by that time and didn't feel anything against him. He said to me, 'I see you've got a car.' I'd just got the Zodiac. I said, 'Do you want to come outside and have a look at it?' He said yes. So we went out and had a look at my car. And that was all. I haven't seen him since or had any contact."

Later that fall, Rory and the Hurricanes appeared at the Palais Ballroom in Aldershot, drawing almost two hundred more people there than The Beatles had the week before. But it wasn't enough, and the work was drying up, so Ringo decided to leave the Hurricanes and accept an offer to join ex-pat British guitarist Tony Sheridan's band in Hamburg.

Sheridan, who was living in Germany after some unspecified "trouble" in England, had a reputation as a terrific guitarist with a mercurial temperament. He was given to fistfights with audience members—and members of his own backing band—and would sometime even switch songs in the middle of a tune without telling his band mates. Ringo knew Sheridan was frustrating, but the offer was a good one. Sheridan offered Ringo his own apartment, a car, and £30 a week for a year's work as his drummer.

On December 31, Ringo returned to Hamburg, joining Sheridan at The Top Ten Club. Derek Fell, of The Executioners (a band based in Blackpool), replaced Ringo in the Hurricanes as Rory's drummer. A little over a year had passed since Ringo's first stint in Hamburg with Rory and the Hurricanes, and he approached his new job with Sheridan enthusiastically. Bassist Colin Melander joined Ringo as part of Sheridan's backing band, The Beat Brothers, which also included pianist Roy Young. (Ringo wasn't the only member of the Hurricanes to leave Rory Storm at this time: Lu Walters departed the group to play bass for Howie Casey and the Seniors.)

"He was a notch above a lot of players," Young said of Ringo. "He styled himself like a metronome, which was great because the qualities of Ringo was definitely recording material, whereas a lot of drummers would play: ooblee, ooblee, ooblee in all fields and that's not necessarily recording material because it gets too busy. But Ringo had the way—I mean he could play busy but he was always able to control himself and keep sort of like a metronome, which is great. He's a very good drummer."

Young also recalled The Beatles asking him about Ringo when he backed John, Paul, George, and Pete at the Star Club. "The Beatles were playing with Pete Best at the time, and one night we were sitting around having a drink with John, George and Paul when they asked what I though about Ringo. I think John and Paul knew they weren't going to pull it off with Pete. They knew I played with Ringo so they asked me what I felt about him, and John was a good friend of Ringo's. I told them he was obviously a great drummer."

But Sheridan was, by all accounts, a pain in the ass, and Ringo's stint as his drummer didn't last long. He quickly grew frustrated with Sheridan's habit of changing songs mid-tune—particularly alarming for a drummer, who's tasked with keeping a steady beat. And Sheridan wasn't above getting rowdy with members of the audience. Ringo thought Sheridan was a terrific guitar player but had trouble controlling his explosive temper. Even while onstage Sheridan would lose his cool if he thought someone was talking to his girl. Sometimes, after a fight, he returned to the stage covered in blood.

So, in mid-January 1962, Ringo returned to Liverpool. Rory welcomed him back with open arms, Derek Fell went his separate way, and Ringo reclaimed his throne as the drummer for the Hurricanes.

Lu Walters also rejoined Rory, and the band, back with its regular lineup of the past three years, began a busy touring schedule. February dates included the Tower Ballroom in New Brighton, the Orrell Park Ballroom in Liverpool, and Knotty Ash Village Hall, where they returned in mid-March to play the "St. Patrick's Night Rock Gala" with The Beatles, who were getting more and more fed up with Pete Best. John Lennon described Best as "harmless" but not on the same intellectual wavelength or as "quick" as the others.

Paul McCartney, only slightly more charitable, said the other Beatles knew Best's talents as a drummer were limited, and that he didn't fit into the group's dynamic. Best didn't help his own cause when he began not showing up for gigs, claiming he was sick—and Ringo would sit in with The Beatles. It just felt right.

The Beatles were now being managed by Brian Epstein, whose well-to-do family owned the NEMS (North End Music Stores) musical instruments and household appliance chain and had recently opened the NEMS music store on Charlotte Street in Liverpool. Epstein was put in charge of the store's record department, but the twenty-seven-year-old—who'd attended the Royal Academy of Dramatic Art in London—had no interest in rock 'n' roll music.

According to Beatles lore, and to Epstein's version of the story, his interest was piqued when several people came into NEMS requesting a recording of "My Bonnie," which Tony Sheridan, accompanied by The Beatles, had recorded in Hamburg several months before. Epstein, intrigued, went to see The Beatles at the Cavern Club in November 1961 and shortly thereafter signed a deal to become their manager.

Ringo first met Brian Epstein in 1962, when he called Ringo at home and asked him to fill in for Pete Best at the Cavern Club. It was around noon and Ringo was still in bed; Elsie knocked on his bedroom door to tell him that Epstein was outside. Ringo didn't know too much about Epstein, but thought it strange The Beatles had a manager—virtually unheard-of for a local band. Epstein asked if Ringo could join The Beatles for the lunchtime session in the Cavern Club. Ringo quickly threw on a pair of pants, downed a cup of tea, and Epstein drove the two of them to the Cavern Club for the gig.

Ringo recalled also playing a session with The Beatles that night in Southport, getting tanked for the session by going to a club and staying there "all afternoon getting' crazy. Mainly just drinking in those days and then driving to Southport for the gig. He got to know the guys a bit more then, and the offer to join the band was floated (but not too emphatically).

Ringo thought nothing more of it, until Epstein came calling again when Pete Best was sick and had to opt out of a performance. Could Ringo fill in? It was a no-brainer; Ringo made good money playing with The Beatles and enjoyed their company and musical talents. This scenario played out several more times; The Beatles were the only band, Ringo said, that he would go to watch in Liverpool.

One time, when The Beatles needed a drummer to sub for Pete that winter, they sent Neil Aspinall around to 10 Admiral Grove to see if Ringo was available. "Neil got me out of bed, and I had no kit," Ringo said. "I got up on stage with only cymbals and gradually Pete's kit started arriving, piece by piece."

Rory and the Hurricanes spent the month of April 1962 playing at United States Army bases in France (Fontenet and Orleans), accompanied by a blond female vocalist named Vicki Woods—a girl singer was required for the army guys in the audience—and a new bass player, Bobby Thompson, who replaced Lu Walters. En route to one of the army bases, Ringo, Rory, and the guys were thrown off the train when it arrived in Paris. The French and Algerians were battling at the time; policemen pointed machine guns at Ringo, who looked suspicious with his drum cases.

In order to cut down on expenses the band stayed in cheap rooms in doss houses, And while the French food was extremely expensive, Rory and the guys didn't really care, since food on the army bases was cheap. Ringo recalled later that Rory and the band were able to use the same rates as the soldiers and indulged in hamburgers and Hershey bars, even though they weren't allowed in the mess hall (but snuck in anyway).

From there, the band traveled to Marbella, Spain. Details are sketchy, so the venue the Hurricanes played there is unknown—it's generally referred to in passing as "a club"— and then it was on to Butlin's, in Skegness, for their third consecutive summer at the holiday camp (and their second time at Skegness).

This time around they were playing in the new Rock and Twist Ballroom, with Ringo and Johnny Guitar once again sharing a room (which was lit by a sad bulb hanging from a frayed wire). The band was working steadily in front of a new audience each week, and Ringo figured he wasn't missing anything back in Liverpool, where the club scene was virtually non-existent during the lazy summer months. "There were different campers every week, so nothing ever got messy," Johnny Guitar recalled.

4

"RINGO WAS THE BETTER BEATLE"

The Beatles had come a long way since starting life as The Quarrymen in 1956. Guitarist John Lennon's group—known as the Blackjacks and Johnny and the Moondogs before settling on The Quarrymen—had, like many other Liverpool bands, embraced rock 'n' roll after the country's skiffle craze died down. Fifteen-year-old Paul McCartney joined The Quarrymen as a guitarist in October 1957, after impressing the seventeen-year-old Lennon with his rendition of Eddie Cochran's "Twenty-Flight Rock," Gene Vincent's "Be-Bop-a-Lu-La," and a medley of Little Richard songs.

George Harrison, Paul's younger school friend from the Liverpool Institute, was recruited into the group in early 1958. Although he had just turned fifteen—nearly three years younger than Lennon, who thought he was too young—Harrison possessed impressive guitar chops for a kid his age, and McCartney implored Lennon, time and again, to give George a chance. The young guitarist won the job after impressing Lennon with his version of the Bill Justis instrumental guitar hit "Raunchy," which he performed atop a Liverpool bus. George was in. He joined Lennon, McCartney, drummer Colin Hanton, pianist John Duff Lowe, and tea-chest bass player Len Garry, who contracted tubercular meningitis and left the group shortly thereafter.

In the summer of 1958, The Quarrymen went into a low-tech Liverpool recording studio and cut two tracks: Buddy Holly's "That'll Be the Day" and a McCartney/Harrison composition, "In Spite of All the Danger." Several days later, Lennon's mother, Julia, with whom he had recently reconnected (he was raised by Julia's sister, Mimi), was hit by a car and killed, sending her son into a months-long funk.

When The Quarrymen regrouped later that year, Lowe was gone (he had to commute too far to rehearse), and he was followed shortly thereafter by drummer Colin Hanton, who departed after nearly getting into a fistfight with McCartney, who had criticized his timekeeping skills after a sloppy Quarrymen performance magnified by large consumptions of alcohol.

By the middle of 1960, after various iterations of the group, including several different lineups and names—Harrison even left for a short time before returning—Lennon cajoled his art school friend Stuart Sutcliffe into joining him, McCartney, and Harrison as the group's bass player. The fact that Sutcliffe couldn't play the instrument, and was far more interested in his art career, didn't matter—his James Dean looks gave the band an aura of danger on which they were keen to capitalize. Sutcliffe hid his inability to play by turning his back to the audience, further adding to his mysterious charisma.

By May 1960 the group was calling itself The Silver Beetles (with a nod to Buddy Holly's backing band, the Crickets) and had a tour of Scotland with Liverpool singer Johnny Gentle under its belt. Tommy Moore, who bore a passing resemblance to Ringo, played drums for The Silver Beetles on the Scotland tour (at least for most of their gigs). In July, the group became The Silver Beatles and then, in August, simply The Beatles. But the band still lacked a permanent drummer.

John Lennon noted how the band went through a string of drummers, since it was so hard to find anyone who owned a drum kit (an expensive commodity). George Harrison recalled a "stream" of drummers, many of whom left behind various pieces of their equipment, giving The Beatles an almost complete patchwork drum set.

But time was now of the essence. Allan Williams, the owner of the Jacaranda Club, also promoted the talent who worked there, and he had wangled a gig for Lennon, McCartney, Harrison, and Sutcliffe in Hamburg. The booking was set to begin August 17, and the group was expected to show up—with a drummer—in the rough-and-tumble German port city. What would they do?

In their former incarnation as The Quarrymen, Lennon, McCartney, and Harrison had played at the Casbah Coffee Club, started by local entrepreneur Mona Best, the previous summer in the basement of her large West Derby house. According to McCartney, they'd even helped paint the place. Mona's older son, Pete, was roughly the same age as The Quarrymen (he was born in November 1941) and played drums in a group called the Black Jacks, who (naturally) were regulars at the Casbah (Pete *did* live there, after all). Pete had also sat in with The Beatles a few times.

After the Black Jacks broke up, and The Beatles needed a drummer for Hamburg, McCartney, who liked Pete's looks more than his talent, asked Pete to join the band. Lennon, naturally, put it more succinctly: "We knew of a guy and he had a drum kit, so we just grabbed him, auditioned him and he could keep one beat going for long enough, so we took him." The audition for Williams at The Jacaranda was unnecessary: Pete already had the job, but Williams didn't want him asking for more than the £15 a week he would be earning in Germany, so he kept him on tenterhooks. Pete Best left for Hamburg the next day with The Beatles as their new drummer.

It was a good ride that lasted for two years.

By the spring and early summer of 1962, John Lennon, Paul McCartney, and George Harrison had grown sufficiently disenchanted with Best to consider making a change in drummers.

(Sutcliffe, whose heart was more into his painting than The Beatles, had left the group in July 1961, with McCartney switching from guitar to bass. Sutcliffe remained in Hamburg with his German girlfriend, photographer Astrid Kirchherr, to pursue his fledgling art career and take classes. He died suddenly in April 1962 at the age of twenty-one from a brain aneurysm, just days after complaining of severe headaches and sensitivity to light.)

It wasn't so much Best's ability behind the drum kit—though, as would be the case with Ringo, opinions on that subject varied wildly—but rather his personality that slowly drove a wedge between Pete and his fellow Beatles. Best was moody and distant, didn't seem to share the same sense of humor as his Beatle brethren and, more often than not, kept to himself after a show rather than banter with the guys. "Pete had never quite been like the rest of us," McCartney said. "We were the wacky trio and Pete was perhaps a little more . . . sensible; he was slightly different from us, he wasn't quite as artsy as we were. And we just didn't hang out that much together."

There was also talk of friction, especially between Pete and Paul McCartney, who liked to think of himself as the group's sex symbol (more so after the smoldering Sutcliffe left the band). It was whispered that McCartney wasn't thrilled with the attention Best commanded on stage from the women in the audience (the same problem he'd had with Sutcliffe). It was also said that McCartney—much as he would do with the next Beatles drummer—had the tendency to micro-manage, telling Pete how to play certain drum parts, which couldn't have sat too well with the group's proud timekeeper.

Ritchie Galvin, the drummer for Earl Preston's band, recalled a scene at the Mandolin Club in 1962, after The Beatles had played a lunchtime gig at The Cavern Club: "Paul was showing Pete the drum pattern that he wanted on a particular song. Pete tried to do it, but he didn't get it."

There were good times, of course, and several Beatles milestones were achieved with Pete Best as the group's drummer. In April 1961, back in Hamburg for a return visit, The Beatles, under cover as The Beat Brothers, backed Tony Sheridan on his recording of "My Bonnie" (the recording which, according to Beatle mythology, turned Brian Epstein on to the band).

On January 1, 1962, The Beatles, with Pete behind his drum kit, traveled south to London to record fifteen tracks (mostly covers, including "Sheik of Araby" and "September in the Rain") for Decca Records. They were turned down two months later. They were told that guitar bands were on the way out.

The Beatles continued to perform regularly in clubs as the group's reputation as terrific performers began to spread. They returned to Hamburg, this time as headliners at Manfred Weissleder's big new venue, the Star Club, where they caught fire.

Five months later, in June, John, Paul, George, and Pete returned to the studio, this time to Parlophone (EMI), to record four songs (including Paul's lead vocals on "Besame Mucho," "Love Me Do," and "P.S. I Love You"). Producer George Martin listened to the finished product once the session was over. While he liked John, Paul, and George, Martin was not happy with Pete's drumming, and he wasn't shy in sharing his opinion with Brian Epstein.

Martin suggested to Epstein that, while Pete might continue to play live gigs, he would need to be replaced in the studio if The Beatles were going to be considered serious recording artists. Martin felt that The Beatles needed a better backbeat than Best could provide—and, besides, no one needed to know who was playing on the studio recordings. Martin wanted to bring in a "hot" drummer, and Epstein agreed.

"It was quite a blow," McCartney recalled. "[Martin] said, 'Can you change your drummer?' And we said, 'Well, we're quite happy with him, he works great in the clubs.' And George said, 'Yes, but for recording he's got to be just a bit more accurate.'"

John Lennon, as usual, gave the bluntest assessment of the Pete Best situation—discounting the myth that Paul was jealous of Best because Pete was better-looking. McCartney and Best didn't hang out much, Lennon said, but only "partly because Pete was a bit slow." Best, Lennon noted, was only in the group because The Beatles needed a drummer when they went to Hamburg—and they always planned on dumping him when a better drummer came along. But by the time they returned from Germany, Lennon said, Best had improved—and the girls liked him.

Throughout the rest of June, July, and early August, The Beatles, with Pete drumming away, kept up a steady schedule of live gigs, including an appearance on the BBC radio show *Northern Dance Orchestra*, after which the group was mobbed by a crowd of girls as they attempted to leave the studio. Their popularity was growing, and word was getting around about the band. Pete was, for all intents and purposes, unaware of both George Martin's remarks about his drumming and about the shared feelings of the three other Beatles. That was all about to change.

In Skegness, meanwhile, Ringo was enjoying his third season at Butlin's, oblivious to all the Beatles melodrama unfolding back in Liverpool. Perhaps he was enjoying himself too much. In early August, he and his Butlin's roommate, Hurricanes guitarist Johnny Guitar, had been kicked out of their stark room after being caught there in the wee hours of the morning playing music—which was *verboten*—and in the company of two young girls (even worse).

Ringo and Johnny were exiled from the premises for "security purposes." Since they were still performing every night with Rory and the Hurricanes, Ringo and Johnny solved their dilemma by renting a trailer for £2 a week—parking it opposite the front gate of Butlin's as a big "fuck you" to the management.

"Ringo had one end, I had the other one," Byrne said of the trailer, which they decorated with posters of American rock 'n' roll stars. And, since they were off the camp grounds, they were able to play music whenever they liked—and as loudly as they liked.

Each night, Rory and his Hurricanes let loose in the Rock and Twist Ballroom. Eric Hunter, who sold hot dogs at Butlin's outside the venue, vividly remembered the power of the band's performance.

> The first part of the show had a group playing jazz standards. After half an hour their music faded, the lights flashed, the music stepped up a gear, and the stage revolved to reveal Ringo raised above and behind the rest of the Hurricanes, his head shaking wildly as he pounded his regulation drum kit, to the group's opening anthem. And then HE [Rory] swept onto the stage and like his name, took the theatre by storm. On the concert stage he was a giant. Others emulated Rory in the 1970s and later, but they had the benefit of more sophisticated amplification equipment.

While at Skegness in that summer of 1962, Ringo received offers to join two Liverpool bands, King Size Taylor and the Dominoes—led by Ted "King Size"

Taylor—and Gerry and the Pacemakers, fronted by fellow Dingle denizen Gerry Marsden, who wanted Ringo to be his bass player. Ringo, of course, didn't play the bass, but that didn't seem to bother Marsden (or Ringo). And Ringo, ever the showman, thought the idea of being up front in a band held some appeal.

King Size Taylor, meanwhile, had lost his drummer, Dave Lovelady, and was in the market for a new stick man. The offer went out to Ringo at Skegness: £20 a week, very good money, and steady work (something that Rory could not always promise). In one of its earlier incarnations, Taylor's band featured singer Cilla Black. She was the same young woman who, before changing her surname (she was erroneously referred to as "Cilla Black" by *Mersey Beat* editor Bill Harry and kept the name), had done Elsie's hair back at 10 Admiral Grove. It was something for Ringo to contemplate.

For the serious musicians in Liverpool, the music business was no longer just a lark. The skiffle craze had given way to rock 'n' roll, which burgeoned into a cottage industry. While the starched-shirt BBC still relegated rock music to off-hours and limited airplay, there was good money to be made—and national fame to be experienced, if the cards fell the right way. Liverpool, in 1962, was still considered provincial, alien territory by the People Who Mattered down south in London, including executives in the record industry. But the emergence of Cliff Richard in the late 1950s as Britain's first bona fide, homegrown pop star, opened the door just a crack—even for bands up north like The Beatles, who were single-minded in their pursuit of success.

The Beatles had a manager—extremely rare for a group, no less a band from scruffy Liverpool—and even had their own tonsorial look, wearing shaggy, bowl-style haircuts fashioned for them by their Hamburg friend Astrid Kirchherr, who was still mourning the death of her boyfriend, ex-Beatle Stuart Sutcliffe. Beatles manager Brian Epstein, ever-cognizant of the importance of publicity—and especially image—was even dressing his "boys" in matching suits, yet even more exotic, particularly for musicians who'd cut their teeth in rough-and-tumble Hamburg (the antithesis of "establishment" behavior).

The Beatles were also extremely aggressive. They knew they were a good band, and had the added benefit, if success was going to be theirs, of nascent songwriters in bassist Paul McCartney and rhythm guitarist John Lennon (lead guitarist George Harrison harbored songwriting ambitions as well—as the youngest band member, however, he was way down on the pecking order). Lennon, McCartney, and Harrison were perfectly happy to play Chuck Berry and Buddy Holly covers (among their impressive arsenal of musical firepower), but John and Paul were extremely confident—cocky, even—in their songwriting abilities and knew success was within their grasp.

"TV and films were a possibility, if we became stars, but records were the main objective," said McCartney. "That was what we bought, that was what we dealt in. It was the currency of music: records." When George Martin opted not to use Beatles drummer Pete Best in the recording studio, John, Paul, and George knew they had to make a move. They decided to dump Best and go after Liverpool's best-known drummer: Ringo Starr.

McCartney recalled that The Beatles needed "the best drummer" in Liverpool. And who was the best drummer? Ringo Starr. Not only that, but he looked cool with his beard and his Zephyr Zodiac. Image was everything (or at least a big part of the package).

Harrison agreed, and pushed for Ringo, talking Lennon and McCartney into the idea. George went to Ringo's house on Admiral Grove; Ringo wasn't there, so George had a cup of tea with Elsie, telling her The Beatles wanted Ringo as their drummer. Ringo, Elsie told him, was at Butlin's with Rory and the Hurricanes—but promised she would have Ringo call George.

Telling Pete Best he was no longer a Beatle after two long and loyal years and many memories, including the momentum-building trips to Hamburg, wasn't going to be easy. That unenviable task fell to Brian Epstein. And there were complicating circumstances; Neil Aspinall—John, Paul, and George's boyhood pal who was now working as the band's road manager/driver/dogsbody—was carrying on an affair with Pete's mother, Mona Best, who was seventeen years older. The relationship resulted in the birth of a boy, Roag, in July 1962. To avoid the whiff of impropriety, the baby was registered under the surname Best. Neil was twenty-one.

If George Harrison was the Beatle pushing the hardest to get Ringo into the group, he was also the band's youngest member and the lowest in its hierarchy. So he stayed behind in Liverpool when John Lennon and Paul McCartney went knocking on the door of the trailer Ringo shared with Johnny Guitar. It was a Wednesday morning, August 15, 1962, and Ringo and Johnny had every intention of sleeping in, since they'd been up late after a show the night before. "It was John and Paul," Johnny vividly remembered. "As soon as I saw them, I knew what they wanted. They wanted Ringo." He invited Lennon and McCartney in, and then came the sales pitch. According to Johnny, Lennon announced that Pete Best was out of the band and they wanted Ringo to join The Beatles.

In Ringo's retelling of that historic moment, Epstein called Butlin's and asked him if he wanted to join the band full-time. (Ringo said he was unaware that George Harrison had been lobbying on his behalf).

If the offer really did come out of left field, it was music to Ringo's ears. As previously noted, he had been growing more and more disenchanted with the stagnating Hurricanes. John, Paul, and George were undoubtedly on the way up, if only in the confines of Liverpool. And they had actually recorded some tracks in the studio, which they were shopping around to the record companies. Real professionals!

Johnny Guitar couldn't really blame his band mate for considering the offer. "They had a recording contract at that time and nobody in Liverpool had a contract," he said.

To sweeten the deal, The Beatles offered Ringo £25 a week, which was £5 more than what King Size Taylor and the Dominoes had on the table. It was a no-brainer.

But Rory and the Hurricanes still had some time left on their Butlin's engagement. Ringo's mind was already made up, but as a courtesy he ran his new job offer past Rory, who told him he should take the gig. (Rory's only stipulation was that Ringo return the pink suit he wore onstage, which would be passed on to the band's next drummer.) The Beatles wanted Ringo to start right away—they were playing at Liverpool's Cavern Club that night—but Ringo, after three good years, felt badly about leaving Rory in the lurch. As a small concession, he promised to stay with Rory through Saturday, when the Hurricanes had the day off (and Butlin's received a fresh infusion of campers), which gave his now-ex-boss three days to find a replacement. That turned out to be sixteen-year-old Gibson Kemp, who had a brief run with the Hurricanes—the first of many drummers Rory used after Ringo's departure.

Ringo was a Beatle. John Lennon told him to shave off his long sideburns and change his Teddy Boy hairstyle—to comb his hair down like the other three Beatles. As for Pete Best, Ringo said he never felt sorry for the man he so unceremoniously replaced—since he was a better drummer.

While the two Beatles were recruiting Ringo into the band, Brian Epstein was preparing to fire Pete Best. John and Paul returned to Liverpool from Skegness to play the Wednesday-night gig at the Cavern Club—with Pete, as usual, behind his drum kit—and Brian waited until the next day to drop the hammer on Pete in a meeting with him in his NEMS office.

"Pete, I have some bad news for you," Epstein told him. "The boys want you out, and it's already been arranged that Ringo will join the band on Saturday." When a stunned Pete asked him why, Epstein told him that John, Paul, and George—and, more importantly, George Martin—didn't think his drumming was up to par. He would have to go. Pete would recall that his "mind was in a turmoil" and that he considered this a "stab in the back." Epstein's consolation prize was an offer to form a new band around Pete which he (Epstein) would manage and promote.

To add insult to injury, Epstein also asked Pete to stay on with The Beatles until Ringo could join the group that weekend—to which Pete initially agreed before thinking better of the idea. "Once I was home at Hayman's Green, I broke down and wept," he recalled. "I wouldn't rate Ringo as a better drummer than me—I'm adamant about that. And when it happened I felt like putting a stone around my neck and jumping off the Pier Head."

"Technically Ringo was a better drummer than Pete Best, but not by much, because Pete Best was quite good," recalled Liverpool promoter Sam Leach. "But compared to Ringo, Pete was only learning. Ringo was the better Beatle . . . and he was a better singer than Pete. He definitely was. Pete was a lovely guy who said some nice things about me but he was very shy and introverted and that didn't help. He didn't want to change his hairstyle. He kept to himself—which is the real reason, in my opinion, that he got the sack. I've always felt that Pete got a raw deal."

In the meantime, Brian Epstein asked Johnny Hutchinson, the drummer for Beatles rivals The Big Three—also managed by Epstein—to fill in for Pete on the three gigs with The Beatles until Ringo could join the group. Hutchinson agreed, and later said that Epstein even offered him the job full-time.

"Brian asked me to join The Beatles and I said, 'I wouldn't join The Beatles for a gold clock.' There's only one group as far as I'm concerned and that's The Big Three. The Beatles can't make a better sound than that, and Pete Best is a very good friend of mine. I couldn't do the dirty on him.'" Hutchinson also had an intense dislike for Paul McCartney, who he felt was a huge phony.

The news of Pete's firing so incensed Neil Aspinall—the new father of Pete's half-brother, Roag—that, for a short time thereafter, he refused to set up Ringo's drum kit. he refused to set up Ringo's drum kit. Given the circumstances, who could blame him? But Neil eventually got over his fit of pique and continued to drive the band's van and operate as their lone roadie.

"We were cowards when we sacked him," Lennon would say later about Pete.

On August 16, *Mersey Beat* broke the news of Pete's firing and Ringo's hiring with a blaring headline—BEATLES CHANGE DRUMMER!—followed by a small accompanying story:

> Ringo Starr (former drummer with Rory Storm & the Hurricanes) has joined the Beatles, replacing Pete Best on drums. Ringo has admired the Beatles for years and is delighted with his new engagement. Naturally he is tremendously excited about the future.
>
> The Beatles comment, "Pete left the group by mutual agreement. There were no arguments or difficulties, and this has been an entirely amicable decision."
>
> On Tuesday September 4th, the Beatles will fly to London to make recordings at EMI Studios. They will be recording numbers that have been specially written for the group.

The news sent a lightning bolt through the Liverpool music scene, igniting a firestorm of controversy.

Pete had been an extremely popular Beatle, despite his ex-band mates' misgivings about his drumming ability and his personality. The group's female fans, in particular, dug Pete's brooding good looks. There was not much of a to-do when Ringo made his official debut as The Beatles' new drummer on Saturday, August 18, at a Horticultural Society dance at Hulme Hall, Port Sunlight (on the Wirral Peninsula in Merseyside) following a two-hour practice session with John, Paul, and George.

That all changed the next night, August 19, when The Beatles took the stage at the Cavern Club in the heart of Liverpool, in front of their homegrown fans. A throng of fired-up, hostile Pete Best supporters turned out to heckle the group in the tiny basement club. The tension was palpable and there was a lot of pushing, shoving, and finger-pointing from the sweaty crowd, crammed elbow-to-elbow in the humid Cavern basement, when The Beatles materialized with Ringo seated behind his drum kit, freshly clean-shaven-and-coiffed as per Beatles regulations.

Shouts of "Pete Forever! Ringo Never!" and "We Want Pete!" rang out. Ringo, who appeared to be extremely nervous, had his own small contingent of supporters ("Up with Ringo!"). When George Harrison stepped off the stage into a small, dark tunnel, one of Pete's more emotional fans punched him in the eye—leaving the guitarist with a shiner that was still visible in Beatles publicity photographs taken with their new drummer shortly thereafter.

But Ringo held his own that first night in the Cavern Club and managed to make it through the set in one piece. "There were riots," he said. "It was okay when I just joined in and played a gig and left, but suddenly I was the drummer. Pete had a big following, but I had been known for years in Liverpool, so I had quite a following too. So there was this whole shouting match, 'Ringo never, Pete forever' and 'Pete never, Ringo forever.' There was this whole battle going on, and I'm just trying to drum away. But they got over it and then we went down to make a record."

For all the hue and cry, the hubbub didn't last far beyond that first night, and Ringo settled into his new role alongside John, Paul, and George. On August 22, Ringo was behind his drum kit for The Beatles when they were filmed at the Cavern Club by Manchester-based Granada Television for a show called *Know the North*, tearing through "Some Other Guy." "Ringo is a much better drummer and he can smile—which is a bit more than Pete could do," George Harrison wrote to a Beatles fan. "It will seem different for a few weeks, but I think that the majority of our fans will soon be taking Ringo for granted."

Two days later, on August 24, John Lennon married Cynthia Powell, who was twenty-three and pregnant with their child. (Julian Lennon was born the following April.) John was the first Beatle to get married, and the newest Beatle was kept out of the loop. He wasn't invited to the wedding, and Lennon didn't tell him, at first, that he'd just gotten married. John and Cynthia were trying to keep it a secret, particularly from Ringo, who was the newest Beatle and hadn't yet earned his stripes. That would change once The Beatles went on tour and got to know one another on a more intimate level.

Ringo, meanwhile, was involved in his own serious romance with Maureen "Mo" Cox, a hairdresser he'd met at the Cavern Club. Six years younger than Ringo—and, like him, an only child—Mary Cox was born in Liverpool in August 1946 (her father was a ship's steward; her mother, a homemaker). When she was fourteen, Mary changed her name to the more posh-sounding Maureen after leaving school to train as a hairdresser and manicurist at the Ashley du Pre salon in Liverpool.

When she was fifteen, the petite Maureen started hanging around the Cavern Club with some friends, including Lorraine Flyte, who would later date Beatles insider Tony Bramwell. Maureen, who had dated Ringo's Hurricanes band mate Johnny Guitar, claimed to have once kissed Paul McCartney on a bet, but her big, dark eyes were firmly set on Ringo, even while she was dating Johnny Guitar. "I fancied him then but couldn't possibly have made the first move. It was up to Richy," she said. "Our eyes met a few times at Rory's gigs but nothing happened. I began to make up my mind that I wasn't his type."

Maureen was so smitten with Ringo that she even memorized the license plate number of his blue-and-cream Ford Zodiac, which she could still remember thirty years later. Shortly thereafter, Ringo asked her to dance one night at the Cavern Club and the two hit it off. He picked her up for their first date at the Ashley du Pre salon and they went to the park, then to hear singer Frank Ifield ("I Remember You"), then to the movies for a double feature and from there to a couple of clubs (The Pink Parrot, The Blue Angel) to drink and dance.

Ringo recalled that, when he first met Maureen at the Cavern Club and offered to take her home, she was game—provided he take her friend home, too. It was a quaint Liverpool custom that grew old very quickly.

They began dating steadily but surreptitiously; in 1962, it wasn't good for a Beatle's romantic image to have a steady girlfriend or, god forbid, a wife, which is why John Lennon had to hide his marriage to Cynthia. "You belong to every girl fan in England," Brian Epstein would tell them.

Ringo and Maureen started going steady—or as steady as they could, given Ringo's touring schedule with The Beatles. But whatever time off he had—usually Mondays, when the clubs were closed—was spent with Maureen. They would go to a pub or a movie or to a restaurant.

Lorraine would help Maureen hide under a blanket in Ringo's car outside of wherever The Beatles were playing. Once Ringo drove out of view of the clamoring fans, she would crawl out from under the blanket so they could be together in private. "I might have been killed otherwise," she said. "The other girls were not friendly at all. They wanted to stab me in the back. It was part of their [The Beatles'] image, that they weren't married and so each girl thought she might have a chance. None of them were supposed to have steadies."

Maureen's time alone with Ringo, at least early on, was something to be treasured, since she was still living at home and her parents enforced a strict midnight curfew, to which she dutifully complied.

She called him "Richy" in private and was smitten, but at the same time she also got an up-close-and-personal look at the growing fanaticism and hysteria of

Beatles fans. "They used to hang round the Cavern all day long, just on the off chance of seeing them," she said. "They'd come out of the lunchtime session and just stand outside all afternoon, queuing up for the evening. Richy and I once went past at midnight and they were already queuing up for the next day. We bought them some pies. They were knocked out."

Maureen saw "fights and rows among the girls . . . knocking each other over" and, before The Beatles came on, going into the bathroom "to get changed and made up" so they'd look their best for John, Paul, George, and Ringo. "It was terrible, the mad screams when they came on," she said. "They went potty."

It could even veer into creepy territory; Maureen recalled some female Beatles fans coming into the Ashley du Pre salon and threatening her—"If you see that Ringo Starr again you're in for it"—then pushing her around when she went outside. She also received threatening phone calls at home. In February 1963, she hid under the blanket in Ringo's car while The Beatles played a Valentine's Day concert at The Locarno Ballroom in Liverpool. She was confronted by a female fan who'd followed her outside, reached through the car window, and scratched her face. It was not an idyllic existence for a sixteen-year-old hairdresser.

5

"RINGO IS A GOOD BEATLE"

The Beatles had secured their new drummer, and now it was time to get down to business, to go into the recording studio and cut some tracks. In early September of 1962 Ringo, with just two weeks as a Beatle under his belt, accompanied his new band mates as they flew from Liverpool to London, where they were booked into EMI's Abbey Road studios for a session on September 4. Producer George Martin was familiar with John, Paul, and George—having met and recorded them the previous June in the now-infamous Pete Best session—but this was his first time meeting Ringo. It was the beginning of an uneasy relationship.

The Beatles, with photographer Dezo Hoffman snapping pictures—George Harrison's black eye from Ringo's Cavern Club debut is visible in the shots—rehearsed for three hours that first afternoon. They practiced six songs, including John Lennon and Paul McCartney's "Please Please Me," and an upbeat number written by Mitch Murray, "How Do You Do It?" George Martin insisted this tune was perfect for The Beatles, although they strongly disagreed. That night, from seven to ten p.m., they hunkered down for their first official recordings, "How Do You Do It?" and "Love Me Do," another Lennon/McCartney original, featuring John's lead-in harmonica and Paul's vocals.

Martin, who was hearing Ringo's drumming for the first time, was not thrilled with his timekeeping abilities on "Love Me Do"—echoes of Pete Best's experience the previous June. "I didn't rate Ringo very highly," he said later, adding the condescending remark, "He couldn't do a roll—and still can't—though he's improved a lot since."

Martin apparently wasn't the only one who thought that Ringo's drumming was not up to snuff. "I've a feeling that Paul wasn't too happy with Ringo's drumming, and felt that it could be better," said engineer Norman Smith, who was recording the September 4 session. "He [Ringo] didn't make too good a job of it. I remember too that there was a fair bit of editing to be done." That assessment is hard to fathom, even with the twenty/twenty hindsight of history. The drum pattern on "Love Me Do" was extremely simplistic and was something Ringo, an experienced drummer by that point in time, could have played in his sleep.

But Martin did not have a pop-music background—he had previously recorded instrumental music and comedians, including Peter Sellers—and had a different standard for drummers. "On all these Lita Roza, Alma Cogan records that were in vogue shortly before us, the drummers were pretty good show drummers, so producers were used to hearing a bass drum in the right place, locking in with the bass guitar like it would now," McCartney said. "George obviously thought that Ringo was a little bit out of time, a little bit unsteady on tempo. We never really had to be steady on tempo. We liked to be but it didn't matter if we slowed down or went faster, because we all went at the same time."

McCartney's backhanded compliment notwithstanding, that's a difficult theory to swallow given Ringo's rock-solid timekeeping skills, which would later prove to be the band's signature calling card.

"Love Me Do" was slated to be The Beatles' first single, and Martin wanted it to be perfect. He wasn't happy with what he'd heard on the September 4 recording, even after all the editing. So he called The Beatles back to Abbey Road the following Tuesday, September 11, to re-record "Love Me Do"—without telling them beforehand that he was going to use session drummer Andy White in place of Ringo. (Martin wasn't present at that September 11 session, which was produced by Ron Richards, who had hired Andy White.) "Andy was the kind of drummer I needed," Martin said. "Ringo was only used to ballrooms. It was obviously best to use someone with experience."

It wasn't unusual for session musicians to replace individual band members in the recording studio. Established drummers like Bobby Graham and Clem Cattini, for example, were brought in to lay down the beat for The Kinks on several of the band's early recordings, including hits like "You Really Got Me"—replacing the group's regular drummer, Mick Avory. "A lot of the time it was a time-saving scenario," Cattini said. "I recorded a whole album with The Kinks in three sessions when it could take that time [to record] one track. It was no reflection on the band's drummer. And playing in a studio and playing live was completely different."

But Ringo's skills had never been called into question. And wasn't he considered by many to be the best drummer in Liverpool? "I was nervous and terrified of the studio," admitted Ringo. "When we came back later to do the B-side, I found that George Martin had got another drummer sitting in my place. It was terrible. I'd been asked to join The Beatles, but now it looked as if I was only going to be good enough to do ballrooms with them, but not good enough for records."

It was a crushing blow, which Ringo later rationalized (to some extent) as being tied to Martin's experience with Pete Best. Martin, Ringo said, didn't want to risk anything and was stuck between a rock and a hard place. But he was, in his own words, "devastated" that Martin doubted his ability, and he was embarrassed that he was being supplanted on the group's very first single by a session drummer. Years later, long after The Beatles reached rock's pinnacle, Ringo said that Martin apologized more than once about that session. But it was a wound that took a long time to heal.

Paul McCartney later said the incident was hard for him and his fellow Beatles to accept, particularly so soon after they'd fired Pete Best. They didn't want to lose another drummer, and this was the ultimate insult to Ringo. (McCartney also claimed that Ringo could never admit to liking the version of "Love Me Do" recorded with Andy White.)

Who could blame him? Ringo prided himself on his drumming, and this turn of events was unbelievably deflating. White, who, at thirty-two was much older, was paid £5 to play drums on eighteen takes of "Love Me Do" while Ringo was relegated to banging a tambourine. (The earlier, September 4 version of "Love Me Do," featuring Ringo on the drums, was included on the albums *Rarities* and *Past Masters, Volume One*. The Pete Best version, recorded in June 1962, was included on *The Beatles Anthology 1*, released in 1995.)

"He had only just joined the group," White said years later. "He was nervous, but he kind of played . . . he said he played a bit behind the beat, which is not really what a drummer should do. The only trouble was they had Ringo playing tambourine quite a way away and I don't think he played it all that great. There was no floundering, but it was more difficult than it should have been."

As if the indignity of being replaced on "Love Me Do" wasn't bad enough, Ringo also sat on the sidelines, gamely shaking the maracas, while White played the drums on another Lennon/McCartney song, "P.S. I Love You." Said Ringo: "The other bloke played the drums and I was given the maracas. I thought, 'That's the end. They're doing a Pete Best on me.' I was shattered. What a drag. How phony the whole record business was, I thought. Just what I'd heard about. If I was going to be no use for records, I might as well leave."

"I didn't realize until quite later on how much I'd hurt him, and I didn't mean to," Martin said, fifty years later, in a joint interview with Paul McCartney.

"Well, he's a sensitive soul, and I don't think we realized how much that hurt him," McCartney answered. "He got over it. He was not precise, and you were used to working with session drummers who were on the ball."

Ringo finally got the chance to play the drums and record with his fellow Beatles on "Please Please Me," a soaring, Roy Orbison–inspired tune, written mostly by John Lennon. White also drummed on a version of the song, which didn't see the light of day until it was released on the *Anthology* album in 1995.

George Martin had returned to Abbey Road as The Beatles were in the process of recording multiple takes of "Please Please Me" and, while he liked what he heard, he thought its pacing was a bit slow (Lennon wrote it as a ballad), and he didn't like George Harrison's habit of replicating Lennon's opening harmonica riff on his guitar throughout the song—again and again. And if Ringo was happy to finally be included in the recording process, he was hampered by the setup that was used to record "Please Please Me."

Geoff Emerick, who was only fifteen at the time, and was training to be an assistant recording director at EMI, recalled Ringo "doing something odd" while playing on the song, holding a maraca in one hand and a tambourine in the other, while using his foot to pound his bass drum. "Look at what that bloody drummer is up to now!" Emerick recalls Norman Smith shouting out in laughter to his colleagues behind the glass.

It's a good story, but likely apocryphal, especially if the version of "Please Please Me" that was eventually released—with Ringo playing a hi-hat with one hand and his snare drum with the other—was akin to his drumming during that recording session.

Martin listened to a few takes of "Please Please Me," and even *he* admitted the song had potential. "I told them to bring it in next time and we'd have another go at it," he said, recommending that the boys increase the song's tempo a bit. Martin was still insisting that "How Do You Do It?" should be the group's first single, but The Beatles (Ringo included) were adamant that "Love Me Do" should be the band's first release, so confident were they that the Lennon/McCartney number spoke more to the group's sound than did Mitch Murray's tune.

Ringo, despite his overwhelming disappointment on being relegated to backup status on "Love Me Do"—and despite having just joined the band—voiced his concern over "How Do You Do It?"

Martin finally caved to the group's insistence and, on October 5, 1962, "Love Me Do" was released as the first Beatles single, with "P.S. I Love You" on the B-side (featuring Andy White on drums and Ringo on maracas).

There would be much confusion over the years regarding "Love Me Do" and the different versions featuring Ringo and Andy White. As Beatles historian and *Mersey Beat* founder Bill Harry points out, the "initial copies" of the "Love Me Do" single released in England featured the Ringo-on-drums version (recorded on September 4); the Andy White-on-drums version was included on the group's first album, *Please Please Me* and on a 1976 re-release of the song.

Ringo wrote to his old Butlin's flame, Doreen Walker, shortly thereafter, excitedly catching her up on all the good news. The letter, written with little, if any, punctuation—and sent from 10 Admiral Grove—was enthusiastic (and non-committal in terms of any future romantic encounters).

Epstein would get the playlists from the local radio stations and let "The Boys" know when "Love Me Do" would be broadcast. The fact that The Beatles had an actual vinyl disc trumped anything the song might do on the charts. That's how exciting it all was.

"I didn't think it was all that brilliant," George Martin said of "Love Me Do," "but I was very thrilled by the reaction to The Beatles and their sound."

The general public shared Martin's sentiments. "Love Me Do" didn't exactly set the world on fire; the BBC, despite producer Ron Richards's entreaties (he knew someone there), refused to play the song, calling it "too amateurish" so airplay was relegated mostly to radio stations up north, on The Beatles' home turf. George Harrison's mother recalled how excited her son was when, late one night, he heard "Love Me Do" for the first time on Radio Luxembourg. His screaming awoke his father, who was angry because he had to go to work early the next morning.

"Love Me Do" entered the charts at Number Forty-Nine and eventually rose to a respectable Number Seventeen—good, but not good enough for a band that knew it was destined for bigger things. There were rumors that a healthy number of copies of "Love Me Do"—the number was estimated at ten thousand—were bought by Brian Epstein on the sly in an effort to pump up the sales figures.

While "Love Me Do" began its crawl up the charts, The Beatles kept up a frantic pace of touring and recording throughout the fall of 1962, including a return trip to Hamburg. In October, a few weeks after the release of "Love Me Do," they made their first television appearance on a Granada show called *People and Places*. It was a regional broadcast and only aired up north, in Manchester, which spoke volumes about the band's status.

On the rare occasions when The Beatles were not on the road somewhere, Ringo slept in his bedroom at 10 Admiral Grove. His proud mother, Elsie, and "stepladder," Harry, adorned the house's parlor walls with publicity photos of their now-well-known son and his band mates. Ringo and Maureen continued to date, and there were whispers that Ringo was also seeing model Vicki Hodge.

As the group's playing grew tighter, so too did Ringo's relationships with his band mates. John, Paul, and George had known one another all too well after four long years together; now, they were just getting to really know their new drummer. "He wasn't too much of a challenge, personally," said George Martin's assistant, Peter Brown. "It was John and Paul's group, with this kid called George and so, though it was never spoken about, the psychological balance had to be kept. Ringo was always the amiable one who was easy to get on with."

Ringo was also confident behind his drum kit, although he was quick to acknowledge that he might not be the most technical drummer.

"I became a drummer because it was the only thing I could do," he said. "But whenever I hear another drummer I know I'm no good. I can only play on the off beat because John can't keep up on the rhythm guitar. I'm no good on the technical things but I'm good with all the motions, swinging my head, like. That's because I love to dance but you can't do that on drums."

But Ringo, with his outgoing personality and his laconic, Liverpudlian sense of humor, was the antithesis of Pete Best and his moody, insular demeanor. Yet Ringo was also the newcomer to a group sharing a long history in which he had no part. He was worried about fitting in and embarrassed about his lack of education, particularly when compared to Lennon and McCartney. He likened his initiation to "joining a new class at school where everybody knew everybody else but me."

"Ringo found his chronic lack of self-confidence difficult to overcome," said Tony Barrow, who began working as a part-time publicist for The Beatles in the fall of 1962 and was an eyewitness to Ringo's integration into the band. "He was acutely aware that he was under-educated academically . . . and the fact that he was such a late arrival in the lineup of the band only added to his feeling of social inadequacy—although this negativity did not extend to his music. He was one hundred percent confident about his drumming. On the other hand, he fitted in perfectly to the image of the group, immediately responding to his appointment as their incoming drummer in the summer of 1962 by giving his haircut a distinctive Beatles fringe."

Barrow also felt that it was Ringo, even more so than George Harrison, who was the quietest Beatle. "He let his backbeat speak for itself. . . . When Ringo came into the picture, John, Paul and George had been together for near enough five years, a particularly long time where formative adolescent years are concerned." But while, in John Lennon's opinion, Ringo was perfect for the group and fit right into its hierarchy, Barrow remembers the band's new drummer struggling to make only a "skin-deep" transformation into the newest Beatle.

"I think he worked hard to overcome his inferiority complex but worrying simply made it worse," he wrote. "Openly, in private and in public, the other three willingly accepted him as a full-blown buddy, pal and mate, treating him totally as their equal, but there was always the underlying feeling that an outsider had become attached to the original unit with ties that were never quite so secure as those that bound the initial threesome together."

Geoff Emerick, who would, in time, become the group's favored engineer, didn't see the "fun" side of Ringo once the band was in the recording studio: "Ringo wasn't especially moody like John was, but there were days when you could tell he was pissed off about something. He could be quick-witted and charming, but he also had a sarcastic sense of humor: you never really knew if he was being funny or if he meant what he was saying. I always felt he used his sarcasm as a defense mechanism to cover his insecurity, like the way some people have a nervous laugh."

Shortly after Ringo joined The Beatles, Barrow was tasked by Brian Epstein with writing vignettes about each of the four band members, which would be distributed to the press to promote the release of "Love Me Do." He asked John Lennon why Ringo was more acceptable to the group than Pete Best. "He told me, 'Pete was a good drummer. Ringo is a good Beatle.' I took this to mean that more was needed of a new Beatle haircut than proficient musicianship. Obviously, John had recognized the dry sense of humor that was a hallmark of Ringo's personality even before the rest of us saw evidence of it.

"To be quite honest, Ringo was also seen as being much more compliant and easy to deal with—whereas Pete had a lot of baggage that made his presence difficult to deal with in the longer term."

In the studio, at least early on, Ringo and George Harrison were quiet and kept to themselves, unlike Lennon and McCartney, who were quite vociferous—both to George Martin and to the EMI engineers—about what they wanted to do and to be done to their songs, even while recording songs they hadn't written themselves.

Ringo often felt like a fourth wheel, relegated to the bottom rung of the band—an afterthought after John, Paul, and George. A "them" and "him" mentality. It would be quite a while until that last remnant of the Pete Best Era finally died down.

"The focus was always on John and Paul; they were the songwriters," Ringo said. "As for the drummer, there could have been a gorilla up there. Drummers aren't really treated like human beings. We're a bit like second-rate citizens. I was doing my best and I was doing some good shit. But I felt as if I was being passed over. I wanted to be considered a member of the band like everyone else.

"In reviews of the records and stories about the music we were playing, very few writers happened to note whether I was playing good or bad. I wouldn't have minded if they said I was crap, as long as they mentioned my name in those days."

The Beatles' frenetic, wide-ranging touring schedule threw them together into very close quarters nearly every waking hour of every week. They spent endless hours in the group's Bedford van, being driven hundreds of miles between gigs by Neil Aspinall—sometimes driving straight through the night through thick fog or pouring rain to get to the next destination on time.

Early on, before they graduated to hotel rooms, John, Paul, George, and Ringo would stay in guest houses, two to a room. McCartney was Ringo's roommate, but that was fine with the drummer—who, unlike John, Paul, and George, had no siblings. Being in The Beatles was like having three brothers, and he loved it all. His fellow Beatles were his brethren. They were his family.

Ringo recalled how the band bonded, driving up and down the M1 highway in their van, freezing, one Beatle sitting in the passenger seat and the other three sitting in the back. Driving. Always driving. Never stopping. Getting to the next gig, no matter how far it was—and trying to keep warm on those freezing days and nights by lying on top of one another, swigging whiskey.

George Harrison described The Beatles, at that time, as "really tight." They were more than a band. They were friends who always stuck together, no matter what, and communicated almost wordlessly whenever an outsider dared to breach the inner circle.

In 1963, when the group's fame in England began to grow, gentle giant Mal Evans, who was working as a telephone engineer, was hired to assist Aspinall in driving the van and functioning as a de facto bodyguard. Ringo was particularly fascinated that Evans could lift a clunky bass amp by himself—no mean feat.

On November 26, The Beatles, even more cohesive than before, returned to EMI for another recording session. George Martin was still adamant about releasing "How Do You Do It?" as the band's next single, but he was intrigued by "Please Please Me," and wanted to hear how the song's writers, Lennon and McCartney, had restructured the song in the two months since the group first recorded the song for him. There was no Andy White in the Abbey Road studio this time around, and, from this point forward—save for a few instances near the end of the band's run—there would never again be anyone but Ringo Starr sitting behind his drum kit for a Beatles recording session.

The version of "Please Please Me" which The Beatles now presented to Martin was quite different; gone were Harrison's guitar licks mimicking Lennon's opening harmonica riff. And John, Paul, George, and Ringo had heeded Martin's advice, quickening the song's tempo and bashing it out like an upbeat pop tune rather than a melancholy love song. Ringo's drumming was sharp and steady and even included a few quick fills. "You've just made your first Number One," Martin told the group, quickly forgetting about "How Do You Do It?" "Please Please Me" would be the band's next single release.

The Beatles, looking for a B-side to "Please Please Me," also ran through several takes of "Ask Me Why" and something called "Tip of My Tongue," which would later be recorded by Tommy Quickly.

"Drummer Ringo Starr had just cause to be pleased with himself after the session," wrote *Mersey Beat* correspondent Alan Smith, who had watched The Beatles in the studio. "During the recording of the Beatles' last disc, George Martin wanted him to do some intricate drumming effects. He was naturally nervous—it was the first time he'd recorded, unlike the rest of the boys—and it took quite a bit of time. On this occasion he had the confidence to perform without worrying."

Terry O'Neill was a twenty-four-year-old photographer working for *The Daily Sketch*, which was based in Manchester near Liverpool, when he was sent by his bosses to take some photos of The Beatles at EMI Studios. O'Neill, who was a jazz drummer before getting into photography, saw it as just another forgettable assignment.

"They all saw this pop thing coming up as being big, and I got hired to go down and shoot this group called The Beatles down at Abbey Road," he said. "They were recording 'Please Please Me.'" O'Neill took John, Paul, George, and Ringo outside, to a small, bricked-in area adjacent to the recording studio and took several photographs.

"I struggled to take this shot of the group and I took this photo of them, with Ringo holding up his drum cymbal and his drum sticks. I mean, this was the first sort of shot of the group, the first musicians of this type, ever to be published in the newspaper." It was also the first photograph of a pop music group to grace the front page of a national British publication. "And it just sold out the day it was published," O'Neill said. "The paper went mad after that."

Over the subsequent decades, O'Neill developed a close relationship with all four Beatles (Ringo even hired O'Neill to photograph his wedding in 1981). "It's obvious from the first picture that John was the leading member [of the group] and the other three are just sort of behind him," he said. "Ringo was the joker of the group. He was always making people laugh. He was a really loveable bloke. You could never fall out with him."

O'Neill, the onetime jazz drummer, was impressed with Ringo's style after watching him that day in the studio. "I knew about drumming, and he was really great . . . he was always different," he said. "He really had something, Ringo. And he doesn't get enough credit for it. They couldn't have gotten a better drummer. He's a good player . . . not flash, good fills and all that, very, very good. He would be a creative jazz drummer if he ever got into it."

In the meantime, The Beatles were booked for two return trips (November and December) to Hamburg's Reeperbahn and to Manfred Weissleder's Star-Club, deals that had been arranged the previous summer. With "Please Please Me" not scheduled to be released until January 1963, the group plodded along with a busy touring schedule, not yet reaping the benefits of the stardom that was just around the corner. They often didn't even top the bill, being relegated to second-tier status to fading performers like Little Richard or Gene Vincent on concerts that Brian Epstein was promoting.

Returning to the smaller hotels after a gig often meant having to forage for something to eat, Ringo recalled having to "beg" for a sandwich one late afternoon. But they pushed on, with loyal Neil and Mal handling the grunt work and making sure everything went off as planned (or as closely as was possible).

After an ill-fated one-off concert in Peterborough supporting Australian crooner Frank Ifield, John, Paul, George, and Ringo headed to Hamburg. Ringo, like his band mates, was not particularly enthused about making the trip; he'd done the "Hamburg Thing" several times already, and the thought of playing multiple shows each night for Manfred Weissleder—*Mach shau!*—wasn't particularly enticing. John Lennon, in particular, was vocal about having to return to Hamburg. What was once exciting was now just a chore.

Besides the November trip, the band was slotted for a second, two-week run beginning in mid-December and lasting through the end of the year; Ringo, who was still living at home, would miss spending the Christmas holidays at 10 Admiral Grove with Elsie and Harry. His band mates shared similar sentiments.

The return trips to Hamburg did include one important perk, however: better accommodations. The band's status as recording artists who had released a single ("Love Me Do") that sold fairly well—with a second single ("Please Please Me") awaiting release—translated into a certain show business cachet. This time around, The Beatles would stay in good hotels and, for the first time, they would enjoy their own rooms (no roommates). Little Richard, accompanied by his pianist, Billy Preston, shared the bill with the group on the November trip; in December, King Size Taylor and the Dominoes joined them at the Star-Club.

Unlike John Lennon, Ringo enjoyed the return trips to Hamburg. For him, it was a homecoming of sorts, and his first time there as a bona fide Beatle. He liked Billy Preston, who was only sixteen at the time, although he thought Little Richard—whom The Beatles had met the previous October when they shared the bill in one of the Epstein-arranged concerts—was a bit of a show-off.

And despite all the carping about returning to Hamburg, The Beatles didn't let that stop them from having a good time. They were still gulping down Preludins, drinking like fishes, and getting away with whatever they wanted—as long as they showed up onstage and played.

Mach shau!

That was about to happen in a big way.

6

BEATLEMANIA

Plase Please Me" was released on January 11, 1963, with "Ask Me Why" on the B-side. Two days later, The Beatles made their first national television appearance, shaking their bowl haircuts and miming to "Please Please Me" on ITV's *Thank Your Lucky Stars*, an influential series that premiered in 1961 and was already a trendsetter with its visual finger firmly on the pop-culture pulse of Britain's music scene. Beatles historians also cite the band's appearance the previous week on *Roundup*, a live Scottish TV show which aired from The Theatre Royal in Glasgow. The Beatles mimed "Please Please Me" but, alas, a copy of this appearance has yet to surface.

Unlike "Love Me Do," which trickled out and was (initially) ignored by the public (outside of Liverpool), "Please Please Me," with its catchy melody, John Lennon's mouth organ intro and lush harmonies, received a lot of airplay upon its release. Radio Luxembourg, in particular, put the single into heavy rotation, and it even crept onto The BBC, a rarity for any pop band, let alone one comprising four unknown, long-haired nobodies from "Up North."

Critics, too, were generous in their praise, with Keith Fordyce from *New Musical Express* calling the song "a really enjoyable platter, full of beat vigour and vitality—and what's more, it's different. I can't think of any other group currently recording in this style."

Thank Your Lucky Stars host Brian Matthew, who also emceed The BBC's popular *Saturday Club* music show, said The Beatles were "musically and visually the most accomplished group to emerge since The Shadows." He would have a long and fruitful association with the band.

The attention was nice—and the growing sales even better—but John, Paul, George, and Ringo were still unknown entities throughout most of England. While "Please Please Me" continued its inexorable climb up the charts, The Beatles embarked on a month-long, nationwide tour of the Moss Empire theatre circuit with Helen Shapiro, joining a bill that boasted Danny Williams,

Kenny Lynch, The Red Price Band, The Honeys, and The Kestrels. Comedian Dave Allen was the emcee. They were all tasked with backing sixteen-year-old British singer Shapiro, owner of several hit singles including "Don't Treat Me Like a Child" and "You Don't Know." (John and Paul wrote "Misery" for Shapiro, which she never recorded. The Beatles recorded it themselves for their first album, *Please Please Me*.)

Kenny Lynch was already a Beatles fan. "One reason I think they'll succeed is because they manage to reproduce their record sound on stage," he told *Melody Maker*'s Ray Coleman. "This is why The Shadows succeeded, and this is why the Beatles will. Apart from that, their sound is so great they can't miss."

The Beatles, as was their wont, were confident in their abilities—but they held no allusions as to who the people were really paying good money to see. "Helen was the star," Ringo said. "She had the telly in her dressing room and we didn't have one. We had to ask her if we could watch hers. We weren't getting packed houses, but we were on the boards, man."

Ringo was still using the same mahogany Premier drum kit from his Rory Storm days, though he had replaced the "R-S" on his bass drum with a more elaborate *Ringo Starr*. With the Helen Shapiro tour about to get under way, The Beatles decided they needed to upgrade their equipment.

Both the group and manager Brian Epstein felt that the *Ringo Starr* stenciled on Ringo's bass drum would call too much attention to the drummer, or maybe even lead people to think Ringo was the leader of the group. It was removed and was replaced by a logo originally designed by Paul McCartney and fine-tuned in Liverpool by a sign writer named Tex O'Hara, whose brother, Brian, played guitar for The Fourmost (also managed by Epstein).

The new "bug" logo featured the word *Beatles* written in script on a piece of cloth. Sprouting from the "B" were two antennae; the logo was stretched across Ringo's bass drum and was held in place by screws under the drum's rim.

Still, it was hard for the band to get noticed. The Beatles were last on the bill, and "made little or no impression on the first few nights of the tour," said singer Kenny Lynch, one of the other performers on the Shapiro tour. "They played their hearts out, like everyone else, but it would have taken a blowtorch to get those audiences to warm to us."

The weather that winter was brutal—the plunging temperatures were the worst in nearly a century, and it snowed virtually every day—but none of The Beatles, especially Ringo, was complaining. They were touring with a top recording star while being showcased as their second single continued to be played on the radio. England's young record-buyers were starting to take no-tice of these four guys with their matching suits (burgundy with velvet collars), funny onstage patter, catchy sound, and, most of all, seemingly boundless ener-gy. And despite the hard-to-impress audiences at most of the Shapiro concerts, the buzz about The Beatles was starting to grow.

New Musical Express reporter Gordon Sampson, who was covering the tour when it stopped at the ABC Cinema in Carlisle, noted that "the audience repeat-edly called for them while other artists were performing." Kenny Lynch noted on that night that "the audience was waiting for them. . . . I think The Beatles shook those crowds up, even scared them a little. They were so different, so tight, so confident, really playing their hearts out. It was like no experience those kids ever had before. Every girl thought they were singing to her, every boy saw himself standing in their place."

"It was a big thrill, going with Helen Shapiro and playing in real theaters," Ringo said. "We'd done the Empire once in Liverpool, when Brian put on a show just to get us on somewhere. We were third on the bill. Some cockney manager of one of the so-called 'stars' had a hassle with us. He didn't want us to be on the show at all. But touring properly round theaters was great. We didn't know anything about things like make-up, because we'd never done proper stage shows. . . . We pranced around like Red Indians, covered in the stuff."

As if the tour with Helen Shapiro wasn't grueling enough, The Beatles were booked into Abbey Road studios on Monday, February 11, to record their first album, while the rest of the Shapiro tour soldiered on to Peterborough. In the span of one full day in the studio, from roughly ten a.m. to eleven p.m., the group tore through ten songs, culminating in John Lennon's "larynx ripper" version of "Twist and Shout." The session produced some of The Beatles' popular early tunes in addition to "Twist and Shout," such as "There's a Place," "Seventeen" (later retitled "I Saw Her Standing There"), "Misery," and "Hold Me Tight."

Lennon and McCartney handled most of the lead vocals, but George Har-rison sang lead on "Do You Want to Know a Secret?" and "Chains." Ringo, too, recorded his first Beatles track, his old Rory Storm and the Hurricanes "Starr Time" number, "Boys." He needed only one take to nail the song, which he belted out enthusiastically—it was perfectly suited to his flat, nasal range—while keeping perfect time on his drum kit and gleefully shouting out "All right, George!" to introduce Harrison's guitar solo. Lennon and McCartney backed up Ringo's lead vocal (*bop shoo op/bop bop shoo op*).

Ringo recalled starting the recording session around noontime and finishing at midnight, when Lennon sang his (hoarse) version of "Twist and Shout." The Beatles were playing songs they'd played live countless times before, making it that much easier to go into the studio and bash them out one after the other.

According to Ringo, the mic setup was simple, with one placed in front of each amp, two mics overhead to capture Ringo's drums, a mic for his bass drum (which he felt didn't do the job), and one for whoever was singing lead vocals.

On February 13, the band resumed their hectic touring schedule with Shapiro and company. The excitement and anticipation surrounding their inevitable appearance on stage—the billing order changed frequently—was growing with each stop on the tour. The press, too, was beginning to take notice of The Beatles (urged on by the savvy Brian Epstein).

"Best of all, there were four young men from Liverpool called The Beatles," wrote *Yorkshire Post* reporter Reginald Brace, "who I predict will go from strength to strength this year. They sing and strum their guitars with enormous, infectious zest." Shapiro noted that the screams, mostly from the young girls in the audience, would erupt only after The Beatles finished one of their songs—quite a change from the nonstop, jet-engine-roar screams that would later drown out the band. "It wasn't out of hand yet," she said.

The Helen Shapiro tour ran through early March. Once that ended, The Beatles jumped right into a tour with Americans Tommy Roe and Chris Montez for £80 a week. "Who are these guys, The Beatles?" Montez reportedly asked. "I try to keep up with the British scene, but I don't know their work." They made a return television visit to *Thank Your Lucky Stars* and to radio shows on The BBC (*Saturday Club*) and *The Radio Luxembourg Show*.

They also returned to the Cavern Club, where the lines to see the band were the longest anyone could remember (snaking around the corner of Mathew Street). Their national visibility received a jolt of adrenaline when, at the end of February, "Please Please Me" finally reached Number One on the *New Musical Express* and *Melody Maker* charts. George Martin's words had come true: The Beatles had their first hit single.

"After Number One, where else is there to go?" Ringo said. "Number One was it." John, Paul, George, and Ringo noticed they were now being treated differently by their friends and particularly by their families, who had seen them on national television, heard them on the radio, and were now related to burgeoning national stars. "We went around boasting," Ringo said. "Professional group, you know. Most groups were still going out to ordinary jobs."

If their tour stopped anywhere within the vicinity of Liverpool, Ringo headed home to 10 Admiral Grove, where a doting Elsie and Harry faithfully kept his untouched room waiting for him. But Elsie, in particular, felt the down side to her son's sudden success: she was losing her little boy to the all-consuming monster known as fame, and she didn't like it. Having raised Richy virtually alone for the first thirteen years of his life, the loss of anonymity bothered her.

"Elsie felt they were taking him away from her," said Ringo's childhood friend Marie Crawford. "And that terrified her." Freda Kelly, who ran The Beatles' fan club in Liverpool, also noticed the change in Elsie. "Of all the parents, she found it quite difficult to cope," she said. "She could have done without any of the success. Elsie would have preferred Richy to be ordinary, to live down the road with four children she could visit every day."

Elsie herself sounded a bit whimsical when talking about her son's newfound stardom. "I always thought Richy would make a career for himself as a musician because he was so keen—but I didn't think it would be like this," she said. "I thought he would eventually find a place for himself in an ordinary dance band. . . . Richy can't get home to see us as often as he'd like to. When he was home at Christmas we had a wonderful time—and he had his camera and was taking lots of photographs of us."

Elsie wondered how Richy would handle the sudden success, and the sudden influx of cash, especially after she found pound notes scattered all over the dressing table in his bedroom. Brian Epstein eventually opened up a bank account for him.

"Mum was frightened when we first got famous," Ringo said later. "She was always getting people telling her I'd been killed or had an accident. Rumors got around and the press would get on to her."

The fans, too, were becoming a nuisance, camping outside of 10 Admiral Grove and often frightening Elsie and Harry with their shenanigans, which included stealing the mailbox, "chipping bits off the door, taking stones away from the outside. We came home one night," Elsie said, "and they'd painted 'We Love You Ringo' all over the front door and on every window. Most of them were nice kids. They did buy the records, so they deserved something. They'd ask for his old socks, or shirts, or shoes. I'd give them some till there was none left."

"When we go home, we go in early in the morning when we've finished a job, and the kids don't know you're at home," Ringo recalled. "But if they find out where I live, they get the drums out and beat it out! 'Cuz it's a play street and, you know, there's no traffic or nothing bothering them.

"Once when the boys came for me —they popped in to see me Mum and me Dad, you know—we had to go out the back 'cause there were twenty or thirty [fans] outside. And they wouldn't believe me mother, you know, knocking and saying 'Can we have their autographs.' So it built up so much. There was about two hundred kids all around the door, peeping through the window and knocking. In the end, me mother was ill, you know— terrified out of her life—with just all these kids and boys and girls, you know."

Sometimes, Ringo was forced to sneak in and out of the house under the veil of darkness; other times, he'd be crouching inside, hiding, while Elsie told some fan or another that he wasn't home.

The temptations of the road were enjoyed by all, but when he was in Liverpool, Ringo only had eyes for Maureen. Their romance continued to blossom. As was indicated earlier, Ringo was also seeing model Vicki Hodge on the side, but publicly it was Maureen who was by his side (when she dared risk incurring the wrath of Beatles fans and inquiries of pesky journalists). Still, it all had to be kept on the sly, lest the public discover a Beatle had an actual girlfriend (or wife, in John Lennon's case).

Ringo was instructed to keep his girlfriend a secret and "to pretend I didn't know Maureen and wasn't in love. Can you imagine what it must have been like for her reading in the papers that I didn't know anyone called Maureen Cox?"

Paul, meanwhile, was dating Iris Caldwell, Rory Storm's younger sister.

Rory Storm and the Hurricanes were never quite the same after Ringo's departure. Their drummer's sudden exit seemed to deflate the band. Rory and the Hurricanes were already starting to hit the proverbial brick wall when Ringo left, and while they continued to tour sporadically, they did so with a series of drummers, none of whom stuck around for any length of time—and none of whom had Ringo's onstage panache.

Ringo's replacement, Gibson Kemp, lasted only a few months with Rory before joining King Size Taylor and the Dominoes in Hamburg (and eventually marrying Stuart Sutcliffe's ex-fiancée, Astrid Kirchherr).

The equanimity with which Rory had publicly accepted Ringo's departure the previous summer started to crack as his fortunes waned and Ringo's fame grew. It didn't help matters that The Beatles were taking off, or that Paul McCartney was dating Rory's sister—a constant reminder of what could have been.

"During the four or five years Ringo was with us he really played drums—he drove them. He sweated and swung and sung," Rory told *Mersey Beat* magazine. "Ringo sang about five numbers a night, he even had his own spot—it was called 'Ringo Starrtime.' Now he's only a backing drummer. The Beatles' front line is so good he doesn't have to do much. This is not the Ringo Starr who played with us."

Still, perhaps to assuage his guilt over leaving Rory so suddenly, Ringo paid a hefty tax bill levied on his old boss by the Inland Revenue. He also talked Brian Epstein into producing Rory and the Hurricanes' first single, "America"—an adaptation of the song from *West Side Story*—and, by some accounts, even helped out in the studio, adding some percussion to the track. "America," backed with "Since You Broke My Heart," was released in late 1964 on Parlophone, The Beatles' label, and quickly faded from view.

With "Please Please Me" topping the charts and the momentum carrying them along, The Beatles returned to the studio to record what they hoped would be their next single. While the group's first album, also entitled *Please Please Me*, was being mixed and fine-tuned, they were back in the acoustic confines of Abbey Road on March 5. That session, which lasted six hours, produced their third single, "From Me to You," another infectious Lennon/McCartney number, which John and Paul wrote during the Helen Shapiro tour while slogging around England on the tour bus.

The Beatles completed "From Me to You" in seven takes, and the song even included a rare drum fill from Ringo, who preferred to keep a steady beat.

The Beatles followed the March 5 recording session by joining the Chris Montez/Tommy Roe tour (which also included The Viscounts, Debbie Lee, The Terry Young Six, and emcee Tony Marsh). As that horrible British winter gave way to a pleasant spring—with temperatures reaching into the low 60s—The Beatles worked more television and radio appearances into their jam-packed schedule, including a return to *Saturday Club* and a visit to EMI's *The Friday Spectacular*, which aired on Radio Luxembourg.

The Montez/Roe tour got off to a shaky start; it became immediately apparent that The Beatles were getting the lion's share of screams and adulation from the audience, which pissed off the tour's headliners (Montez was riding high with "Let's Dance"; Roe hit it big with "Sheila"). It had to be especially galling since The Beatles were sometimes only a threesome, since John Lennon missed several stops on the tour due to a bad cold. (The Beatles rearranged their set list in lieu of their missing rhythm guitarist/lead singer.)

"The Beatles stole top honors for entertainment and audience reaction," wrote a journalist covering the show in East Ham. "This all-action quartet from Liverpool has everything—exciting new sound, terrific instrumental attack, exhilarating solo and group vocal effects and a fresh energy that leaves them (they told me later) limp at the end of each act." Tommy Roe, in a later interview, admitted that he and Montez had been upstaged: "It was complete mayhem, with hundreds of screaming girls rushing the stage like lemmings. . . . How could you possibly follow that?"

The Beatles first album, *Please Please Me*, was released on March 22, nine days before the end of the Montez/Roe tour. The LP's cover featured a photo of all four Beatles looking down at the camera from an inside stairwell at the EMI building in Manchester Square. Among the album's fourteen tracks were Ringo's lead vocal on "Boys" and his drumming—not Andy White's—on "Love Me Do."

Three weeks later, on April 22, their third single was released. "From Me to You" hit Number One on the British charts nearly two weeks later, on May 4, though reviews were mixed. Some critics, like *Melody Maker*'s Ray Coleman, carped that the song lacked the verve of "Please Please Me." (Coleman was a Beatles supporter and fan of the group, but he thought the melody was "so-so" and the song "average.")

The critics, though, weren't the ones buying "From Me to You," and Beatles fans gobbled it up. Down south in London, in the heart of England's record industry, people were starting to take notice of these four shaggy-haired guys from Liverpool who now had their second consecutive Number One. There was no looking back.

***

April 1963 marked eight months since Ringo joined The Beatles. In that short span, the group's remarkable trajectory included recording three singles, cutting their first album, and appearing on influential television and radio shows as their fame grew—eventually overshadowing the headliners with whom they toured the nation.

As the first signs of Beatlemania began to stir—frenzied, screaming fans, an adoring media ready to push the Next Big Thing—Ringo's bond with John, Paul, and George was solidified. There was no other alternative, but it was never a question of whether he would fit in—only a question of how long that would take.

"The Boys," as Beatles manager Brian Epstein liked to call his band, spent nearly every waking hour of every day of every week together—playing live, killing time in hotel rooms and on long bus rides, or driving hundreds of miles, crammed into the van, to yet another far-flung gig in the provinces. (The Beatles always honored their commitments, even as their star began to rise.)

The guys, with Neil Aspinall or Mal Evans at the wheel, often drove straight through the night to their next destination, or back, to rejoin the Helen Shapiro or Chris Montez/Tommy Roe tours. Days off were rare, and if they weren't performing they were cloistered for hours on end in the recording studio, where they kept to themselves or chatted only with their producer, George Martin.

In his memoir *Here, There and Everywhere*, Abbey Road engineer Geoff Emerick remembered Ringo as "very uptight and nervous" in the studio when he had to sing (à la "Boys") while keeping to himself in the drum booth, leaving only when John or Paul or George put down their guitars. "That was his signal that they were taking a break. Then he'd come out and sit down with Neil or Mal," Emerick recalled. "Ringo was like a machine, drumming away for hours on end. . . . Ringo would leave the studio totally knackered, completely drained," he wrote. "I was always impressed at how he'd rebound the next day, though, fresh and ready for another bout of marathon drumming."

Squabbles among the four Beatles were common, but were quickly smoothed over and forgotten. Ringo was no longer considered the outsider, the stranger to be kept at arm's length and away from internal band business or gossip. He'd earned his stripes. His laconic, sometimes biting humor, so typically Liverpudlian, endeared him to his fellow Beatles (and eventually won over Neil Aspinall, Pete Best's chief defender, the father of Pete's half-brother and the group's de facto driver/confidante). The press loved Ringo, and enjoyed pointing out how he was the most talkative of the four Beatles, the most willing to answer any of the repetitious questions asked him.

"Ringo was a nice guy, he did the job and he didn't make any particular waves in the psyche of the [Beatles] family," a Beatles intimate, who wished to remain anonymous, told the author. "I think he did help keep the peace because there were moments when the other three had their own axes to grind. I don't think he was a peacemaker, per se, because I don't think he was assertive, but I think he was a comfortable person who they respected. He didn't preach and didn't intrude too much, but they felt secure with him as a person.

"If you had time on your own with Ringo you would start to realize that he was someone nice and comfortable—a very nice person who knows a few things."

The Beatles, meanwhile, weren't the only Liverpool group to top the charts. Gerry and the Pacemakers, who were now also under Brian Epstein's management, shot to Number One with "How Do You Do It?" the same Mitch Murray song George Martin had unsuccessfully lobbied The Beatles to release as their first single. But John, Paul, George, and Ringo *were* the only chart-topping group with four individual personalities. Could anyone but a hardcore Pacemakers fan name their drummer? The Beatles had a distinctly singular look and sound, which made a huge difference in an industry—and a genre (pop music)—experiencing this phenomenon for the first time.

George Martin's original concerns about Ringo's drumming ability were brushed aside after "Please Please Me" and "From Me to You" went to Number One, although he and Ringo would continue to be wary of each other in the studio. Ringo never totally forgave Martin for using Andy White on "Love Me Do" and "P.S. I Love You," and Martin could be patronizing when asked about Ringo's drumming skills.

"I did quickly realize that Ringo was an excellent drummer for what was required," he once said. "He's not a technical drummer. Men like Buddy Rich and Gene Krupa would run rings around him, but he is a good solid rock drummer with a steady beat, and he knows how to get the right sound out of his drums. Above all, he does have an individual sound. You can tell Ringo's drums from anyone else's and that character was a definite asset to the Beatles' early recordings."

Martin's read-between-the-lines attitude was shared by his trusted studio lieutenant, EMI engineer Geoff Emerick: "Ringo had a definite talent and style, but little imagination. I always felt, however, that he knew his limitations." Buddy Rich, who was never shy in sharing his opinions, was once asked about Ringo. "Ringo Starr was adequate. No more than that," he said.

Ringo's ego was strong enough to brush aside the naysayers. He was, from the very beginning, extremely confident in his drumming ability, pointing out that he did his job setting the "feel" for the song, which, combined with Paul McCartney's melodic bass riffs, gave The Beatles a unique sound.

Repeating a drum fill was a different story; Ringo admitted he couldn't do it, try as he might, because he played to however he was feeling at that moment. He preferred "solid" drumming over a "busy" style.

The only validation he needed was from his band mates. They were now the brothers he never had growing up in the Dingle. "Ringo's a damn good drummer," John Lennon said. "He was always a good drummer. He's not technically good, but I think Ringo's drumming is underrated the same way as Paul's bass-playing is underrated." George Harrison, who had pushed the hardest to recruit Ringo into The Beatles, was even more emphatic: "Ringo's got the best backbeat I've ever heard," he said.

While his fellow Beatles appreciated Ringo's timekeeping skills, and the intangibles he brought to the group, they could be very controlling—sometimes obnoxiously so—in the recording studio. Lennon and McCartney, particularly Paul, were not shy in telling and/or showing Ringo how they wanted the drums to be played on their songs which, to be fair, comprised the lion's share of the band's output on vinyl. Ringo was compliant and did not complain in the early days, although this scenario would evolve and change in the coming years.

"When we first started, they basically went John and Paul's way because they were the writers and they would say, 'This is the song,' and I would play as creatively as I could," he said. "Sometimes I would have three people telling me how to do it. They were saying, 'Play this like on that track. I'm saying, 'For Christ's sake, there are two drummers there.' They could never hear that, you know. You'd have to have four arms to do half the stuff they wanted me to do."

"We always gave Ringo direction on every single number," McCartney admitted. "It was usually very controlled. Whoever had written the song, John for instance, would say, 'I want this.' Obviously, a lot of things came out of what Ringo was playing, but we would always control it."

George Harrison, the youngest Beatle, was also not immune to scathing comments from John and Paul in the studio. In 1963, when the group first took a stab at recording Lennon and McCartney's bouncy tune "The One After 909," Lennon was so incensed at Harrison's twangy guitar solo that he turned to him and sneered, "What kind of solo was *that*." Like Ringo, Harrison would eventually defend himself vigorously as his stature within the band's hierarchy's grew.

In late April 1963, with "From Me to You" speeding up the charts—and some rare time off before beginning another tour—Ringo, Paul, and George went on a vacation together to Tenerife in the Canary Islands. John left for a sojourn to Spain with Brian Epstein, ignoring his wife, Cynthia, who had just given birth to their son, Julian.

In Tenerife, the three Beatles stayed in a house owned by the parents of their Hamburg pal, Klaus Voormann. The house had no electricity—they roughed it—and Ringo recalled it was the first time he'd ever seen black sand. All three Beatles got terribly sunburned, and Ringo and George suffered sunstroke several days into the vacation. Paul almost drowned after being pulled into a riptide.

With the newfound success came more changes to the band's onstage appearance. Ringo, who was still using his old Premier drum kit, decided he needed a more elaborate, prestigious (and expensive) set of drums. While in London, with Brian Epstein in tow, he paid a visit to the well-known drummers' mecca Drum City (yes, they sold only drums), where he picked out a Ludwig drum kit with an oyster pearl black finish.

"I remember Ringo was looking at my desk, and on the desk I had a swatch of colors," recalled Drum City owner Ivor Arbiter. "We didn't talk about which brand at this point. Ring said, 'I like this color.' We didn't get too heavily into what the drums were or what they sounded like. They chose Ludwig because of the color, and I made some sort of deal with Brian. I have a feeling that they paid a bit of money for the drums . . . we had the kit in stock."

Ringo's new Ludwig drum kit needed a new logo, so the "bug" logo was jettisoned and replaced on Ringo's bass drum with *The Beatles* written in block lettering, both the *B* and the *T* in Beatles enlarged in the now-iconic logo. William F. Ludwig Jr., who owned the company at the time, claims the logo was designed by Ivor Arbiter. "He alone took out a piece of stationery, drew a circle, and created The Beatles logo with the exaggerated capital B and the exaggerated capital T. That became the official Beatles logo known all around the world. And all that Ivor ever got out of it was that he sold them a drum set."

As with many pieces of Beatles mythology, Ludwig's story was changed a bit by Arbiter himself, who says that while he might have had the idea, the actual logo was designed by a local sign writer named Eddie Stokes. "There were about three or four options, and they chose the one with the drop-T. Eddie did it in front of me; he painted it by hand on the first drum that we supplied. I think we charged £5 extra for the artwork. And when I see the drop-T logo today on everything, how I wish we could have registered it."

Ringo premiered his new drum kit with the new Beatles logo when the band appeared on *Thank Your Lucky Stars* in May.

"Ringo put Ludwig drums on the map," said drummer Max Weinberg. "Before Ringo, to play a Ludwig drum set in England was very unusual. They didn't have a distributor over there. Gretsch was the jazz drum set and there was Slingerland. Ludwig was kind of the also-ran. . . . And before Ringo, drummers didn't typically have the name of the band on the bass drum. The name was usually shielded with the drummer's initials—suddenly Ludwig had space for advertising."

"From Me to You" hit Number One on May 4. Two weeks later, The Beatles embarked on a national tour, this time with American artist Roy Orbison, who'd hit it big with "Only the Lonely," "Pretty Woman" and "In Dreams." Fellow Liverpudlians Gerry and the Pacemakers, who were on their way to another Number One with "I Like It," were also on the bill, along with The Terry Young Six, Erkey Grant, Ian Crawford, David Macbeth, and Louise Cordet. Tony Marsh was the emcee.

But if The Beatles had been the show-stoppers since the February tour with Helen Shapiro, they found a worthy competitor in Orbison, who had the falsetto voice of an angel and a mysterious, near-mystical onstage persona with his dark sunglasses and his penchant for dressing completely in black.

George Harrison recalled how effortless it was for Orbison; how he just stood stock-still onstage "like marble" and only moved his lips—even when reaching for his trademark quavering high notes.

Ringo, John, Paul, and George were cowed.

"It was terrible, following Roy," Ringo recalled. "He'd slay them and they'd scream for more. In Glasgow we were all backstage, listening to the tremendous applause he was getting. He was doing it just by his voice. Just standing there singing, not moving or anything. He was knocking them out. As it got near our turn, we would hide behind the curtains whispering to each other, 'Guess who's next, folks. It's your favorite rave!' But once we got on stage it was always OK."

The Orbison tour also marked the first time The Beatles were pelted onstage with jellybeans (or "jelly babies," as the Brits called them). Both John Lennon and George Harrison had told an interviewer they each had a weakness for the soft, flavored candy, and once their remarks appeared in print, Beatles fans began throwing jellybeans at their heroes when the group appeared onstage. Ringo used his cymbals to deflect the candy missiles, which littered the stage after every Beatles appearance. It was harmless and all in fun, but nonetheless it annoyed all four Beatles, who were trying to play their music while dodging jellybeans and attempting to be heard above the raucous din that was growing shriller by the day.

A fan named Dave Ward, who was in the crowd when the tour stopped in Southampton, described the scene when The Beatles took the stage. "They opened with 'Some Other Guy.' Their presence was electric. I was in the second row from the front nearest to where John Lennon stood onstage. The girls were going frantic. Then George approached the microphone and raised his hands to quiet the audience. Then he made the announcement: 'We are very flattered by the screams. Thank you for that, but we would appreciate it if you could save them for in-between the songs because we want you to hear our music.'"

As The Beatles continued to surge, they were in demand elsewhere and had to leave the Orbison tour several times, traveling to London to appear, once again, on The BBC's *Saturday Club* radio show and on another show, *Stepping Out*, where they performed live.

They returned to television on ITV's *Thank Your Lucky Stars*, performing "From Me to You" and, four days later, visited the BBC TV kiddie show for their only appearance on *Pops and Lenny*, where they sang "From Me to You" and a shortened version of "Please Please Me," hanging around to kibbitz with host Terry Hall and his cast of characters (including Lenny the Lion).

In June, they appeared on *Lucky Stars (Summer Spin)*, miming "From Me to You" and "I Saw Her Standing There." John Lennon also sat in as a juror on the BBC TV show *Juke Box Jury* that month.

The Beatles now even had their own BBC radio show called *Pop Go The Beatles*, which began in early June and ran through the end of September 1963. On the show, which aired nationally, they would play six or seven songs and joke around with hosts Lee Peters and Rodney Burke. The importance of the exposure was immeasurable.

In late May, *Please Please Me*, the album The Beatles recorded that frantic day in February, reached the top of the charts. It would remain there for the next thirty weeks, supplanted only when The Beatles topped themselves with their follow-up LP.

But the success of *Please Please Me* in England was not replicated in America, where The Beatles were virtually unknown. One big early Beatles fan in the U.S. was George Harrison's older sister, Louise, who lived in Illinois. George visited her there in 1963, and also traveled to New York City and to St. Louis. "Please Please Me" tanked in the States when it was released by the Vee-Jay label, and quickly disappeared from view. "From Me to You," issued by Vee-Jay in late May, experienced a similar fate.

In England, of course, it was a different story. The group's fan mail, sporadic earlier in the year, now began pouring into The Beatles fan club in Liverpool, which was run by Freda Kelly. The letters, like this one sent to Ringo at 10 Admiral Grove, were gushing, innocent and indicative of the group's early fan base (mostly young girls).

My darling, dear, delightful Ringo,

Could you please send me something of yours? Anything, a lock of hair, a smoked cigarette a thread from your coat, a button from your shirt, a piece of old toast or a bristle from your toothbrush. I would treasure it forever.

At first, the bulk of pleading letters from fans asking for autographs—or declaring their everlasting love—were sent to John, Paul, and George. Ringo, the last Beatle to join the group, had won over most of the fans but received the least amount of mail.

"Richy came in [the office] one day and asked politely if I would do his mail," Kelly recalled. "I told him he must be joking. 'Get your mum and dad to do it. All the other parents do.' But he just stood there pathetically and said, 'Me mum doesn't know what to put. Anyway, I don't get a lot.' I felt so sorry for him, so I said, 'All right, bring it in, but just this once.' The next day he came in with one of those small poly bags that tights come in—that was all his mail, stuffed inside. Paul got two feet of mail, but Richy only had that small sack, with ten letters in it."

Ringo, who "put the sad eyes on," had written the answers to the fans' questions on the top of the letters he'd received, Kelly recalled.

> He must have thought I was terrible. I looked at him and said, "Is this all you get?" He said, "Would you help me? Would you come show my mum what to do?" I ended up going round and knocking at 10 Admiral Grove and Elsie opened the door and I said, "I'm Freda from the office" and she went, "Oh, thank God, come in, love. Have you had any tea? Would you like egg and chips?" Then we started talking and we got on like a house on fire. Every week, for years, I went to that house.

Elsie had grown close to Cilla White several years earlier when Cilla came to wash her hair. But Cilla was off now chasing stardom as Cilla Black, and Freda stepped into her place in Elsie's affections. Elsie and Freda grew very close, and Freda would spend hours at 10 Admiral Grove, sometimes until the wee hours of the morning, chatting with Elsie and Harry and going through the mail, describing "the joy and happiness and laughter" that enveloped Ringo's parents.

"I loved coming here every week. . . . I spent a lot of my life here . . . going through the mail and talking and laughing [about] who I was going out with at the time," she said. "Elsie would give me motherly advice. She was very jolly, very outgoing with a really strong laugh. I told her all my secrets when I was a teenager; maybe she looked on me as the daughter she didn't have."

At one point, Elsie decided that Freda should get a raise and, after downing a few at a party, she chided Brian Epstein, telling him how important Freda was and how much she meant to the group. "I got a raise two weeks later," Kelly recalled. "[Elsie] was the nearest to a mother figure for me."

Before too long, Ringo was being deluged with knickknacks from Beatles fanatics. He counted a collection of sixty dolls—dogs, fish, kewpie dolls, elephants—and, on his birthday, he was sent a model of the American cartoon character Fred Flintstone playing a bass drum. When he admitted to not liking Donald Duck, Beatles fans naturally sent him fifteen Donald Duck dolls.

It also helped to know a Beatle or to be related to a Beatle, at least in Liverpool. When a local Merseyside group called The Bluejeans was looking for a drummer, they placed an ad in a music trade publication. "One day a guy called John Foster answered the ad," recalled Bluejeans member Mike Gregory. "He was Ringo Starr's cousin and he had Ringo's old Ajax drum kit. Well, that almost made him a god in our eyes. The job was his!"

But not for long; Foster's gig as the drummer for The Bluejeans was short-lived, and he was replaced shortly thereafter.

As June turned into July, The Beatles were about to embark on another summer of hectic touring. On July 1, they were back in London at EMI to record what they hoped would be their third single.

"She Loves You" was written by Lennon and McCartney in a hotel room less than a week before, during a stopover in Newcastle-Upon-Tyne. The song, a paean to young romance, opened with Ringo's booming roll on his floor tom, and its upbeat flight, culminating in an exuberant crescendo of *Yeah Yeah Yeah* stamped it, and The Beatles, into pop culture history. The song's energy was as infectious as its *Yeah Yeah Yeahs*.

"She Loves You" also marked a technical development in recording The Beatles' sound, most evident in the aural crispness and clarity of Ringo's drums and Paul McCartney's bouncy bass guitar riffs. EMI engineer Norman Smith had suspended a microphone over Ringo's drum kit, resulting in a more immediate, prominent drum sound. You can almost hear Ringo attacking his drums with an urgency that's more evident than before. Smith also used an electronic device called a "compressor" that boosted McCartney's bass.

John, Paul, George, and Ringo also recorded one more song, "I'll Get You," in the latter half of that same session, which was almost sidetracked before it even began. A group of shrieking, nearly hysterical Beatles fans, mostly teenage girls, were crowded outside the EMI studios. Somehow, through some hormonal telepathy, they knew John, George, Paul, and Ringo were inside, and were hoping to get a glimpse of or—*gasp!*—maybe even touch one of their idols.

A hysterical fan barged in right before the first take of "She Loves You." As she charged toward Ringo, who was seated behind his drum kit, she was tackled by Neil Aspinall and then dragged, sobbing, out of the studio by Mal Evans.

Meanwhile, a gaggle of other fans had managed to get inside the studio and were now running riot through the hallways of EMI: "Scores of hysterical, screaming girls racing down the corridors, being chased by a handful of out-of-breath, beleaguered London bobbies. Every time one would catch up with a fan, another two or three girls would appear, racing past, screeching at the top of their lungs."

But that was only a taste of things to come.

The Beatles spent the rest of July and August touring up and down England, sometimes fulfilling commitments in small venues that were scheduled months before, when their star had yet to rise. Brian Epstein believed in keeping his word, no matter how insignificant it might seem now to play a one-nighter in some far-flung province. Twice in July, on the 18th and 30th, the foursome returned to the studio to record tracks for their second LP, including a version of Chuck Berry's "Roll Over, Beethoven," "Till There Was You," "All My Loving," "It Won't Be Long," and "You Really Got a Hold on Me."

The Beatles' rise in popularity naturally fueled speculation among a cynical press corps—at least those in the media who were paying attention to them—that there was some discord within the group, particularly towards the relative newcomer Ringo Starr. "We hear rumors that he's leaving, but there's absolutely no truth in them," Paul McCartney proclaimed.

An article in *New Musical Express* claimed that there was talk of moving Ringo out from behind his drum kit to become a Beatles dancer—with other members of the group rotating as the band's drummer. McCartney didn't deny it.

"It would only be for certain numbers," he said. "But it's an idea we're working on. We all mess around on drums a bit and we could take his place now and again. Mind you, we could never be as good as Ringo," he added somewhat condescendingly. "He's the best drummer we've ever had. The rest of us have always got on well, but he's fitted into the group like a glove. We've had other drummers we've got on well with, but no one could beat Ringo. If it all comes off, it's going to be quite a novelty to announce him as 'The Singing-Dancing-Drummer!'" Given Ringo's pride in his abilities behind the drum kit, this couldn't have sat too well with him. But if he was pissed off, he kept his mouth shut when this strange bit of news was reported.

That talk was quickly forgotten. The proverbial shit hit the fan on August 23, 1963, when "She Loves You" was released and England heard *Yeah, Yeah Yeah* for the first time (the rest of the world would catch up soon enough).

The single, which already had a massive pre-order of half-a-million copies, shot straight to Number One.

"It exploded with a fury into the number-one position, selling faster and harder than any single ever released, and became the largest-selling single in the history of Great Britain," wrote Peter Brown. "A simple 'yeah, yeah, yeah' . . . became not only The Beatles' trademark but an international euphemism for rock music."

By early September, "She Loves You" passed the five-hundred-thousand sales mark and The Beatles hit the trifecta: A Number-One album (*Please Please Me*), a Number-One single ("She Loves You") and even a top-selling EP ("Twist and Shout"). "She Loves You" surpassed the one-million milestone by the end of November and kept on going . . . except to America, where it didn't yet have an impact.

But the success of "She Loves You" had Brian Epstein thinking big; if the single was so huge in England and the UK, why shouldn't it translate across the Atlantic? Epstein began working the phones, trying to line up something—anything—for The Beatles in the United States. He hoped that the past failures of British pop stars like Cliff Richard and Adam Faith to make a dent across the Atlantic would be forgotten once The Beatles stormed America's shores.

The impact of "She Loves You" and all that quickly followed was mind-blowing for all four Beatles; for Ringo, it was as if he was living in an alternate reality. A year before he was playing with Rory Storm and the Hurricanes at Butlin's; now he was thrust into the eye of a hurricane as the phenomenon dubbed "Beatlemania" swept across England.

John, Paul, George, and Ringo inherited the headlines that, just weeks before, were dominated by political scandal (the Profumo affair, which resulted in a suicide and Harold Macmillan's subsequent resignation) and crime (a Royal

Mail train that was robbed of £2.6 million while traveling between Glasgow and London—the biggest heist in history).

England was emerging from a gloomy period; the country, and especially its youth, was ready to embrace The Beatles and their energetic, euphoric sound. Ringo recalled that The Beatles knew they were a great band, but had no idea what was in store. He was making good money, which he was spending—on cars and clothing—and on the apartment he shared with George Harrison. That first year, he was earning fifty quid—a small fortune, in his eyes and double what he'd been earning when he first joined The Beatles.

The Beatles were now in the public eye. And Ringo also noticed a glaring, sudden shift in his personal life. Richy Starkey still lived at 10 Admiral Grove with Elsie and Harry, but Ringo Starr was now the nationally famous drummer for the country's biggest pop group. John, Paul, George, and Ringo were household names. Privately, Ringo was still the same guy—self-deprecating and sensitive, with a biting sense of humor. But he now found that his friends and family treated him differently, as if the sudden fame made him special in a way he hadn't been before.

He noted how, in 1963, his family began to treat him differently. On one occasion, while visiting his aunt, someone bumped into a table and jostled Ringo, who spilled his tea into his saucer—causing quite a bit of consternation. He was a Beatle, after all. He knew then that his life was taking a drastic turn.

He knew he was being treated differently now by his family, by people who'd known him since he was a baby. He was still the same old Ringo—just not to them. He felt like he was living in an alternate universe.

The Beatles fans in Liverpool, who had supported the group through thick and thin for the past three years, also felt the toll that success was taking on the group. *Their* group. The tremors sent by "She Loves You" throughout the country and the London-dominated music industry meant that The Beatles were no longer just "four lads" from up north; they belonged to the entire country now, and that did not sit well with the insular, Merseyside Beatles backers, who were already suspicious of outsiders (particularly Londoners).

There was a whiff of resentment among the hardcore fans and palpable jealousy from other Liverpool bands who felt they were just as talented, if not more so, than The Beatles. John, Paul, George, and Ringo were lucky, that's all—they'd gotten the break some of the other bands felt *they* deserved.

"Home and family were the two things I didn't want to change, because it had all changed 'out there' and we were no longer really sure who our friends were, unless we'd had them before the fame," Ringo said. "The guys and girls I used to hang about with I could trust. But once we'd become big and famous, we soon learnt that people were with us only because of the vague notoriety of being 'a Beatle.' And when this happened in the family, it was quite a blow. I didn't know what to do about it; I couldn't stand up and say, 'Treat me like you used to,' because that would be acting 'big time.'"

Pete Best could only grit his teeth over the success of his now-famous former band mates. After being fired by The Beatles, he remained under Brian Epstein's managerial thumb and joined Lee Curtis & the All Stars, which morphed into Pete Best & the All Stars. The group's only single, "I'm Gonna Knock On Your Door," was released by Decca Records but failed to chart, and Best's music career hit a dead-end. By March 1964, after The Beatles stormed America, Best was already a pop-culture footnote, appearing as a guest on the CBS television show *I've Got a Secret*. (His tagline: "I used to be one of The Beatles.")

Best eventually left the business completely but stayed in Liverpool, beginning a long civil-service career and wondering what might have been. He would have to wait over thirty years to finally reap a huge financial windfall from his status as the original drummer for The Beatles. But in the fall of 1963, despite their success, no one could have imagined The Beatles being anything more than a short-lived lark, something for the fans to pass the time until the next guys came along. Kids were fickle that way.

Ringo's popularity, meanwhile, meant that Beatles fans expected at least one "Ringo Song" on each album. His rousing version of "Boys" on the *Please Please Me* LP struck a chord with fans, and he was slated to sing lead vocals on two songs for the group's second album, which they had been recording in bits and pieces since July. Lennon and McCartney wrote "I Wanna Be Your Man" and "Little Child" with Ringo (and his limited vocal range) in mind.

In mid-September, with "She Loves You" saturating the airwaves, The Beatles were back in London at EMI's Abbey Road studios. Ringo sang lead vocals on "I Wanna Be Your Man," a task made more difficult because he had to play his drums simultaneously while singing into a microphone (there wasn't much overdubbing of vocals done in those early days). Lennon, however, changed his mind regarding "Little Child," and decided to sing lead vocals on the track himself. That song was recorded, along with several other tracks, including "Don't Bother Me," George Harrison's first written contribution.

Lennon and McCartney also decided to give "I Wanna Be Your Man" to their new pals in London, The Rolling Stones; their version, with Mick Jagger on lead vocals and Brian Jones backing him up, was released in early November and climbed to Number Twelve on the British charts. McCartney claimed that songs for Ringo were kept "fairly simple," not only because of his flat vocal range but because "if he couldn't mentally picture [the song], you were in trouble."

Lennon, as usual, was more direct, particularly regarding the laissez faire attitude toward "I Wanna Be Your Man."

"It was a throwaway," he said. "The only two versions of the song were Ringo and The Rolling Stones. That shows how much importance we put on it: We weren't going to give them anything great, right?"

The tsunami otherwise known as "She Loves You" meant that The Beatles were in demand, now more than ever. Brian Epstein, a wizard at promoting his group, lined up a seemingly endless round of newspaper and magazine interviews, personal appearances and radio and TV appearances (*The Mersey Sound, Big Night Out, Ready Steady Go*). Epstein even commissioned a magazine devoted to the group; called *The Beatles Monthly*, it was edited by Sean O'Mahony under the pen name Johnny Dean. He had unlimited access to John, Paul, George, and Ringo, though his "reports" on the group ignored the more salacious aspects of Beatlemania.

"My first impression of Ringo was of a very nice bloke, a great drummer, typical Liverpudlian with a great sense of humor," O'Mahony said. "As far as I can recall, he fitted in [with The Beatles] very well indeed. Within a few weeks [of my working with the group] it seemed as if he'd always been there. If there was any pecking order in terms of the fans, it was John and Paul and then George and Ringo.

"Obviously you couldn't get 'round the fact that he wasn't one of the original Beatles, but for someone who had just joined an established band he fitted in incredibly well. I wouldn't agree at all that he felt like a bit of an outsider in the early days."

The media blitz, of course, had to be coordinated with the group's grueling touring schedule, which meant that Ringo rarely had time to visit Elsie and Harry, who refused to move from 10 Admiral Grove despite the incessant line of fans who camped out in front of the house when it was rumored that Ringo might be there. But if his mother and stepfather didn't want to leave the Dingle, Ringo had had enough. London was the place to be now.

The fans made it nearly impossible for him to visit 10 Admiral Grove, and, besides, the real scene was down south in London, in the big city where he would be just one more celebrity.

Ringo and George moved in together, staying first in the Hotel President in Russell Square before shelling out £45 a week for an apartment in Green Street, Park Lane, in the city's Mayfair district. (John and his wife, Cynthia, were already living in London.) Their downstairs neighbors, Harry and Carol Finegold, helped the boys (Ringo was twenty-three, George was twenty) make the adjustment to living as bachelors. They were living on their own for the first time and needed help with the creature comforts; Ringo admitted that he and George couldn't look after themselves without a little bit of help.

They were like two kids in a candy store, often frequenting the Saddle Room, a posh club that counted Prince Philip as a member. The club kept a horse and coach outside; according to Ringo, he and George, both drunk—"two shit-kickers from Liverpool"—would ride the coach up Park Lane back to their apartment.

Living in London also meant hanging out with "happening" bands, and Ringo and George, along with John and Paul, took full advantage. It wasn't uncommon for The Beatles to be seen, in one club or another—the Bag O'Nails was a favored haunt—rubbing shoulders with members of The Animals or The Rolling Stones.

Ringo had a tougher time adapting to the custom, in sophisticated London, of men greeting each other with a kiss on the cheek, which he found "weird" and quite different from social mores in Liverpool, where a handshake sufficed. But he eventually came around (not that he had much choice).

That September, during a rare two-week lull, Ringo and Maureen took a trip to Greece with Paul McCartney and his girlfriend, Jane Asher. John and Cynthia went on a belated honeymoon to Paris, while George Harrison visited his sister, Louise, in the United States.

When all four Beatles returned to England, they embarked on a short, week-long tour to Sweden and then heard the stunning news from Brian Epstein: They were booked to appear October 13 on ITV's *Sunday Night at the London Palladium*, one of the country's biggest, most prestigious and influential television shows, which was hosted by comedian Bruce Forsyth and was seen by an average audience of fifteen million viewers each week (huge viewership numbers for England's small television universe). Not only were The Beatles appearing on the show, but they were topping the bill (at Brian Epstein's insistence). Other guests included Des O'Connor and Brook Benton.

For Ringo and his three fellow band mates, it was a dream come true. Ringo remembered how, years before, he and the Eddie Clayton group would practice in the living room at Admiral Grove, with family friend Annie Maguire jokingly telling them she'd see them at the Palladium—the absolute top rung of the British show-business ladder. It wasn't a joke anymore.

Before the show, Ringo was so nervous that he vomited into a bucket just before running onto the stage with John, Paul and George, following in the (apocryphal) show-biz tradition. Hearing the introduction to a show, he said, always made him want to run onto the stage in a spurt of nervous energy.

Beatles fans crowded the Palladium's entrance on Argyll Street in the hours before the show, pushing, shoving, and hoping to get a glimpse of John, Paul, George, and Ringo, who were in a nearby rehearsal hall practicing for their big night. The press was alerted to the near-hysteria in front of the Palladium (probably by Brian Epstein) and newspaper reporters and radio and television crews descended on to what was quickly becoming an "event."

Some, however, remember it differently. In his book, *The Love You Make*, Peter Brown writes that photographer Dezo Hoffman, who was there, claims that only eight girls were present—and that the resulting photos were cropped to show a much larger crowd. The handiwork, Brown suspects, of Brian Epstein. Philip Norman, in his book, *Shout!* went Brown one better, quoting Hoffman as saying, "There were no riots. I was there. Eight girls we saw—even less than eight. Later on, the road managers were sent out to find The Beatles a girl each, and there were none."

The Beatles played four songs on *Sunday Night at the London Palladium*— "From Me to You," "I'll Get You," "She Loves You," and "Twist and Shout"— shaking their heads in perfect synchronicity with their *ooooohs!*, with their voices and instruments barely audible over the screams emanating from the audience. Even Ringo got into the act: high up on his drum riser, he bobbed his head back and forth and from side to side while keeping a steady beat for John, Paul, and George.

The next morning, *The Daily Mirror* headline said it all:

BEATLEMANIA!

Then, just three days later, it was announced that The Beatles would play for the Queen Mother and Princess Margaret in the annual Royal Command Variety Performance on November 4, which would air November 10 on ATV. (The Queen was pregnant with her third son, Prince Edward, and could not attend.)

The gala, held at London's Prince of Wales Theatre, was hosted by Harry

Secombe, who comprised one-third of BBC Radio's madcap *The Goon Show* (along with Peter Sellers and Spike Milligan), and was, by extension, a Beatles favorite. (All four band members loved The Goons, and Ringo eventually developed a particularly close friendship with Sellers.)

The Beatles would appear on a bill that boasted among its stars Marlene Dietrich, Wilfrid Brambell and Harry Corbett (the stars of BBC TV's *Steptoe and Son*), comedian Eric Sykes, and singer Sophie Tucker. A coterie of forgettable acts rounded out the roster of performers.

In the meantime, there were more television appearances—*Thank Your Lucky Stars, Drop In*—more touring and an offer from United Artists to make a movie in which The Beatles would star. The group, who only weeks before were largely ignored by the national press, were now being inundated with interview requests through their press officer, Tony Barrow. Derek Taylor was added to Brian Epstein's growing stable to help with press and publicity. Everyone, it seemed, wanted to know what John, Paul, George, and Ringo thought of even the most inane topic—and they were all happy to comply (as per Epstein's instructions).

"I don't like talking," Ringo told one interviewer. "Some people gab all day and some people play it smogo. I haven't got a smiling face or a talking mouth." Before long, he, too, was caught up in the moment and was ready, willing, and able to answer any question put to him by a reporter, no matter how trivial or inane."

He admitted that fame went to his head. When asked about a variety of topics, he would comment "as if I suddenly knew" the answers. (Hint: He didn't.) Ringo Starr was a Beatle, after all, with a country (and soon the world) bestowing upon him a sudden wisdom that came with being the drummer for a band selling millions of records. Only much later, after all the madness of Beatlemania, would he admit that "life" was his best education.

The Beatles, building on the momentum of their three Number One singles—"Please Please Me," "From Me to You," and "She Loves You"—were also busy that fall in the recording studio.

They hunkered down in EMI's Abbey Road (Studio Two) multiple times in September and October to record tracks begun that summer for *With the Beatles*, their second album. The LP included "I Want to Hold Your Hand," which was slated to be the fifth Beatles single. Written, once again, by Lennon and McCartney, "I Want to Hold Your Hand" was recorded in fifteen takes on October 17.

Unlike the group's previous three Number Ones ("Love Me Do" was not considered a "hit" single), "I Want to Hold Your Hand" was devoid of The Beatles signature *ooooohs!* It did, however, feature syncopated hand-clapping and an upward-spiraling crescendo emphasized by Paul McCartney's falsetto—*It's such a feeling that my love, I can't hide, I can't hide, I can't hide!* In bootlegged studio outtakes of "I Want to Hold Your Hand," McCartney can be heard urging Ringo to attack his crash cymbal to emphasize the song's opening bars.

In England, The Beatles marketing blitz also began in earnest, particularly after 250,000 advance orders of *With the Beatles* set the groundwork for the LP's release on Friday, November 22—the same day that President John F. Kennedy was assassinated in Dallas, Texas. Earlier that day, before the horror, the *CBS Morning News with Mike Wallace* featured a story, filed by CBS News' London correspondent Alexander Kendrick, on The Beatles phenomenon unfolding across the pond in England.

Kendrick's report was preceded a week earlier, on November 18, by NBC News reporter Edwin Newman, who filed a four-minute report on The Beatles for *The Huntley-Brinkley Report*, NBC's daily evening newscast. Video of Newman's report is (thus far) lost to history, but the audio is available.

Newman's recitation on The Beatles features a snippet of "their smash hit" "From Me to You" and some snarky editorializing, calling them "A quartet of young men with pudding-bowl haircuts . . . they've sold two-and-a-half million records and they earn five thousand dollars a week." Newman categorized Beatles fans as "compulsive screamers, mostly female, mostly between the ages of ten to sixteen. . . . Those who study such things say that at last the British juvenile has someone immediate to identify with, not some distant American rock and roll hero." He opines that "one reason for The Beatles' popularity may be that it's almost impossible to hear them," and closes by citing a "sobering report" in the *London Times* that "The Beatles may bring their Mersey sound to the United States, to which it may be rejoined, 'Show us no Mersey.'"

But that was in America. In England, *With the Beatles* immediately topped the charts. A week later, on November 29, with over one-million advance orders already tallied, "I Want to Hold Your Hand" was released as a single in the UK and, a week later, went to Number One—eclipsing "She Loves You" (enjoying its second run in the top spot). It was the fourth consecutive smash-hit Beatles single.

The Royal Command Variety Performance, which aired on November 10, drew an audience of twenty-six million viewers who heard John Lennon, introducing a rollicking version of "Twist and Shout," ask "the people in the cheaper seats [to] clap your hands. And the rest of you, if you'll just rattle your jewelry."

"It was the only time I felt British," Ringo said. "You know, you never think about royalty. But the Queen Mother, she was a nice lady."

By Christmas 1963, store shelves in England were stocked with Beatles wigs, jackets, sweaters, Beatles dolls, plastic Beatles guitars and drums, aprons, record racks, chewing gum, Beatle boots, handkerchiefs, pencils, buttons, bedspreads, shoulder bags, and even a candy called a "Ringo Roll." Virtually every product available had some sort of Beatles tie-in.

Lancashire-born actress Dora Bryan, who was forty at the time, sucked it up and recorded a Christmas song called "All I Want for Christmas Is a Beatle," in which the singer asked her mother for a Fab Four gift (*Ringo, Paul, John, George they're all the same*).

Young boys started growing their hair longer to emulate their heroes; there were newspaper stories aplenty of teenagers being sent home from school, or from their apprenticeships, because their hair was too long. There was panic among Beatles fans when Paul missed a concert in Portsmouth because of the flu; Ringo, stricken with an ear infection in Lincoln, had to be rushed to the hospital wearing a disguise (an overcoat, hat, and glasses) that "made him look like [playwright Bertolt] Brecht being smuggled out of Germany."

The accompany media blitz following The Royal Command Variety Performance fed the frenzy and pushed John, Paul, George, and Ringo further into the gaping, unquenchable maw of interest in and fascination with The Beatles. In America, *Time* magazine took note of Beatlemania:

> They look like Peter Pans, with their mushroom haircuts and high white shirt collars, and onstage they clown around endlessly—twisting, cracking jokes, gently laughing at the riotous response they get from their audience. . . . "We're not interested in living it up," says Ringo. "All of our money goes into Beatles Ltd., and we take only enough out for clothes and a few ciggies."

Before the year was out The Beatles were everywhere. They made multiple appearances on television, including spots on *Thank Your Lucky Stars*, *It's The Beatles*, *Late Scene Extra*, and *Juke Box Jury*. In early December, The Beatles appeared on *Two of a Kind*, ATV's popular television show, hosted by Eric Morecambe and Ernie Wise (or "Eric and Ern," as they were lovingly called by a country that warmly embraced the two stars). The Beatles performed "This Boy," "All My Loving," and "I Want to Hold Your Hand" and played along as Morecambe donned a Beatles wig while John, Paul, and George gamely sang "Moonlight Bay" with Ernie.

Ringo, wearing a jacket and straw boater, kept time further back and high up on his drum riser.

Eric: Where is he?

Ernie: Where is he?

Eric (walking toward Ringo): Hello, Bongo!

Ernie: That's Ringo!

Eric: Oh, is he there as well?

With the new adjective "Beatlemania" having already entered the British lexicon, the English press began to scramble for other terms to describe the group. "The Fab Four" and "The Four Mop Tops from Liverpool" were commonly used, and the individual Beatles were quickly pigeonholed with embellished identities: John (the intellectual), Paul (the cute one), George (the quiet one), and Ringo (the funny one).

"In all our handouts and in all our press dealings, Brian only stressed what was good about them. He never created any nonexistent good points," said Tony Barrow. "The Beatles were four lads from down the street, the sort you might have seen at the local church hall. This was the essence of their personal communication with the public. This was the appeal. People identified with them from the beginning. Brian realized this and never tried to hide it."

But being put under the microscope of fame meant the (sometimes unwanted) magnification of each Beatle's personality and physical looks. While Ringo would be described as having "puppy dog" eyes, he was also mocked for the size of his nose. One intrepid reporter from *Melody Maker* even asked him if he'd ever considered having plastic surgery on his proboscis. *The Jewish Chronicle* called Brian Epstein's office, wanting to know if Ringo was Jewish—strangely perpetuating the stereotype of Jewish people having big noses. On television, Eric Sykes and Hattie Jacques poked fun at Ringo's (and France's president, Charles de Gaulle's) schnozzola in an episode of their BBC sitcom, *Sykes and a . . .*

Boyfriend, a teen magazine aimed at young females (read: Beatles fans), defended Ringo's nose as "a sign of distinction, one of the things that makes him attractive."

As for Ringo's take on the matter: "I've come to terms with my own nose. It's the talking point when people discuss me. I have a laugh, and it goes up one nostril and out the other."

He didn't always laugh it off, however. "You know, I went through a stage of thinking seriously about having plastic surgery on my nose because that was all the papers seemed to write about," he said. "I never noticed 'my feature' until the press pointed it out. It didn't hurt me, but I get fed up reading about it."

Despite the CBS News and NBC news reports, The Beatles were still virtual nobodies in America. Ed Sullivan hoped to change that. Sullivan and his wife, Sylvia, on a trip to England that fall, had witnessed the frenzy at Heathrow Airport that accompanied a Beatles homecoming following the group's trip abroad to tour Sweden. Sullivan was impressed by what he saw and, in late 1963, met with Brian Epstein in New York City when Epstein flew there to introduce one of his acts, Billy J. Kramer, to record executives.

Going on a hunch, Sullivan signed The Beatles for several February appearances on his popular Sunday-night CBS television variety series, *The Ed Sullivan Show*, which was a popular (and highly rated) showcase for up-and-coming acts—including hip-swiveling Elvis Presley, whom Sullivan famously ordered be shown only from the waist up when he appeared on his show in 1956.

Sullivan offered The Beatles three appearances at $4,500 per appearance, plus round-trip airline tickets. He also agreed to foot the bill for the band's expenses while they were in America. Epstein accepted the deal.

Sullivan hoped he was right, and he had reason to be fairly optimistic. Toward the end of the year, word was starting to spread throughout the American media. The *New York Times* weighed in on the group—"There has been adulation before but no one has taken the national fancy as they have"—and stories appeared in both *Time* and *Newsweek*.

Tony Barrow, acting under Brian Epstein's orders, began courting the American teen magazines, particularly *16* and its editor, thirty-seven-year-old Gloria Stavers, who bought into Beatlemania and ran breathless fanzine profiles of the group. In late December, Capitol Records, caving in to Brian Epstein's entreaties, released "I Want to Hold Your Hand," backed with "I Saw Her Standing There," in the States a month earlier than planned.

7

"IT WAS MAD . . . BUT IT WAS INCREDIBLE"

I n January 1964, "I Want to Hold Your Hand" still had yet to make an impact, entering the charts at Number Eighty-Three. But it was a start, and both The Beatles and their new single were given a nudge early that month by former *Tonight Show* host Jack Paar, who showed footage of The Beatles performing "She Loves You" (shot the previous summer in Southport for a British TV special called *The Mersey Sound*) on his new NBC prime-time show, *The Jack Paar Program*. Paar was encouraged to do so by his teenage daughter, Randy, who'd met John, Paul, George, and Ringo in England and was a big Fab Four fan.

Back in England, "I Want to Hold Your Hand" was knocked out of the top spot by the Dave Clark Five's "Glad All Over" and, for all intents and purposes, it looked as if Ed Sullivan might have lost his gamble on The Beatles hitting it big in the States. Even the British press took some shots at The Beatles, wondering if their time in the sun was about to eclipse.

The band's three-week stint at The Olympia Theatre in Paris in mid-January got off to an inauspicious start, with unenthusiastic audiences and lukewarm press coming as something of a shock to a group already accustomed to adulation. The screaming teenage girls, so prevalent elsewhere, were in short supply in France—in fact, The Beatles, and Ringo in particular, seemed mostly to be attracting what George Harrison called "a bunch of slightly gay-looking boys" shouting "Ringo! Ringo!" and chasing the band's car through the streets, in a gender reversal of the group's English fans.

Ringo said the boys chased the band all over the city. Once The Beatles took the stage, they were greeted with a roar they hadn't heard before (different from the shrieks of young girls back in England).

Meanwhile, The Beatles started to heat up in America as "I Want to Hold Your Hand" ascended the charts around the time Brian Epstein was closing a deal with Sid Bernstein for The Beatles to appear at Carnegie Hall on February 12, three days after their *Ed Sullivan Show* appearance. By January 18, "I

Want to Hold Your Hand" hit Number Forty-Five on the charts; a week later it climbed to Number Three.

The Beatles were in their rooms in the George V Hotel in Paris on February 1 when the news hit: "I Want to Hold Your Hand" was Number One in America after only three weeks on the charts. "We couldn't believe it," Ringo recalled. "We all just started acting like people from Texas, hollering and shouting, 'Ya-hoo!' I think that was the night we finished up sitting on a bench by the Seine; just the four of us and Neil. In those days we'd promise Neil £20,000 if he'd go for a swim. He'd go for a swim and we'd say, 'No, sorry.'"

John, Paul, George, and Ringo celebrated the mind-blowing news with a lavish dinner, accompanied by Brian Epstein and George Martin, who was in Paris to oversee the group's German-language recordings of "She Loves You (*Sie Liebt Dich*)" and "I Want to Hold Your Hand (*Komm Gib Mir Deine Hand*)." The timing couldn't be better, with the first trip to America less than week away. The gods, Ringo said, were on the side of The Beatles, but it wasn't just luck; Lennon and McCartney were writing terrific songs, the band was a cohesive unit, and they were already seasoned veterans who'd toured (and conquered) several countries. In Ringo's mind, the chips were falling into place—capped off by "I Want to Hold Your Hand" hitting Number One in the United States just as The Beatles were on their way to America.

On February 7, The Beatles were seen off to America by a throng of four-thousand enthusiastic fans at Heathrow Airport. They couldn't even begin to imagine what awaited them across the Atlantic at John F. Kennedy Airport in New York, newly renamed for the president slain three months before in Dallas. "There's twenty-billion kids out there," Ringo recalled. It just fitted into place all the time, you know?"

Local New York City radio stations WMCA and WINS, home of popular disc jockey "Murray the K" Kaufman, were giving minute-by-minute accounts of The Beatles' progress as their Boeing 707 began its descent into JFK Airport. Both stations that day played "I Want to Hold Your Hand" nearly nonstop, pausing only to give the time and temperature in "Beatle time" and "Beatle degrees." Kaufman divulged the exclusive news that The Beatles would be staying at The Plaza hotel, sending an army of frenzied fans scurrying to the hotel's Central Park entrance to camp out for the band's imminent arrival. Ringo recalled the excitement on the plane as New York came into sight, describing the pull of the city "like tentacles" wrapping themselves around the aircraft as it began its descent into John F. Kennedy International Airport. Big crowds in the U.K. were one thing; arriving to thousands of screaming fans in America was a whole other level of excitement for The Beatles, a "madness" they hadn't yet experienced.

The Beatles were greeted by thousands of screaming teenage fans upon their arrival at JFK and an army of press ready to capture this fleeting phenomenon for posterity. Paul McCartney remembered the captain of Pan Am Flight 101 checking in with ground control at JFK, then relaying the message back to the cabin: "Tell the boys there's a big crowd waiting for them."

Many of the kids who'd cut school that cold Friday afternoon to welcome their new heroes—and maybe get a glimpse of John, Paul, George, and Ringo— were armed with signs ("Ringo for President!" "We Love John!" "Beatles Forever"). They had to be held back by a phalanx of New York City cops, straining to keep the hysteria in check, as the throng of kids ran to meet the plane carrying The Beatles. It was Sinatra and the Bobby-Soxers and Elvis making the girls squeal by shaking his hips—but on a more massive scale and for four young men who, the year before, were unknown even in their own country.

"Three thousand teenagers stood four deep on the upper arcade of the International Arrivals Building," the *New York Times* reported. "Girls, girls and more girls."

The Beatles, looking a bit shell-shocked, held a memorable press conference inside the Pan Am terminal. They were the calm at the center of a storm, the likes of which had never been seen as newspaper reporters jostled with television and film cameramen—and crying, pleading fans—in the pandemonium amid a sea of exploding flash bulbs and microphones pointed at (standing left to right) Paul, Ringo, George, and John.

Question: What about you, Ringo? What do you think of Beethoven?

Ringo: I love him. Especially his poems.

Question: Some of your detractors allege that you are bald and those haircuts are wigs. Is that true, John?

John: Oh, we're all bald—yeah. And I'm deaf and dumb, too.

Question: Will you sing something for us?

John: We need money first.

Question: How do you find America?

Ringo: Turn left at Greenland.

The Beatles, of course, were thrilled with their reception, but none more so than Ringo. Why? Well, for starters, Beatles fans in America were new to the party and were, for the most part, unfamiliar with the band's history—or with Ringo Starr's place in the annals of Beatles lore. For Ringo, the American fans' blind acceptance of him as a true, equal Beatle was quite different than back home, where hardcore Pete Best fans, and many Beatles fans in Liverpool, considered Ringo an interloper.

Ringo was giddy with the immediate embrace he felt from fans in the States. They didn't know about Pete Best, nor were they interested. Ringo felt like the proverbial kid moving to a new town, where he could start with an uncluttered, clean slate. It helped that Brian Epstein's publicity machine, in hyper-drive, scrubbed any mentions of Pete Best from the band's sanitized story.

In America, Ringo had his own identity. He had a huge fan base who loved him because he was a Beatle, and nothing more. Here, he was the *only* Beatles drummer. Here, there was no emotional baggage.

He loved the energy, the "hip" radio and television and the club-hopping. Most of all, though, he loved the fact that, in America, his name was often mentioned first in The Beatles pantheon. Here, he was an equal member of the band.

It was Ringo—and not John Lennon or Paul McCartney—who was considered by many American observers in the American press to be the most popular Beatle—not the group's leader, not by any stretch of the imagination, but the wittiest and zaniest Beatle whose teddy-bear countenance, offset by his sad blue eyes, diminutive size and funny name, struck a chord with the group's stateside fans.

The Saturday Evening Post assigned reporter Al Aronowitz to follow The Beatles around for a few weeks after they landed in New York. Aronowitz, in an article published in March, went so far as to call Ringo "the most popular of the Beatles in America" who "evokes paroxysms of teen-age shrieks everywhere by a mere turn of his head, a motion which sends his brown hair flying." John Lennon, of course—perhaps a bit jealously—put his drummer in his place: "I just look at Ringo and I know perfectly well we're not supermen." Aronowitz, despite his opinion of Ringo's stateside popularity, was also a keen observer of the group's dynamic:

> He sits with his drums behind the group as the other three perform, and he rarely sings, although that is what he would most like to do. At twenty-five [sic] he is the oldest of the Beatles, but he is at the bottom of what sociologists would call their pecking order. When he joined the group it already had a record contract, and the unspoken feeling in the quartet is that Ringo was hired by the other three.

When they disagree on anything, Ringo is the last to get his way. "You'd be nowhere," Paul McCartney says to him in the ultimate squelch, "if it weren't for the rest of us."

If Ringo cared what Aronowitz, or anyone else, thought about him he wasn't letting on. The drummer from the Dingle was embraced wholeheartedly by his newfound American fans and he was having a blast basking in their love and adulation—even if the emotional outpouring was filtered through thick hotel-room walls, car windows, or local television reports of the "invasion."

Frenzied Beatles fans surrounded The Plaza hotel near Central Park in the two days leading up to *The Ed Sullivan Show*, shouting for their heroes ("We love you, Ringo!") and chasing official-looking limousines in the general vicinity, hoping to get a glimpse of a live flesh-and-blood Beatle inside. Back in England, the press and public were keeping tabs on John, Paul, George, and Ringo and were as amazed—if maybe a little jealous—at the ruckus "The Boys" were causing across the ocean.

John, Paul, George, and Ringo did a round of telephone interviews with disc jockeys back home at they sat cloistered in their suite in The Plaza, watching TV (*The Huntley-Brinkley Report*), listening to the radio and talking on the phone to blowhard Murray the K on 1010 WINS—who dubbed himself "The Fifth Beatle"—reading about their JFK press conference in the papers, autographing photos and peeking out the window at the gathered throng below, screeching their names.

Ringo loved everything about it, from the horse-drawn carriage they rode in Central Park to the fact that there was a TV set blaring in each room of their hotel—and that each Beatle had a radio with earphones. This was living.

America met The Beatles at eight p.m. Eastern time on the night of February 9, 1964, when it seemed like the entire country turned their television sets to CBS to watch *The Ed Sullivan Show*.

The hype had been building for weeks, and New York's music radio stations, particularly 1010 WINS, were playing nothing but Beatles songs. The theater from which *The Ed Sullivan Show* aired could accommodate seven-hundred people, in stark contrast to the fifty-thousand fans who tried to get tickets for that night.

It was feared that George Harrison, who was running a fever and had a sore throat, might not make it to the show. He'd already missed an earlier Beatles photo shoot in Central Park (Paul, John, and Ringo went and gamely mugged for the cameras in the freezing temperatures). His older sister, Louise, was caring for him in his suite, with Cynthia Lennon, kept hidden from Beatles fans, in the next room. A doctor was dispatched to The Plaza to pump George full of medicine (and amphetamines, according to Brian Epstein's assistant Peter Brown). He was bundled up, tossed into the back of a waiting limousine, and made it to the theater just before show time.

"You know something very nice happened and The Beatles got a great kick out of it," Sullivan said, opening the show. "We just received a wire, they did, from Elvis Presley and Colonel Tom Parker wishing them a tremendous success in our country and I think that was very, very nice." After a commercial break, Sullivan was back. "Yesterday and today our theater's been jammed with newspapermen and hundreds of photographers from all over the nation, and these veterans agree with me that the city has never witnessed the excitement stirred by these youngsters from Liverpool who call themselves The Beatles."

Sullivan could barely be heard over the shrieking din as he introduced the group ("Ladies and gentleman, *The Beatles*! Let's bring 'em on!") as John, Paul, George, and Ringo launched into a rousing rendition of "All My Loving." They followed that with the quiet ballad "Till There Was You," during which the black-and-white CBS cameras panned to each individual Beatle, introducing America to The Fab Four.

Each Beatle's smiling face was accompanied by a blocky white graphic identifying "Paul," "Ringo," "George," and "John" (in that order). The fans in the theater screamed when Ringo was shown (he looked a bit dazed from it all); underneath John's name, to the horror of Brian Epstein—working so hard to keep The Beatles single and available—were the words *Sorry, girls, he's married*. The farsighted Lennon, who could barely see five feet in front of him without his glasses, smiled unwittingly as the graphic was flashed on the screen and the audience screamed.

The Beatles then sang their Number One hit single "She Loves You," which, Sullivan told his audience, they were dedicating to *The Tonight Show* host Johnny Carson, Randy Paar (daughter of Carson's predecessor, Jack Paar), and *New York Post* columnist Earl Wilson. (It's doubtful The Beatles knew who any of these people were—despite Randy Paar's influence in getting her father to show footage of The Beatles on his NBC show.)

The Beatles returned later in the broadcast to perform "I Saw Her Standing There" and "I Want to Hold Your Hand." *The Ed Sullivan Show* producers gave Ringo some solo camera time during both numbers, particularly on "I Want to Hold Your Hand" when the CBS camera panned up to Ringo high on his drum riser, thumping away and shaking his head to the beat as he grooved on his hi-hat cymbal.

The shrieking from the fans in the *Ed Sullivan Show* studio audience that night made it nearly impossible for the CBS camera operators to hear their directions from the control booth, even though they were wearing headphones. Shortly thereafter, CBS ordered specially made headphones for their camera operators. Call it "The Beatle Effect."

Those first nights in New York were frenetic and exciting. The Beatles made various pit stops around the city, including a visit to The Playboy Club and a well-documented foray with Murray the K to the Peppermint Lounge—where they drank Scotch and Cokes (the "official" Beatles drink), smoked heavily, and danced the night away under Brian Epstein's watchful eye. Newspaper reporters and fan magazines trailing the group reported that Ringo spent the night boogeying with the Peppermint Lounge dance captain. But that was for public consumption. The Beatles needed to maintain their squeaky-clean image.

In reality, Ringo had spotted Geri Miller, a dark-haired go-go dancer and Peppermint Lounge regular from Passaic, New Jersey, and struck up a conversation with her. Miller, a future member of Andy Warhol's motley ensemble, was only too happy to oblige a Beatle. "He was dumb," she said later. "You see I'm stupid in the way he was stupid and I like someone who's really intellectual."

Miller gave a (highly sanitized) narrative of her night with Ringo a few months later to *Movieland* magazine.

> Sure enough, at half past twelve, the Beatles were sitting ring-side, sipping Scotch and coke and watching our revue! I flipped immediately over George. I thought he was gorgeous. After the show, all the girls (still in costume) were brought to their table and introduced. I didn't see George and asked for him. I was disappointed to learn he had a sore throat and had to leave. Oh well, I thought, he must be a dead-head. I probably wouldn't have liked him anyway. While at the table I noticed Ringo staring at me. I knew one of the other girls dug him, so I decided to go back to the dressing room and change

into street clothes. When I came out, dozens of girls were swarming about them. I figured I'd never stand a chance with all the competition, so I got up on stage to dance with some friends. Then the band played a real wild Monkey, and I danced as I've never danced before. As I spun around, I caught Ringo staring at me intently. Afterwards he invited me over to join his table, there were no chairs vacant, so I did the next best thing . . . I SAT ON HIS LAP!

In Miller's version of events, she went back home, stopping along the way for some groceries. Even though she'd forgotten to tell Ringo her apartment number, he miraculously answered the door when she heard the television set blaring from outside in the hallway and rang the bell. "He explained he met a neighbor in the lobby and she told him which apartment I lived in. I pictured my neighbor wondering why the one and only RINGO STARR was asking about silly ol' Geri Miller's apartment."

Miller wrote that she made Ringo breakfast "and we talked and talked" until he left at seven a.m. "to leave and get some sleep. . . . I ran into the hallway and gave him a Peppermint Lounge souvenir key-chain and told him to 'use it and think of me.' . . . He kissed me again and said goodnight."

The Beatles' appearance on *The Ed Sullivan Show* sent the viewing numbers skyrocketing. It was estimated that a record-setting U.S. television audience of seventy-three million people watched the telecast. Among the viewers was evangelist Billy Graham who, according to a UPI report, broke his cardinal rule and watched television on the Sabbath. Crime in New York City that night was virtually non-existent.

The other acts on *The Ed Sullivan Show* that night, forever relegated to footnote status, included impressionist Frank Gorshin, the comedy team of Mitzi McCall and Charlie Brill and a number from the British musical hit *Oliver!*—whose cast on the stage that night included future Monkees lead singer Davy Jones.

Not everyone was impressed with *The Ed Sullivan Show* appearance. "Visually, they are a nightmare: tight, dandified, Edwardian/Beatnik suits and great pudding bowls of hair," sniffed *Newsweek* magazine. "Musically, they are a near-disaster: guitars and drums slamming out a merciless beat that does away with secondary rhythms, harmony, and melody. Their lyrics (punctuated by nutty shouts of 'yeah, yeah, yeah!') are a catastrophe, a preposterous farrago of Valentine-card romantic sentiments . . . the odds are they will fade away, as most adults confidently predict."

The *Washington Post* referred to The Beatles as "asexual and homely," while the *New York Herald Tribune* called them "75 percent publicity, 20 percent haircut and 5 percent lilting lament."

But those were the exceptions. The majority of the press reports were glowing but, more importantly, America's youth fell in love with John, Paul, George, and Ringo that night. And that was all that mattered. If the older people disliked the four shaggy-haired boys from Liverpool, well, that made it even better. To hell with them. Young girls could fantasize with puppy-dog crushes about their favorite Beatle, while an untold number of rock 'n' roll groups were formed right then and there.

"I was a kid running around outside with my brother in Stockbridge, Massachusetts, where I grew up and there was nothing to watch on TV," recalled drummer Kenny Aronoff, who would one day play with Ringo and Paul McCartney, "and my mom said, 'You gotta watch this thing on TV. The Beatles are going to be on *Ed Sullivan*. We went flying in there and the tornado stopped. And there was complete silence. I'm watching this thing, flipping out. I turned my head and I was like, I want to be in The Beatles. Who do I call? I want to grow my hair, I want girls going crazy over me, I want to play the drums. Who do I call? What do I do? What's a ten-year-old kid going to do? So I started a band the next week."

Beatles slang ("gear," "fab," "grotty") was all the rage, as were Beatles haircuts and Beatle boots (like the ones they wore on *The Ed Sullivan Show*). Sales of guitars and drum sets skyrocketed.

Among the group's legion of young female fans was fourteen-year-old high school student Marilyn Crescenzo, who lived in the New York City area and began keeping a diary of her favorite group. She quickly fell in love with Ringo, although her first diary entry, dated February 22—thirteen days after The Beatles first appearance on *The Ed Sullivan Show*—described her future love as "not too good looking either. But as all the rest—very talented." Only Paul McCartney, in that first entry, emerged as "very good looking."

The black-and-white image of a smiling, head-shaking Ringo, thwacking away on his drum kit to a sea of hysterically screaming girls, drove untold numbers of young boys toward the drums. Ringo made it look so cool. "More than any other drummer, Ringo Starr changed my life," said Max Weinberg, longtime drummer for Bruce Springsteen's E Street Band and for Conan O'Brien's *Late Night* and *Tonight Show* bands. "The impact and memory of that band on *The Ed Sullivan Show* in 1964 will never leave me. I can still see Ringo in the back moving that beat with his whole body, his right hand swinging off his sock cymbal while his left hand pounds the snare. He was fantastic, but I think what got to me the most was his smile. I knew he was having the time of his life."

"Not since Gene Krupa thirty years earlier had any one drummer inspired so many youngsters to take up the sticks," wrote drumming historian John H. Beck. "Ringo was the leading reason that rock drummers began using the matched grip, and his signature Oyster Pearl kit was so popular that it made Ludwig the number one drum manufacturer for the next two decades."

In September, when The Beatles tour stopped in Chicago, Ludwig Drum Company president William F. Ludwig Jr. presented Ringo with a gold-plated Ludwig "Super-Sensitive" snare drum. "I have never known a drummer more widely acclaimed and publicized than you, Ringo Starr," Ludwig said. "Your millions of fans have honored you and the other members of The Beatles by their overwhelming acceptance of your recordings and concert appearances."

William F. Ludwig Jr. had reason to be pleased; according to the company, Ludwig had sales of $6.1 million in 1964. Overnight, after Ringo's appearance on *The Ed Sullivan Show*, the company's factory in Chicago (on Damen Avenue) began running twenty-four hours a day, seven days a week—in order to keep up with the demand for drums. *The Ed Sullivan Show* appearance, Ludwig joked, was "the show that launched a thousand purchase orders." Within two years, Ludwig's sales had doubled to $13.1 million, and the company expanded its factory.

The Ed Sullivan Show was the proverbial slingshot which propelled The Beatles onward with a lightning-speed momentum, with seemingly no end in sight. The Beatles left New York for Washington, D.C., and their first live U.S. concert, traveling by train to the nation's capital after a raging snowstorm closed all the airports.

Three months before, Washington was cloaked in funereal solemnity following President Kennedy's assassination. Now The Beatles were coming to town, and, like a gigantic, mass catharsis, people were ready to celebrate (notwithstanding the bitter cold). The Beatles, and Ringo in particular, kept the press contingent, cloistered with them on the train ride to Washington, entertained with a nonstop string of gags and one-liners.

The Beatles weren't afraid to give it back in spades to the press corps, which only endeared them to the grizzled reporters. Ringo, Paul, John, and George would yell back at the reporters barking out questions or trying to get a rise out of these shaggy-haired Liverpudlians—who scored extra points by joining the press corps in smoking and drinking.

The show at the sweaty Washington Coliseum was pure bedlam. The Beatles were hit with a nonstop barrage of jelly beans—"We were absolutely pelted by the fucking things," George said—while cops tried to hold back the swelling crowd of mostly young girls. A jet-engine din of noise made it impossible for John, Paul, George, and Ringo to hear themselves; a theater-in-the-round effect was accomplished by manually turning Ringo's drum riser around after each number.

"Ringo, in particular, played like a madman, revealing a fire that nobody had ever glimpsed before beneath his workmanlike surface," Albert Goldman wrote in his biography of John Lennon. Ringo loved every second of it. "They could have ripped me apart and I wouldn't have cared," he said afterward. "What an audience! I could have played for them all night."

The attention was great, of course, but the drawbacks to being a Beatle were just starting to seep into the band's consciousness. Now that they had conquered the American market, red flags were being raised with alarming frequency. Such was the mythology surrounding the group that handicapped people would often be wheeled in to see them before or after concerts, hoping they could be cured by a Beatle's magical touch.

Invited for a meet-and-greet at the British Embassy following their concert at the Washington Coliseum, The Beatles were mingling with the tuxedo-and-jewelry set, making small talk, when someone came up behind Ringo and, with a cuticle scissors, cut off a locket of his hair (behind his ear) for a keepsake.

Ringo, pissed off, swung around, and hissed at the unsolicited barber, asking him what the hell he thought he was doing—and wondering why he was carrying around a pair of scissors. John Lennon was so incensed at the incident that he walked out, swearing.

Ringo was now a household name in America, which translated into worldwide acclaim. The Beatles continued their U.S. tour, following up their historic *Ed Sullivan Show* appearance with two sold-out concerts at Carnegie Hall on February 12 and a return engagement to *The Ed Sullivan Show* the following Sunday, February 16, in sunny Miami, where Sullivan was doing his show from the Deauville Hotel.

Ringo, so accustomed to the harsh English winters, basked in the sun with his band mates, drove a motor boat and tooled around the area with George Harrison in a borrowed car. In-between, The Beatles hung out of their beach-front Miami hotel-room window, shouting back "Which one are *you?*" to the fans who shouted that same question up to them while writing each Beatle's name in the sand.

They even caught a show headlined by the caustic comedian Don Rickles, who poked fun at them and was dubbed "not cool" by George Harrison because he apologized for making fun of everyone at the end of his act. George figured Rickles should have just exited after his last barb, leaving the room abuzz.

If Ringo loved New York, he was absolutely ecstatic about the warmth of Miami. The Beatles were given anything they wanted, including a yacht to tool around in and a sixty-foot speedboat. Ringo experienced his first drive-in movie in the comfort of a Lincoln Continental—with two female companions.

Beatlemania, meanwhile, took on a life of its own. In Southern California, an eighteen-year-old young singer named Cherilyn Sarkisian, who was living with her boyfriend Sonny Bono—and hadn't yet changed her name to Cher—recorded her first single under the name of Bonnie Jo Mason. "Ringo, I Love You," was produced by Bono's pal Phil Spector and flopped out of the gate, since too many people thought the singer sounded like a man.

British singer Penny Valentine released a single called "I Want to Kiss Ringo Goodbye," while Australian entertainer Rolf Harris of "Tie Me Kanga-roo Down, Sport" fame cut "Ringo for President." The Four Sisters released "I Want Ringo for Christmas," while Christine Hunter also got into the act with "Santa, Bring Me Ringo" (*Santa bring me Ringo/I want to hold his hand*). There was also Neil Sheppard's "You Can't Go Far Without a Guitar (Unless You're Ringo Starr)."

Even pop-culture parody king Allan Sherman ("Sarah Jackman," "Al 'n' Yet-ta"), who'd had a huge novelty hit several years before with "Hello Muddah, Hello Faddah" tried to cash in on Beatlemania. Sherman's star was on the wane after President Kennedy's assassination dampened America's enthusiasm for his type of humor. On his album *Songs for Swingin' Livers* (A play on the 1956 Frank Sinatra LP, *Songs for Swingin' Lovers*, "Livers" replacing "Lovers" to em-phasize the generation gap), Sherman recorded "Pop Hates the Beatles," which he sung to the tune of "Pop Goes the Weasel," singling out Ringo as "the one with the drum." In an episode of the ABC sitcom *F Troop*, one of the characters, a jinxed soldier, was named Wrongo Starr.

One Beatles fan, who was fifteen at the time, told author Hunter Davies several years later that she was annoyed with George Harrison after seeing The Beatles at Carnegie Hall. "He seemed to be standing in the way of Ringo and we couldn't see him. We all shouted at him to get out of the way and let us see Ringo." It was John, though, whom she really loved: "I gave him three whole years of my life from then on."

Ringo knew how popular he was in America, that he'd "made it" as a personality. That meant little to his family back in Liverpool; to them, it was good enough that Ringo and The Beatles were hometown heroes who'd played the Palladium. Popularity in America was just gravy.

The Beatles returned to England on February 22 as conquering heroes. Thousands of screaming fans and dozens of reporters were on hand to greet "The Boys" at Heathrow Airport when they stepped off their Pan Am flight. Girls fainted. British Prime Minister Sir Alec Douglas-Home referred to them as "our best exports." Ringo, who'd left school at the age of fifteen, was elected a vice-president of Leeds University. The Beatles were even immortalized in wax by Madame Tussaud's.

And that was just the start.

They now held the top five positions in the U.S. singles charts while their first two albums were holding steady at Number One and Number Two. It was unprecedented; America, up until now, had failed to embrace British talent. Now The Beatles unleashed what the U.S. press was calling "The British Invasion."

The four soldiers leading the charge didn't have much time to think about the pop-culture history they were creating. Beatlemania was already in full swing in England and, by now, had spread to the rest of the continent.

Back in Liverpool, Elsie and Harry, still living at 10 Admiral Grove, tried to go about their lives as best they could. But being the parents of a Beatle meant the end to a normal life, and now, more than ever, they bore the brunt of having a son who was one of the most famous people in the world.

"The first time I really noticed how well they were known was when we woke up one morning to find a busload of fans knocking at the front door," Elsie said. "It was seven o'clock on a Sunday morning. They'd traveled overnight from London. Well, what could I do? I fetched them all in and gave them tea and biscuits. I thought it was marvelous. All that way, just for our Richy. They never ate anything. They just wrapped them up to take back as souvenirs."

And those were some of the tamer Beatles fans. Others, mostly girls, "used to climb over the back yard wall, or sleep in the street for days," she said. "They were physical wrecks, most of them, but they were just too excited to rest or eat. They'd ask 'which is his chair?' I'd say "sit on them all, love, he has.' They always wanted to go up to see his bed as well. They'd lie on it, moaning."

Back in London, there was a movie to be made—and a soundtrack for that movie that needed to be recorded. In late February—after taping an appearance for the television variety show *Big Night Out*—John, Paul, George, and Ringo returned to the EMI studios at Abbey Road. Once again they were paired with producer George Martin to start recording songs that would be used as the soundtrack for their first of a three-movie deal brokered by Brian Epstein. The movie was tentatively titled "Beatlemania."

"We were making records and, wow, the records were taking off and then we're playing to bigger and bigger audiences and that's taking off, and now we're doing a movie," Ringo said. "It was mad . . . but it was incredible."

The movie was being produced for United Artists by Walter Shenson, with a script by Welsh writer Alun Owen, both of whom spent time with The Beatles in Paris and in Britain earlier that year. For Owen, in particular, it was a chance to witness Beatlemania firsthand and to observe the interpersonal relationships of the four band members. It was also a chance to pick up some of their Liverpool slang and to gauge their individual attitudes—elements Owen incorporated into his screenplay.

The writer accompanied The Beatles on a leg of their British tour, eventually incorporating the chaos that went along with all of that into his screenplay—a snapshot, really, of several days in the life of The Beatles.

The cast for the movie, which began shooting March 2, included Wilfrid Brambell, co-star (with Harry Corbett Jr.) of the BBC's popular sitcom *Steptoe and Son*, who was playing Paul's "clean" grandfather. (It was an inside joke, since Brambell's *Steptoe and Son* character, Shepherd's Bush "rag and bone man" Albert Steptoe, was constantly called "a dirty old man.")

The grandfather was a recalcitrant codger who was traveling with John, Paul, George, and Ringo on their way to a Liverpool television performance, all the while meddling in their affairs, poking fun at Ringo's appearance (particularly his nose) and generally causing trouble. Veteran actors Victor Spinetti, Norman Rossington, and John Junkin were also in the movie's cast.

The director was Richard Lester, an American from Philadelphia who spent his early career working in the fledgling medium of television before relocating to London in 1953. More importantly for The Beatles, Lester had worked with Peter Sellers, so he was already golden (The Beatles revered Sellers). Lester helped Sellers adapt BBC Radio's *The Goon Show* (with Sellers, Harry

Secombe, and Spike Milligan) to British television (for two short-lived series), and collaborated with Sellers and Milligan on *The Running, Jumping & Standing Still Film*, a short (eleven-minute) anarchic film that was nominated for an Academy Award.

Beatlemania began shooting March 2 at London's Marylebone Station. Owen's screenplay encompassed two frenetic days in the life of The Beatles (though the group's name was never mentioned) as they prepared for a television appearance in Liverpool. Ringo couldn't believe that he was making a bona fide movie, something he'd dreamed of as a kid in the Dingle, when he and Davey Patterson would go to the Saturday-morning pictures.

He recalled how much he'd loved the movies as a child, going to see a Saturday-morning picture at the Beresford and Gaumont theaters and becoming, for 90 minutes, a pirate or a cowboy or one of the Three Musketeers. Now, he was starring in a movie; it was all so "romantic," he said, arriving at the studio in a limo just like one of his Hollywood heroes.

"Romantic," though, would not be the word to describe the movie's shooting schedule. The Beatles had a six a.m. call every morning, which meant they had to be up and awake by five a.m. "Getting up early in the morning wasn't our best talent," Ringo said. Ringo's "talent" was on display in one of the movie's key scenes, a three-and-a-half-minute scene which was constructed around his character, who's been told by Paul's troublemaking grandfather (Brambell) that he's not appreciated by the other Beatles. (The scene is underscored musically by "Ringo's Theme," a twangy, instrumental version of "This Boy," composed by George Martin.)

Feeling forlorn and morose, Ringo goes for a walk, snapping pictures with a camera and ducking into a second-hand clothing store to "disguise" himself after being chased down the street by two young girls. The disguise works too well; he approaches a pretty young girl to say hello. "Get outta here, shorty," she snaps back.

Ringo ends up near a riverbank, tries to take a self-portrait (the camera falls into the water) and encounters a dirty-faced ten-year-old boy, another "deserter" with whom he bonds in an engaging sequence. When the movie opened, critics singled out this scene when praising Ringo's acting chops; little did they know there was absolutely no acting on Ringo's part. He had arrived to film the scene that morning after a sleepless night of carousing in London.

He was a little hung over, which posed a problem since he was scheduled to shoot the key scene with his fellow "deserter." Ringo was sluggish and feeling crappy, and though Lester shot the scene in several different ways, nothing seemed to work. Exasperated, Ringo suggested that he walk around with the cameras filming him; maybe something would happen they could use in the movie. Hence the now-famous riverbank scene. Sometimes you just get lucky.

Most of the film was scripted; Ringo said later most of what ended up on the cutting-room floor was "the ends of scenes," with the four Beatles improvising little bits of business. None of them memorized the script as expected; instead, he said, they learned their lines on the way to the studio each morning.

The movie was rechristened *A Hard Day's Night*. This came from one of Ringo's many malapropisms, a "Ringoism," John Lennon said, that he used in his first book, *In His Own Write* ("He'd had a hard day's night that day") and which Richard Lester wanted to use for the movie's new title. "So Dick Lester said, 'We are going to use that title,' and the next morning I brought in the song."

George Harrison noted that Ringo's frequent malapropisms would break the guys up. One time, driving back to Liverpool from Luton in Ringo's Zephyr Zodiac, the wind blew the car's hood onto the windshield. "Don't worry, I'll soon have you back in your safely beds," Ringo said.

Ringo's response? "Don't worry, I'll soon have you back in your safely-beds."

Ringo chalked it up to thinking of one thing while saying another; his brain was moving too fast to process the information. Other Ringo malapropisms would find their way into Beatles songs and Beatles lore; Lennon used "Tomorrow Never Knows" as the title for a song he wrote for the *Revolver* album. He also loved the Ringo phrase "slight bread." No one knew what it meant, but it was funny and sounded groovy.

A Hard Day's Night wrapped after six weeks of filming. The movie's closing scene featured The Beatles (finally!) performing on the television show to which they were headed in the movie's first scene. To capture the moment as realistically as possible, the scene was shot at the Scala Theatre in London in front of an audience of several hundred screaming teens, mostly drama students from nearby London schools.

Among the horde was thirteen-year-old Phil Collins, the future world-renowned rock drummer and lead vocalist for Genesis, who was studying at The Barbara Speake Stage School. Collins recalled:

> We didn't know when we went that day to the Scala Theatre, which is no longer there, but . . . the drama school that I was at, as well as all the other drama schools in London, got a call for however many kids

they could handle to go along to that theater for a job. No one knew really what the job was. It was only when we walked in the theater and saw the drum kit set up on the stage that we realized that this has something to do with The Beatles.

One of the many reasons that I didn't actually end up as one of the screaming teenagers in the audience [in the movie] was because all I wanted to do was listen. I didn't want to scream. I mean, people used to scream when I went to see the film in [the] cinema, without The Beatles, just on the movie screen, kids were screaming in the cinema. I just wanted to listen.

And years later, in fact it was 1994, when they did the thirtieth anniversary of *A Hard Day's Night*, Walter Shenson got a hold of me. He heard I was in it, and he gave me the outtakes and I found myself eventually, you know, sitting there. It was very cool. But, I mean, I was sitting there, with my hands in my lap, listening, not doing what the director wanted at all.

During the filming of *A Hard Day's Night*, the next Beatles single, another Lennon/McCartney number called "Can't Buy Me Love," was released and shot immediately to Number One, selling two million copies in the U.S. within a week and going gold on its first day in release. Advance orders in Britain topped one million.

George Harrison met his future wife, Pattie Boyd, during filming and the group's first extensive tour of America was being planned for later that summer. It would be the culmination of a worldwide tour set to start in June. The Beatles also made their first appearance on the BBC television show *Top of the Pops* (miming to "Can't Buy Me Love" and "You Can't Do That").

England, and now the world, was in a full-on Beatles frenzy.

On paper, The Beatles were now millionaires, though, to them, it was an abstract concept at best. Brian Epstein was a whiz at promotion but a mess at economics; he'd made a slew of shitty business deals, including selling himself and The Beatles short, financially, on *A Hard Day's Night* and dropping the ball on Beatles merchandising in the U.S.

Theoretically, each Beatle was rich beyond his wildest dreams, but nothing really changed too much. Besides, there was no time to enjoy their new-found wealth. Their lives were now largely confined to hotel rooms, recording studios, planes, and the backs of limousines. They gave endless interviews, answering the same inane questions over and over again but only occasionally letting their cynicism seep through. Privacy was at a premium.

Ringo enjoyed himself at night—the Ad-Lib club in London was a Beatles favorite—but Maureen was the love of his life. She remained, for the most part, back in Liverpool, mostly out of sight. Sometimes she accompanied Ringo to a concert or for part of a tour, where she was identified as the drummer's secretary. If an interviewer asked Ringo what he planned on doing once the group disbanded—since no one, let alone The Beatles, expected this to last—his usual answer was that he would like to open a bunch of hair salons (a nod toward Maureen's stated vocation).

"I've always fancied having a ladies hairdressing salon," he told an interviewer in Manchester in 1963. "You know, a string of them, in fact! Strut 'round in me stripes and tails, you know. 'Like a cup of tea, Madam?'" Besides, there was a practical side to his plan. "I figure it would be a good business move," he said. "Girls will always want their hair doing, and if The Beatles ever fell through I'd have a good sideline."

After about a year, Ringo moved out of the apartment he was sharing with George and into his own place, the ground floor and basement of a Georgian town house in Montagu Square. Once Ringo was settled in, Maureen left her parents in Liverpool and moved in with him. Beatles roadies Neil Aspinall and Mal Evans, who were sharing a place, were just down the road.

But Ringo wasn't sold just yet on The Beatles' magical run continuing. He felt the group was established—especially after the release of *A Hard Day's Night*—and obviously they were selling lots of records. He was living in the now and wasn't thinking of the future or a life after The Beatles. He was going with the flow.

Ringo finally convinced Elsie and Harry to sell the house at 10 Admiral Grove, which was overrun nearly every day of the week by Beatles fans and gawkers. It was becoming too much for the aging couple to handle, although they never complained too strenuously and they were always affable if approached outside the little two-up, two-down residence. Their neighbors tolerated the intrusion, but it was obvious it couldn't go on this way much longer.

"Elsie wanted to be close enough to come back and see her friends," said Elsie's friend, Marie Maguire. "Admiral Grove was surrounded by fans twenty-four hours a day, which was awkward, particularly as the toilet was still in the yard." According to Marie, she helped Ringo (or "Richy," as she still called him) find a place for his parents.

"So I went and found three houses which I thought could be acceptable. She and Harry chose the bungalow in Heath Hey in Woolton, which was a lovely house." Ringo paid £24,000 for the modern, ranch-style bungalow in the nearby Gateacre neighborhood—picking Elsie and Harry up at 10 Admiral Grove and driving them over to see the new house. "It was so beautiful, I couldn't resist," Elsie said. "I just hope the fans don't come 'round too much, as it might bother the neighbors—and then they'd wish us to move."

In May, Ringo finally got the chance to spend some quality time with Maureen when they went for a three-week-long vacation to St. Thomas in the Virgin Islands with Paul and his girlfriend, Jane Asher. Everyone needed to unwind after a typically frenetic period that saw The Beatles finish shooting *A Hard Day's Night*, go back into the studio to record the soundtrack for the movie, star in their own TV special, *Around the Beatles*, accept their awards from the Variety Club as Show Business Personalities of the Year (for 1963) and play Wembley's Empire Pool as winners of the New Musical Express artists of the year.

Ringo recorded "Matchbox," written by his idol Carl Perkins, for the Beatles' next EP, insisting on singing and playing his drums simultaneously, rather than recording his vocals separately. Perkins, who was in London touring at the time, stopped by the Abbey Road studio to watch Ringo record his song.

Brian Epstein wanted The Beatles' separate holidays to be "gloriously private," and had gone to great lengths to ensure that Ringo, Paul, George, and John would be able to unwind in anonymity. He hired a private company to create a "fool-proof secret route" for both parties to arrive at their destinations, and each Beatle and his girlfriend (or wife, in Cynthia's case) was given a code name: Paul was "Mr. Manning," Ringo was "Mr. Stone," Jane was "Miss Ashcroft," and Maureen was "Miss Cockroft." John was "Mr. Leslie" and Cynthia "Mrs. Leslie," while George and Pattie became "Mr. Hargreaves" and "Miss Bond," respectively.

Two of The Beatles were given the other two's passports by mistake, but customs officials didn't seem to care, since one Beatle was the same as the other in their eyes. It was becoming that insane.

The company hired by Epstein rented a thirty-foot motor boat (the *Happy Days*) for Ringo, Paul, Jane, and Maureen. It came with a captain (Captain Bolyard), his wife, Peggy, and a deck hand; John and George, meanwhile, took off for Tahiti with Cynthia and Pattie. It was the second time that Ringo, Maureen, Paul, and Jane vacationed together, having traveled to Greece the year before. But, even miles away from Beatlemania there wasn't much privacy to be found. Despite Epstein's best efforts, the group was only there a few days when word leaked out that two Beatles were on the boat in St. Thomas and the press showed up, demanding at least a few pictures if Paul and Ringo wouldn't talk to them.

Back in Liverpool, Maureen's parents, Joe and Florence Cox, didn't flinch when they heard the news about two Beatles (and their girlfriends) cruising around the waters of St. Thomas. Maureen, who was still only seventeen years old, had told them that she was going to visit Ringo in London for a few days.

"It really did not surprise my wife nor myself when we learned she was halfway across the world," Joe Cox told a reporter. "In any case it wouldn't have made any difference. I would have given her permission anyway. Maureen is a sensible girl and well able to take care of herself."

The trip was eventful; Jane couldn't go in the sun and Paul suffered a severe sunburn, which kept him writhing loudly in pain all night. Privacy was at a minimum, with the bedrooms separated only by curtains (everything was audible).

The vacation wasn't a total loss, though. Paul wrote "Things We Said Today," which The Beatles recorded for their upcoming album, *A Hard Day's Night*, while sitting in the bottom of the boat, strumming an acoustic guitar and getting nauseated from the combination of gasoline fumes and the rocking of the boat.

8

"HE IS LIKE A SILENT COMEDIAN"

Ringo survived the blazing St. Thomas sun and returned to London with Maureen, Paul, and Jane Asher in late May 1964. The Beatles were scheduled to embark on a tour of Holland, Hong Kong, Australia, and New Zealand the following week. First, though, they had to return to Abbey Road studios on June 1 for three days of recording songs for *A Hard Day's Night*, the album scheduled to be released in July in conjunction with the movie's premiere.

The medical maladies that afflicted young Richy Starkey only ten years earlier were now a distant memory. The only reminder of his past medical afflictions was his sensitive stomach (he hated onions and spicy food). He was still slight of build, packing 157 pounds onto his five-foot-seven-inch frame. Like the other Beatles, Ringo tended to gain some weight whenever one of the group's singles went to Number One, triggering a round of celebratory dinners with plenty of food, wine, and, of course, Scotch and Cokes.

Gulping speed (Preludin) in Hamburg, and later while on tour with The Beatles, did little to effect Ringo's constitution or, more surprisingly, his demeanor. He was still affable Ringo, the "Clown Beatle" who kept the others loose with his joking, malapropisms, and good nature. "His fame has brought Ringo other treasures, but he seems not to have forgotten what it was like to grow up amid the grimy row-house streets of Liverpool," a magazine reporter noted at the time.

Calamity struck the world of The Beatles on June 3 when Ringo suddenly collapsed that morning during a photo shoot for *The Saturday Evening Post* in southwest London. He had a fever of 102 degrees and was rushed to nearby University College Hospital, where he was diagnosed with tonsillitis and pharyngitis (a swelling in the back of the throat between the tonsils and larynx). He was ordered to strict bed rest for at least a week.

Ringo's throat was so sore he could only eat jelly and ice cream—and it didn't help that he smoked like a chimney.

The Beatles were set to begin their five-country tour the next day in Copenhagen. They wouldn't go without their drummer.

Or would they? Brian Epstein didn't believe in cancelling any commitments and was adamant that his "Boys" would fulfill their contractual obligations. Like it or not, they would begin the tour with another drummer. Session man Jimmy Nicol got the call and hastily rehearsed with John, Paul, and George. He would go on tour with The Beatles until Ringo had recovered enough to join his band mates. Even Pete Best's name was thrown into the mix in the mad rush to find a drummer.

"Not good for him," Lennon said. "It would have looked as if we were taking him back."

The decision to start the tour without Ringo did not set well with his fellow band mates, particularly George Harrison, who had been so instrumental in recruiting Ringo in the first place. George felt the tour should have been cancelled, and likened touring without Ringo like The Rolling Stones touring without Mick Jagger. He resented the dismissive "Off you go" attitude, and the fact that The Beatles had little to no say in anything of importance.

Harrison threatened to boycott the tour if Ringo was left behind. George Martin said that he and Brian Epstein had to persuade George that if he didn't do the tour, he'd be disappointing everyone.

Ringo was horrified at his bad luck and was crushed that the worldwide tour would begin without him. Epstein's decision, and his band mates' willingness to go along with the plan, certainly didn't do much for his self-esteem. He was "miserable," he said, and thought that, just maybe, Paul, John, and George didn't love him anymore.

Adding insult to injury, Nicol would be wearing Ringo's stage suit (the pants were too short) and using Ringo's by-now-iconic Ludwig drum kit. The good news, as far as the three other Beatles were concerned, was that Nicol didn't need too much practice to learn most of the group's songs. He'd been the drummer on *Beatlemania*, an album of fourteen note-for-note Beatles songs recorded for the Pye label and released that spring. He was reportedly paid £2,500 per gig for the Beatles tour, plus a £2,500 signing bonus. Out of deference to Ringo, "I Wanna Be Your Man" was removed from the group's set list.

"This could only have happened with Ringo," said Beatles press officer Tony Barrow. "The Beatles would have insisted on cancelling the trip altogether if John, Paul, or George had fallen ill."

The Beatles, with Jimmy Nicol in tow, left for Copenhagen on June 4. Even more discouraging for Ringo—but reassuring to Brian Epstein—was the wild reception The Beatles were getting in each country they visited and performed in, while their regular drummer recuperated in University College Hospital, confined to his bed and feeling forgotten. He was told that, eventually, he would need to have his tonsils removed.

The fans overseas had not been told about Ringo's absence beforehand—there just wasn't enough time—but they didn't seem to care that it was Jimmy Nicol now thwacking away on "She Loves You" and "I Want to Hold Your Hand." Paul sent several get-well cables to Ringo: "Didn't think we could miss you so much. Get well soon." That was followed by "Hurry up and get well, Ringo, Jimmy is wearing out all your suits." But the hospitalized drummer with the very sore throat found little consolation in the missives.

Ringo left the hospital on June 11, a week into The Beatles' overseas tour and the same day they arrived in Sydney, Australia, in the driving rain. Jimmy Nicol's short-lived Beatles career had encompassed a nonstop supply of girls and shows with John, Paul, and George in Denmark, The Netherlands, Hong Kong, and now, a few gigs in Australia.

"I thought I could drink and lay women with the best of them until I caught up with these guys," he said in summing up his short-lived Beatles career. An estimated three hundred thousand people welcomed The Beatles to Adelaide, where Nicol marked the end of his brief time in the spotlight and played his last gigs as a member of the Fab Four (four concerts over two nights in Adelaide). Ringo was on his way back to meet John, Paul, and George in Melbourne.

On June 12, Ringo and Brian Epstein left London for the thirty-four-hour flight to Australia. Actress Vivien Leigh, who was traveling to America to begin what would be her last movie, *Ship of Fools*, was on the same plane; there are several black-and-white photos of Ringo and Leigh posing outside the plane, though Ringo had no idea who Leigh was (or so he professed—it's hard to believe, given that he was a movie buff and she was an A-list actress). The flight was scheduled for a layover in San Francisco, which was serendipitous, since Ringo left his passport back home and it had to be rushed to him before he and Epstein could undertake the next leg of the arduous Qantas flight to Sydney. The process was expedited. This was a *Beatle*, after all.

Ringo recalled the flight to Australia as "horrendous" and lonely without the other three Beatles. But, once he landed, he was elated to be reunited with John, Paul, and George, who'd brought him presents in Hong Kong.

A scene of bedlam awaited Ringo and Epstein upon their arrival in Sydney on June 14. They had a two-hour layover before flying to meet John, Paul, and George in Melbourne. A shrieking crowd of fans, estimated at four thousand, and a contingent of Australian press greeted the plane, while Ringo endured yet another inane press conference.

Question: Ringo, do you miss anything now being a Beatle, or do you think you've got everything now?

Ringo: Umm, no. I don't miss anything, you know. Well, I can't remember. I just have a good time. It's good fun, you know.

But the reception in Sydney was nothing compared to what awaited Ringo at Essendon Airport in Melbourne and carried over into the rest of the day. John, Paul, George, and Jimmy Nicol were due to arrive later in the day, but the frenzy that accompanied Ringo's arrival was unprecedented, at least for a Beatle without his band mates. "It was a madness we had not seen in Adelaide," Beatles press officer Derek Taylor said.

Following the standard airport press conference in Melbourne, Ringo and Epstein were chauffeured to the Southern Cross Hotel along a route lined with screaming kids. Their limo arrived at the hotel and was greeted by three-thousand fans, who pounded on the hood of the car and, if they were lucky to get close enough, pressed their eager faces to the windows, hoping to get a glimpse of the famous drummer.

Getting from the car and into the hotel was a typically madcap adventure, underscored by danger and the threat of bodily harm. Beatlemania often veered into sinister territory, and this instance was no different. A Melbourne cop named Mike Patterson literally slung the five-foot-seven-inch Ringo over his broad shoulders and barreled through the crowd. But he knocked into a hotel official in the process and all three tumbled to the ground, where the crowd engulfed them. Patterson quickly picked Ringo up and managed to get him through the hotel doors to safety. "His first words were, 'Give us a drink. That was the roughest ride I've ever had,'" Patterson related later.

Ringo went straight up to his room to recover from the ordeal and to get some much-needed rest after his two-day odyssey to the Land Down Under. "I was starting to get a little panicky. But the police did a great job," Ringo said later when queried by the Australian press.

Later that day, he was finally reunited with John, Paul, and George. They held a press conference which included Jimmy Nicol, the first and only time all five men appeared together. "The boys were very kind but I felt like an intruder," Nicol said. "They accepted me, but you can't just get into a group like that—they have their own atmosphere, their own sense of humor. It's a little clique and outsiders just can't break in." He left Australia early the next morning, quietly slipping into the shadows of history.

That night, The Beatles began a three-night run (six concerts) at Festival Hall, with Ringo back behind his drum kit, pounding away and singing "Boys" and "I Wanna Be Your Man." Life was good.

The Beatles followed their run in Australia with six equally frenzied concerts in New Zealand—where Ringo met three long-lost Starkey cousins who'd immigrated there—and finally returned home to England on July 2 (one day before Pete Best released his first post-Beatles single, "I'm Gonna Knock On Your Door"). This first world tour was exhilarating for all four band members but, at the same time, underscored the darker side of Beatlemania.

John, Paul, George, and Ringo had taken on mythical proportions around the world—their first tour of the U.S. still awaited them—and some people were imbuing the four scruffy young men from Liverpool with magical powers, to the point of believing they could heal the sick and handicapped. (They conveniently forgot how sick Ringo had been as a child and as a teenager—or did his status as a Beatle now render him forever immune from illness?) The Beatles were trapped in a corner; did they ignore these people to the detriment of their public profiles or gamely soldier on?

Ringo recalled one instance of standing on a rooftop building in Australia with John, Paul, and George and waving to the crowd when a man suddenly discarded his crutches—and declared himself suddenly able to walk before falling flat on his face. So much for miracles.

As their fame grew, The Beatles were increasingly bombarded backstage with similar scenarios. It was particularly ironic for John Lennon, who would sometimes break into immature "spastic" gyrations on stage, mimicking a disabled person, which angered many in the group's entourage who didn't appreciate Lennon's insolence and insensitivity.

Lennon, George Harrison said, was "allergic to cripples," perhaps out of some kind of fear. Eventually it reached a point where The Beatles would call on their roadie, Mal Evans to bail them out of these situations.

Ringo recalled handicapped people constantly being brought backstage, in Britain as well as overseas, to be "touched by a Beatle." Some children would literally be brought backstage in baskets; others were casualties of Thalidomide who would be left in the group's dressing room—prompting cries of "Mal, cripples!" from The Beatles.

A Hard Day's Night premiered in London on July 6, 1964, a day before Ringo's twenty-fourth birthday and seven years to the day since Paul McCartney first met John Lennon in Liverpool. The Beatles watched the movie in a private screening earlier that day with producer Walter Shenson, Brian Epstein, and Derek Taylor—and, for the most part, enjoyed seeing themselves on the big screen.

The premiere that night was a glittering affair, with all four Beatles (looking uncomfortable in tuxedoes) joined by Princess Margaret and Lord Snowdon at the London Pavilion—and a crowd of twelve-thousand Beatles fans jammed into Piccadilly Circus, which was closed to traffic, hoping to get a glimpse of "one of them."

Afterwards, The Beatles celebrated with a party at the Dorchester Hotel, drinking the night away. Ringo took a tour around the dance floor with a beaming Elsie, who was in town for the premiere. George danced with his mom, Louise.

Ringo celebrated his birthday with Elsie and Harry the next day and gladly took possession of his birthday present from Brian Epstein: a pair of diamond cufflinks. *A Hard Day's Night* opened on July 8 to mostly enthusiastic reviews and brisk business, with lines snaking around corners almost everywhere the movie was playing. All four Beatles were lauded for their acting and were compared to The Marx Brothers for their comedic chops. They were playing themselves, but it didn't matter. London's *Daily Mail* referred to John, Paul, George, and Ringo as "Merseybeat Marxes." It was that over the top.

Ringo was rewarded with his own share of praise, particularly for the "Ringo's Theme" scene where he wanders aimlessly around London taking pictures and acting like a sad sack. "In the first place, it's a wonderfully lively and altogether good-natured spoof of the juvenile madness called 'Beatlemania,' the current spreading craze of otherwise healthy young people for the four British lads with the shaggy hair," opined the *New York Times*, whose review was accompanied by a photo from *A Hard Day's Night* showing Ringo and Wilfrid Brambell. "Unless you know the fellows, it is hard to identify them, except for Ringo Starr, the big-nosed one, who does a saucy comic sequence on his own."

Leonard Mosley, reviewing the movie in the *Daily Express*, focused on Ringo for his words of praise. "He is the only one of The Beatles who doesn't really like the sound of his voice. Now I see why. He is a natural clown in the Chaplin-Harpo Marx class," his "sad face crowned by the most elegant nasal organ since Schnozzle Durante and Cyrano de Bergerac."

For distinguished British culture critic Penelope Gilliatt, it was Ringo who "emerges as a born actor. He is like a silent comedian, speechless and chronically underprivileged, a boy who is already ageless."

The powers that be in the British film industry were intrigued by Ringo's performance in the movie. "I had lots of films offered after that, but they were all big star things, expecting me to carry the show," he said. "I nearly agreed to one about Sherlock Holmes, with me as Dr. Watson, but I thought it was too big. I don't want to try to carry anything yet. It would be awful if it was a flop. But a minor part would be okay, then I wouldn't have the responsibility. If that was okay, I could try bigger stuff."

The kudos, however, could not quell the nervousness The Beatles felt in returning to Liverpool for the July 10 "northern premiere" of *A Hard Day's Night*. "Friends kept coming down to London saying, 'You're finished in Liverpool,'" Ringo said, echoing the apprehension of his band mates. Their worry turned to relief once John, Paul, George, and Ringo arrived at Speke Airport and saw some three-thousand fans on hand to greet them, just like the good old days of the year before.

They each received a key to the city and were amazed at the two-hundred-thousand fans who lined the route on their way to city hall, cheering their home-town heroes. The Liverpool police implemented the biggest security detail in its history to protect John, Paul, George, and Ringo. Over six-thousand fans lined the street in front of the Odeon Cinema that night for the movie's premiere, with an estimated fifteen-hundred people forming a line for tickets to the next day's showing. It was pure bedlam—and Ringo loved it all.

Ringo loved it all; the decoy cars and elaborate schemes worked out to smuggle The Beatles to their next gig. They were mingling with actors and fellow musicians, the *creme de la creme* of British pop culture. Ringo didn't yet feel trapped by his fame, and took full advantage of the club scene.

That couldn't have been pleasant for Maureen, who was the shy and retiring type, but she and Ringo were seen more and more in public together as the year started to wind down. Still, that didn't stop the rumor mill from churning out stories of Beatles romances.

The American scandal magazine *Confidential*, which was known to embellish or even fabricate stories from whole cloth, printed an article entitled "How

Ringo Flipped for Ann-Margret." It went on to relate how Ringo was romancing the curvy singer/actress and had "bent her shell-pink ears with an hour of long-distance oggly-googling, all in a special Teddy Boy lingo that left little Annie limp."

Ringo denied that there was any romance between them and, when questioned about it, couldn't even seem to pronounce her name properly. "Ann-Margaret? 'Anned' Margaret and, um, you know, saying I don't phone her anymore 'cause she can't understand me. I write twice a week, you know, which is ridiculous 'cause I don't even write to my mother, I just phone 'er. I've never met the girl or anything, there's all this big thing, Ringo and Anna Margaret going steady and all." Such was the life of a Beatle.

There were more television appearances—*Top of the Pops, Lucky Stars (Summer Spin), Scene at 6:30, Blackpool Night Out* with comics Mike and Bernie Winters—and more touring around Britain in a nonstop barrage of appearances from north to south. It culminated in a tour of Sweden and the release of *A Hard Day's Night* in movie theaters across America on August 12, just six days before The Beatles arrived in California (on their private plane) to begin the twenty-five-city American tour.

The American film critics were just as enthusiastic about the movie as their British compatriots. "*A Hard Day's Night* suggests a Beatle career in the movies as big as they've already been in stage and dancehall," wrote the *New York Post*. "They have the songs, the patter, and the histrionic flair. No more is needed."

Capitol Records, meanwhile, had released the single of "A Hard Day's Night," backed with "I Should Have Known Better," in the U.S. in mid-July. It shot to Number One on August 1, remaining in the top slot for two weeks and selling over one-million copies in its first five weeks in release. "America was now very aware of The Beatles," said roadie and confidante Neil Aspinall. "And things were crazy." The Beatlemania monster was out of its cage and raging wildly.

Back in New York, fourteen-year-old Ringo fanatic Marilyn Crescenzo won two tickets to the American premiere in August of *A Hard Day's Night*. "Most of the Beatlemaniacs liked Ringo," she confided to her diary. "(He's the Best)." But what's this about rumors that Ringo will have surgery in New York?

> My aunt Nita's friend went to get her nose fixed at Big doctors hospital. She called and said the [sic] Ringo's coming to N.Y. to get his nose fixed. He suposto [sic] come on the 18th of August with the group to tour the U.S. but he's coming sooner to get his nose fixed.

No body [sic] knows about it but if I find out where and when I'll be there. I'm gonna go see him. I hope I can. I love Ringo!! As for Maureen, Eck! I hate you. She's ugly to me. She just wants his money. That's all. Ringo just can't realize this. I hope he does! A columnist said that Maureen is now Ringo's personal secretary and he made her quit her beautician gob [sic]. (Who knows?)

Ringo made less of an attempt to hide his romance with Maureen now. They liked to hit the clubs and go dancing, chauffeured around by their driver, Alan. If they weren't seen at the movies, they could often be found in London clubs like the Crazy Elephant or Dolly's. They socialized with fellow Liverpudlian Cilla Black, who was being managed by Brian Epstein, and her husband, Bobby.

Beatles press officer Tony Barrow described Ringo and Maureen acting "like a pair of loverbirds" within the group's inner circle "for as long as we could remember."

The American tour kicked off on August 19 at the Cow Palace in San Francisco, where The Beatles played a half-hour set before seventeen-thousand hysterical fans. "Although it was publicized as music, all that was heard and seen of the Mersey Sound was something like a jet engine shrieking through a summer lightning storm because of the yelling fans," the *San Francisco Examiner* reported. "It had no mercy, and afterwards everyone still capable of speech took note of a ringing in the ears which lasted for as long as The Beatles had played."

One kid suffered a dislocated shoulder in the melee enveloping the concert; it was reported that when The Beatles first took the stage, the girls in the audience screamed for nearly five minutes. In all, fifty fans were injured, nineteen girls fainted and needed medical attention, and two fans were arrested for unruly behavior. The Beatles played for a half hour then rushed into a waiting limousine, which was nearly crushed by throngs of fans who pounded on the car roof.

Ringo found time in San Francisco to visit a local bar, where he met one of his heroes, actor Dale Robertson, a veteran of over sixty Westerns who also starred in the NBC/ABC television series *Tales of Wells Fargo*. The group was kicked out of the place at two a.m., closing time for California bars at that time, and carried the party back to The Beatles' hotel.

That first stop in San Francisco was a snapshot of what awaited The Beatles at every city and town they visited on that tour. Girls lined up and were pre-sented to the group in their hotel suite, often doing whatever it took (including pleasing roadie Mal Evans) to meet a Beatle. Other girls dressed up like hotel maids and tried to sneak into the band's suite. Cops everywhere worked over-time, or on their days off, when The Beatles came to town, trying to control the unruly crowds at concerts, drag screaming girls away as they fainted, and then patrol the entrance to whatever hotel in which the group was hunkered down.

John, Paul, George, and Ringo were pelted with jelly beans on stage (Ringo would turn his cymbals upward to deflect the candy missiles) and were unable to hear themselves over the deafening roar. John, Paul, and George would rely on their drummer to keep a steady backbeat as a visual and auditory aid—even though he couldn't hear anything, either.

Ringo said he would try to read the others' lips to see where they were in a particular song, or would watch how they moved. He didn't bother playing his tom-toms, since no one could hear him anyway.

George Martin, who was recording the group's concert at The Hollywood Bowl with the thought of releasing a live album on Capitol Records, realized when he listened to the tapes afterward that the screaming—"like putting a microphone at the tail of a 747 jet"—would make that virtually impossible. The idea was shelved. (Martin revisited the project over a decade later when more sophisticated noise-separating technology was available. Capitol Records re-leased *The Beatles at the Hollywood Bowl* in 1977, covering the group's August 1965 and 1965 concerts there.)

Martin said later that Ringo told him all he could do was hang on to the backbeat in an effort to keep everyone together. He would also "follow their three bums wiggling" to gauge where they were in a song.

Ringo fell in love with Hollywood when The Beatles arrived in Los Angeles on August 23 for the Hollywood Bowl concert. They stayed at a rented house, owned by British actor Reginald Owen, which was situated in the posh neighborhood of Bel Air. Philadelphia radio reporter Larry Kane, who was traveling with The Beatles, referred to the mansion as having "the grandeur of an F. Scott Fitzgerald novel."

The neighbors couldn't have been too happy with the hundreds of fans mill-ing around the house at the foot of the street, hoping to get a glimpse of a Beatle. They weren't as lucky as Sandra Dee, Peggy Lipton, Joan Baez, and Jayne Mans-field, who partied with The Beatles at their rented home. That party was followed the next day by a shindig held in the sun-drenched back yard of Capitol Records

Top Left: Richy Starkey (left) and his best friend, Dave Patterson, in the early '50s, posing for a portrait at Jerome's, a "proper" Liverpool photography studio. Dave remembers they paid for the photograph themselves. (Courtesy of Dave Patterson)

Top Right: Dave (left) and Richy looking dandy on the pier at New Brighton. (Courtesy of Dave Patterson)

Left: The newly rechristened Ringo Starr sporting his "Teddy Boy" look, circa 1959. (Photo by Michael Ochs Archives/Getty Images)

August 1961: Rory Storm and the Hurricanes at the Jive Hive (St. Luke's Church Hall). From left: Rory Storm, Johnny Guitar, Ringo, and Lu Walters. (© Michael Ochs Archives/Corbis)

Elsie and "stepladder" Harry Graves revel in their son's fame in the sitting room at 10 Admiral Grove. A poster of Ringo hangs on the wall. (Associated Newspapers/Rex/Rex USA)

An early shot of The Beatles with their new drummer. Note the short-lived "bug" logo on Ringo's bass drum and the shorter hair. From left: Paul McCartney, Ringo, John Lennon, and George Harrison. (Photo by Keystone-France/Gamma-Keystone via Getty Images)

John, Paul, George, and Ringo on the cusp of Beatlemania, October 1963. Their lives were about to change forever. (Evening News/Rex/Rex USA)

February 7, 1964: The famous press conference at New York City's John F. Kennedy International Airport. Q: "What do you think of Beethoven?" Ringo: "I love him. Especially his poems." It was love at first sight. (Associated Newspapers/Rex USA)

America meets The Beatles: Paul, George, Ringo, and John on *The Ed Sullivan Show*, February 9, 1964. (Photo by Bernard Gotfryd/Hulton Archive/Getty Images)

Ringo gets some advice from Paul's "clean" grandfather (Wilfrid Brambell) in *A Hard Day's Night* (1964). (Photo by United Artists/Courtesy of Getty Images)

The kid from The Dingle shakes hands with royalty: Meeting Princess Margaret at the London premiere of *A Hard Day's Night* as Paul, John, and George look on (July 1964). (Photo by Daily Sketch/Rex/Rex USA)

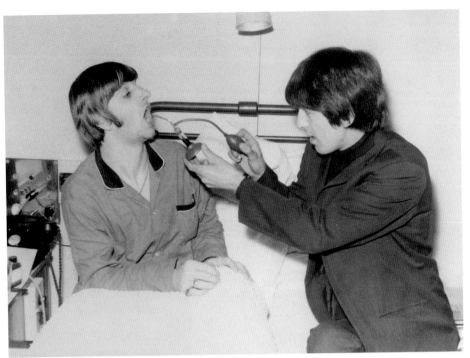

December 1964: Clowning with George Harrison in University College Hospital after The World's Most Famous Tonsils were removed. (© Bettmann/CORBIS)

Wedding bells for Ringo and Maureen, February 1965. Flanking the happy couple (from left): Joseph Cox, Cynthia Lennon, Florence Cox, John Lennon, George Harrison, Brian Epstein, and Harry and Elsie. (© Bettmann/CORBIS)

And baby makes three: Ringo and Maureen with newborn Zak at Queen Charlotte's Maternity Hospital in London. (Photo by Keystone/Getty Images)

With John Lennon on the set of *How I Won the War* in October 1966. (© Bettmann/CORBIS)

Jason Starkey arrived in August 1967, with Maureen and Ringo looking appropriately groovy. (AP Photo)

chief Alan Livingston, where The Beatles met Hollywood's elite, including Jack Palance, Shelley Winters, Edward G. Robinson, Rita Hayworth, Dean Martin, Eva Marie Saint, and Jack Lemmon. Many of the stars brought their children to the party so they could brag to their friends that they'd met The Beatles.

Later, Ringo and Paul went to a party at actor Burt Lancaster's house to watch a private screening of the new Peter Sellers movie, *A Shot in the Dark*. Ringo thought Lancaster was great; he arrived at the actor's home dressed like a cowboy, carrying two toy guns in his "holster." Lancaster later sent Ringo two real guns along with a real holster.

Lancaster's house represented everything Ringo loved about the glamor of Hollywood—including an indoor/outdoor pool that ran underneath the glass floor of Lancaster's living room. He loved the palm trees and the warm climate, but those moments were fleeting.

It was the same everywhere they went—Las Vegas, Denver, Cincinnati, Milwaukee, Atlantic City, Chicago, Detroit, Dallas, Kansas City—an endless blur of cities fed by pill-popping (speed), alcohol (Scotch and Coke), and willing groupies. The festive air turned to panic in Indianapolis, when Ringo disappeared the night before a concert at the State Fair Coliseum and showed up just minutes before the band was scheduled to greet its shrieking fans.

In his memoir *The Love You Make*, Brian Epstein's right-hand man, Peter Brown, revealed that Ringo had been awake for three straight days "fueled by 'purple hearts,' the amphetamine tablets that had replaced Prellys." Ringo himself admitted that he and his band mates often got the pills from the cops who were assigned to protect them and shepherd them to and from their gigs. The police, he said, were very good to The Beatles, taking whatever pills they'd confiscated from the kids and giving them to the band members.

According to Brown, Ringo had slipped out of the Speedway Motel that night, informing roadie Neil Aspinall that he was going to kill himself—a threat Aspinall laughed off until Ringo failed to return hours later. When Ringo was still missing the next morning, the entire Beatles entourage was in a high state of panic, until the drummer magically appeared just before the State Fair Coliseum concert, accompanied by two Indiana state troopers.

It turned out that almost as soon as Ringo left the hotel the night before, he encountered the troopers, who offered to give him a tour of the city. Ringo "casually mentioned he had always wanted to see the Indianapolis auto racing track," home of the Indianapolis 500, so the cops drove him there, convinced the night watchman to open the gates (they had a Beatle with them, after all), then watched as Ringo "spent much of the night driving the police car around the track to his heart's content." At dawn, one of the troopers took him back to his house, where his wife cooked Ringo breakfast before the big concert.

"By the time Ringo took his place at his drum kit on stage, his legs were so weak from his seventy-two-hour binge, they went out from underneath him, and he was unable to use the drum pedals for his bass [drum]," Brown wrote.

"The funniest bit that no one else knows is that we were chased by another cop car," Ringo said almost twenty-five years later. "And we had to drive up an alley and turn the lights out and I'm hiding with this cop in an alley so we didn't get caught."

The tour landed in New York in late August. The Beatles played a concert in front of thirty thousand shrieking fans at the Forest Hills Tennis Stadium in Queens adjacent to the brand-new Shea Stadium, which opened that April as the home for the New York Mets. John, Paul, George, and Ringo, along with the rest of the world, admired folk musician Bob Dylan from afar, but they were in a position to do something about it.

He was their hero, writing "great songs," Ringo said, which tapped into the zeitgeist of his generation.

They met Dylan for the first time when he showed up at their Delmonico Hotel suite and turned them on to marijuana—accompanied by his road manager, Al Aronowitz, who doubled as a music journalist. (Aronowitz wrote the in-depth article on The Beatles' first visit to the U.S. for *The Saturday Evening Post*, quoted earlier in this book, and also wrote for the *New York Post*.)

According to Aronowitz, Dylan handed a marijuana joint to John Lennon, who "commanded" Ringo to try it first, which "instantly revealed The Beatles' pecking order." Ringo hesitated, but acquiesced after Lennon made a wisecrack about his drummer being the group's "royal taster." This was a new experience, even for the four young men who'd already been through a lifetime's worth of eye-opening situations by their early twenties, and Ringo had no idea how to smoke a marijuana joint.

Aronowitz wrote later that he told Ringo to "inhale with a lot of oxygen. Take a deep breath of air together with smoke and hold it in your lungs for as long as you can." But Ringo, unaware of the etiquette of sharing a marijuana joint with his fellow tokers, was smoking it like a cigarette, inhaling luxuriantly and taking his sweet time before finally passing the joint around.

"Soon, Ringo got the giggles. In no time at all, he was laughing hysterically,"

Aronowitz wrote. "His laughing looked so funny that the rest of us started laughing hysterically at the way Ringo was laughing hysterically. Soon, Ringo pointed at the way Brian Epstein was laughing, and we all started laughing hysterically at the way Brian was laughing."

With the hindsight of history in his rear-view mirror, Aronowitz cited that meeting of pop-culture icons as a turning point in musical history: "Until the advent of rap, pop music remained largely derivative of that night at the Delmonico. That meeting didn't just change pop music, it changed the times."

Having Ringo so close at hand also threw Marilyn Crescenzo's world into a tizzy, as evidenced by her August 28 diary entry:

> Oh well—the Beatles are here—I say it this way because I thought I'd go downtown to see them. My *Mum* and Pop said no. They were afraid I'd get hurt! I don't care—even if I did! As long as I saw them. Just to see them, to hear them, to breathe the very air they breathe! As I walk along the ground I think so near get so far! They are walking along this same soil! N.Y.C. soil! This may sound stupid but it's the closest I've come to them and I think this will be the closest ever. My girlfriend Pat gave me the name of a bird from England and she will give me a Pen-Pal form [sic] Brittian [sic]. I mailed her a letter. I hope she answers back! (He did. He was from Leeds. We wrote for a few years.)
>
> This morning ten o'clock, I heard a report from the Beatles hotel and Ringo and George were talking—I said to my mother "why didn't you let me go down there—Everybody is there." I then walked into the bathroom and couldn't hold back - I just cryed! [sic] I couldn't help it! I just wish I had them standing near me—Even just in my view! Oh well—I just don't have the luck.

The New York trip was notable for Ringo for another reason. Shortly after meeting Dylan, Ringo's beloved St. Christopher medal was ripped off his neck, along with the rest of his shirt, by a crazed Beatles fan as the group made their typically mad dash into the Delmonico Hotel. The incident was played up big by local AM radio station WABC, home to popular DJs "Cousin Brucie" Morrow and Scott Muni, who were competing intensely with Murray the K on WINS and the WMCA "Good Guys" for Beatles "exclusives," however inane they might be. (WABC's newest jingle was "WA Beatle C," at least while The Fab Four were in town.)

New York radio listeners learned about Ringo's missing St. Christopher medal in an interview he gave to Morrow and Muni. "I got it when I was twenty-one for me twenty-first [birthday] and I've never taken if off," Ringo told them (to the accompaniment of audible screams in the background). "He's supposed to be the patron saint of travelers and we do a lot of traveling and we've been all right up until now so I'd like to keep it." Who gave him the medal? "An auntie." Naturally, this passed for huge news in the Beatles universe.

The mother of Angie McGowan, the teenager who'd ripped the medal from around Ringo's neck, heard the interview and called Morrow and WABC officials to tell them Angie had the medal—and that she, along with three of her friends, wanted to return it to Ringo. The station realized it had a huge public relations "scoop" and put Angie and her mother up at the hotel for the night, then held a widely covered press conference the next day, which aired on WABC radio and on WABC TV, so Angie could return the St. Christopher medal to Ringo, who gave her (and her friends) a kiss and thanked her. She also got a kiss from Paul McCartney.

"There were good nights and bad nights on the tours," Ringo said. "But they were really all the same. The only fun part was the hotels in the evening, smoking pot and that."

While Lennon and McCartney continued to frantically write songs amidst the touring chaos for the group's next album release in England, *Beatles for Sale*, the good vibes took a sinister tone when The Beatles flew to Canada in early September to play two concerts at the Montreal Forum. "Les Beatles" received death threats from French-Canadian separatists, who singled out Ringo as "an English Jew," which necessitated the presence of sharpshooters in the crowd in case anyone took a potshot at Ringo or one of his band mates. Ringo was terrified.

Ringo and his band mates were used to the threats. It came with the territory, but this one was different with its sinister overtones. Once The Beatles took the stage in Montreal, Ringo—up on his drum riser—purposely turned his cymbals outward toward the audience for whatever little protection that afforded him. There was a plainclothes policeman stationed nearby. The concerts went off without a hitch, but The Beatles were so disgusted they left Montreal that night as soon as they could. Adding insult to injury, the shows at the Forum failed to sell out. That *never* happened at a Beatles concert. The Beatles spent a total of ten hours in Montreal and never returned. Ringo called the concerts "the worst gig of my life."

The North American tour finally came to an end on September 20. The Beatles played a final concert at the Paramount Theater in New York City called "An Evening with the Beatles," which benefitted the United Cerebral Palsy Fund of New York. (How ironic, given John Lennon's proclivity for doing his imitation of a "spastic" while on stage—which he no doubt refrained from that night.)

Steve Lawrence and Eydie Gormé co-headlined the show. Sprinkled throughout the audience of nearly four thousand, many of whom paid upwards of one hundred dollars for a ticket, were Beatles fans who'd won tickets to the show—including Marilyn Crescenzo.

> Oh God—they were beautiful—I'm still shaking for hysteria. There [sic] really different then there [sic] pictures. Paul's hair is black and wavy. George's hair is redish [sic] brown, and very straight. Ringo's hair is a silver brown and John's hair is very light brown and boy do they have lots of it too. There [sic] really so beautiful. I'll never forget this day as long as I live. I'll never forget their faces. I'll never forget Ringo—I cryed [sic] my eyes out for I knew I'd never meet him. I love Ringo so much I could die! I'll never forget this day, never!

The Beatles flew back to England on September 21, where they were greeted by thousands of screaming fans who'd been amped up (not like they needed it) by continuous Beatles music that played in the terminal all that day.

Three days later, Ringo and a business partner, Barry Patience, formed The Brickey Building Company, a construction, design, and decorating firm that was intended to help Ringo's fellow Beatles (and other celebrity friends) with projects that required these types of services.

While Ringo still occasionally talked of opening a string of hair salons, he put that on the back burner for now, given the continued success of The Beatles. Everyone kept waiting for the bubble to burst, but Beatlemania had surprising staying power.

It seemed like it would go on forever.

Ringo had been a Beatle for a little over two years, yet only now did he really feel completely at ease with John, Paul, and George. The forced togetherness of the manic U.S. tour had a lot to do with that. There were the endless hours cloistered in hotel suites, literally being thrown into cars going to and from concert venues. There were the requisite inane press conference in every city and town, when Ringo would remain silent when the inevitable questions came up about how the group formed. But the ordeal, fun as it was at times, brought the four Beatles together in a way they hadn't been united before. After all, no one but John, Paul, George, and Ringo knew what it was like to be four of the most famous people in the world—while living in a vacuum, the calm at the center of a massive storm. It was a brotherhood only they shared.

"It took about two years to get each other sorted out," Ringo said. "But from then on I had the feeling there was four of us in it. I suppose we get on together because there are only four people like us; we're the only ones who really know what it's like. When there was all that Beatlemania we were pushed into a corner, just the four of us. A sort of trap, really. We were like Siamese quads eating out of the same bowl."

Their return to England didn't mean The Beatles were about to get a break, however, and their touring schedule began in earnest that fall. They were now playing smaller venues, which was something of a comedown from their raucous U.S. shows performed before thousands of screaming fans.

By this time it was estimated that The Beatles had sold over ten million records in the U.S. and that their just-concluded tour had grossed over $1 million (a mind-boggling figure in 1964). *A Hard Day's Night* had earned $5.8 million at American theaters in just over six weeks, and, in the UK, EMI was reporting sales of $256 million, largely boosted by sales of Beatles music. Capitol Records in America, meanwhile, said its revenues were up by 17 percent thanks to The Beatles.

John, Paul, George, Ringo, and Brian Epstein were said to be millionaires "several times over" and had grossed an estimated $56 million in total income beyond what they'd earned in the UK. Lennon and McCartney were reaping extra financial benefits by collecting additional royalties on the songs they wrote for The Beatles (and for others).

But the group would never see a lot of that money, given the huge tax bills, particularly in England, and the bad business deals brokered by Brian Epstein. Yet despite their worldwide popularity and all that (assumed) money, Epstein insisted his "boys" fulfill their obligations back in England, no matter how famous they were. And he never renegotiated their fees.

The Beatles weren't thrilled; they sometimes went from a packed house of thousands to a small dance hall in the middle of nowhere. But they seemed to appreciate the way in which Epstein honored his commitments. And it was good for the band's image.

There was also a new single and a new album to record. The single, written mostly by John Lennon, was called "I Feel Fine." Lennon based the song's signature guitar riff—which he played in tandem with George Harrison—on Bobby Parker's twangy 1961 tune, "Watch Your Step," which The Beatles played live onstage in 1961 and 1962. Lennon, of course, put his own singular stamp on "I Feel Fine" with his lead vocal, backed by George and Paul, and with the song's opening discordant feedback, which Lennon claimed to be a recording first.

Whatever the case, the song was brilliant and catchy, and is complemented by Ringo's propulsive drumming, which particularly impressed Paul McCartney. "The drumming is basically what we used to think of as "What'd I Say" drumming," McCartney said. "There was a style of drumming on 'What'd I Say' which is sort of Latin R&B that Ray Charles's drummer Milt Turner played on the original record and we used to love it. One of the big clinching factors about Ringo as the drummer in the band was that he could really play that so well."

In late November, four days after its release in the U.S., "I Feel Fine," backed with Paul McCartney's "She's a Woman," was released in England and climbed to Number One two weeks later, eventually selling nearly one-and-a-half-million copies. It hit Number One in the U.S. shortly thereafter.

The album, meanwhile, was called *Beatles for Sale* and was recorded that fall amidst touring, television appearances (*Lucky Star's Special, Shindig*—recorded in London and shown later in the U.S. on ABC—*Scene at 6:30, Top of the Pops, Top Gear, Ready Steady Go!*) and more radio specials. The "Ringo Song" for the new album was a Carl Perkins country-flavored tune called "Honey Don't," which he recorded in late October.

The Beatles already knew the song well, since it was a staple of almost every Liverpool band. Ringo had sung it with Rory and the Hurricanes as part of his "Starr Time" segment. (John Lennon took lead vocals on "Honey Don't" during one of The Beatles live radio performances on the BBC.)

Recording on *Beatles for Sale* was finished by late October. In addition to Ringo's "Honey Don't" contribution, *Beatles for Sale* boasted, among other memorable tracks, "No Reply," "I'm a Loser," "Baby's in Black," a rousing version of Chuck Berry's "Rock and Roll Music," and "Eight Days a Week" (the title of which, according to Paul McCartney, came from a comment made to him by a chauffeur driving him to John Lennon's house). Like Ringo, George

Harrison's solo vocal contribution was a Carl Perkins song, "Everybody's Trying to Be My Baby."

The album was released in the UK on December 4, three days after Ringo entered University College Hospital in London to finally have his "dodgy" tonsils removed. The event, of course, necessitated a press conference. This was worldwide news, after all. Screaming fans greeted Ringo upon his arrival at the hospital, and he grudgingly opened his mouth widely several times to placate reporters' requests before sitting down to answer the inane questions. ("Why are you here?" he was asked. "Is he kidding?" Ringo responded.) He was chauffeured to the hospital in a Rolls-Royce, although he'd passed his driving test in October and bought a new Facel-Vega car for £5,500.

Ringo told the reporters that he'd brought some records with him to help pass the time—Bob Dylan, The Supremes, James Brown—and informed the packed press room that he would have ten days off after he left the hospital before starting rehearsals for The Beatles' Christmas show at the Hammersmith Odeon.

Back in New York, Mary Crescenzo was worried, as she revealed in her diary.

> Ringo—My Ringo is getting his tonsils out. Dec. 1 this year. I hope he'll be alright and his throat won't be to [sic] sore when its all over! And most of all I hope his voice doesn't change permently [sic]. I know when your tonsils are removed your voice changes for a while, and sometimes stays that way. I hope he stays the same! He's voice is so tough-like. I'll be thinking of him every minute that day. I know this sounds a little disgusting and messy, but if I could, I'd like to have Ringo's tonsils preserve [sic] in famaldihide [sic] Oh—I now [sic] I'm sick—but I love him so much I think I've gone crazy when it comes to the Beatles or—Ringo—my Ringo!

The World's Most Famous Tonsils were removed on December 2, and Ringo spent the next week in the hospital, recovering from the surgery and downing lots of ice cream for his sore throat. George and Paul visited him on successive days—causing pandemonium near the hospital entrance—and there were constant television and radio news reports in London keeping eager fans up to speed on his recovery.

Fans calling "The Official Beatles Fan Club" in London were greeted with a recorded announcement from Anne Collingham: "Hello there. Ringo's condition is improving all the time. His personal physician is seeing him regularly, and he's telling me that Ringo is making excellent progress. He's been eating lightly boiled eggs, jelly, ice cream and warm tea, and the doctor says Ringo is a cheerful and very helpful patient. There will be a further weekend bulletin at 5:30 p.m. on Friday." Anne Collingham, in fact, did not really exist; the role was played by a number of young women. It just made things easier. (Anne's name also appeared on fan-club correspondence.)

Maureen, who was now more visible than ever, spent a lot of time at Ringo's bedside, keeping him company while he recovered from his surgery. She stayed with Elsie in Ringo's London apartment, and it was during that time that Ringo asked her to marry him.

"I wasn't trying to take advantage of the situation and I had no idea whether me visiting him would lead to anything more," Maureen said. "To tell you the truth, the idea of having to move to London permanently was putting me off."

Ringo's discharge from the hospital on December 10 was even bigger news and was covered by many outlets, including British Pathé, which produced newsreels for movie theaters. It sent a camera crew to record the "event" for posterity, entitling the proceeding ninety-second newsreel "Tonsils Good-Bye":

> University Hospital. Early-morning drama.
> The rumor is right. Ringo is restored, good as new.
> Even nurses are so excited they're running a temperature.
> Minus those troublesome tonsils, fit as a drum, he's out!

9

"I'M THE LITTLE FELLOW"

Ringo Starr became the second Beatle to tie the knot when he married Maureen Cox on February 11, 1965.

Two weeks earlier, he'd proposed to her at three o'clock in the morning at the Ad-Lib club in London, getting down on one knee to pop the question while his friends whooped in unison. The mid-morning wedding ceremony took place in the Caxton Hall Registry Office, near the couple's apartment in Montagu Square. Their friends and family were startled by its suddenness.

Brian Epstein swore everyone to secrecy about the wedding ceremony and issued veiled threats to anyone who dared leak the news. "Maureen hated the spotlight and was worried that fans might disrupt things," said Roy Trafford, Ringo's old friend from his Henry Hunt and Sons days, who wasn't invited. "I didn't want hundreds of people around the register office," Ringo said. "I always think the wedding is the woman's day. . . . So it was Maureen's day and I didn't want hundreds of people standing around cheering for me."

There was a bigger, unspoken reason for the rushed wedding and the secrecy. "We went to the Ad-Lib and in the ladies' room Maureen confessed how hard everything was for her," said Ringo's neighbor and old friend from Liverpool, Marie Crawford. "I recognized that weekend that Maureen was pregnant. She was very sick in the morning and was beginning to show."

Peter Brown, Brian Epstein's right-hand man, was especially blunt. "Like any northern girl, Maureen ensnared her man the northern way; by mid-January she was pregnant," he wrote. "Ringo, like any good northern man, did what was expected."

Ringo alluded to the pregnancy in a read-between-the-lines comment he made during an interview with *Photoplay* magazine several months later. "I didn't know till three weeks before I got married that I was going to get married," he said. "About last November, it got that we just went out together with each other and nobody else, you know. And then I asked her to marry me and she said yes and we got married. It was a bit of a rush, you know. But we both knew it was going to happen. I knew because Maureen was always there. Even when we first started going out on dates I always enjoyed going out with her more than anybody else.

"When we got famous and we used to take girls out, we never knew whether they went out with us for ourselves or because of who we were. With Maureen I always knew it was because I was what I was, not because I was a Beatle."

John and George were told only the day before about Ringo's marriage; Paul was on vacation with Jane Asher in Tunisia and learned about Ringo's wedding hours later when Brian Epstein sent him a cable: "RICH WED EARLY THIS MORNING." McCartney had trouble understanding the Tunisian operator and couldn't quite decipher the message. "Eventually I saw the wedding story when we picked up a newspaper and realized it referred to Richy and Moe getting married," he said. "It was just a drag I wasn't there because I would have enjoyed it."

George, arriving on a bicycle, and John attended the wedding, along with Elsie and Harry and Maureen's parents, Joseph and Florence Cox. Brian Epstein was the best man, and Lennon noted that Ringo hadn't even bought his male guests boutonnieres, joking to a reporter that they were "going to wear radishes, actually." Lennon (probably knowing that Maureen was pregnant) said of his band mate, "He's the marrying kind, a sort of family man." Ringo wore a brown tweed suit, a polka-dot tie, and a carnation; Maureen wore a pink suit with a matching pink hat.

Thousands of miles away, Mary Crescenzo received the devastating news.

It's 7:00 AM and I just got up to go to school. I'm startled! I don't know what to do—you see the first thing my mother told me was Ringo got married—It's true! I'm crying now—I don't know how I'll make it in school. I just can't believe it! Just a few days ago I wrote in a sence [sic] of speaking—My Ringo—Now I'm not allowed to do that!

I knew it had to happen sometime—but in my heart that sometime meant when his Beatle days are over. Well, that will be a very long time from now—and now is today. He's married to Maureen Cox. She's 18 years old but she has loved him since he was Rickie [sic] with Rory Storm.

Ringo and Maureen hurried off to Sussex for a short honeymoon, during which they stayed at the house of Beatles solicitor David Jacobs. They were hoping to unwind and enjoy themselves before The Beatles began work on their next movie, this one to be shot in the Bahamas.

But two hours into their honeymoon word leaked out about the couple's whereabouts, and they were besieged by reporters just one day into their new marriage. "Are you taking a honeymoon?" they were asked. "Well, this was supposed to be it, but it didn't work," Ringo responded, looking slightly annoyed. "Well, you know, we took a chance. We tried to keep it quiet and we tried to arrive here quiet, but we must've been spotted and that's the end of it, you know. So from now on, it's not really a honeymoon, it's just—we're just stayin' here."

Ringo was also asked if he thought his marriage would affect the band's image. "On The Beatles as a whole, I don't think any great effect—as much as that everyone will sort of say, 'Well, we can't sorta like them anymore 'cuz Ringo's married,' you know. I don't think I've got that image. I don't think it'll bother them too much. It may help, in fact, you know. We don't know yet. It's too early to say."

Privately, he worried that he would be excoriated by Beatles fans, particularly the group's core fan base of young girls who had always showered him with adulation. He admitted to having "qualms," not only for the effect the marriage would have on The Beatles but "if it was the finish" for him.

"But then Maureen and I got a lot of letters and cards and gifts and everything from around the world. About 99 percent seem happy for me. There aren't very many people shouting, 'You shouldn't have done it.' I haven't read any nasty letters. Oh, I read one that said 'Dear Ringo, How could you?' And that was it."

Back in London, Ringo and Maureen returned to their ground-floor apartment in Montagu Square. The only way they could avoid the constant mob of fans camped outside was to climb over the kitchen sink and out of a small window into the garden into the back-yard mews. They didn't plan on staying there much longer but, in the meantime, Ringo hired architect Ken Partridge, who had renovated John and Cynthia's house in Weybridge, to give their apartment a complete overhaul during the four weeks Ringo was on location shooting the next Beatles movie.

Peter Brown wrote that the apartment "was stocked with the latest electronic inventions, including TVs, stereos, burglar alarms, and telephones. There were telephones everywhere, literally every four or five feet, and there was a red telephone in the bedroom that was connected directly to the NEMS office."

Principal shooting on the movie, which had the working title "Eight Arms to

Hold You," began in late February in Paradise Island, twelve days after Ringo and Maureen's wedding. In the meantime, The Beatles returned to the Abbey Road studios in mid-February to record songs for the movie's soundtrack album, including "Ticket to Ride," "I Need You," "Another Girl," "You Like Me Too Much," and "The Night Before."

Ringo returned from his honeymoon on February 14 and the group started recording the next day.

Ringo took (double-tracked) lead vocals on an upbeat Lennon/McCartney rocker called "If You've Got Trouble," but the song just didn't work and was not released until nearly thirty years later, when it was included on *The Beatles Anthology* CD. "To be brutally honest, it's not difficult to see why," wrote Beatles historian Mark Lewisohn about the song. "It was not one of the better Lennon-McCartney numbers by any stretch of the imagination, nor was it brilliantly performed in the one and only take . . . which was recorded."

Unlike *A Hard Day's Night*, which was filmed primarily in London on a shoestring budget, "Eight Arms to Hold You" took The Beatles not only to the Bahamas (including New Providence Island) but on location to the Austrian Alps and elsewhere in England (the Salisbury Plain). Several scenes were also shot in London at Twickenham Film Studios.

Maureen did not accompany Ringo to the Bahamas. She stayed with her parents in Liverpool for a little while, then traveled back to London, where she bunked with Cynthia Lennon. She was, however, with Ringo for the eight days of shooting in Austria. "She won't be traveling with me, ever, not while I'm working," Ringo said. "It's ridiculous to take a wife with you, she couldn't stand it. We're used to moving at this wild pace, but wives aren't. They'd collapse after a couple of weeks."

Richard Lester was once again directing The Beatles, but it would be difficult for him to recapture the spontaneity of *A Hard Day's Night*. That movie was filmed almost one year before in the first flush of Beatlemania, when it was all so new and the world was just getting to know John, Paul, George, and Ringo. But producer Walter Shenson and distributor United Artists had high hopes that "Eight Arms to Hold You" could replicate the financial success of *A Hard Day's Night*, even though the new movie was estimated to be costing three times as much—$1.5 million—as its predecessor.

This time around, The Beatles would be filmed in color, with a stellar supporting cast, including Leo McKern, Eleanor Bron, John Bluthal, Patrick Cargill, and, once again, Victor Spinetti, who played the harried television producer in *A Hard Day's Night*. (Spinetti was a favorite of The Beatles, and later went on a vacation with John and Cynthia Lennon to Marrakesh.) In addition to their own songs written for the movie, they were backed by a lush orchestral soundtrack.

What could possibly go wrong?

Well, for starters, a lot had changed in one year, particularly the drug culture, which The Beatles embraced with all eight arms after their encounter with Bob Dylan the previous fall. They were stoned for most of the movie and felt the script was a jumbled mess, not that it bothered them all that much (they were too high to pay much attention). The Beatles were playing themselves, and Ringo, who'd been singled out for his acting chops in *A Hard Day's Night*, was the movie's main focus this time around.

He thought his enthusiasm with the group's first movie might have helped land him the central part this time around. He admitted to smoking a lot of pot, which, no doubt, attributed to the giggly mood on the set. George Harrison recalled smoking dope with actor Brandon De Wilde on the plane ride to the Bahamas—with Mal Evans lighting up cigars to mask the odor of marijuana.

The convoluted plot of "Eight Arms to Hold You"—the title, suggested by Ringo, was later changed to *Help!*—has an Eastern cult leader trying to come into possession of a sacrificial ring being worn by Ringo, who attempts to protect the sister of a high priestess (who secretly sent him the ring in order to save her sister). Ringo himself eventually becomes the cult's sacrificial target, but is saved after a series of farcical events that unravel like an episode of the loony 1950s BBC radio comedy *The Goon Show*, which The Beatles loved so much.

Lennon said later that The Beatles were so high that communicating with them was difficult. They were glassy-eyed and giggly most of the time, even when having to wake up at the ungodly (to them) hour of 7 a.m.

The shooting schedule for *Help!* took The Beatles to Austria, where they donned skis to film a scene in the Austrian Alps. Ringo remembered the scene in the movie featuring Victor Spinetti and Roy Kinnear sliding big curling stones, one of which was armed with a bomb. The Beatles, knowing it's about to explode, run away; Ringo and Paul ran, as instructed by director Richard Lester, and smoked a joint before walking back to the set.

The group's new single, "Ticket to Ride," was released in the UK on April 9, five days before The Beatles finished filming *Help!* at Twickenham Studios. Backed by "Yes It Is," "Ticket to Ride" went to Number One in the UK and in the U.S., where it was released on April 19 and spent a week in the top spot. The song featured George Harrison's jingly twelve-string Rickenbacker, Ringo's distinctive snare-tom-snare-tom percussion—topped off with a drum-roll flourish—and John Lennon's double-tracked lead vocals. "That was one of the earliest heavy-metal records made," Lennon said later. "Paul's contribution was the way Ringo played the drums."

If Ringo was being told how to play a particular drum part, usually by Lennon or McCartney, it usually didn't take him more than once to get it right. There's no record of him having trouble with the drum pattern on "Ticket to Ride," but Beatles engineer Geoff Emerick noted how "John and Paul could be quite rude to Ringo when he was having trouble with his fills, but once the song was recorded and done with, they would be fine with him again."

The new album, like the movie, was called *Help!* The decision to scrap "If You've Got Trouble" meant that another "Ringo Song" was needed for the album. That turned out to be "Act Naturally," a Buck Owens song which Ringo, who loved country music, had discovered. "I said, 'This is the one I am going to be doing' and they said 'OK,'" he recalled. "We were listening to all kinds of things. John sang "Dizzy Miss Lizzy." We were all listening to that, too."

Ringo's contribution was overlooked once *Help!*, the fifth Beatles album to be released in the UK, hit the stores in August, for two big reasons: "Help!," the title song written and sung by John Lennon, and "Yesterday," which was written and performed on an acoustic guitar by Paul McCartney, backed by a string quartet (which he produced along with George Martin). Lennon considered the rousing, plaintive "Help!" to be one of the best Beatles songs he'd ever written, and it kicked the album off with a charge. The quiet, introspective "Yesterday," by comparison, was the first Beatles song to be performed solo and would go on to become one of the most recorded tunes in pop music history.

McCartney said that, when he played the song in the studio for band mates, Ringo told him it wouldn't make any sense to add drums; John and George felt the same way about adding extra guitars. Although it was credited to "Lennon/ McCartney," it was all McCartney.

On March 22, 1965, Ed Sullivan ran the following item in his newspaper column: "Sir Stork en route to the Ringo Starrs." The item was accurate, and on April 7, while The Beatles were filming scenes for *Help!* at Twickenham Studios, Ringo and Maureen officially announced they were expecting their first child in the fall. With a baby on the way, Ringo began looking around for a bigger place, even though he'd just spent a small fortune renovating the couple's Montagu Square apartment.

(The apartment at 34 Montagu Square had a storied history after Ringo moved out. In 1966, when counter-culture hero William S. Burroughs was living in London, he met Paul McCartney, who, like Burroughs, was interested in experimenting with stereo sound. McCartney rented the apartment from Ringo and set up a small recording studio. McCartney and Burroughs both used the studio to record experimental ideas. Jimi Hendrix later lived there, and John Lennon and Yoko Ono used the apartment to take the naked photograph of themselves that was used on their *Two Virgins* album. Ringo, who still held the lease, eventually sold it in 1969 to avoid any more trouble.)

Ringo eventually settled on a large mock Tudor estate in Weybridge, Surrey, in the exclusive St. George's Hill estate, about an hour's drive from London. He paid £37,000 for the house, called Sunny Heights, which was located on the bottom of a wooded hill, less than a mile from John and Cynthia Lennon's twenty-seven-room estate, Kenwood. (The Lennons were frequent guests at Sunny Heights.) The house's property backed onto St. George's Hill Golf Course, though neither Ringo nor John was a member of the club, and neither played golf.

Ringo and a very pregnant Maureen moved into the place that summer, and Ringo used his Brickey Building Company to renovate the house, spending £40,000 on a complete overhaul. If he thought the job would be done quickly, since he co-owned the construction company undertaking the assignment, he was sorely mistaken.

"The thing about being in Weybridge in that house was that I bought half the building firm that was working on it because I thought they'd get the job done much faster," he said. "Not a chance in hell! Builders do things in their own good time. And the foreman would cook Maureen and [me] dinner because she couldn't cook."

According to Peter Brown, "Ringo spent money on the house like a poor man who had just won the Irish Sweepstakes" and shelled out £10,000 alone on a semi-circular wall in the rear of the house. He even flew in his own pool table from the U.S., since only billiard tables were readily available in England. The table's two-day journey from America cost him twice as much as the table itself.

Sunny Heights sat on a large expanse of property. The sloping lawns, or "the grounds," as Ringo liked to say (with just a bit of pretension), included a goldfish pond, a tree house, an old air raid shelter, a kennel for the couple's three dogs (a poodle and two Airedales), and a large garage housing his four cars, all maroon-colored (a Rolls-Royce, a Facel Vega, and two Mini Coopers). Eventually, a huge amphitheater was dug out of the ground in the back yard.

There was a line strung between two trees onto which a tin can was fastened; Ringo and Maureen used it for target practice. Ringo, the kid from the Dingle, often traipsed around "the grounds" using a silver-tipped walking stick, looking every inch a true country gentleman. "When I walk round I often think, 'What's a scruff like me doing with this lot?'" he said. "But it soon passes. You get used to it. You get ready to argue with anyone who is trying to get too much of your money."

Ringo and Maureen spent a lot of time with their neighbors John and Cynthia. "I mainly saw John in that period because we lived a couple of blocks from each other. We used to spend practically every weekend together," Ringo said. "We'd edit 8mm film and have fun—sometimes hysterical fun. I'd walk home....We'd try and do manly things, too; we'd go to the pub and bring Maureen and Cynthia a Babycham [a brand of sparkling wine] or something—a real Liverpool attitude."

While a portrait of Lennon and McCartney "loomed" over the mantelpiece, Ringo underplayed his "other" life as a Beatle—there was no drum kit to be found anywhere in Sunny Heights. "When we don't record, I don't play," he said. His good friend Keith Moon, who played drums for The Who, followed the same rule, never keeping a drum kit in his house.

Ringo hired an interior decorator named Ronnie Oke to design the interior of the house, which boasted a sunken tub in the main bathroom that was accessed by carpeted steps (about which Ringo complained). The main sitting room seated around thirty people, and Ringo had an office with a big desk. He started painting his game room, but never finished the job; guests were invited to paint whatever they liked on the other walls.

Maureen Cleave, a reporter for the *Evening Standard* who was a Beatles favorite (John Lennon, in particular), visited Maureen and Ringo for a newspaper article headlined "How Does a Beatle Live?" that detailed the couple's domestic bliss.

> There are shelves full of trophies, neatly arranged: gold disks; a piece of fossilized wood from the Libyan Desert, millions of years old; books (one shelf for science fiction, another for the Asprey leather-bound); a miniature cannon. "A present off of my wife," said Ringo grandly.

"She's always buying me presents." There is a perfectly horrible small brown stuffed puppy dog standing on a carpet in a glass case—a present from John. "I think it's nice," said Ringo. . . . The roof of the house is stuck all over with television aerials that enable him to get four channels. "Might as well get everything that's going," he said. "I get all my knowledge from TV."

The house was filled with tape recorders, movie cameras, telephones, and television sets (even in the bathrooms). Ringo's love of photography was evident by the many cameras lying around. (A book of his photographs was scheduled to be published in the U.S., but the project never came to fruition.) Ringo, according to Beatles biographer Hunter Davies, "made some excellent and ingenious" home movies, including a twenty-minute color film of Maureen's eye "with a background of music concrete" which also included a scene Ringo shot by sitting in a swing and shooting his house and garden as he swung up and down. But he didn't like to show the movies to anyone, since he didn't think they were of any significance.

Sunny Heights also boasted a bar, which Ringo named the "Flying Cow." It was memorialized by its own plaque (a cow with wings hanging on antlers just inside the entrance). "I've always wanted a pub, from movies, I think," he told Cleave. "What I like would be for about fifteen of my friends to pop in here without being asked, without me being here even. I would love to have a real pub in my house. My mother was a barmaid once."

The man whose mother was once a barmaid was now also a Member of the Order of the British Empire—an MBE. On June 12, 1965, the news broke that John, Paul, George, and Ringo had been recommended for MBEs by British Prime Minister Harold Wilson, a Merseyside member of Parliament (he was born in Yorkshire, about seventy-five miles from Liverpool). There were murmurings that Brian Epstein was not on the list since he was both Jewish and a homosexual, "an accurate assumption," according to Peter Brown.

Ringo wondered if Brian minded not being awarded the MBE but figured he would have been knighted—an even higher honor—had he lived long enough.

The Beatles were scheduled to officially receive their awards from Queen Elizabeth in October, during a ceremony at Buckingham Palace. The MBEs weren't a total surprise; six weeks earlier, paperwork addressed to each individual Beatle arrived from 10 Downing Street, informing them of Wilson's recommendation on the annual Queen's Birthday honors list. Ringo, like the others, had to provide a written acceptance of the MBE; the letters from Wilson's office were rushed to The Beatles while they were filming *Help!* so they could sign them and not miss the deadline.

The news of The Beatles and their MBEs ignited some controversy, not only among the British upper crust but also in the media, taken aback that four northerners—from Liverpool, no less—were being included among war heroes, lords, and titans of industry. The nerve!

"It seems that the road from rebellion to respectability is much shorter than it used to be," sniped an editorial writer for the *Sun*. "In the name of all that's sane if not sacred, isn't pinning a royal medal onto four Beatles jackets just too much?" wondered Donald Zec, the entertainment columnist for the *Mirror*. Never mind that the annual MBE list numbered in the hundreds.

Others returned their MBEs in protest. A Col. George Wagg sent back all twelve of his medals and was so incensed he quit the Labour Party; Paul Pearson, a war hero, returned his MBE to the Queen with a note: "Its meaning seems to be worthless."

John, Paul, George, and Ringo took it all in bemused stride, as the following exchange attests:

Reporter: Ringo, how do you feel about going to the palace in morning suit and all that?

Ringo: I don't mind, you know. It's alright. When I buy one.

Reporter: You haven't got one?

Ringo: No, not yet. I've got an evening suit, if that will do.

Reporter: I don't think it will.

Ringo: Well, I'll just go in my pajamas then.

Ringo said later that he and his fellow Beatles were happy to receive the honor, at least initially, and that their families were thrilled at the idea that the boys were going to meet The Queen. The fact that some "old soldiers" sent their MBEs back in protest went almost unnoticed in the group's immediate circle.

Maureen spent the summer moving into Sunny Heights and preparing for the arrival of the baby amid the clatter of the Brickey Building workmen. Ringo supervised the renovations when he was around, but his schedule was predictably frenetic. The Beatles spent most of June in the studio, cutting songs for the *Help!* album and crafting their next single, Lennon's title track, backed with McCartney's "I'm Down" (sung by Paul in the "larynx-tearer" style of Lennon's rendition of "Twist and Shout").

The *Help!* album was released in the UK on August 6 and reached Number One two days later, remaining in the top spot for nine weeks. Its U.S. release followed on August 13. It hit Number One in the States the following month and spent nine weeks in the top spot. Beatlemania was showing no signs of slowing down.

The *Help!* movie opened to brisk business on July 29—Princess Margaret attended its glitzy London premiere—and so-so reviews which, for the most part, spared John, Paul, George, and Ringo, but criticized the movie's structure and nonsensical plot. As in *A Hard Day's Night*, Ringo was once again singled out by many critics for his performance, some even going so far as to compare him to Charlie Chaplin.

"Why expect reason in a picture that jumps from London to the Alps to Salisbury Plain without any explanation, or brings Ringo face to face in a wine cellar with a tiger that can only be appeased by the discomposed Ringo singing a snatch of Beethoven's Ninth Symphony?" wrote *New York Times* critic Bosley Crowther. "There's nothing in *Help!* to compare with that wild ballet of The Beatles racing across a playground in *A Hard Day's Night*, nothing as wistful as the ramble of Ringo round London all alone. Those were episodes that gave a welcome respite to the frantic pace and mood of that film. This one, without sense or pattern is wham, wham, wham, all the way."

It didn't matter, of course. The Beatles were The Beatles—anything new was huge news—and fans flocked to see *Help!*

By the time Crowther's review appeared in print, John, Paul, George, and Ringo were well into their second tour of America. The ardor of Beatlemania was still in full swing, but the cracks were beginning to show in the band's young fan base. The floodgates they'd opened after their February 1964 appearance on *The Ed Sullivan Show*, which the press dubbed "The British Invasion," saw the likes of The Dave Clark Five, Herman's Hermits, The Animals, The Rolling Stones, and Gerry and the Pacemakers topping the U.S. charts with their own hit singles, each band staking a claim to the hearts of America's youth (and making the requisite appearance on *The Ed Sullivan Show*).

The first leg of their summer tour took The Beatles to Italy, France, and Spain. Ringo was appalled when he went to his first and last bullfight in Madrid—"the saddest thing I ever saw. . . . I always thought it was such a miserable end"—before they landed in New York on August 14 for a stretch of sixteen shows in sixteen days.

Their hair and sideburns were longer now and John Lennon, in particular, had put on some weight (reflected in his chunky face). Upon their arrival in New York they taped their final in-studio appearance on *The Ed Sullivan Show*—a total of six songs, including Ringo singing "Act Naturally" (the performance aired September 12 on CBS).

They braced themselves for the following night's historic concert at the year-old Shea Stadium in Flushing, Queens. The stadium was packed with nearly fifty-six-thousand hysterical fans in what was the largest outdoor concert in rock history. Teenager Barbara Goldbach, who was about to turn eighteen, and Linda Eastman, soon to be twenty-four, sat somewhere in the mass of humanity that night at Shea Stadium—never imagining in their wildest dreams they would both marry Beatles one day.

The Shea Stadium concert was sheer insanity from start to finish. Brian Epstein wanted his "boys" to be plopped onto the field from a helicopter (the stage was near second base, on the edge of the outfield). That was ruled out by city officials, so John, Paul, George, and Ringo took a limo from the Warwick Hotel to a heliport, where they were airlifted over Manhattan via helicopter to the roof of the World's Fair building adjacent to Shea Stadium. From there, they were hustled into a Wells Fargo armored van. Each of them was given a Wells Fargo agent badge, which they proudly affixed to the jackets they wore on stage. It was perfect for Ringo, who loved Westerns.

Ed Sullivan, who introduced The Beatles to the Shea Stadium crowd, hired a twelve-man camera crew to document the historical concert; the city provided an estimated two-thousand security personnel (cops, etc.) to control the raucous throng, mostly teenagers, some of whom stormed the field and had to be chased down by cops when The Beatles appeared onstage. (The Shea Stadium scoreboard flashed a futile message asking fans to please remain in their seats. Good luck with that.) Several girls fainted and had to be dragged off to be treated. Others just cried and cried.

Brian Epstein, dressed in a suit and tie, stood coolly off to the side of the stage, nodding his head to Ringo's beat and soaking in what he had unleashed on the city of New York, and the world. It was all over in the blink of an eye, a sweaty, half-hour set of twelve songs, including "Act Naturally," which was introduced by Paul McCartney. "We'd like to introduce you, at great expense, brought specially from the other side of the earth for you tonight, singin' a song off our new album . . . *Ringo!*"

Even though The Beatles were using new, specially made 100-watt amplifiers, the din of those fifty-six thousand fans drowned out everything. Ringo recalled how the band used the house public address system, even at Shea

Stadium. But no one came to hear The Beatles, only to scream and drown everything out once the band started to play.

The last number they performed that night was a raucous version of Paul McCartney's "I'm Down," with John Lennon shedding his guitar for the organ, careening along the keyboard with his elbows and laughing maniacally whenever he and George Harrison shared a microphone to back up McCartney's lead vocal. Ringo felt his band mate was acting up from all the excitement and tension. John, he said, went "mad," not certifiably insane, of course, but carried away with the excitement of it all. What stood out for Ringo was how far away the audience was at Shea Stadium. Even for The Beatles, who were used to mobs of people, it was disconcerting. They'd cut their teeth in small clubs; playing before fifty-thousand-plus people was unprecedented in the annals of music history.

The rest of the tour was the usual chaos, and it was starting to wear thin: the half-hour sets played in front of fans screaming so loudly that the group couldn't hear themselves beyond their woefully inadequate amplifiers and microphones. Ringo didn't even bother trying to replicate the drum fills he'd performed in the studio, preferring to just bash away on his hi-hat and snare drum trying to keep John, Paul, and George in some semblance of a rhythmic balance.

Their musicianship didn't seem to matter anymore in the live shows; missed notes, fluffed drum patterns and forgotten lyrics went unnoticed by the shrieking crowds who seemed to scream just for the sake of screaming. Girls fainted and had to be dragged away by security guards; fans pounded on the limos going to and from the concert venues. Another city, another faceless hotel suite, another press conference. Answering the same questions over and over. Who needed it?

"We'd get in the car. I'd look over at John and say, 'Christ. Look at you. You're a bloody phenomenon!'" Ringo said. "And just laugh, because it was only him. Elvis went downhill because he seemed to have no friends, just a load of sycophants. Whereas with us, individually, we all went mad but the other three always brought us back. That's what saved us. I remember being totally bananas thinking, I am the one, and the other three would look at me and say, ''Scuse me, what are you doing?' I remember each of us getting into that state."

Ringo got into another state of mind when the tour stopped in Los Angeles in late August for two shows at the Hollywood Bowl. The Beatles hunkered down for a week in a rented house off Mulholland Drive in the Hollywood Hills, where they partied away in the days leading up the their live shows. Peter Fonda, David Crosby, and Jim (later Roger) McGuinn from The Byrds and others came to visit in various stages of consciousness.

Harrison said he and John decided that Ringo and Paul needed to experience their first acid trip in order to keep up with their band mates—who couldn't relate to them anymore on a spiritual (chemically induced) level.

In Ringo's version of events that August day, "a couple of guys" came to visit the band and persuaded Ringo to take his first trip, dripping some acid onto a sugar cube with an eye-dropper. Ringo was joined by John, George, Neil Aspinall, and Mal Evans.

Everyone was nervous, not just because they didn't know what to expect or how they would react while on the acid, but because a reporter, Don Short, was hanging around that afternoon and needed to be kept unaware of what was happening. What would the world think if it was revealed that John, George, and Ringo were taking drugs? Ringo recalled that day fondly, but the acid trip extended into the evening, when it seemed like it would "never wear off."

During the gang's acid trip, Peter Fonda kept whispering into Lennon's ear, "I know what it's like to be dead," describing how he'd shot himself in the stomach when he was ten years old and how, while undergoing surgery, his heart stopped three times. Lennon found Fonda annoying, but later used the phrase for "She Said She Said," one of his contributions to the group's *Revolver* album.

The Beatles, including McCartney this time, took another trip several days later to Elvis Presley's nearby mansion in Bel-Air to meet their idol. But this wasn't the hip-thrusting, rebellious Elvis of 1955; he was now jaded and bored, a thirty-year-old, burned-out pop idol living a life of seclusion surrounded by his yes-men "Memphis Mafia" and reduced to churning out a string of crappy movies—including the one he'd just finished, *Blue Hawaii*—under the inscrutable eye of his manager, Colonel Tom Parker. Parker and Brian Epstein worked hard behind the scenes to arrange the historic meeting of their superstars. And, as these situations often are, it turned out to be a disappointment for both camps.

Ringo was excited about meeting Presley and was glad to have his band mates along for the historic sitdown. But they found Presley's big house very dark inside, with Elvis sitting in front of a TV set playing a bass, surrounded by his "Memphis Mafia." He was shy and appeared to be a bit disinterested—the complete opposite of how the four guys from Liverpool felt meeting one of their idols.

Paul McCartney called it "hero worship of a high degree" on the part of The Beatles. Their first stop upon arriving at Presley's house was to be ushered into his pool room, where they were shown The King's pool table, which swiveled to become a craps table. Then they sat down with Elvis in front of the television set, which had a remote control (the first John, Paul, George, or Ringo had ever seen). The conversation was stilted until the guitars were broken out and they jammed together a little bit; eventually, Elvis's fiancée, Priscilla, was trundled out to be shown off before she disappeared just as quickly.

Journalist Chris Hutchins, who accompanied The Beatles to the Presley mansion, wrote later how surly John Lennon was toward Elvis throughout the visit—and how the encounter was underscored by "uncomfortable undertones" and "superficial cheerfulness."

"We didn't jam with Elvis," Ringo recalled years later. "I don't care who says it. The big memory was [we] walked in, and he was on the settee watching TV, and he had a TV commander. We were like, 'Wow!' We were fans of Elvis . . . for me, [he] was the first one who wasn't like your dad. He was a couple of years older, that's all. So anyway, those were the big memories, and we didn't jam. We didn't really play American football, although him and his guys did. We didn't know how to play that."

So much for The King. Ringo, for his efforts, received a much-cherished gun holster from Elvis, which he proudly displayed in a showcase back home in Sunny Heights.

———

Ringo was the second Beatle to get married and, on September 13, 1965, he became the second Beatle to become a father when Maureen gave birth to a boy. They named the baby Zak, and his birth at Queen Charlotte's Maternity Hospital was, naturally, international news. The British Pathé cameras were on hand nine days later to shoot a sixty-second newsreel documenting the baby's departure from the hospital. Zak, swaddled in a blanket, was held by a private nurse as Ringo and Maureen looked on and croaked out a few words to the mass of reporters gathered outside the hospital's main entrance.

They looked tired and annoyed at all the attention in such a private moment, but it was unavoidable. "Zak's a lot too young to know he's been born in the Beatle clan but his father is now prouder than he's ever been before and that his mother, nineteen-year-old Maureen, is so happy she can't put it into words," chirped the British Pathé narrator. "Fancy having a son who's automatically top of the pops the day he's born!"

The trio quickly jumped into a Rolls-Royce and sped off for Sunny Heights. A report across the pond in *Time* magazine noted that the baby "inherited the magnificent Ringo nose along with the basset-hound jowls."

It wasn't reported at the time, but Valerie James, the wife of actor/comedian Sid James—who was famous in England for teaming with Tony Hancock on the radio and television show *Hancock's Half Hour*—was also at Queen Charlotte's, expecting her third child. Ringo paid a visit to Valerie's room to offer some comfort after she suffered a miscarriage. "Ringo was bitterly disappointed for us," she said. "I'd never met him before, but the next day he came in to see me and he was really sweet. I was lying there when he came to my room and he tried so hard to cheer me up."

Zak's arrival was a joyous occasion for the young couple, and Ringo admitted to having some jitters—no different from any other first-time dad. "I was frightened at first, you know, when Maureen had the baby and I went in to see her, you know, just after she'd had it—it was all purple and crinkly," Ringo said. "And the doctor says, 'Here you are. Here he is.' And they laid it on my arms saying, 'Ok, can you take it?' And I couldn't move because I just thought it would break.

"I used to be terrified of dogs and babies. Babies cried and dogs bit me. But what knocks me out about this baby is him shouting his head off in his own senseless way—laughing at bits of wood. That's what I like about babies." He doted on Zak, using his new Nikon camera to take lots of pictures of the baby. "Nothing made him happier than sitting at the kitchen table, eating Corn Flakes with Maureen and Zak," said Ken Partridge.

Ringo admitted to doing "one nappy [diaper] change" for the new baby, but he wasn't spending much time at home that fall. The Beatles returned to the studio in October and November to work on songs for their next album, including "Run for Your Life," "Norwegian Wood," "Nowhere Man," "Day Tripper," and "Drive My Car," the latter two Lennon/McCartney originals featuring Ringo's snare-heavy, pulsating beat.

Ringo fulfilled his one-song-per-album vocal quota with "What Goes On," a twangy country-western tune featuring George and John's guitar-picking and McCartney on backing vocals. Ringo was given his first co-writing credit, as Richard Starkey, on "What Goes On," alongside Lennon and McCartney.

"I used to wish that I could write songs like the others—and I've tried, but I just can't," he said. "I can get the words all right, but whenever I think of a tune and sing it to the others they always say, 'Yeah, it sounds like such-a-thing,' and when they point it out I see what they mean. But I did get a part credit as a composer on one—it was called 'What Goes On.'"

He still grew very nervous when he had to record a lead vocal—"he had to be coached and nurtured around the mic," Abbey Road engineer Geoff Emerick remembered—but he usually pulled it off with a minimum number of takes. "If he did make any kind of comment during a session, it would most often be about the drum sounds, which he knew were critical," Emerick said of Ringo. "Funnily enough, he would often go into a near panic whenever he had to do a drum fill. You can almost hear him freezing, trying to decide what to do as he's doing it."

Emerick was one of the group's favored Abbey Road engineers, and was particularly close to Paul McCartney. He thought Ringo kept steady time on the drums—and that his small physical stature gave his style a particular sound, since it took his arms longer to reach the drums, giving him a "laid-back" feel.

"I would constantly be saying to Ringo, 'Can you hit the snare a little harder? Can you stomp on the bass drum pedal harder?' and he would reply, 'If I hit them any harder, I'm going to break the skins,' but it did make a huge difference to the sound, and he did hit those drums hard." Emerick noted "a big pile of wood chips" around Ringo's drum kit, the after-effects of all the drumsticks he splintered during a recording session.

On October 26, 1965, John, Paul, George, and Ringo received their MBEs in a ceremony at Buckingham Palace. Fortunately, someone was there to take down what was said:

The Queen (to Paul): How long have you been together now?

Paul: Oh, for many years.

The Queen (to Ringo): Are you the one who started it?

Ringo: No, I was the last to join. I'm the little fellow.

They may or may not have been stoned when they met the Queen—accounts differ, even among the four Beatles—but there was no denying that their use of recreational drugs was becoming more and more prevalent. John and George, in particular, were adding lysergic acid (LSD) to their marijuana use. Ringo smoked a lot of pot and occasionally joined them on their acid trips.

Marijuana, in Ringo's estimation, was a big influence on the ways in which The Beatles were changing and evolving, particularly for Lennon and McCartney, who were writing the bulk of the group's songs.

They weren't alone, of course; by late 1965 the counter-culture movement was expanding as more and more people began to follow psychedelic drug guru Timothy Leary's mantra to "turn on, tune in, and drop out"—particularly postwar baby boomers, who experimented with pot, LSD, and anything else that might alter their consciousness and take them to a higher cosmic plane. While The Beatles certainly weren't the only musicians dabbling in drugs, they were the movement's highest-profile adherents—keeping their exploits hidden from their fans, of course.

Ringo admitted the music was "absolute shit" when too many chemicals were involved; what The Beatles thought was terrific turned out to be crap, once they were back on planet Earth and listening to what they'd recorded with clear heads.

George Harrison remembered how John Lennon would pick him and Ringo up in his Rolls-Royce, which had blacked-out windows, on the way to the studio. They would smoke "double doses" of marijuana; by the time they pulled up to Abbey Road studios, Harrison said, they would literally tumble out of the Rolls-Royce.

It didn't affect their music, at least in the studio. In their live performances, The Beatles played virtually the same repertoire all the way through the summer of 1966, when they finally threw in the towel and stopped touring. They couldn't replicate a lot of the newer, more intricate studio sounds on stage. A song like "Yesterday," in which Paul McCartney accompanied himself on an acoustic guitar, was fine; it was a different story for a song like "Norwegian Wood," which utilized a lot of studio enhancement and—gasp!—a sitar, or "In My Life," on which George Martin added a Bach-influenced, classical-sounding piano solo. Only John Lennon, of course, could sum it up unequivocally: *Rubber Soul*, he said, was the "pot album." *Revolver* was "the acid" album.

Ringo noted how *Rubber Soul* was a departure for the band; they were integrating a lot of their influences into the music on tracks like "Nowhere Man," and "The Word." The lyrics, too, were changing, particularly on "Drive My Car," "Norwegian Wood," "You Won't See Me," "Nowhere Man," and "Michelle."

Rubber Soul, the sixth Beatles album to be issued in the UK, was released there on December 3, 1965, and went to Number One sixteen days later, knocking out *The Sound of Music* soundtrack and remaining in the top spot for eight weeks. It was the eleventh Beatles album released in the States when it debuted on December 6, selling 1.2 million copies in its first nine days and topping the Billboard charts a month later, on January 8, 1966.

The U.S. version of *Rubber Soul* omitted "Drive My Car," "Nowhere Man," Ringo's "What Goes On," and George Harrison's "If I Needed Someone," replacing them with "I've Just Seen a Face" and "It's Only Love" from the UK version of the *Help!* album. The reconfigured and bastardized Beatles albums put out by Capitol Records in America frustrated The Beatles, and their fans, to no end.

By the end of 1965 it was a given that anything The Beatles touched turned to gold. Beatlemania might have waned just a bit in the zeitgeist, but, professionally, John Lennon, Paul McCartney, George Harrison, and Ringo Starr were the most famous musicians in the world, bar none. They had only to look back over their shoulders at the sold-out tours in America that summer—accompanied by the now-expected mass hysteria—to see that the Beatles freight train was showing no signs of slowing down.

In his memoir, *A Cellarful of Noise*, published in 1964, Brian Epstein remembered thinking that his first impression of meeting Ringo was of "a little chap with a beard." Well, that "little chap" was now a millionaire several times over, with a huge country estate for his wife and baby, filled with the toys with which he indulged his growing passions: car collecting, photography, and electronics. But what good was all of that if he wasn't around to enjoy it?

Ringo had been a Beatle for over three years now, and while it brought him unimagined fame and wealth, the down side, such as it was, included the non-stop blur of touring, marathon recording sessions, television and radio appearances too numerous to count, a litany of redundant press conferences answering inane questions and, yes, those two movies thrown into the mix.

He wasn't complaining—that wasn't in his nature, and, besides, Richy Starkey from the Dingle wasn't about to look this gift horse in the mouth—but the thrill of it all was starting to wear thin. Sure, Ringo could say he was on a first-name basis with A-list friends like Elizabeth Taylor, Richard Burton, and Peter Sellers—but what price glory?

Where once Ringo and his fellow Beatles were exhilarated by touring, the prospect of yet another worldwide tour in 1966—and one more trip to America—was daunting and depressing. They were expanding musically and spiritually—both with and without the drugs—and they looked with weary eyes at spending yet more time in more anonymous hotel rooms in a blitz of cities and countries where they couldn't even hear themselves playing onstage (or see the scenery, for that matter). They'd been there and done that.

Ringo noted how, at the end of 1965, the touring "started to hit everybody." The band held a meeting to talk about the drop-off of their live musicianship, the tedium of touring, the endless hotel rooms, the unrelenting pressure—it was a long laundry list of grievances.

Ringo agreed with his band mates that, more than anything else, their live performances were suffering. Or, more to the point, why even play live when they were drowned out by hysterical fans whose screams made it a pointless exercise?

"No one heard us, not even ourselves," he said. "I found it very hard. I mean, looking at amplifiers thinking the sound is going to come through my eyes instead of ears. . . . I couldn't do any fills because I'm just there to hold it together somehow, you know? So if I go off for a fill which isn't as loud as all your force on an off-beat it would get lost anyway. And the timing usually went all to cock. And that's why we were bad players. That's when we decided to stop, in '66."

10

POUNDING "RAIN"

The acrimony and the lawsuits would come later, but as the calendar changed to 1966, the four Beatles were still extremely close, not only as band members, but as friends. If Ringo felt inadequate on an intellectual level due to his lack of schooling, he more than compensated for it in the way he complemented the three others with his sunny disposition and "gee-whiz" attitude. The four young men from Liverpool shared the shackles of fame that only they could understand, particularly on an emotional level. They had their squabbles—what family doesn't?—but they felt a kinship that seemed unbreakable as they helped usher in the burgeoning mod scene in London.

To Ringo, his fellow Beatles were the closest friends he'd ever had, his "three brothers" who looked out for each other and shared lots of laughs. He remembered how, in those heady first days of worldwide success, they would stay in posh hotel suites, sometimes taking up the entire floor of a hotel but ending up together, the four of them, in the bathroom—"just to be with each other." They would drive into London together, work all day in the studio, then leave together, stopping off at home long enough to change their clothes and reconnoiter at a club later that night.

Harrison became the third Beatle to tie the knot when he married model Pattie Boyd on January 21, 1966. Ringo and John Lennon were off on vacation and couldn't attend the nuptials, but Paul McCartney, now the lone bachelor Beatle, served as Harrison's best man.

This was the "Swingin' '60s," where everything British was hip, a movement teetering on the verge of psychedelia where the fashions of Carnaby Street coalesced with rock and mind-altering drugs into a pop-culture phenomenon—with The Beatles at the forefront, holding court like four kings at the Ad-Lib Club while continuing to experiment in the studio.

To Ringo, it marked a definite shift in their attitudes and in their lives, particularly during the *Rubber Soul* recording sessions. They were "doing great stuff" in the studio, he said; everyone was happy with the results.

"I feel The Beatles were doing what they wanted to do, and a lot of it was that youthfulness of trying to change ideas. I think it allowed people to do things they wouldn't have done if we hadn't been out there. Because so many people have always said, 'Oh, it's OK for you to dress like that or to do that,' but it's OK for anyone, really."

The experimentation and psychedelia spilled over into their next album, *Revolver*, which was released in early August 1966. Ringo's adaptability to the group's changing sound is evidenced throughout the album, with his innovative drum fills on tunes like "She Said She Said" (on which George Harrison played bass, after a McCartney-Lennon argument), "Doctor Robert," and "I'm Only Sleeping"—all of which include complex time changes—and his flat-out power drumming on two John Lennon compositions, "Tomorrow Never Knows" and "Rain." The latter song was not included on *Revolver* but was the B-side to McCartney's "Paperback Writer," released as a single in June 1966.

As he'd done with *A Hard Day's Night*, Lennon borrowed the title to the trippy "Tomorrow Never Knows," inspired by either *The Tibetan Book of the Dead*, Timothy Leary's *The Psychedelic Experience*—or both—or from another of Ringo's jumbled sayings. (Ringo had uttered the phrase in a press conference back in 1964 after the episode in which a lock of his hair was snipped off during a party at the British Embassy.)

"I took one of Ringo's malapropisms as the title, to sort of take the edge off the heavy philosophical lyrics," Lennon said. Lennon's electronically altered lead vocal (he told producer George Martin he wanted to sound like "thousands of monks chanting") was underscored by Ringo's cymbal-heavy backbeat and his snare-tom-snare syncopation. George Martin referred to Ringo's drumming on this song as "very characteristic." Ringo was proud of his drumming on the song—and on the album as a whole.

Geoff Emerick, who was engineering the *Revolver* sessions at Abbey Road, said he helped create the aural "hypnotic" sound of Ringo's drums on "Tomorrow Never Knows" by moving the bass drum microphone "*thisclose*" to Ringo's bass drum, something that hadn't been done before. "There's an early picture of The Beatles wearing a woolen jumper with four necks. I stuffed that inside the drum to deaden the sound," he said. "Then we put the sound through Fairchild 660 valve limiters and compressors. It became the sound of *Revolver* and *Pepper* really. Drums had never been heard like that before."

Ringo, Emerick said, "loved" the idea. "They all loved the sounds. It was exactly what they wanted."

On "Rain," which fades out with the song playing backwards (Lennon's idea after a night smoking hash), Ringo simply pounds away on his snare drum, both for the backbeat and for the fills. "The drumming on 'Rain' stands out for me because I feel as though that was someone else playing—I was possessed!" he said. "'Rain' blows me away. It's out of left field. I know me and I know my playing, and then there's 'Rain.' I think it was the first time I used this trick of starting a break by hitting the hi-hat first instead of going directly to a drum off the hi-hat. But to me, the drums, I felt, had another quality. I've never played like that since, I don't feel."

But it was Ringo's lead vocal on another *Revolver* track, "Yellow Submarine," that provided him with one of his most memorable Beatles showcases. Paul McCartney said he wrote "Yellow Submarine" as a children's song while lying in bed in the attic of girlfriend Jane Asher's parents' house—though he knew, given the tenor of the times, that it might be taken as a nod to the burgeoning drug culture (given its psychedelic overtones).

"I was thinking of it as a song for Ringo, which it eventually turned out to be, so I wrote it as not too rangey in the vocal," he told author Barry Miles. "I just made up a little tune in my head, then started making a story, sort of an ancient mariner. . . . It's pretty much my song . . . written for Ringo in that little twilight moment."

McCartney also said that Ringo fluffed one of the words, turning "everyone of us has all *he* needs' into "everyone of us has all *we* need." "It's wrong but it's great," McCartney said. "We used to love that." Scottish-born rocker Donovan also contributed a few lines to the song ("Sky of blue/And sea of green"), which was underscored with a plethora of studio sound effects, including Lennon and McCartney talking through tin cans to create the "captain's orders" and Ringo yelling "Cut the cable! Drop the cable!" that he recorded outside the recording studio doors.

"Yellow Submarine" also included a thirty-second spoken intro from Ringo, which was underscored by the sound of marching feet. According to Beatles archivist Mark Lewisohn, "The theme of the lesson was the walk from Land's End to John O'Groats [the southernmost tip of England to the northernmost tip of Scotland]." The intro was eventually dropped from the finished track.

Ringo claimed the song "had no hidden meanings," and even took it one step further. "Many people have interpreted it to be a war song, that eventually all the world would be living in yellow submarines," he said. "That's not the case."

"Yellow Submarine" was released as a "Double-A-side" single in the UK, along with "Eleanor Rigby," and went to Number One on August 5, 1966. It remained in the top spot for four weeks and, later that year, won an Ivor Novello Award for the year's top-selling single in the UK. In the U.S., "Yellow Submarine" reached Number Two on the *Billboard Hot 100* chart. It was first Beatles hit to showcase Ringo on lead vocals.

The band, Ringo felt, was really starting to discover its potential in the studio, just the four of them playing, adding improved overdubbing (tricky because of the lack of extra tracks available) and the occasional cool special effect.

"I think the drugs were kicking in a little more heavily on this album. I don't think we were on anything major yet; just the old usual—the grass and the acid . . . we never did it to a great extent at the session. We were really hard workers. We worked like dogs to get it right."

The 1966 world tour kicked off with a return trip to Hamburg in June, and there was trouble from the very start.

The bad vibes, in fact, were sparked in March, when The Beatles gathered in a London studio to pose for a series of photos that were intended for the cover of their next U.S. album release, *Yesterday and Today*, and for the UK release of *Paperback Writer*.

Photographer Robert Whitaker dressed John, Paul, George, and Ringo in white butchers outfits and photographed them smiling and holding severed dolls (heads and other body parts), with butchered, bloody meat draped on their overalls. Once EMI chairman Sir Joseph Lockwood saw the photos he ordered the cover killed—forcing the record company to paper over the "Butcher Cover" with a photo of The Beatles posing in and around a steamer trunk. EMI also has to recall around 750,000 copies of the album, which were sent to Capitol Records in America.

Returning to Hamburg, where they'd started as nobodies six years earlier, had its drawbacks. The Beatles were now the world's most famous pop band, and everyone wanted a piece of them. With the fame came the "ghosts" who came out of the woodwork; people George Harrison likened to a "best friend" from one night years before.

But it only got worse once The Beatles traveled to Japan. They were greeted in Tokyo by right-wing nationalists, who thought that a rock band playing a concert in the city's Nippon Budokan arena was an insult to the country—and to the aura of the arena, which was built for martial arts competitions and was considered a shrine to the sport. It didn't go any further than some protests—the two Budokan shows went off without further incident, though the Japanese fans were somewhat subdued—but all four Beatles were keenly aware they weren't exactly welcomed with open arms.

It was a different, more sinister story once The Beatles reached the Philippines, which was under the rule of dictator Ferdinand Marcos. The group felt bullied from the moment they landed, which "was a very negative vibe from the moment we got off the plane, so we were a bit frightened," said George Harrison.

And it went downhill from there.

They were whisked off to their hotel by sullen, gun-toting policemen, barking orders and pushing them. It got worse when The Beatles declined an invitation to visit the Presidential Palace to meet First Lady Imelda Marcos and a group of Philippine children, which was an egregious snub to The Leader's wife and to her minions. John, Paul, George, and Ringo likely had no idea the visit was on their itinerary—they went where they were told to go and had little say in anything of that sort. It was also their scheduled day off, so they would've been pissed had Brian Epstein not declined the invitation on their behalf.

Ringo and John, who were sharing a room, woke up in the morning and ordered some breakfast, also requesting that day's newspapers. They puttered around for a while, then turned on the television—only to see Madame Marcos screaming about how The Beatles had let her down, the cameras focusing on little children's crying faces as if to emphasize the point.

The Beatles stayed in their hotel rooms the rest of the day, but the screaming newspaper headlines, including a story in the *Manila Times* accusing them of "snubbing the First Lady and the three Marcos children," set the tone for the rest of their short, tense visit. Their room-service food turned dodgy (sour milk, inedible rolls, foul-smelling meat) and Brian Epstein's public apology, which aired on television, was blacked out by Ferdinand Marcos.

The group's July 4th concert at Rizal Memorial Football Stadium went off largely without incident, but when they returned to the Hotel Manila they were greeted by a surly staff which refused to handle their luggage or lift a finger to help transport The Beatles to Manila International Airport. It was getting ugly—and physical.

The Beatles were rousted out of their beds and packed quickly. Ringo noticed that there was only one motorbike outside the hotel to escort them to the airport—quite a change from the impressive motorcade that had accompanied the band on the way in.

It was worse at the airport, where Philippine officials cut off power to the escalators and, suddenly, no one was around to help the world's most famous rock band with their luggage as they schlepped amps and suitcases to the gate. Nasty, shirt-sleeved policemen, brandishing pistols, were snapping orders at them—"Get over there! You treat like ordinary passenger!"—while, at the same time, a throng of Beatles fans were pushing and shoving to get up-close to their idols. It was chaos.

Ringo claimed that, once The Beatles arrived at the airport, people began spitting on them. He and John took refuge behind some nuns, figuring they'd be safe (who would beat up a nun?). Beatles chauffeur Alf Bicknell suffered a fractured rib, and burly roadie Mal Evans "was kicked in the ribs and tripped up but he staggered on across the tarmac towards the aircraft with blood streaming down one leg."

It didn't end once The Beatles and their entourage were safely on board the plane: Philippine officials hauled Evans and Beatles press officer Tony Barrow off the plane. They feared for their lives. Barrow was forced to pay an enormous tax bill before the plane was finally allowed to take off around forty-five minutes later.

The Beatles feared they would be put in jail. The country was a dictatorship and anything could happen. Once Mal Evans and Tony Barrow got back on the plane, the entourage got the hell out of there. It was Ringo's first and last time in Manila.

The experience in Manila left an extremely sour taste in everyone's mouth, and gave The Beatles yet one more reason to stop touring altogether. It wasn't fun anymore—it hadn't been, for quite some time—and with the technological innovations in recording, and their interest in experimenting in the studio, the allure of live shows just wasn't there anymore.

The band was having more fun in the studio and was starting to spend more time together there, producing more intricate sounds and songs. The pressures of touring seemed like a distant memory as The Beatles hunkered down in Abbey Road.

But they still had to get through the American leg of the tour.

After a pit stop in India, their first trip to that country (which left an indelible impression on George Harrison), The Beatles arrived in the States in mid-August, opening the tour with two shows at Chicago's International Amphitheatre. The previous March, during an interview with *Evening Standard* reporter and Beatles favorite Maureen Cleave, John Lennon had pronounced The Beatles "more popular than Jesus now" in trying to draw a parallel to the stagnation of Christianity and his band's influence on pop culture. "Christianity will go. It will vanish and shrink," he said. "I needn't argue about that; I'm right and I will be proved right. . . . I don't know which will go first—rock and roll or Christianity."

No one paid much attention to Lennon's comments when the article first appeared, but on July 29, right before The Beatles were set to arrive for their U.S. tour, a teen magazine called *Datebook* published a front-page article entitled "The Ten Adults You Dig/Hate The Most" (a picture of Paul McCartney graced the magazine's cover). The article included a section on Lennon and ran his "more popular than Jesus now" quote totally out of context.

The shit hit the fan, particularly in the South, where outraged fundamentalist Christian groups organized boycotts and exhorted their followers to burn Beatles albums and memorabilia. Many of them happily complied. The Ku Klux Klan came out in force, spewing (hooded) hatred toward The Beatles. Many Southern radio stations banned Beatles music, death threats were leveled at the group, and Brian Epstein was forced to issue a statement explaining Lennon's analogy: "What he said, and meant, was that he was astonished that in the last fifty years the Church in England, and therefore Christ, had suffered a decline in interest. He did not mean to boast about The Beatles' fame." It did not go unnoticed in the South that Epstein was Jewish.

That was followed by a tired-looking Lennon holding a press conference on August 11, before the tour kicked off in Chicago, to apologize and clarify his remarks. Ringo felt Lennon's remarks caused "a real mess" in America, whose public had twisted John's words or simply misunderstood what he was trying to say. Yes, Ringo admitted, The Beatles were "punks" who occasionally shot their mouths off. But this was just making a mountain out of a molehill, in his opinion.

Lennon's apology went a long way toward mollifying those who'd been angered by his original remarks, and the tour continued onward—but all four Beatles were nervous. For the first time, they'd been roundly criticized in a heretofore-safe haven. They took the death threats seriously. It was yet one more reason to stop touring.

Ringo admitted it was a scary time to be a Beatle and that John apologized not because of what he said, but because the band really did fear for their lives in a hostile environment.

During a show in Memphis, with the Ku Klux Klan burning Beatles records outside, someone set off a firecracker. Each Beatle thought the other had been shot. That's how bad it had become. In Cincinnati, a downpour caused The Beatles to cancel their show—a first—but they soldiered on and played a midday show at Crosley Field the next day, then turned right around, packed up their gear and flew to St. Louis to play their next scheduled thirty-minute concert that night at Busch Stadium.

They were still selling out in most venues, but the hysteria was now replaced by more orderly audiences. Young girls weren't screaming, shrieking, and fainting like before. Even the group's second visit to Shea Stadium, on August 23, lacked the electricity of their triumphant appearance the year before. It didn't even sell out, with an estimated eleven-thousand seats left unfilled.

The lure of the road, once so bright, had dimmed considerably. John, Paul, George, and Ringo each felt like caricatures, paraded out to the screaming masses who shrieked out of habit, ignoring the music. Ringo felt it was a waste of time, and he was unhappy with the way he was playing, going through the motions while trying to keep the semblance of a backbeat.

"The awful thing was, I used to go and cover the concerts, and you couldn't hear a bloody thing," said Ringo's friend, photographer Terry O'Neill. "People screamed and they only did twenty minutes, half an hour. You just couldn't hear them. They could be making every mistake in the book, but you'd never hear it."

The final stop on the tour was a concert at Candlestick Park in San Francisco on August 29. Privately, each band member felt this could be The Beatles' last live performance, at least for the foreseeable future. The live touring had to end. They all needed to rest, to spend some time with their families, recharge their batteries, and get back into the studio. That's where all the action was.

The feeling of finality was there, but nothing was decided until The Beatles returned to London. There was no formal announcement, no public proclamation that The Beatles would cease to perform live concerts—or what Lennon called "bloody tribal rites."

George Harrison remembered placing cameras on the amplifiers onstage at Candlestick Park and putting them on a timer. The group stopped between tunes, Ringo jumped down off his drum riser, and they faced the amps, taking pictures with their backs to the audience. They knew.

For Ringo, freedom from touring meant more time to spend at home—and more time trying to keep himself busy in-between dates in the recording studio. Unlike John, Paul, or George, he wasn't writing any music and wasn't working on other projects outside The Beatles universe. Ringo and George Harrison participated in *The Music of Lennon and McCartney* the previous fall, but they were more sidemen than stars of the Granada television special, which paid tribute to John and Paul's prolific output. (Ringo and George joined Lennon and McCartney on "Day Tripper" and "We Can Work It Out.")

Outside of The Beatles, McCartney spent part of 1966 writing the soundtrack for *The Family Way*, a big-screen movie starring Hayley Mills that was released in 1967. Lennon had inked a deal to co-star alongside Michael Crawford and Roy Kinnear in a movie comedy called *How I Won the War*, which began shooting in the fall of 1966 in England and on location in Spain, with *A Hard Day's Night* and *Help!* director Richard Lester once again behind the camera. Lennon, who'd taken to wearing the "granny glasses" with which he would be so identified, said he made the movie because "I didn't know what to do," but he used his down time on the set to begin writing a song with the working title "Strawberry Fields Forever."

Ringo used the time to indulge his love of photography. One of his favorite subjects was his year-old son, Zak, who was photographed eating, sleeping, and doing what babies do. The renovations at Sunny Heights, meanwhile, were spiraling, and ended up costing Ringo £90,000, nearly three times as much as he paid for the house (£37,000).

He admitted that buying the house was the "daftest" thing he'd ever done, but enjoyed the time off, acclimating himself to his new domestic life with Maureen and Zak, now a year old.

Running his Brickey Building Company wasn't going to take up much of Ringo's spare time; the company never got off the ground and eventually went bankrupt. "We built a lot of very good houses but nobody had the money to buy them," he said. "I didn't lose money when the firm closed, except that I was left with a dozen new flats and houses which stood empty for a long time."

Cynthia Lennon, who had to tiptoe around her moody, unpredictable husband, admired the domestic bliss that permeated Sunny Heights, how Maureen "would wait up until [Ringo] came home and serve him a wonderful roast dinner, even it if happened to be five in the morning." Maureen concurred:

"When he's recording I often stay up till four-thirty in the morning. He's usually got up late the day before and perhaps not had a proper meal before going out. So I try to have something for him when he comes home, however late. Then I know at least he's got a meal inside him. They all just peck at things when they're working."

Maureen still answered Ringo's fan mail, even thanking fans who sent Ringo birthday wishes and telling them their idol was just too busy to answer back himself. Once in a while, she would get Ringo to autograph a few photos. "I like answering the letters," she said. "I've been doing it for five years now. I get some lovely replies back from the parents. . . . I don't do it just because people are polite. I know that if I liked someone enough to write a nice letter to them I would like some sort of reply. I've had letters from fans saying this is their fifteenth letter. They must feel awful."

Even with the baby at home, Ringo and Maureen still enjoyed driving into London and going out to the clubs. They both loved to dance, and would often follow a night out on the town with stops at the Crazy Elephant or Dolly's. They counted Cilla Black and her husband, Bobby, as close friends; Elizabeth Taylor and Richard Burton were also pals, and often dropped in on Ringo and Maureen whenever they were in England.

The singer Lulu and Maurice Gibb, one-third of The Bee Gees, were neighbors and close friends. Gibb, in particular, became a trusted confidante; he and Ringo teamed for a series of very funny color home movies in which they played different characters, including Ringo as a king and Gibb as a fey prince, with little Zak and Ringo's pet collie wandering in and out of the frame (the movies are posted on YouTube). By early 1967, Maureen was pregnant again; the couple's second son, Jason Starkey, arrived on August 19, 1967.

But visitors to Sunny Heights around that time came away with the distinct impression that Ringo was uncomfortable in that environment since most of his neighbors (save for the Lennons) were successful businessmen—stockbrokers, investment bankers, and the like. No matter how much he adored the exterior of his rock-star public life, Ringo Starr was still Richy Starkey from the Dingle.

One particular friend of The Beatles around this time was Ray Connolly, a newspaper reporter for the *Liverpool Post*, then the *London Evening Standard*. Regarding Ringo, he observed:

> He didn't seem to have a lot of ego. He seemed to be grateful for what
> had happened to him. Quite happy with what happened to him. He

missed the Liverpool background, because where he lived was totally different. . . .

He was surrounded by rich people in nice houses with big gardens and all that, and he sort of missed the Liverpool community spirit. I remember he was talking at Sunny Heights about a friend of his [in Liverpool] having only ten or twelve albums or whatever and how much he loved them. And Ringo said, "I've got thousands [of albums] I don't play, because I have so many records, I don't play them all." But his friend only had a few albums, and played them all the time. I understood that. I thought, these are very honest things to come out with.

With time to kill before The Beatles entered the recording studio in late November—and perhaps missing his band mates more than he let on—Ringo, accompanied by Maureen, flew to Spain (Almeria) to keep John Lennon company on the set of *How I Won the War* (Neil Aspinall was already there). George Harrison had returned to India to study sitar with Ravi Shankar, and McCartney was busy working on the soundtrack to *The Family Way*. Ringo was the only Beatle not working on an outside project.

Lennon was feeling lonely on the set of the movie, and Ringo was there to lend him some support. Ringo and Maureen stayed with Lennon's co-star, Michael Crawford, in a succession of sketchy location houses with which there was always something wrong—and the hot weather didn't make it easier.

———————————————

The times were changing, and The Beatles, as usual, were at the vanguard of the movement. Gone were the "Beatle Boots" and the collarless jackets they'd made so popular two short years before. They were no longer the "Four Moptops from Liverpool," not with their hair and sideburns longer (and bushier) and each of them sprouting mustaches.

George Harrison grew his mustache during his six-week sojourn to India that fall, while McCartney attributed his new facial hair to covering up a split lip, the result of falling off a moped in Liverpool and smashing his face on the pavement. John Lennon complemented the re-grown hair on his head (shorn for *How I Won the War*) with a walrus mustache that, along with his ever-present granny glasses, became part of his "look."

Facial hair was nothing new to Ringo. He'd worn a beard (and longer hair and sideburns) during his time with Rory Storm, and might have continued to do so had The Beatles not entered his life. He hated shaving, anyway, so he decided to join the mustache brigade. After all, it "was just a part of being a hippy," he said. And it was "The Look" for cool cats, as 1966 turned into 1967, and bell-bottom pants, Nehru jackets, floppy hats, and flowery shirts—the more jarringly color-ful the better—became the norm for any rock star worth his weight in cool.

It was all part of the look of the times, what Ringo likened to going through a metamorphosis. John Lennon met Japanese performance artist Yoko Ono for the first time in November 1966 at a London art gallery, The Indica; he, too, would go through a "metamorphosis" of his own.

The cessation from touring also meant fewer media appearances for the group, since there was nothing to promote. The endless parade of inane press conferences was a thing of the past, too, as The Beatles retreated into their private lives and into the studio. They made only two television appearances in 1966—one on *Top of the Pops* and when accepting an award from *New Musical Express*; their lone small-screen appearance in 1967 was the historic *Our World* telecast beamed around the globe, on which they performed "All You Need Is Love."

The new album, which they started to record in the fall of 1966, didn't yet have a title, but Lennon, McCartney, and Harrison were all contributing songs. Lennon arrived at Abbey Road studios with "Strawberry Fields Forever," "Lucy in the Sky with Diamonds," and "A Day in the Life"; McCartney with "Penny Lane," "When I'm Sixty-Four," and "Fixing a Hole"; and Harrison with his East-ern-influenced, sitar-heavy "Within You Without You."

Ringo had not written anything for the new album—he wasn't expected too, really—and while he claimed at the time that he "loved" working on the new al-bum, he was starting to grow a bit uneasy with his role as the band's drummer.

John, Paul, and George, along with an enthusiastic George Martin, were experimenting in the studio with overdubs, sound effects, orchestral strings, Harrison's sitar and Tabla and even a Mellotron, an electronic keyboard which was used on "Strawberry Fields Forever." The days of banging out basic live tracks—lead guitar, rhythm guitar, bass, and drums—were in the past.

Ringo, for the most part, was called upon only when he was needed to lay down his drum part, usually after most of the components were finalized. His input wasn't required as the songs were taking shape and, more and more, it seemed like he was being exiled to play cards with Mal Evans while John, Paul, and George tinkered with their tracks.

"I never really liked *Sgt. Pepper*," he said, ten years after the fact. "I mean, I think it's a fine album. All the work we do is fine. But I think I felt like a session man on it. We put so much on it—strings and brass—and you'd sit around for days, you know, while they were overdubbing other things." Ringo did accrue one benefit from all the down time while working on the album: he learned how to play chess from Neil Aspinall. It was one more way to keep himself busy in the studio.

Hunter Davies interviewed John, Paul, George, and Ringo at length for his book, *The Beatles*. Published in 1968, it was the first comprehensive biography of the group. Davies, who spent time with them both at their homes and in the studio, described Ringo at the time as "restless and worried-looking," concerned about his future now that the band was no longer touring "and he knew that in the studio, especially with all the new synthesizer equipment then coming in, his drumming was not really as vital as it used to be."

Davies recalled how Paul McCartney "would take over the drums in the recording studio, to explain what was wanted." He wrote that Ringo "couldn't see what else there was for him to do," besides a possible future acting career.

But Ringo's band mates didn't completely exclude him from taking a role in what they were now calling *Sgt. Pepper's Lonely Hearts Club Band.* McCartney envisioned the album as a "concept" vehicle in which all four Beatles would adopt alter-egos as part of the LP's mythical titular foursome. Ringo was transformed into "the one and only Billy Shears," and was given his lone lead vocal on the album in a tune written by Lennon and McCartney called "With a Little Help from My Friends."

The song, which may or may not have been about drugs (the so-called "friends") was prominently featured as the album's second song on Side One, and Ringo sang it with gusto in his flat, nasally baritone, with his band mates gathered around him, mere "inches behind the microphone, silently conducting and cheering him on as he gamely tackled his vocal duties."

McCartney originally wrote the line, "Would you stand up and walk out on me?" as "Would you stand up and throw tomatoes at me?" But Ringo balked at the line, and for good reason. The memories of being pelted with jelly beans on stage were still fresh in his mind; there was no way he was going to be bombarded with tomatoes when singing those words.

"With a Little Help from My Friends," recorded in late March 1967, was a perfect vehicle for Ringo and his vulnerable, unassuming persona; McCartney said he and Lennon had Ringo in mind from the very beginning, when they were calling the tune "Bad Finger Boogie." As Paul explained, "Ringo's got a great sentimental thing. He likes soul music and always has, though we didn't see that scene for a long while 'til he showed us. I suppose that's why we write these sorts of songs for him, with sentimental things in them, like 'With a Little Help from My Friends.'"

McCartney told biographer Barry Miles that he and Lennon wrote "With a Little Help from My Friends" at Lennon's house in Weybridge, and that Ringo was "to be a character in this operetta, this whole thing we were doing, so this gave him a good intro, where he came in the album. . . . It was a nice place for him. . . . Again, because it was the pot era, we had to slip in a little reference: 'I get high!' It was a challenge, it was something out of the ordinary for us because we actually had to write in a key for Ringo and you had to be a little tongue-in-cheek."

Ringo always hated "flashy" drumming, but he came through with flying colors on the album's closing song, "A Day in the Life," with innovative fills and a sound which Abbey Road engineer Geoff Emerick achieved by removing the bottom heads of Ringo's tom-toms, miking them from underneath and wrapping a microphone in a towel and placing it in a glass jug to record Ringo's floor tom.

The album's "concept" idea was eventually abandoned, save for several thematically linked songs and its famous cover, designed by Peter Blake—in which John, Paul, George, and Ringo (and their mustaches) posed in full military-style regalia as Sgt. Pepper's Lonely Hearts Club Band.

Despite his worldwide fame and his immense wealth, Ringo never forgot where he came from, and though he'd spent a small fortune purchasing and renovating Sunny Heights, he still lavished his generosity on Elsie and his "stepladder," Harry. He was very close to and protective of them both, even while trying to balance some semblance of a home life: Maureen, infant Zak, and another baby on the way.

And, unlike John Lennon—who had to deal with the re-emergence of his father, Freddie Lennon, once The Beatles became famous—Ringo didn't have to worry about the man who'd abandoned his family years before.

Richard Starkey, to his credit, never bothered Ringo nor did he lay any claim to his famous son; when asked, occasionally, if they were related—the father/son facial resemblance was strong, particularly their noses—he'd claim to be Ringo's "uncle." Richard Starkey was proud of his son, but kept his distance, preferring instead to keep a running scrapbook of clippings about Ringo and The Beatles. Apparently, he had no regrets regarding his lack of a relationship with his son—he never made any serious attempts to foster any paternalism and made it a point never to contact Ringo or Elsie. But he was sorry that *his* father, Grandfather Starkey, didn't live to see all that "Little Richy," his favorite, had accomplished.

Starkey Sr. was remarried but had no other children, and while he didn't readily admit to being Ringo Starr's dad, it bothered him when newspapers and magazines referred to Harry Graves as "Ringo's father." As noted Beatles author Hunter Davies wrote, "He would like to correct it, but on the other hand he doesn't want the press to find out who he is and where he lives. He has no wish to get involved in Ringo's fame."

Ringo was generous to his parents, and insisted on helping Elsie and Harry financially, though they didn't really need the money. Harry was only fifty-one in 1965 when he retired from the Liverpool Corporation, but he did so only because Ringo urged him to stop working.

"I could have gone on another fourteen years if I'd wanted to," Harry said. "The Corporation was very good. They were almost as proud of the boys as I am. I had to take jokes, of course, '*You* don't have to queue up for your wages, do you!' That sort of thing. Richy was at me for a long time to retire, but I didn't think I should. Then one day one of his mates saw me up a forty-foot ladder in the snow painting a council house, and he forced me to give it up. It's funny, after all these years, not wanting for money," he said. "After all the years of pushing along. We still go second-class on trains. You get just as good a seat."

Elsie and Harry were the only "Beatle parents" still living in Liverpool, but they missed Admiral Grove, despite all the hassles that went along with it. Hunter Davies described them as "the most stunned" by Ringo's success, "caught like rabbits in the searchlight of fame" and feeling "completely isolated" in the Woolton bungalow, missing the chumminess of their neighbors in the Dingle (who never begrudged them Ringo's success). They were on their guard when giving interviews, and only a phone call from Ringo, assuring them it was okay to talk to Davies for his book, helped them to relax and open up a bit.

Inside their house—the interior was furnished by and paid for entirely by Ringo—the walls were adorned with mementos of The Beatles, including three gold records and two silver records. "I will say this, he's never got big-headed," Elsie noted admirably. "He's never changed his life. Maureen's very quiet, very natural."

She did, though, worry about the toll that Ringo's fame was taking on her only child. "It's still very difficult for the boys. . . . I've seen Richy sit here till it's dark because he's scared to go out in the light. Not being able to go out in the light. Isn't it terrible! But you can't have everything, can you?"

Harry, for his part, let his wife do most of the talking, but occasionally offered up an opinion. "I think I preferred their earlier music. The rock and roll stuff. But they've got to change, haven't they? You've got to in this business. You've got to listen to their tunes properly now, more than once." He sent some songs he'd written to "Richy," who sent them back, since "he only plays one instrument, so he couldn't do any music."

Ringo visited Elsie and Harry when he could and spent nearly every Christmas with them in Liverpool. His parents were frequent visitors to Sunny Heights, giving Maureen a breather from the baby. It also allowed them to dote on their grandson.

When they were at home, Elsie and Harry spent most of their evenings watching television, playing Bingo, and going to dinner dances. Often they were asked for their autographs once people found out who they were. Their "fame," such as it was, was not limited to Liverpool; Harry recalled visiting his family in Romford, and having to sign "about three hundred autographs" when he accompanied a nephew to a school concert. Beatlemania, it seemed, extended to anyone in the group's orbit.

"It's all out of this world, isn't it?" Elsie said. "There's not much more that they can do. They've done everything. The last five years has been like a fairy story. But I still worry about him, about his health, after all he went through."

Ringo's physical health was fine and money wasn't an issue. Due to The Beatles' tangled financial web, and the fact that he never touched hard currency, even *he* didn't know his net worth: "If I said give us my money tomorrow I want it in me hand, I would have no idea what it would come to," he said.

He wasn't earning the enormous royalties paid to the band's songwriters— John Lennon, Paul McCartney, and, to a lesser extent, George Harrison— though he reportedly did receive a small percentage of the profits generated by Lennon and McCartney's publishing company, Northern Songs, Ltd. As it was, the British government took a whopping 90 percent of his income. Ringo was never very political, but he was outspoken about the high taxation rate and would eventually become a tax exile, explaining that "All governments are the same." The Beatles tried to alleviate their tax concerns with a weird scheme pitched to Brian Epstein: hire someone to live in the Bahamas and hold their money for them there, so it couldn't be taxed. Naturally it didn't work; in the end, all the money was brought back, and The Beatles had to pay the taxes—plus the person who'd moved to the Bahamas for them.

Ringo rarely walked around with money in his pockets; if he signed a bill, it was sent back to the group's accountant, who, in turn, sent it back to Ringo for verification. If Maureen went shopping, she "just uses a card which says this is money," he noted. He had a checkbook for emergencies but never used it; he claimed he didn't know how and, besides, he'd lost the checkbook almost as soon as it was given to him.

He once borrowed Peter Brown's car so he could drive Maureen home from Brian Epstein's house. They ran out of gas in the middle of nowhere, and Ringo managed to flag down a car and ask the driver for "five bob" so he could buy gas for the ride home. The driver of the car said he'd take Ringo and Maureen back to Sunny Heights, since it was a Sunday night and no gas stations were open. They could retrieve Brown's car the next day. The driver turned out to be a reporter for the *Daily Telegraph*, but he kept his mouth shut about the embarrassing story after Ringo invited him in to the house and gave him a signed album.

Maureen, like her husband—whom she always called Richy—lacked pretense, and was well-aware of how lucky she was to be enjoying such fabulous wealth. She never forgot her humble roots in Liverpool and didn't take the riches for granted, running a relatively tight ship at home. She did the family's food shopping at a supermarket in Weybridge, near Sunny Heights, and always got trading stamps with every purchase. She didn't intend to use them, but enjoyed collecting them and sticking them in her book.

She bought "cheap remnants" if she was going to make a dress for herself, which she did quite often, and liked to "mess around" the house, rearranging the furniture, making her own curtains and, on one occasion, putting sequins on an old lampshade.

Their marriage, at least in those early days, was typical of their generation, particularly for two people who'd grown up as only children in Liverpool. Ringo was the dominant force and Maureen was docile, although she could keep her husband in line when necessary. It worked for both of them in the mid-1960s, with the Women's Liberation movement still a few years off.

Hunter Davies noted that Ringo and John Lennon, both of whom he knew very well, had "a bit of Andy Capp in them." (Andy Capp was a cockney comic-strip character who regularly came home drunk and beat his wife.) Ringo readily admitted that he was the master of his domestic domain: "That's how it is. My grandfather [Starkey] always had his seat in the house, which only he sat in. I'm the same, I suppose.

"I don't think women like to be equal," Ringo said when asked about his marriage. "They like to be protected and in turn they like looking after men. That's how it is." During a 1966 interview with *Evening Standard* reporter Maureen Cleave, who was visiting Sunny Heights for a "Ringo at home"–type feature, he went one step further, noting of Maureen, who was then still only twenty: "I own her, of course. When I married her, her parents signed her over to me. That just knocked me out; she's still a minor, you see. When you're married it's not like when you're courting, as they say. You both become different people because you get to know each other so well. She can shout at me without opening her mouth—that's being married."

Now that The Beatles weren't touring anymore, there was a lot more down time, meaning more time for Ringo to reflect on how far he'd come in the five years since joining the band. He was The World's Most Famous Drummer and was known universally by his first name—a pop-culture phenomenon shared by a rarefied group with Ringo in the company of Elvis and Marilyn and Frank.

But fame was a double-edged sword, and he wasn't emotionally immune to the barbs tossed in his direction by people who considered him "The Lucky One," the last Beatle to jump on the gravy train as it pulled out of the station, transporting the group on their remarkable journey as a cultural force whose creative engine was stoked by the talents of John Lennon and Paul McCartney. George Harrison? He was "The Quiet Beatle," the kid who was overshadowed by Lennon and McCartney but was slowly coming to the fore as his songwriting skills blossomed with each album release.

But Ringo? Justifying his contributions to The Beatles was growing more difficult, no matter how often his band mates—his "brothers," as he liked to call them—emphasized how vital a component he was to the group's core DNA. And if the press and the public weren't making fun of Ringo for his large nose, there was sniggering about his creative contributions to the band—or lack thereof. He never wavered in believing he was a skilled drummer, but he was acutely aware of the public's perception of him.

"If all four of us had to stand up there in front of millions of fans and they had to line up behind the one they liked best, I think Paul would get the most," he said once. "John and George would be joint second. Ringo would be last. That's what I think. You can tell, from the letters and the fans screaming and mobbing."

To his credit, though, he never backed down when questioned about his lack of songwriting skills. He knew his limitations and accepted them—to a degree. It didn't help that he was constantly being called on the carpet, especially by journalists who questioned him about why he didn't contribute more to The Beatles canon, notwithstanding his drumming and the occasional vocal on a song written by someone else.

In revealing comments he made to Hunter Davies, Ringo put it all out there for everyone to see: Yes, he was bothered that he couldn't write a decent song. Yes, he was bothered by his inability to play another instrument besides the drums. And, yes, it even bothered him that he was often credited for drum fills he was instructed to play, usually by Lennon or McCartney. (George Harrison appears, for the most part, to have left the drumming on his songs to Ringo's discretion.) Even in *that* regard he was doing someone else's creative bidding. He told Davies:

> I'm not the creative one. I know that. But people expect I must want to be. They write and say why don't you try. I did try a couple of years ago to write two little songs, but they were such pinches, without me really realizing it. . . .
>
> It can get you down, not being creative. You know people are thinking you're not the creative one. But out of four people, you wouldn't expect them all to be creative, would you? Fifty percent is enough. Think of all the groups, good groups, who can't write anything at all. [I'd] love to be able to, of course. It's a bit of a bind when I realize I can't. I've got a piano, but I can't play it, really. I often get a feeling. I just feel like writing a lovely song today, but I go and I can't, I don't know how to. I can knock out things in C, as long as it's a twelve-bar. That's a musical joke. It means nothing.
>
> I do sometimes feel out of it, sitting there on the drums, only playing what they tell me to play. Often when other drummers of groups say to me that was great, that bit, I know the others have usually told me what to do, though I've got the credit.

Several years earlier, around the time of the *Rubber Soul* album, Ringo had described in glowing terms the excitement of working in the studio, of rehearsing and completing songs and describing how Lennon, McCartney, and Harrison would play their new tunes for him on an acoustic guitar or a piano. But if studio-heavy albums were The Beatles' future path, would there be room on the creative journey for their loyal drummer?

"People were comfortable with him, they felt secure with him as a person," said Peter Brown. "I mean, if you went into a crowded room, and he wasn't Ringo Starr, you wouldn't necessarily seek him out, but if you had time on your own with him, you would start to realize that there is something here which is rather nice and comfortable. Not a great intellect, but a very nice person who knows a few things."

In 1967, The Beatles, who were now in the forefront of pop-culture, played a starring role in "The Summer of Love." The *Sgt. Pepper's Lonely Hearts Club Band* album was released worldwide, simultaneously, on June 1 and was immediately hailed for its sonic innovations and exquisite songwriting. It entered the UK album charts at Number One—holding that position for twenty-two weeks and reportedly selling 250,000 copies in seven days. It went to Number One in the U.S. a month later, on July 1, and spent fifteen weeks in the top spot.

The *New York Times* called the album "a new and golden Renaissance of song; *Newsweek* critic Jack Kroll compared the lyrics of "A Day in the Life" to T. S. Eliot's "The Waste Land."

In late June, John, Paul, George, and Ringo were asked to spearhead the UK segment of *Our World*, the first-ever live global satellite telecast representing fourteen nations, with appearances from opera singer Maria Callas and artist Pablo Picasso, among others. The black-and-white telecast was beamed to thirty-one countries and was seen by an audience estimated somewhere between four-hundred-million to seven-hundred-million people.

The broadcast was intended to present an alternative to the problems then plaguing the world: the Vietnam War was raging in Southeast Asia, U.S. cities including Detroit and Los Angeles were ablaze with race riots, and Israel had triumphed two weeks before in its "Six-Day War" with Egypt, Jordan, and Syria. (The Soviet Union reportedly pulled out of the telecast to protest Western support of Israel.)

The Beatles were, perhaps, the only music act big enough (and audacious enough) to pull it off, to command a worldwide audience of that size. And it was all for peace and love—two words that would become important to Ringo further down the road.

The Beatles, dressed in their finest Flower Power clothes, performed a new song, "All You Need Is Love," written by John Lennon. EMI's biggest studio, No. 1, which was used for the telecast, was festooned with colorful balloons;

seated on the floor were celebrity pals including Keith Moon, Eric Clapton, Mick Jagger and Brian Jones from The Rolling Stones, Marianne Faithfull, Jane Asher, Hunter Davies, and Graham Nash, all of whom joined in singing the chorus on "All You Need Is Love." Ringo wore a "bloody heavy" beaded suit designed for him by Simon Posthuma and Marijke Koger from a psychedelic Dutch band called The Fool.

Except for a drum roll to introduce "All You Need Is Love," Ringo was the only Beatle not to play live in the studio that day, for the sole reason that the sound of his drums would have drowned out the live orchestra; his drum track, recorded at Olympic Studios along with the backing vocals, could be modulated during the four minutes Lennon, McCartney, and Harrison were playing live.

Ringo's live drum roll, along with part of Harrison's guitar solo and a snippet of Lennon's lead vocal, was tweaked in the studio after the telecast. "All You Need Is Love," backed with "Baby, You're a Rich Man," was released as a single in the UK on July 7 and shot straight to Number One, where it remained for three weeks. It was released ten days later in the U.S. and spent one week at the top of the charts.

The good vibes were shattered on August 27 with word that Brian Epstein was found dead, his body discovered in his Chapel Street house after he'd failed to answer repeated knocks on his bedroom door. He was thirty-two. Epstein's death was later ruled an accidental overdose of the sleeping pill Carbitral, which he'd been taking for some time to help with his insomnia.

Just four days before, on August 23, Epstein visited The Beatles in Chappell Recording Studios in Central London, where they relocated for several days (the EMI studios on Abbey Road were booked). The group was working on a Paul McCartney track called "Your Mother Should Know," which ended up on the *Magical Mystery Tour* album. Epstein "came in to hear the playbacks looking extremely down and in a bad mood," Chappell engineer John Timperley told Beatles historian Mark Lewisohn. "He just stood at the back of the room listening, not saying much."

The Beatles learned of Epstein's death while in North Wales with the Maharishi. John, Paul, and George (but not Ringo) had seen the Maharishi Mahesh Yogi speak at the Hilton Hotel in London on August 24, and afterward were invited to his "summer conference" in Bangor, set to get underway several days later. The trip, which began on August 25, was organized by George Harrison, who was immersing himself in Eastern culture and philosophy and persuaded the others to join him. Ringo was hesitant to go, since Maureen had just given birth to Jason.

"I rang Maureen in hospital," Ringo said. "She said I had to go. I couldn't miss this." When he got home, there was a message from John: they were going to Wales and Ringo had to join them. Then a message from George: they'd seen the Maharishi. He was great. Ringo needed to be with them when they left for Wales on Saturday.

The Beatles joined the Maharishi on the train ride to Bangor accompanied by George's wife, Pattie, her sister, Jennie Boyd, Mick Jagger, and Marianne Faithfull. Jennie Boyd had just moved back to England from San Francisco; George and Pattie had visited her there earlier that month. Cynthia Lennon was supposed to accompany John on the trip, but the train pulled out of Euston Station in London, leaving her behind. She never joined up with everyone else, which, according to Paul McCartney, was the moment her marriage to John Lennon ended.

The Maharishi claimed not to have any clue as to who The Beatles were; if that was really the case (which is doubtful), he quickly found out when their train pulled into Bangor and was greeted by a horde of shrieking Beatles fans. As Ringo described the scene, "They ran right past him and were looking in our faces, and I think he realized that these boys could get his message across real fast." The Maharishi, according to Ringo, broached the idea of The Beatles accompanying him on a worldwide tour. They politely declined.

It was in Bangor that John, Paul, George, and Ringo heard about Brian Epstein when Peter Brown called from Chapel Street and broke the shocking news to McCartney. The group was stunned; Ringo said he didn't know how to process the information, especially in the midst of all the hope and flowers in Bangor. So they headed home.

As the last Beatle to join the group, Ringo didn't share the same history with Epstein as did his band mates, but he'd known Brian for five years now and loved him dearly. "He was a generous man," he said. "We owe so much to him. We have come a long way with Brian along the same road."

When The Beatles returned to the studio in early September, they were still reeling. Ringo "appeared close to tears." Lennon seemed "to be in a state of shock." George Harrison "seemed shaken but offered words of comfort" while McCartney "seemed the most composed."

None of The Beatles attended Epstein's funeral on August 29, knowing their presence would only turn the solemn occasion into a circus and upset Epstein's grieving family, which was dealing with their second tragedy within a month (Harry Epstein, Brian's father, had died in July in Liverpool at the age of sixty-three). All four Beatles did attend a memorial service for Epstein in October at the New London Synagogue, not far from the EMI studios. Still, according to Peter Brown, once the "shock" of Epstein's death had worn off they "made foolish jokes about him."

Ringo was "so gutted" by Epstein's death that the night before the funeral he asked Cilla Black (who was also managed by Brian) to join him in a séance in an attempt to contact his spirit. "In the end, the Maharishi told Ringo not to hold on to Brian—to love him but let him go, because we were all powerful forces who could halt him on his natural progression to heaven," Black wrote. "The message helped all of us."

Everything changed for The Beatles the moment they learned about Brian Epstein's death. Nothing was ever the same again. It was true that the gulf between the band and their manager had been widening since The Beatles stopped touring and devoted themselves to studio work, but they still considered Brian a father figure of sorts, a mentor who believed in them from the very beginning and charted their course to worldwide fame and fortune. Epstein's five-year contract with the band was set to expire that October, and it was believed by everyone that it would be renewed.

Still, there was no getting over the feeling that, without Epstein, they were rudderless.

Although Epstein's role with the band had changed—especially after The Beatles stopped touring—each of them still felt close to their manager, as close as they'd been to him in the "early days," according to Ringo.

To George Harrison, Brian "was at a bit of a loss" since the band stopped touring, while Lennon, as was his wont, was brutally succinct: "We collapsed. I knew that we were in trouble then. . . . I thought, 'We've fuckin' had it!'"

In the meantime, Epstein's brother, Clive, became the de facto manager of The Beatles after inheriting NEMS, Brian's management company. But he was far more interested in running his Liverpool furniture store than in managing The World's Most Famous Band.

Several other industry types came sniffing around the band, including Robert Stigwood. Unbeknownst to The Beatles, Brian had given Stigwood the option to acquire 51 percent of NEMS. But it all came to naught. The Beatles quickly bought their way out of the deal and heard that Allen Klein had expressed an interest in the group. They ignored him.

No one could replace Brian Epstein. John, Paul, George, and Ringo were on their own.

Changes were afoot.

11

"SOMETIMES I FEEL I'D LIKE TO STOP BEING FAMOUS"

Filming on *Magical Mystery Tour* began two weeks after Brian Epstein's funeral. The project was largely conceived by Paul McCartney, with smaller contributions from Lennon, Harrison, and Starr. It was a way for The Beatles to be seen by their fans, now that they were no longer playing live. The hour-long film, which reportedly cost the band £40,000 of their own money, aired on BBC1 on December 26, 1967—Boxing Day in the UK.

There was a sense of unease from the very start of filming, since McCartney et al. didn't have much of a plot, and no real script, on which to hang *Magical Mystery Tour*. Brian was no longer around to organize the project into a cohesive plan of attack, and The Beatles were left to their own devices—a case of the lunatics running the asylum.

The movie's premise played off the popular British "mystery tours," in which a group of thirty or forty people would travel by bus to an unknown destination—finding the fun in guessing where they would end up. As in *A Hard Day's Night* and, more significantly in *Help!*, Ringo was front and center in *Magical Mystery Tour*.

Its flimsy plot was built around "Mr. Richard Starkey" (Ringo) and his Aunt Jessie (Jessie Robins), recently widowed, embarking on a "mystery tour" of the English countryside, along with a busload of about forty other passengers. (McCartney, Lennon, and Harrison were along for the ride, of course, as was Beatles pal Victor Spinetti and Viv Stanshall of The Bonzo Dog Band.)

The movie is a mishmash of improvised scenes and dialogue with no coherent center, and Ringo and Aunt Jessie spend most of their time bickering. Ringo explained that Paul's directing, such as it was, consisted of a blank piece of paper with a circle drawn on it—and trying to get from one point to another, improvising as they went along.

How disorganized was the project? After filming in Brighton, Paul, John, George, and Ringo discovered they were thirty lunches short of feeding the cast and crew; on the first night of filming on the road, McCartney and Neil Aspinall "spent hours" breaking up fights between the fat ladies and little people in the cast, who refused to share rooms.

The Beatles spent two weeks filming *Magical Mystery Tour* with no concrete idea as to what they were accomplishing (or what they *thought* they were accomplishing). "They'd blithely expected to do a week in the studios at Shepperton after Devon, thinking you could just turn up," wrote Hunter Davies. "Instead they had to use an airfield in Kent."

That was followed by eleven more weeks trying to edit what they'd shot into something resembling a movie. As Tony Bramwell described it, "Paul would come in and edit in the morning. Then John would come in, in the afternoon, and re-edit what Paul had edited. Then Ringo would come in . . ." Ringo, who was credited as "Director of Photography Richard Starkey, M. B. E.," even had a giant drum kit built for a scene in the movie. "This is what happens when you don't really think it out," he said.

In one of the scenes in *Magical Mystery Tour,* filmed outside Sunny Heights, Ringo projected slide images onto George Harrison's face. The scene was underscored by Harrison's song, "Blue Jay Way." Ringo later admitted, "I didn't photograph all of it. But I had all the crazy lenses, all the prism lenses, and I was making slides. So I knew that stuff."

Magical Mystery Tour received a critical drubbing from the British press when it finally aired to an audience of fifteen million viewers in December. The movie was shown in black and white, since color wasn't yet available on BBC1; it aired in color ten days later on BBC2, but there were so few color television sets in Britain at the time that it didn't make much of a difference.

"It didn't do very well in England because the first time the BBC showed it, they showed it in black and white," Ringo said. "By then we participated in some sort of mind medication and color was important."

The *Daily Express* television critic called the movie "blatant rubbish" and "tasteless nonsense" and his sentiments were widely echoed elsewhere. "Whoever authorized the showing of the film on BBC1 should be condemned to a year squatting at the feet of the Maharishi Mahesh Yogi," sniffed the *Daily Sketch* critic.

In the U.S., *Daily Variety*'s snappy headline screamed, "Critics and Viewers Boo: Beatles Produce First Flop with Yule Film." The Fab Four, so accustomed to everything they touched turning to gold, were taken to task by the media and their public.

On a more positive note, the movie's soundtrack album, also called *Magical*

Mystery Tour, was released in the UK on December 8 and contained several Beatles classics, including "Fool on the Hill," "Your Mother Should Know," and "I Am the Walrus"; on its B-side were the singles "Strawberry Fields Forever," "Penny Lane," "Hello, Goodbye"—which went to Number One in the UK and in America—"Baby, You're a Rich Man," and "All You Need Is Love."

Shortly after *Magical Mystery Tour* aired in Britain, Ringo boarded a flight for Rome to film a small role as a horny Mexican gardener named Emmanuel in *Candy*, a big-screen adaptation of the 1958 Terry Southern/Mason Hoffenberg novel, scandalous for its time, about a naïve eighteen-year-old stunner who finds herself in a mélange of farcical sexual situations.

Buck Henry, who co-created the hit mid-'60s NBC sitcom *Get Smart*, wrote the screenplay for *Candy*, with Christian Marquand directing an all-star cast, including Marlon Brando, Raquel Welch, Ringo's pal Richard Burton, and Charles Aznavour. Seventeen-year-old Ewa Aulin, a former Miss Teen Sweden, played the titular role.

For Ringo, who loved the process of moviemaking and was a natural in front of the camera, the role was a welcome break from life as a Beatle, and a chance to unwind after the loss of Brian Epstein and the disappointment of *Magical Mystery Tour*. It was also a chance to prove he could do more than provide a steady backbeat for The Beatles, and to build upon the cinematic promise he'd shown in *A Hard Day's Night* and *Help!*

A year before, Ringo had visited John Lennon on the set of *How I Won the War* in Spain; now, like Lennon, he was venturing outside the constricting Beatles inner circle to dip his toe into uncharted waters. It felt good.

"I'd read the book . . .and I thought, 'You're joking. How can they make that into a film?'" Ringo said. "'Randy' isn't the word for it. No wonder it's been banned! It was the mind-blowing thrill of my life. I was filming with Marlon Brando, Richard Burton, Walter Matthau and those guys. Wow!"

A *Life* magazine article chronicling life on the set of *Candy* provided a snapshot of Ringo:

> Ringo Starr waits nervously in his hotel room, meditating per instructions from the Maharishi Mahesh Yogi.
>
> What parts were you offered? [the reporter asked.]
>
> "They didn't offer me a choice. They only asked me to play the lust-mad Mexican gardener. But I end up on the pool table with the girl."

Would you have preferred another role?

"Yes, the hunchback."

Why?

"It must be nice rubbing your hunch against a tree and swearing."

Ringo didn't have much screen time in the movie; his only scene lasts about three-and-a-half minutes. Wearing a droopy mustache, and doing his best (read: pretty bad) Mexican accent, Emmanuel is invited indoors by Candy and instructed to bring an ironing board down to the basement, where he and Candy do the nasty on a pool table while being watched by an eccentric poet, MacPhisto (Burton), who goads them on as he makes love to a blowup doll. Emmanuel climaxes with a triumphant "¡Viva Zapata!" Oh, and legendary boxing champ Sugar Ray Robinson is also there in the basement, mixing drinks. It's that kind of movie.

While filming, Ringo spent his down time on Richard Burton's yacht. Burton's wife, Elizabeth Taylor, was also there—Ringo already knew her from their nights of partying in London—and Burton delighted Ringo during a break in filming by reading the lyrics to John Lennon's "I Am the Walrus" in "that voice of his." (Peter Sellers, another of Ringo's celebrity friends, had recorded comic versions of "A Hard Day's Night" and "She Loves You," the former as Laurence Olivier-doing-Richard III; the latter in his best *Dr. Strangelove* voice.)

When *Candy* premiered in December of 1968 it angered and mystified the critics almost as much as had *Magical Mystery Tour* the year before. *New York Times* critic Renata Adler opined that "the movie, directed by Christian Marquand, manages to compromise, by its relentless, crawling, bloody lack of talent, almost anyone who had anything to do with it. Richard Burton, as a poet-seducer, gives a firm, delighted, irrefutable demonstration of his lack of any comic talent whatsoever. John Huston and Ringo Starr look as though they had been drawn in by a regrettable, humorless beautiful people syndrome."

The New Yorker's Pauline Kael called the movie an "incomprehensible mess. *Candy* keeps getting worse than seems possible."

Roger Ebert, writing in the *Chicago Sun-Times*, was more sympathetic, calling the movie "a lot better than you might expect. . . . When you look at the cast—Burton, Brando, Ringo, Matthau, Coburn and everybody—you dread it'll turn out to be another *Casino Royale* (1967) with lots of names mugging the camera and then disappearing into the void. That doesn't happen, except with Ringo, who didn't get much of a role."

After wrapping his small role in *Candy*, Ringo flew back to England to prepare for what promised to be an interesting trip to India in February. The Beatles had unfinished business with the Maharishi after their trip to Bangor the previous August was cut short by Brian Epstein's death. A planned October visit to the Maharishi's "learning center" in India was postponed because The Beatles were too busy working on *Magical Mystery Tour.*

But John, Paul, George, and Ringo had cleared their schedules for mid-February 1968 and were intent on trekking to the Himalayan foothills to cleanse their minds, bodies, and souls, contemplating the meaning of life at the feet of the Maharishi. The Maharishi, who was now billing himself as "The Beatles' Guru," would enlighten them in the ways of Transcendental Meditation at his International Center for Meditation, a fourteen-acre compound surrounded by lush jungle and located in the mountains across the River Ganges near Rishikesh.

The Beatles wouldn't be alone in their quest for enlightenment: Welsh rocker Donovan, actress Mia Farrow and her sister Prudence, Mike Love from The Beach Boys, journalist Louis Lapham, Mal Evans, Neil Aspinall, and a retinue of reporters and photographers joined the traveling circus. And that was on top of dozens of other non-celebrities who had paid a pretty penny to attend the three-month retreat.

Ringo and Maureen left Zak and Jason with the nanny and made the arduous trek to India with Paul McCartney and his girlfriend, Jane Asher, arriving on February 19. John and Cynthia Lennon were already there, as were George and Pattie Harrison. (Yoko Ono, with whom Lennon was involved by that time, was conspicuously absent—although Lennon said later he thought about bringing her along.)

Ringo and Maureen had problems in India from the get-go. When the group arrived in Delhi, Ringo felt some pain in his arm, and thought he was having a bad reaction to an inoculation he'd received prior to the trip. He pleaded with Beatles roadie Mal Evans to take him to a doctor. Evans, who kept a diary dating back to his early years with The Beatles, took note of Ringo's condition:

"Mal, my arm's killing me, please take me to a doctor right away." So off we go looking for one, our driver leaving us to a dead end in the middle of a field, soon to be filled with press cars as they blindly follow us; so we explain to them that it's only Ringo's inoculation giving him trouble. When we arrived at the local hospital, I tried to get immediate treatment for him, to be told curtly by the Indian doctor,

"He is not a special case and will have to wait his turn." So off we go to pay a private doctor ten rupees for the privilege of hearing him say it will be all right.

The situation didn't improve much once the group reached the Maharishi's compound. Ringo had a notoriously bad stomach—he hated spices, particularly garlic and onions—and arrived with one of his suitcases filled only with cans of baked beans. Maureen, meanwhile, had a deathly fear of insects, of "moths and flying things," which didn't bode well, since the jungle compound was infested with bugs. Ringo remembered having to "fight off" the scorpions and tarantulas in the bathroom, making a lot of noise to get them to scurry away. By the time his bathing was completed and he left the room, the insects had returned.

To make matters worse, the group ate breakfast outside, and monkeys would swoop down from the trees and grab the bread off the table.

Ringo and Maureen tried to be good sports about the excursion—along with the rest of the group, they wore traditional Indian garb, meditated, and joined in the endless discussions—but after two weeks of bug infestations, dodgy food, and stolen bread, they'd had enough. They missed the kids and wanted to go home.

"Suddenly . . . excitement," Mal Evans noted in his diary. "Ringo wants to leave . . . Maureen can't stand the flies any longer." Paul McCartney corroborated Evans' assertion, noting how Maureen seemed to know the exact location of a fly in the room—and how she refused to leave a room when there was a fly perched over the door. Rishikesh was not the place for The Beatles drummer or his wife.

Ringo and Maureen left for London on March 1 after only ten days in the Himalayas. McCartney and Jane Asher followed them several weeks later. The Lennons and Harrisons stayed the longest in the compound, six weeks, but they, too, decided it was enough. Lennon, in particular, was disillusioned with the Maharishi, and wrote the biting song "Sexy Sadie" ("You made a fool of everyone") about his onetime guru, which was included on *The White Album*.

"We had to leave the others there because we had children at home but we also left because we only planned to go for two weeks in the first place," Ringo wrote later. "Maureen had this fly/moth phobia and to be in the jungle of India didn't help. John and George got up to seven hours of mediation. Paul got two and a half. We never got that far—an hour at the most.

"This was a really good time because it relieved all that pressure of being The Beatles . . . in many ways it was also our first experience of being left alone, although the press caught up with us and photographed us leaving. I'm still glad I went and feel so blessed I met the Maharishi—he gave me a mantra that no one can take away and I still use it."

With his schedule freed up—and the other Beatles still in India—Ringo had time to kill. He puttered around the house in Sunny Heights and waited for his fellow band members to return. Journalist Ray Connolly paid a visit to Ringo and Maureen in March 1968 and reported on his visit for the *Evening Standard*.

> You step through a large, white hoop like an airlock on a submarine to get to Ringo's playroom. It's the top floor of an annex built to the living room end of his home, and it's a splendid place of flashing lights, panda rugs, a fruit machine, a table for snooker, another for table tennis and miles and miles and miles of taped music. It is, in fact, like the last word in youth clubs.

Ringo, Maureen, Zak, and Jason were tended to by a live-in nanny, a chauffeur, a gardener, and a woman who did the housework. The family had nine cats, most of them Siamese. Maureen's mother, Florence, was staying with them when Connolly visited. "Maureen's dad's at sea," Ringo told him. "He wouldn't give it up for anything." Ringo described a life in which most of their neighbors were strangers—save, of course, for John and Cynthia, who lived very close nearby.

"I've always had crazes, but now if I want to do something I go out and buy all the equipment," Ringo said of his constantly changing hobbies (which included developing his own photographs, making amateur movies, playing pool, making light machines with colored slides, and painting giant sunflowers on his garden walls. He told Connolly,

> I don't stay with one hobby for much more than a couple of weeks at a time. Sometimes I'll have a week and I'll just play records; then I might spend a day just playing with my tape recordings; and sometimes I put the videotape machine on and film myself playing snooker.
>
> I supposed I get bored like anyone else, but instead of having three hours a night to get bored in I have all day. . . . Sometimes

I feel I'd like to stop being famous and get back to where I was in Liverpool. There don't seem to be so many worries in that sort of life, although I thought there were at the time. But I had to come to realize that they counted for very little.

━━━━━━━━━━━━━━━━━●

There was more work to do back in London. Before they'd left for India, The Beatles had begun recording songs for their next album, including John Lennon's "Across the Universe" and "Hey Bulldog," which was included on the soundtrack for the *Yellow Submarine* movie and featured Ringo's thundering drums, a terrific guitar solo from George Harrison, and some fun ad-libbing between Lennon and McCartney in the song's fadeout ("Whaddya say?" "I say 'woof!'" "You know any more?").

The Beatles were contractually committed to United Artists for another movie, and *Yellow Submarine* was a way to fulfill their duties without breaking too much of a sweat. The soundtrack was their only involvement with the animated film, save for appearing briefly as themselves in a live-action sequence (shot in January) at the end of the movie.

Actors were hired to replicate the familiar inflections of John, Paul, George, and Ringo. (The voice of "Ringo" in *Yellow Submarine* was supplied by Liverpudlian actor Roy Angelis, best known in England for a role on the long-running BBC television cop drama *Z-Cars*. Angelis was also the voice of the "Chief Blue Meanie." His younger brother, Michael Angelis, later replaced Ringo as the narrator of *Thomas and Friends*.) *Yellow Submarine* was released in the UK in July 1968, and in the U.S. that November; it took its title from the tune sung by Ringo on the *Revolver* album released in 1966.

In 1967, months before Epstein's death, the group had purchased a three-story building in London at 94 Baker Street, primarily as a real-estate investment to keep the taxman at bay. In December 1967, the ground floor of the building opened as the Apple Boutique. The boutique was the retail-clothing arm of Apple Corps., The Beatles' new company founded to manage their business holdings.

In addition to the Apple Boutique, the multi-faceted Apple Corps. encompassed a recording company, Apple Records (with the now-iconic green-apple logo), Apple Publishing, Apple Films—ostensibly run by Ringo, who, after all, had appeared in *Candy*—and Apple Electronics. Apple Records was not only The Beatles' new record label, but would give heretofore-unknown artists a chance to be heard—and possibly recorded—without having to knock on so many doors.

The basic idea, as Ringo explained, was for artists to tell Apple their ideas and, hopefully, procure funding for their projects. The Beatles didn't want anyone to beg, having been through that humiliating experience themselves.

The company was officially incorporated in January 1968 and, that May, before The Beatles started work on their next album, Lennon and McCartney flew to America to announce the start up of Apple. They held a press conference and appeared on NBC's *Tonight Show* (guest-hosted by Joe Garagiola, subbing for the vacationing Johnny Carson) to publicize their new Beatles baby.

"We decided to play businessmen for a bit, because . . . we've got to run our own affairs now," Lennon said when asked about Apple. "So, we've got this thing called 'Apple' which is going to be records, films, and electronics—which all tie-up. And to make a sort of an umbrella so people who want to make films about . . . grass . . . don't have to go on their knees in an office, you know, begging for a break. . . . I mean, we'll find out what happens, but that's what we're trying to do."

Ken Mansfield, who'd worked at Capitol Records in L.A. since 1965, and met The Beatles on their first trips to the U.S., was hired to run the Apple offices in America. His new position took him to London, on occasion, to touch base with the home office.

"The front of the Apple building was very nondescript in the middle of the business district," he recalled. "Just little teeny steps and a porch; you'd go through the crazies outside, the girls and then you'd go through the door and there was this other madness, almost like if you shot a surreal movie. There might be Hell's Angels in there, there might be a famous actor, maybe some Hare Krishnas. You just didn't know. Derek Taylor holding court in his bizarre big wicker chair. It was madness. It was absolute madness."

The seven-month lifespan of the Apple Boutique was marked by mismanagement and chaos. Lennon enlisted his boyhood friend Pete Shotton to manage the boutique, along with George Harrison's sister-in-law Jenny Boyd, but by the end of July 1968 the boutique was £200,000 in the red. Merchandise was stolen, both by customers and employees, inventory was woefully mismanaged and the utopian ideal gave way to brutal reality. The night before the boutique closed, The Beatles took what they wanted off the racks—"We cleaned a lot of stuff out," Ringo said—and, the next day, they gave away the remaining inventory to the public for free (whatever people could carry—or take via wheelbarrow, as some did). "Everything about it seemed to be a disaster of poor planning and incompetence," Peter Brown noted. Ringo was more matter of fact about the endeavor, calling it a lark and "silly." Besides, The Beatles had accomplished their goal, he joked, of opening up a store and dressing everyone like them.

Apple Records fared marginally better. There were some success stories vis-à-vis the artists who were recruited by The Beatles—James Taylor ("Carolina In My Mind"), Jackie Lomax ("Sour Milk Sea"), Mary Hopkin ("Those Were the Days"), Badfinger ("Come and Get It," written by Paul McCartney)—but it, too, lost money hand over fist.

To differing degrees, each of The Beatles did what he could to support the company, and each band member dutifully attended the requisite business meetings at Apple's Savile Row headquarters. But, once again, chaotic mismanagement, insane budgets, freeloaders, scattershot planning—or no planning at all—and rampant drug use eventually weakened, and then destroyed, the utopian venture.

A bearded, fast-talking, Greek-born electronics wizard named Alex Madras—"Magic Alex," as he was known in hip London circles—became a Beatles confidante. John Lennon introduced "Magic Alex" to Paul, George, and Ringo and they hired him as their point person for Apple Electronics. He hoodwinked the band with promises of fantastic recording innovations and gadgets—wallpaper doubling as loudspeakers, "electrical paint," a toilet with a built-in radio—and, finally, a seventy-two track, state-of-the-art recording studio for Apple.

The studio's computers sat, collecting dust, mice, and birds, in Ringo's garage in Sunny Heights. "Alex never came through," Ringo said. What he did do was waste a ton of The Beatles' money before disappearing into the wind.

Ringo wasn't as involved as his band mates in the Apple endeavor; he wasn't in the office every day, but neither were the others, for the most part. Lennon, McCartney, and Harrison discovered, along with Ringo, that being businessmen was not their forte. They were all in their twenties, all idealistic and all willing to give Apple a chance, funding a large part of the corporation with their own money—but the concept of running a business was overrun by its economic (and human) realities.

"I mean, we started it [Apple] as like a toy—because we weren't businessmen, and we didn't know what it involved, and we'd just started this great empire thinking we could do it whenever we felt like," Ringo said. "But it ended up that we couldn't, you know, we had to go in. So what we're really doing now is paying for when we opened it and played about. Because we used to keep everybody on forever, you know, just because they were like a mate or a pal. They never did the jobs what we used to keep them on . . . it's like another time we were being played on. So now, if they can't do the job then they have to leave. . . . It's not a playground anymore."

When The Beatles weren't working in the studio, Ringo preferred to stay at home in Sunny Heights with Maureen and the kids—which, ironically, led to his most important contribution to the artistic component of Apple Records.

In mid-1968, Ringo was having some work done at Sunny Heights. The building firm doing the renovations on Ringo's house was run by Roger Tavener, who knew about Apple Records and regaled Ringo with stories about his very talented older brother, John, a graduate of the Royal Academy of Music. He had won a distinguished Prince Rainier award while still a student and, after graduating, composed *The Whale*, a dramatic cantata (a musical composition accompanied by song) based on the Biblical story of Jonah.

In 1968, *The Whale* was performed at the London Sinfonietta and as the opening concert at the Queen Elizabeth Hall. Roger Tavener persuaded Ringo to give it a listen. "I loved it," Ringo said. "We were very open to all different kinds of music, so we thought we'd put it on Apple. That was my contribution." Tavener went on to an illustrious career in the classical music field and was knighted by Queen Elizabeth in 2000.

"My association with The Beatles in general, before I met Ringo, was when I was invited by an American producer to a dinner party in Chelsea, where I met John Lennon," Tavener recalled in 2013, shortly before his untimely death at the age of sixty-nine.

> I vividly remember meeting Ringo at my brother's place for a cup of tea and I remember my brother had ordered caviar and champagne, and Ringo and Maureen had come for tea and they ordered jam sandwiches and cup of tea. Although there was a tremendous interest in John Lennon, it was Ringo who practically arranged for *The Whale* to be recorded. I remember him coming to the recording sessions, and he's one of the voices that shouts in the background in that recording.
>
> He [Ringo] was very easy to work with, very down-to-earth. He was very keen to get things done quickly. They had been talking about [*The Whale*] for some time, and about Apple recording my mu-

sic, and I know that when Ringo came onto the scene, it all happened very quickly. I look back at all that with great affection because I think it was so important. Classical music at that time was more than classical music . . . it wasn't going anywhere, and I think it was enormously important in every respect that Apple recorded it.

Ringo was also responsible for a 1968 recording, ostensibly for Apple, that was not publicized at the time but which has achieved near-mythical status among Beatles fans and memorabilia collectors through the years. And he did it all for love—specifically for his wife, Maureen, who was turning twenty-two that summer.

Maureen was a huge fan of Frank Sinatra, and Ringo wanted to surprise her with a special birthday gift. He got in touch with Sinatra's representatives—via Peter Brown or Beatles assistant Ron Kass, depending on who's telling the story—with the idea of approaching Sinatra about recording a special birthday wish for Maureen.

Sinatra, who was at the peak of his powers, could have laughed off the request. He had enough to do, wasn't much of a pop-music fan, and had enough reasons to resent The Beatles, who knocked him off the charts for a while after they stormed America in 1964. But Sinatra was Sinatra—in his world, The Beatles didn't even come close—and he didn't hold a grudge.

In 1967, he'd lent his private jet to Paul McCartney and Mal Evans for a flight out of Denver. Now, when Ringo approached him, Sinatra was in the final stages of his divorce from Mia Farrow, who'd accompanied The Beatles to Rishikesh earlier that year. Their divorce was finalized in August.

Sinatra agreed to Ringo's request, although they had never met, and took it one step further. In the 1950s, Sinatra had a hit with the 1937 Lorenz Hart/ Richard Rodgers tune "The Lady Is a Tramp," which he recorded and also sang in the 1957 movie *Pal Joey*. He now had his favorite songwriter, Sammy Cahn, rework the lyrics into "Maureen Is a Champ," recording the song at Capitol Studios in Los Angeles accompanied only by a piano (which was played by Cahn, according to Peter Brown).

The new lyrics included the line: *She married Ringo, and she could have had Paul/That's why the lady is a champ.* Ringo had the recording pressed and gave it to a thrilled Maureen on her birthday. (It's been said that the Sinatra recording was pressed as "Apple 1," meaning it would be the label's first official recording, but that's never been verified.) Maureen kept the original pressing but its whereabouts are unknown; the recording was bootlegged and a scratchy copy of "Maureen Is a Champ" now resides for posterity in cyberspace on YouTube.

The Sinatra recording was a sweet interlude in what was a sour summer for Ringo and his band mates. In May, they began recording their first album for Apple, tentatively titled *The Beatles*—later simply called *The White Album* (which is how it will henceforth be referenced). They laid down tracks for different versions of John Lennon's "Revolution." Also on the recording docket in May was "Don't Pass Me By," a country-western-flavored tune, credited to "Richard Starkey" and sung by Ringo, who first mentioned the song five years earlier in several interviews, including an appearance on the BBC radio show *Top Gear*.

Lennon joked that Ringo "composed it himself in a fit of lethargy"; Ringo said he wrote the tune while sitting at home; since he only played three chords on both the guitar and piano, his range was limited, but if a melody came to him, he ran with it. It felt great to write his first song totally on his own, and he loved Jack Fallon's violin playing on the tune.

Besides Fallon's violin, "Don't Pass Me By" featured only Ringo (drums, sleigh bells, maracas, and other percussion) and McCartney (grand piano and bass), who also teamed for another *White Album* track, "Why Don't We Do It in the Road?"

But tensions within the group were running high. By the summer of 1968, The Beatles were going their separate ways: George Harrison was exploring his interest in Indian music and that country's culture; Paul McCartney was chasing new experiences in pop art; Ringo was making movies (he'd signed a deal to co-star with Peter Sellers in *The Magic Christian*); and John Lennon, still married to Cynthia, was in love with Yoko Ono. The Beatles, once Lennon's entire life, were now just an annoyance.

Despite the exhilaration of *Sgt. Pepper's Lonely Hearts Club Band*, recording together was becoming a chore, the long hours in the studio giving way to increased internal bickering. Lennon, McCartney, and Harrison—still only in their mid-to-late twenties—had spent over ten years together as a band and were getting on one another's nerves. George, the youngest Beatle and always overshadowed by Lennon and McCartney, was coming into his own as a songwriter and was expressing his dissatisfaction with being relegated to second-tier status.

Ringo, a Beatle for six years, wasn't immune to the others' barbs but wasn't shy about speaking out, if necessary. "At one time we used to change together, then we started changing separately in different directions," Ringo said. "We were just living our own lives, you know?"

And, when The Beatles weren't arguing among themselves that summer, Paul, George, and even the usually amiable Ringo, were pissed that John was now bringing Yoko Ono into the studio. There she sat, passively watching the band's recording sessions, rarely saying a word but keeping her eyes trained on John.

"I remember being freaked out by Yoko," Ringo said. "The four of us had been through a lot together and we were very close . . . most of the time. I thought we were very possessive of each other in a way. The wives and girlfriends never came to the studio—*that* was when *we* were together. But then [Yoko] is sitting in the studio on [John's] amp . . . so we all got a bit weird."

Recording *The White Album* continued into June, when Ringo recorded his solo vocal for "Good Night," a sweet bedtime lullaby written by Lennon for his five-year-old son, Julian. Lennon originally intended to sing the song himself but changed his mind, apparently embarrassed by its tender tone. (McCartney claimed that Lennon "sang it very tenderly" in the studio when instructing Ringo on how he wanted it vocalized.)

Ringo's nervousness in carrying the song is apparent in his quavering voice, which is accompanied only by an orchestral score arranged by George Martin. But Ringo, with his innate charm, gullibility, and vulnerability, succeeds in a fine effort, and "Good Night" was used to close out *The White Album*.

The band members' tempers began to flare as the summer progressed. In June, Ringo and Maureen joined George Harrison on a trip to California—Harrison was filming a project with his sitar guru, Ravi Shankar—but the journey did little to appease the bad feelings all-around. Everyone was getting pissed off at the situation.

Ringo, around this time, knew there were problems but was hopeful they could be solved internally, as The Beatles had done with past disagreements. "There's that famous old saying, you'll always hurt the one you love. And we all love each other and we all know that," he said. "But we still sort of hurt each other, occasionally. You know . . . where we just misunderstand each other and we go off, and it builds up to something bigger than it ever was. Then we have to come down to it and get it over with. . . . Sort it out. And so we're still really very close people."

But even Ringo had his limits, and he reached his boiling point on August

22. Frustrated with the in-fighting, the mixed signals, and his own drumming—and "freaked out" by Yoko Ono's immutable presence—he walked out, quitting the band. Just the day before, John, Paul, George, and Ringo sullenly plodded through a marathon twelve-hour recording session. It was almost six years to the day that Ringo had joined The Beatles.

"Ringo probably had the hardest job in the band, playing for hours and hours, and he probably shared the same view that we occasionally had, 'I played that last night for nine hours. Do I have to do it again?'" said EMI insider Richard Lush. "He had a hard job trying to please them."

Ringo just couldn't take it anymore, and he made his feelings known to his band mates. He said he left because he felt he wasn't playing well enough in the studio, and because he felt alienated from John, Paul, and George. Little did he realize that each of the other three felt like the outsider. It was that kind of group dynamic. Everyone was suspicious of the other guy (or gal, since John was never separated from Yoko Ono).

"Ringo was always sitting in the reception area waiting, just sitting or reading a newspaper," recalled producer Ron Richards. "He used to sit there for hours waiting for the others to turn up. One night he couldn't stand it any longer, got fed up and left. George [Martin] told me that he was having trouble with Ringo but I'm not surprised." Beatles author Hunter Davies, who was an eyewitness to the band's life in the recording studio, noted how Ringo "was often virtually ignored. John and Paul would break off for sometimes hours at a time. . . . There was often no need for Ringo to be there at all—his contribution could be dubbed on any time."

Ringo's sudden departure from The Beatles was covered up, lest word leak out that The World's Most Famous Drummer had just quit The World's Most Famous Band. Despite the internal strife, The Beatles were putting on a happy public face, trying to retain the "all-for-one" façade they'd spent so many years cultivating. Everyone in and around The Beatles orbit was sworn to secrecy about Ringo's hasty departure. Lennon, McCartney, and Harrison carried on in Ringo's absence—after all, there was an album to record, and time was money.

McCartney, who fancied himself a respectable drummer (he was pedestrian, at best), filled in (somewhat clumsily) for Ringo on the rousing rocker "Back in the USSR," although it's been noted that several drum tracks were added and that Harrison and Lennon might have also drummed on Ringo's vacant drum kit. McCartney also played a simple drum track on Lennon's song "Dear Prudence," written about Mia Farrow's sister who'd accompanied them to Rishikesh earlier that year. ("Every time I went for a cup of tea, [Paul] was on the drums!" Ringo noted.)

Ringo couldn't get out of London fast enough. His pal Peter Sellers offered him the use of his yacht, which was anchored in the Mediterranean off the coast of Sardinia, near Italy. In his own mind, Ringo had left The Beatles. He was done. The magic was gone, the once-rock-solid relationships frayed beyond repair. He couldn't get past the feeling of being an outsider.

McCartney, always somewhat condescending toward Ringo, blamed his departure on paranoia about his drumming skills, particularly Ringo's disdain for solos. Shortly thereafter, McCartney sent Ringo a postcard: "You are the greatest drummer in the world. Really."

Ringo accepted Sellers's offer and, joined by Maureen, Zak, and Jason, flew to Sardinia to clear his head, unwind, and mull his future. The trip was restful and the family enjoyed themselves in the warm, sunny climate.

Ringo used part of his time to write his second song, "Octopus's Garden," while lolling on Sellers's yacht. The family had requested fish and chips for lunch one day, but were surprised when their plates arrived with the requisite French fries ("chips" in England) but some funny-looking fish, which turned out to be squid (and not the expected cod).

It was Ringo and Maureen's first time dining on squid. Ringo struck up a conversation with the yacht's captain, who told him how octopuses liked to hunker down in their caves, building "gardens" from stones and other things they found in the sea nearby. A light bulb went off in Ringo's head; he, too, felt like living under the sea, particularly at this low point in his professional life.

Ringo wrote "Octopus's Garden" in the kid-friendly vein of "Yellow Submarine": *I'd like to be, under the sea/In an octopus's garden, in the shade.* The song was credited to "Richard Starkey" and ended up on The Beatles' final album, *Abbey Road.*

Two weeks into his Sardinia sojourn, Ringo received a telegram from his band mates: "You're the best rock and roll drummer in the world. Come on home. We love you." Back in London, George Harrison instructed Beatles roadie Mal Evans to decorate the entire studio, including Ringo's drum kit, with hundreds of flowers. Ringo, already emotional and vulnerable, was touched by the gesture when he returned to Abbey Road in early September.

McCartney said he thought that Ringo felt insecure, so he told him he was "the best drummer in the world for us" and led the celebration welcoming the drummer back into the band.

"It was just a beautiful moment," Ringo recalled years later.

A week later, The Beatles resumed recording McCartney's raucous "Helter Skelter," which they'd started in July. Ringo pounded away on his drums as hard and as loud as he possibly could, egged on to "just beat the shit out of the drums, just kill them" in the manner of his friend, The Who's drummer Keith Moon. "I've got blisters on my fingers!" he shouted at the end of the take that was used on *The White Album*.

Those blisters healed, and the remainder of *The White Album* recording sessions ran much more smoothly, at least on the surface. Hurt feelings were, for now, pushed to the side, despite Paul, George, and Ringo's irritation at Yoko Ono's constant in-studio presence. Ringo would always say that he loved *The White Album* because because he thought The Beatles were playing and interacting like a band again. Just like the old days. It took his two-week defection to wake everyone up.

"John and Paul weren't writing together, but we would all support the songs as a band," Ringo said of that time. "It didn't matter who wrote them. That's why I've always felt we were more of a band at that time. We weren't like session players trying to get the bloody arrangement down pat. We were a band."

But the wake-up call didn't last for long. In early January 1969, The Beatles began working on their next album, *Let It Be*, at Twickenham Studios in London—the same movie studio at which Ringo was scheduled to film scenes for his upcoming role in *The Magic Christian*. The idea for *Let It Be* was to film The Beatles rehearsing new songs for their next album, with cameras recording their ongoing creative process. The plan was to have the rehearsals culminate in a live concert performance at the end of the movie, which was slated to air on television. A live album, culled from the television special, would follow. (The filmed live concert idea was eventually abandoned.)

Several ideas for *Let It Be* location shoots were broached, including shooting the movie aboard a floating ocean liner or in an open-air stadium in Tunisia (Ringo was dead-set against both) before they settled on Twickenham. In theory, the concept for *Let It Be* would be another groundbreaking achievement for The Beatles. In November 1968, *The White Album* was released (to uneven reviews) as a double-LP with an unprecedented thirty songs over four sides; its snow-white jacket had no identifying marks save for "The Beatles" embossed in small lettering on the cover—a first for a rock band.

But Twickenham was a cold, sterile place "like a big barn," Ringo said. The warehouse-type environment was depressing, the lighting was bad (despite the movie cameras) and the acoustics were terrible. It was literally very cold, and the band was asked to report for work early in the morning—anathema for any rock star. The old tensions immediately resurfaced as John, Paul, George, Ringo—and now Yoko Ono—were once again thrown together for long, tedious, boring hours on end.

"Yoko came in," Ringo said. "And that was fine, as John's relationship when we all said hello to her, because she was with John. But then she's sittin' in the studio on his amp. I mean, the pair of them were amazing. So we all got a bit weird, and I was wondering what was happening one day. So I was saying to John, 'What is going on here? You're always together all the time, you know. You're freaking me out a bit. What's happening?' And he told me what they were trying to do, so then I was fine after that. I sort of relaxed a lot around Yoko."

Most of the band's verbal anger was directed at McCartney, who'd assumed the leadership role from a strung-out Lennon. (The hostility that Paul, George, and Ringo harbored toward interloper Yoko Ono was mostly under the surface and etched on their faces.) Harrison was particularly prickly, and the *Let It Be* cameras caught his tense exchanges with Lennon and his quarrels with McCartney. "I'll play what you want me to play. I won't play at all if you don't want me to," George growled at Paul, who was trying to explain how he wanted a guitar solo to sound. "Whatever it is that will please you, I'll do it."

Harrison became the second Beatle to quit the group, walking out of Twickenham on January 10 after Lennon criticized him for his lack of both enthusiasm and contributions to the project. George drove to his parents' house in Liverpool, where he hunkered down for a few days.

He didn't tell John, Paul, or Ringo that he was leaving; there had been some trouble brewing in the studio that morning, Ringo said, but no one realized until they broke for lunch that George was nowhere to be found. He eventually returned—after some persuasion from his band mates—but the damage was done. Ringo was mostly an observer of the arguments. He'd made his big statement by leaving the band once before; now he just looked sad, dejected, and defeated.

In late January, The Beatles vacated Twickenham and relocated to the more cozy environs of Apple's basement recording studio at 3 Savile Row. (One of Harrison's conditions for returning for the group was to cancel the live concert film and get the hell out of Twickenham.) The new location didn't do much to improve the group's mood, although the appearance of Billy Preston, who played keyboards on several tracks, lifted the clouds a bit.

Ringo noted that the "bullshit" disappeared once Preston came on the scene. The Beatles loved recording at Apple—it was home to them—but the tension was bubbling under the surface, occasionally rising to an argument or heated discussion.

On January 30, 1969—a cold, raw, rainy day in London—The Beatles performed live for the last time. They had been searching for a way to end the *Let It Be* movie, and someone suggested the grand finale: a mini-concert on the roof of the Apple building.

The idea was okayed by everyone, and after Mal Evans and Neil Aspinall schlepped the band's equipment up to the roof, John, Paul, George, and Ringo—joined by Billy Preston on keyboards—launched into a set, including "Don't Let Me Down," "I've Got a Feeling," and "Dig a Pony." An amazed crowd gathered in the street below, gawking, while others watched out of office windows, straining to see what was happening on the rooftop. No one, not even The Beatles, realized this was their last live performance.

Ringo wore a red raincoat against the chill and was in top form, keeping fluid time (no mean feat in the cold weather) and rocking out, particularly on "The One After 909," an old Lennon/McCartney tune they first tried recording in 1963. The Beatle wives were there, and Maureen elicited a "Thanks, Mo" from McCartney for her enthusiastic whooping and clapping at the end of "Get Back."

Someone called the London cops, who were captured by the *Let It Be* cameras breaking up the concert. Ringo said later he has hoping the cops would drag him away from his drums; since it was all being filmed, it would make for a great scene, with Ringo kicking his cymbals.

Ken Mansfield, who was running Apple's U.S. offices, was up on the rooftop that day, lighting cigarettes so George Harrison could warm the tips of his fingers. "When we were on the roof, you could just feel it. It wasn't like, 'Oh my gosh, this is historical' or 'Wow, this is the last time The Beatles are playing together' or 'Gee whiz, they are going to break up now.' We just knew something, and the strangest thing is, all of us walked off the roof and down to our offices and nobody talked. I think we just didn't quite know what happened."

Lennon, of course, got in the last word: "I'd like to say thank you on behalf of the group and ourselves and I hope we passed the audition."

Ringo's friendship with Peter Sellers dated back to the mid-1960s, but they grew close during the filming of *The Magic Christian*, which got underway at Twickenham Studios in early February, several days after The Beatles wrapped the *Let It Be* project. Ringo had read Terry Southern's book and said all it took to get the movie made was a knock on Sellers' door. The deal was made after a flurry of phone calls.

Sellers, born in 1925 in Portsmouth into a traveling show business family, was fifteen years older than Ringo. Like Ringo, Sellers was also a drummer, having started his career playing for dance bands throughout England before and after World War II. (Sellers served in the RAF and was a member, from 1943–45, of Ralph Reader's *Gang Show* unit, which entertained the troops.) In the 1950s, Ringo, like many British teenagers of the time (including his fellow Beatles), was entranced by Sellers's funny voices on *The Goon Show*, the anarchic, loony, trailblazing BBC radio comedy also starring Spike Milligan and Harry Secombe. (Original "Goon" Michael Bentine left the show early in its run.)

Ringo's friendship with Sellers paid other dividends. In 1968, after three years at Sunny Heights, Ringo and Maureen were looking to move into a new place. Sellers, in the process of divorcing Britt Ekland, told Ringo he was in the market to sell his huge estate in Elstead, Surrey, which was called Brookfield. The fifteenth-century oak-beamed Brookfield estate was on several acres, had its own private lake, walled gardens and barns, a gym, sauna, and private movie theater. Ringo jumped at the opportunity. Sellers had just pumped £50,000 into renovating Brookfield, but told Ringo he'd sell it to him for £70,000. John Lennon, meanwhile, also wanted the house—located twenty-five miles outside of London—and offered Sellers £150,000. But Sellers kept his promise. Ringo, Maureen, and the kids moved into Brookfield in November 1968.

Ken Mansfield described the sumptuous estate,

> You'd pull up to the front of Brookfield and there are these big steps and two giant lions on each side. It's like walking up into the Four Seasons Hotel. You go in the big front door and [there is] the staircase and all that, and to the left there's this giant den on the wing of the left side of the house with a big fireplace in there; they stuck a TV in the fireplace and the crib was over in one corner and Maureen's sewing stuff was in another corner and Ringo had his drums set up in another part of the room. It's almost like, here they were, they had this big mansion but they were just simple people, like a family living in a one-room place.

The Magic Christian marked the second time Ringo was working on a movie written by Terry Southern, though *Candy*, shot the year before, had yet to premiere when production began on *The Magic Christian*. Southern was adapting *The Magic Christian* from his 1959 satiric novel of the same name; also contributing to the screenplay were future *Monty Python's Flying Circus* troupers John Cleese and Graham Chapman, director Joe McGrath, and Sellers.

Unlike his three-minute appearance as Emmanuel the gardener in *Candy*, *The Magic Christian* was a major role for Ringo, who was in nearly every scene and received top billing alongside Sellers (whose star was eclipsing and wouldn't rise again for another five years). The movie also boasted an all-star cast of cameos from the likes of Raquel Welch, Laurence Harvey, Yul Brynner, Spike Milligan, Christopher Lee, Dennis Price, Richard Attenborough, Wilfrid Hyde-White, and Roman Polanski (whose wife, pregnant actress Sharon Tate, was murdered in Los Angeles that summer by the Manson Family).

Ringo recalled that the producers would phone whichever big star was in town and have Southern write them into the movie. Southern would slip a script under Ringo's door and, about an hour later, he'd be called to the set to shoot his scene(s).

"Because of the name Ringo as a Beatle, I was allowed to walk right into a good slot," Ringo said of the role. "[Sellers] started with, like, walk-on parts and then he got a bigger part, and then he got his own films. I didn't have to stand-in, or do any of the small jobs."

The plot of *The Magic Christian* revolves around Sir Guy Grand (Sellers, with fashionably graying hair and a mustache), an eccentric billionaire intent on proving, via the almighty dollar and elaborate practical jokes, that everyone has his price. Ringo plays Youngman Grand, a long-haired, mustachioed twenty-something orphan who's adopted by Sir Guy. Youngman is Sir Guy's sidekick, helping his "dad" pull his outlandish pranks. (The Youngman character did not exist in Southern's book and was written especially for Ringo.)

In the meantime, there was a lot of movement in The Beatles' universe. Engineer Glyn Johns was trying to salvage the *Let It Be* sessions at Abbey Road; Paul married Linda Eastman; George had his tonsils removed; The Beatles' management was in flux—should their business affairs be handled by Allen Klein or Paul's brother-in-law, John Eastman?; John married Yoko in Gibraltar and they later staged a week-long "bed-in" for peace in Amsterdam; and *Candy* finally premiered in London (at the end of February, with Ringo attending the opening).

The Magic Christian's thirteen-week shooting schedule was rigorous and kept Ringo busy, so he'd be forgiven if he wasn't exactly keeping up with his band mates' lives. Ringo, George, and John were not in attendance at Paul and Linda's March 12 wedding (though George and his wife, Pattie, were at the reception, just hours after their apartment had been raided and they were busted for possession). Ringo, working closely with Sellers virtually every day, was now discovering the chameleon actor's dark side: his severe emotional tics, wild mood swings, churlish behavior, and strange affectations.

They would work together all day, have dinner that night, and enjoy each other's company. Ringo found Sellers hysterical. But when they met up the next morning, Ringo he felt as if he had to begin the relationship all over again. Sellers would often sulk, or would ask to be left alone on the set.

Still, all in all, Ringo enjoyed his time with the mercurial actor. They would often break into hysterics in the middle of a take as soon as Sellers opened his mouth.

One day, while they were filming a scene in which Ringo, as Youngman, had a lot of lines of dialogue, Sellers purposely stood across from him, in camera range, picking his nose. He wanted to teach Ringo a lesson: that the movie audience would focus on Ringo's eyes. He needed to maintain his concentration.

After *The Magic Christian* wrapped in early May, Ringo and Sellers hosted a joint party at Les Ambassadeurs in London. John and Yoko were there, as were Paul and Linda (no George or Pattie) and many stars, including Michael Caine, Richard Harris, Sean Connery, and George Peppard.

Later that month, Sellers joined Ringo, Maureen, George, and Pattie on the brand-new *Queen Elizabeth 2* as it set sail from Southampton to New York. The trip was funded by *The Magic Christian* producers, Commonwealth United, as a sort of very expensive "thank you" gesture for getting the film done on time and under budget. After arriving in New York, everyone left for a two-week vacation in Paradise Island in the Bahamas before Ringo and George were scheduled back in London to join Paul and John. The Beatles were recording a new album.

The trip was also supposed to include John and Yoko when it left Southampton. They were planning to stage their next "bed-in" for peace in New York City, but U.S. immigration authorities denied Lennon a visa because of his conviction for cannabis possession the previous November. He and Yoko were left behind, along with Yoko's daughter, Kyoko, Apple chief Derek Taylor and John and Yoko's assistant, Anthony Fawcett. They eventually flew to the Bahamas, then on to Montreal, where they staged their "bed-in."

(Coincidentally, Lennon used the line "Standing on the dock at South-ampton" in "The Ballad of John and Yoko" to describe the couple's Gibraltar marriage odyssey two months before. Despite their now-adversarial relation-ship, Lennon and McCartney recorded the song in mid-April without Ringo or George, who were both unavailable, with Ringo working on *The Magic Christian* and George away in the U.S.

"The Ballad of John and Yoko," with Lennon on guitar and McCartney on piano, bass, and drums, was released at the end of May, backed by George's "Old Brown Shoe." It was the final Beatles single to reach Number One in the UK, reaching Number Eight on the U.S. charts. Lennon and McCartney joked during the recording, with Lennon telling McCartney, "Go a bit faster, Ringo!" and McCartney answering back, "Okay, George!")

The Beatles' Apple venture, meanwhile, was slowly going down the tubes. The seventy-two-track recording studio promised by "Magic Alex" Madras turned out to be a pipe dream, which John, Paul, George, and Ringo discovered when they moved from Twickenham to the basement of Apple to record the rest of *Let It Be*.

Over on the music side, the talented British group Badfinger, one of the first acts inked to an Apple recording deal in 1968 (when they were known as The Iveys), contributed a song to *The Magic Christian* soundtrack called "Come and Get It," which was written and produced by Paul McCartney. But little else was happening while the business continued to hemorrhage money.

Ringo's biggest contribution to Apple, the signing of John Tavener, gave the label a bit of much-needed cachet early, but didn't make a dent in the mar-ketplace. In 1969, with the future of The Beatles a murky one, Ringo used his connections at Apple to become partners in his second business venture, this time with London designer Robin Cruikshank.

Ringo met Cruikshank in 1968, when the London furniture designer signed a production deal, aligning his company, Robin Ltd., with Apple. At the time, Ringo and Maureen had just moved into Elstead. Now, after only a year, they were looking for another place. "It was just a drag coming into town every day in the car, you know," Ringo said. "It took an hour-and-a-half, and then an hour-and-a-half to get out again. So I just hated the idea of three hours a day of my life wasted, sitting in a car. And also, it's better for Maureen if we come into town because . . . at least I go into the office and . . . see a lot of people. Whereas I think she's getting a bit fed-up with being stuck out in the country. So if we're in town then she can leap about as much as I do."

Just days before Ringo made those remarks, in an interview with BBC2's *Late Night Line-up* in mid-December, he'd purchased a roomy house in North London. It was called Round Hill and was located on a private cul-de-sac, on Compton Avenue, in the prestigious suburb of Highgate, in Hampstead. The drive to Apple was only minutes (instead of hours) and Kenwood Park was close by, a bonus for Zak and Jason. (Ringo sold Brookfield to musician Stephen Stills. They'd met at Apple a few years before and would record together several times in the future.)

Ringo and Maureen asked Robin Cruikshank for his help in furnishing their new house. Cruikshank designed a stainless steel fireplace for Round Hill. He also designed some mercury-filled discs used for a board game, which Ringo gave to Maureen for a Christmas present. Ringo, who liked Robin as soon as they met, offered a few suggestions for a line of steel-and-glass furniture Cruikshank was designing. They discovered they shared a mutual interest in hi-fi and audio equipment. Before too long, through word of mouth—and, no doubt, because of Ringo's name—they were being asked to design furniture as a team.

A request came from the chairman of Cunard, asking if Ringo and Robin would design a disco for one of the company's London hotels. Cunard eventually abandoned the project, but Ringo and Robin, who enjoyed each other's company, decided to create a new furniture design company called ROR Ltd., which stood for "Ringo or Robin." They incorporated the company and set up offices on the top floor of the Apple building on Savile Row, hiring a secretary and an architect to help flesh out their designs. Ringo owned a 51 percent stake in the business to Robin's 49 percent. They decided that any disagreements between them would be solved by flipping a coin. That was Ringo.

ROR snagged several big design contracts, including the upscale Harvey Nichols store in Knightsbridge and Liberty on Regent Street (where Cruikshank had some contacts). The firm's designs were put on display at both stores.

"ROR are undoubtedly a success, and it is worth looking a little more closely at the possible reasons for this success," wrote *London Times* reporter Penny Radford. "First, and I hope without being unfair, because Robin Cruikshank, a talented and experienced designer, has had as an equally hard-working and imaginative partner Mr. Ringo Starr—and there is no doubt that a Name does help. . . . Their first range was a collection of spectacular, expensive stainless steel furniture, an exciting visual stimulus but one in which only the rich could afford to indulge."

ROR designed a stainless steel table which had a Rolls-Royce radiator at the center; it was Ringo's idea after passing a car store near Round Hill and noting the gleaming devices. British Steel was so impressed by the design that it used the table in its advertisements. Another popular ROR design was a tall stainless steel audio unit, shaped like a long, wide tube, which had openings in the front for stereo equipment.

By the time ROR closed up shop in the mid-1980s—Ringo was no longer a British resident and was less involved in the business—the company had exhibited its designs around the world (Lagos, Paris, and New York).

A bevy of celebrities bought ROR furniture, including British Prime Minister Edward Heath (immortalized in The Beatles song "Taxman"), Rod Stewart, Harry Nilsson, David Bowie, Elton John, and Christopher Plummer.

Ringo spent the summer of 1969 in the studio. The Beatles were back at Abbey Road, recording their next album, which didn't yet have a title when work began on July 1. (Lennon, who rarely drove because of his bad eyesight, was missing after crashing a car in Scotland during a family outing—injuring himself, Yoko, her daughter Kyoko, and Julian Lennon.)

Of the four Beatles, it was Paul who pushed the hardest to get the band back into the studio to record another album; after the debacle of *Let It Be*, no one was jumping at the chance to work together again. That was apparent in March, two months after the rooftop concert at Apple, when Ringo was asked by a reporter if The Beatles would ever perform live again. "I suppose it's a bit nasty on the fans," he said. "I'm sorry for them but no more public shows—never." Lennon, who was honeymooning with Yoko Ono in Amsterdam—and who seemed to be the least interested in ever rejoining his band mates—issued a surprising rejoinder. "Ringo can't say this," he said. "We will give several public shows this year."

Despite all the hard feelings and the bickering, McCartney convinced George Martin that all four Beatles were on board for another album and would behave themselves in the studio. The goal, with the new record, was to get back to basics and record as they'd done in the early days—bashing it out without too many overdubs or studio tricks. Good old rock 'n' roll.

Ringo was excited to be back with his mates, and even more psyched because he was using a drum kit with new calf-skin heads, which made his drum sound pop. He was extremely pleased with the way his tom-toms sounded—they really popped on vinyl, and you can hear the difference while listening to that record.

The album boasted the famous cover photograph of The Beatles crossing Abbey Road: George dressed all in blue, Paul in bare feet and holding a cigarette, Ringo dressed in black, and John wearing a white suit. (All of those elements on the cover—Paul's naked feet, a Volkswagen with the license plate "28 IF" seen in the background, and even the color of The Beatles' clothing—fed the "Paul is Dead" rumors.) They decided to call the album, simply, *Abbey Road*, and it was the perfect title for a near-perfect piece of work.

The LP marked the emergence of perpetually overlooked George Harrison as a top-flight songwriter in his own right. His two contributions, "Something" and "Here Comes the Sun," are classics that are considered just as good, if not better, than anything written by Lennon or McCartney (or both of them together). The sessions, which took up most of July and August, didn't come close to the rancor of the *Let It Be* sessions, although there were moments when it threatened to boil over. (Yoko Ono was, once again, a constant presence in the studio, but by this time she was grudgingly accepted by Ringo, George, and Paul—who didn't have much of a choice in the matter.)

The album also featured Lennon's "Come Together" and "Because," McCartney's "Maxwell's Silver Hammer" and "Oh! Darling," and (finally!) Ringo's "Octopus's Garden."

For the first and only time on a Beatles record, Ringo played a drum solo, reluctantly, on "The End," the album's last track (notwithstanding the twenty-second "Her Majesty," added by Apple engineer John Kurlander). "The End" also featured dueling guitar solos from Lennon, McCartney, and Harrison and capped off the Side B medley of Lennon and McCartney song snippets: "You Never Give Me Your Money," "Sun King," "Mean Mr. Mustard," "Polythene Pam," "She Came in Through the Bathroom Window," "Golden Slumbers," and "Carry That Weight" (on which Ringo's nasally baritone voice is clearly heard on the backing chorus).

Ringo shied away from drum solos, which he found boring, and his solo at the end of "Carry That Weight" is his only recorded drum solo on a Beatles album. George Martin convinced him to do it and counted him in; it was a tricky time measurement (thirteen bars long), but Ringo pulled it off.

In 1971, Ringo and Paul went to see an Iron Butterfly concert. The band, of course, played its signature hit, "In-A-Gadda-Da-Vida," which featured drummer Ron Bushy's distinctive solo. "Ringo sent his man backstage and invited me out to a private club called Tramps," Bushy said. "We had dinner and drinks and were up all night shooting the shit. He told me then that he kind of copped my solo for their song 'The End' on *Abbey Road*. And I just thought that was cool. It was the biggest compliment that I could ever get."

Abbey Road was released in the UK on September 26, 1969, and entered the charts at Number One. It spent the next eleven weeks in the top spot, was replaced by The Rolling Stones album *Let It Bleed* for a week, then was back on top for another six weeks. Its performance in the U.S. was no less impressive; released on October 1, it spent twelve weeks at Number One.

Reviews for *Abbey Road* were generally, but not always, favorable: music critic Nik Cohn, while praising the fifteen-minute medley as "the most impressive music they've made since *Rubber Soul*," heaped scorn on the rest of the album in a scathing review in the *New York Times*, calling *Abbey Road* "an unmitigated disaster" with "limp-wristed, pompous and fake lyrics." Ringo took a drubbing as well, with Cohn calling "Octopus's Garden" a "Ringo Starr nursery rhyme" and the song itself "purest Mickey Mouse."

<hr>

By the fall of 1969 it was obvious, if not yet official, that The Beatles were going to break up. The *Abbey Road* sessions were relatively harmonious compared to the bitterness and bile of *The White Album* and *Let It Be* sessions and produced some great music on par with anything in The Beatles canon. But the writing was on the wall.

"By now everything was tough except the moments when we played and that was the saving grace," Ringo said. "Once the music started we were always okay because we still did our best." The Beatles had managed to hold it together for *Abbey Road*, but everyone intrinsically knew it was all over by then.

The band that defined the sixties looked like it would dissolve as the decade ended. In September, John and Yoko started recording an album with their Plastic Ono Band, which featured an interchangeable lineup—and Ringo's familiar, steady drumming on "Cold Turkey," Lennon's ode to drug-withdrawal, which also featured old Hamburg pal Klaus Voormann on bass and Eric Clapton on guitar. ("It rocked," Ringo recalled. "John was in a good space.")

Despite his original aversion to Yoko Ono, Ringo—always the least combative, most easygoing Beatle—had come to peace with her constant presence and her quirky personality. That, in turn, drew him closer to John Lennon, who now enlisted Ringo and George Harrison in his fight against Paul.

McCartney wanted his father-in-law and business manager, Lee Eastman, to take over management of The Beatles; Ringo and George, siding with John, were in favor of Allen Klein steering the sinking ship. Klein's management portfolio included The Rolling Stones, The Kinks, Donovan, and Herman's Hermits. Lee Eastman, by comparison, had no track record in managing a rock band. Klein won the battle—he moved into the Apple offices in February 1969—but, in the end, it made no difference.

In mid-September, back in London after performing in Toronto with The Plastic Ono Band, John Lennon officially quit The Beatles, announcing his decision during a contentious meeting—just a day after the group renegotiated a new record deal with EMI/Capitol. The news was kept quiet, for now—although, internally, everyone knew this was it—and it would not be made public until the following April, when Paul McCartney issued a statement announcing the news, driving the final nail into the coffin of The World's Most Famous Band.

Ringo was not shocked by the breakup, although he held out a faint hope that The Beatles could regroup and get it together, maybe just one more time. He sunk into a deep depression that fall, sitting in his garden and wondering about his future sans John, Paul, and George.

What was he going to do now?

John Lennon, the toughest, most acerbic of The Beatles, always had a soft spot for Ringo. They'd vacationed together in the early days and were neighbors in Weybridge, spending many weekends in each other's company outside of the studio. Ringo and John shared that singularly sharp scouse sense of humor.

John was worried about Ringo, too, now that The Beatles ceased to exist (at least on paper, at this point). Paul McCartney was half of the most successful songwriting team in pop history, and had his hand in a number of pies, including (very quietly) his first solo album. No need to worry about him. George Harrison was coming into his own as a songwriter and producer, working with Billy Preston and with Delaney and Bonnie. He had a bright future.

But Ringo? True, he was The World's Most Famous Drummer, known universally by his first name. He was a millionaire several times over and owned 25 percent of Apple. But was it enough to sustain the gravy train?

Everything is relative, of course—especially when discussing The Beatles—

but Ringo was not as wealthy as Lennon and McCartney, who reaped additional mega-royalties from their Beatles songwriting and all their hits. While George Harrison was always overshadowed by John and Paul, he managed to get a song or two (or three) onto each Beatles album, and had big hits with "While My Guitar Gently Weeps," "Something," and "Here Comes the Sun."

Ringo's solo songwriting credits ("What Goes On," "Octopus's Garden," and "Don't Pass Me By") were nice, but minuscule by comparison to his band mates. He wasn't involved in any production work for Apple and did not have any outside projects, other than contributing to The Plastic Ono band's "Cold Turkey." His entire professional identity was wrapped up in The Beatles.

"I remember John talking about Ringo when we were in Tittenhurst Park and he said, 'I don't want Ringo to end up poor, having to play the Northern nightclubs,'" journalist Ray Connolly recalled. "Because the worst thing in the world for an ex-pop star in England is to end up playing Bradford or Darlington, the northern nightclubs, because they are really awful places. . . . The people eating chips and scampi while you're trying to be heard."

"I was lost for a while," Ringo admitted. "Suddenly the gig's finished that I'd been really involved in for eight years. 'Uh-oh, what'll I do now?" In mid-September, stressed out, he checked into Middlesex Hospital in London, suffering from severe stomach pains and an "intestinal blockage." After a few days in the hospital he went home.

In November 1969, Ringo shook himself out of his stupor. He needed to get back into the studio and do *something*. "I called George Martin and said, 'I'm going to do an album of standards that will get me out of bed, out of the house and get me back on my feet."

For his project, which evolved as his first solo album, *Sentimental Journey*, Ringo went back to his childhood roots in Liverpool and to the old familiar standards sung by Elsie, Harry and his aunts and uncles at family get-togethers, where everyone had a favorite "party song."

They were familiar, comfort-food types of tunes; besides, Ringo was fresh out of other ideas. Although neither John, George, nor Paul played on the album, McCartney was one of its musical arrangers. Ringo, Martin, and Neil Aspinall compiled a list of songs that Ringo could sing on key—no easy task, considering his limited vocal range.

Ringo sang vocals on each of the album's twelve tracks but didn't play the drums or any instruments (that was left to The George Martin Orchestra). Each song featured a different arranger, including heavy hitters Quincy Jones

("Love is a Many-Splendored Thing"), Elmer Bernstein ("Have I Told You Late-ly That I Love You?"), Paul McCartney ("Stardust"), George Martin ("Dream"), Richard Perry ("Sentimental Journey"), and Ringo's pal and former neighbor Maurice Gibb ("Bye Bye Blackbird").

Ringo worked on the album through early March 1970, recording his vocals in several studios, including Abbey Road, Trident, and Olympia Sound Studios. Several of the arrangements, including "Love Is a Many-Splendored Thing," were recorded at A&M Studios in December (Ringo was not present at these sessions).

"We had Quincy Jones and all these great arrangers, but if it did nothing else it got me off my bum, back into recording," he said. "The great thing was that it got my solo career moving—not very fast, but just moving. It was like the first shovel of coal in the furnace that makes the train inch forward."

On the cover of *Sentimental Journey*, which was released March 27 in the UK, Ringo used a photograph of the Empress pub, located just around the cor-ner from 10 Admiral Grove. The album's title was emblazoned in caps across the middle of the pub's façade; the words *RINGO STARR* were written across the top of the three-story building. Photographs of Ringo's relatives adorned each of the windows.

Officially, *Sentimental Journey* was the first solo album released by a Beatle; McCartney's self-titled album, *McCartney*, followed three weeks later, in April, coinciding with his public declaration that The Beatles were finished.

The reviews of Ringo's solo venture were mixed. "*Sentimental Journey* may be horrendous, but at least it's classy. Or is it?" Greil Marcus wrote in *Rolling Stone* magazine. "There *is* a certain thrill to hearing Ringo swing immediately and finally flat on 'Stardust' . . . Not exactly *Octupus Garden* [sic], but what the hell."

John Lennon said he was "embarrassed" by the effort, while George Har-rison praised *Sentimental Journey* as "a great album . . . really nice." Paul Mc-Cartney's reaction isn't known—but, then again, he had his own solo album on the horizon.

When all was said and done, it didn't matter *what* the critics thought. Ringo's name alone was enough to vault *Sentimental Journey* to Number Fifteen on the British charts. In the U.S., where it was released by Apple in late April, it sold half-a-million copies in three weeks, rose to Number Twenty-Two, and remained in the Top 30 for five weeks.

To promote the album, Ringo starred in a three-and-a-half-minute film, directed by Neil Aspinall, in which he sang "Sentimental Journey," wearing a big pink bow tie and the same black suit he'd sported on the *Abbey Road* album cover. The film was shot at Talk of the Town, a cabaret near Leicester Square, on the same day in March that Ringo was photographed (wearing a blue suit) for the *Sentimental Journey* album cover. The promotional clip featured backup dancers (male and female, all dressed in white); Ringo sang (and danced, awkwardly) on a stage flanked by the Union Jack and U.S. flags to an anonymous audience sitting at tables in the darkened club.

"The thing was, after I made that album, these people flew me to Vegas because they were thinking, 'Oh, now he can play Vegas!,'" Ringo said. "I went to see Elvis there, actually. And that was good. But I just knew at the time, that was not what I wanted to do. I did not want to wear a bow tie but, because the video we made for it had me with the bow tie and the dancing girls, they just dived in and thought that was me now."

There was more good news for Ringo as The Beatles continued to bicker behind closed doors—when they were even speaking to each other, that is. *The Magic Christian* premiered in mid-December, and Ringo made several high-profile appearances to promote the movie, including an hour-long interview for BBC2's *Late Night Line-Up* and an appearance with co-stars Peter Sellers and Spike Milligan on *Frost on Saturday*, the London Weekend Television show hosted by David Frost.

Ringo and Maureen attended the movie's star-studded London premiere with John and Yoko—a public-yet-misleading sign of Beatle unity. John and Yoko, not to be outdone in their grab for attention, marched past the public and press carrying a banner that read "Britain Murdered Hanratty," a reference to convicted killer James Hanratty, whose guilt was questioned by many when he was hanged in a British jail in 1962.

The reviews for *The Magic Christian* were a mixed lot. Ringo, by and large, was spared any viciousness. A *New York Times* critic wrote that "Ringo is fine, and Sellers is finer," while *Time* magazine thought that it was "just another flagging satire, with ludicrous overtones of homosexual lubricity."

Hollywood show business bible *Variety*, meanwhile, praised Sellers, while criticizing "Ringo Starr's effort to project himself as a non-Beatle actor" as "a distinct non-event."

The reviews did little to dampen enthusiasm for the movie, which wasn't exactly a blockbuster success but performed reasonably well at the box office. It also scored a big hit for Apple's showcase group, Badfinger. Their version of

"Come and Get It," written and produced by Paul McCartney, was included on *The Magic Christian* soundtrack. It hit Number Four on the British charts and rose to Number Seven in America.

Ringo knew it was really over for The Beatles in April, when he paid a visit to McCartney in his role as a stop-gap peacemaker. Ringo might have beaten McCartney to the punch by releasing *Sentimental Journey* in March, but it was only after a protracted argument with McCartney, who wanted to be the first Beatle to release a solo album and grudgingly agreed to let Ringo have the honor. Besides, Ringo's album of standards was regarded as a lightweight throwaway, with none of the buzz surrounding *McCartney*, Paul's impending solo effort, which was shrouded in mystery.

"I put my album out two weeks before, which makes me seem like a good guy," Ringo said, "but it wasn't really, because I needed to put it out before Paul's album, else it would have slayed me."

McCartney was now pushing for his album to drop in April; John, George, and Ringo, with Allen Klein's backing, were pushing him to delay its release, since they feared it would dull the impact of the *Let It Be* movie and the accompanying album, due to be released later that month.

None of The Beatles wanted any part of the *Let It Be* album, but were contractually committed to its release. The songs they'd recorded during that traumatic period lay dormant for around six months, until legendary producer Phil Spector, famous for his "Wall of Sound" mixing technique, stepped in and added his technical flourishes—infuriating McCartney. In April 1970, McCartney sent a letter to Allen Klein, voicing his displeasure with Spector's tinkering of McCartney's song "The Long and Winding Road," to which Spector had added strings and a harp. He ended his letter with "Don't ever do it again." He was ignored.

McCartney had even called George Harrison, telling him he wanted to get off the Apple label so he could release his solo record on his own. Harrison told him he would "stay on the fucking label," added a "Hare Krishna," and slammed the phone down.

With a civil war brewing, Harrison penned a letter to McCartney on March 31, leaving it at the Apple offices to be delivered to McCartney via messenger. In the letter, Harrison told McCartney that "it's stupid for Apple to put out two big albums within 7 days of each other (also there's Ringo's and *Hey Jude*)—so we sent a letter to EMI telling them to hold your release until June 4th (there's a big Apple-Capitol convention in Hawaii then.)" He signed it "Love, John and

George," leaving Ringo out of it, perhaps to protect the amiable drummer from McCartney's wrath.

Ringo "didn't think it was fair" for a messenger to deliver such an important letter to McCartney, so he volunteered to personally take the letter to McCartney's house on Cavendish Avenue. "The gentlest of The Beatles, the only one who never uttered a bad word about his band mates, who genuinely loved the others and wanted only their love in return" thought he could soothe McCartney's anger by talking it out and trying to reach a compromise. "I was talking to the office and they were telling me what was going on, and I said, 'Send it up, I'll take it round,'" Ringo said. "I couldn't fear him then."

He was wrong.

The meeting started out pleasantly enough, but as soon as Ringo broached the *McCartney/Let It Be* kerfuffle, pulled out the letter, and told Paul he agreed with everything in it, Paul lit into him like he'd never done before—cursing Ringo out and literally throwing him out of his house. McCartney admitted later he was "fairly hostile," and while they didn't come to blows, both men were shaken by the encounter. McCartney regretted that it was Ringo who bore the brunt of his wrath; he was angrier at Lennon and Harrison, but Ringo was the "fall guy."

Ringo was stunned and said he couldn't believe this was actually happening while McCartney was jabbing his finger in Ringo's face.

It was the straw that broke The Beatles' back. Paul, incensed at what he saw as John, George, and Ringo's truculence and betrayal, released *McCartney* on April 17, 1970—and, along with the album, a questionnaire in which he made his feelings known. The Beatles, as the world knew them, no longer existed. The final question read: "Do you miss The Beatles and George Martin? Was there a moment, e.g., when you thought, 'Wish Ringo was here for this break?'"

Paul's answer: "No."

"There was always the possibility that we could have carried on," Ringo said. "We weren't sitting in the studio making *Abbey Road*, saying, 'OK this is it: last record, last track, last take. But Paul put his solo record out and made the statement that said that The Beatles were finished. I think because it was said by one of The Beatles people understood it was over."

It was. Ringo was the last Beatle to play on a recording session for a group project. On April 1, he arrived at Abbey Road studios and laid down his drum and percussion tracks for George Harrison's "I Me Mine" and McCartney's "Across the Universe" and "The Long and Winding Road."

12

"IT DON'T COME EASY"

Ringo Starr turned thirty years old on July 7, 1970. While The Beatles no longer existed, there was a lot to which he could look forward, both person-ally and professionally.

Maureen was pregnant again, and their first daughter, Lee, was born that November. Bolstered by the success of *Sentimental Journey*, plans were afoot for Ringo's second solo album. There was talk of Ringo starring in a twelve-part television series—a project that never came to fruition—and, of course, there were movie roles being offered, although it would be another year until he would be on the big screen again.

Ringo and Klaus Voormann were even invited to play on a Howling Wolf blues album for Chess Records, but Ringo sensed he was in way over his head. Shortly into the session, he asked the album's producer, Glyn Johns, what the hell he was doing there and then tried to get both he and Voormann out of their commitment. Johns was able to book Charlie Watts (on drums) and Bill Wyman (on bass) from The Rolling Stones to replace Ringo and Voormann.

He remained on good terms with his ex-band mates, which was a huge plus. Paul McCartney, George Harrison, and John Lennon couldn't stand the sight of one another, but they all loved Ringo (Paul's anger at Ringo during the band's tumultuous breakup eventually subsided), and their favorite drummer would continue to work with each of them for years to come on their projects and on his own solo albums.

George, in particular, wasted no time in regrouping with Ringo after the break-up of The Beatles, inviting him to play drums (and tambourine) on *All Things Must Pass*, Harrison's mammoth triple album which he started to record in May. Ringo joined a galaxy of other A-list contributors, including Eric Clapton, Badfin-ger, Klaus Voormann, Gary Wright, and Billy Preston. He's credited with playing drums on "My Sweet Lord," "Wah Wah," "Isn't It a Pity," "Beware of Darkness," "All Things Must Pass," and "I Dig Love" (and tambourine on "If Not for You").

During their years together as band mates, George was always ready to lend Ringo a helping hand when he was struggling to write a song. Although "Octopus's Garden" is credited to Ringo, it's been long-rumored that Harrison's contribution was extensive.

The previous January, while Ringo was working on *Sentimental Journey*, he asked George to help him with a new tune that needed some help, both lyrically and structurally. The song, which morphed into "It Don't Come Easy," was released in 1971. It was Ringo's first solo single in the UK and is one of his best-known hits.

Ringo's involvement on *All Things Must Pass* led to his second solo album through an unlikely ally: noted Nashville producer and pedal steel-guitarist Pete Drake. In May, Drake—known for his hit 1964 album *Forever* and for his work with Bob Dylan, including Dylan's *Nashville Skyline* album—flew to London to play on *All Things Must Pass*.

Ringo sent his car to retrieve Drake from the airport, and on the ride to Abbey Road, where Harrison et al. were recording, Drake noticed a lot of country-western tapes strewn throughout the car. When he finally met Ringo in person, he asked about his interest in country.

"I said, 'I love country music.' So he said, 'You must come to Nashville and do an album.'" But Ringo was not about to pick up and move to Tennessee for six months, especially with Maureen pregnant and expecting their third child in the fall. "He said, 'Six months! *Nashville Skyline* took two days.' So I said, 'Okay, I'll come to Nashville and let's see what happens.'"

Ringo flew to Nashville in late June. It was his first time in the city. (The closest he'd been to Nashville previously was in 1966, when The Beatles played Memphis, 210 miles away.) With Drake behind the console as producer, and Elvis Presley's original guitarist, Scotty Moore, engineering, Ringo began recording what would evolve into *Beaucoups of Blues*. Like *Sentimental Journey*, Ringo only sang on the album, though he got behind the drums for a couple of impromptu jam sessions which were not included on the album's original release.

Drake lined up an all-star roster of musicians to back Ringo, including guitarist Charlie Daniels, Drake on his pedal steel guitar, and Presley's drummer, D. J. Fontana. Fontana knew a thing or two about playing with a huge star, and had high praise for Ringo's timekeeping skills and for his personality:

> He's one of the finest drummers. People say, "He don't do a lot." Well, he don't have to do a lot. He played that steady tempo. He was

the glue for The Beatles. He put it together for them. That's what they needed. That's the whole secret of drumming. If you wanna do something fancy, go ahead and do it. If not, just play the beat. What amazed me, he never varied from that tempo. He had the greatest conception of tempo I've ever heard in my life. I have never heard anybody play that steady in my life, and that's a long time.

We were thinking he was going to be a jerk. I mean, The Beatles, the number-one act in the world. This guy's got all these big monster records. But he came here and it was, "Whatever you guys want to do, let's do it. You guys play the way you've been playing and I'll try to catch up."

He played that backbeat and never got off of it. Man, you couldn't have moved him with a crane. It was amazing. He played a hell of a backbeat, man, and *that's* where it's at.

It was country all the way. Ringo and Drake spent their mornings listening to tracks submitted by a bevy of songwriters; they chose five songs each day, which were then recorded that afternoon at Music City Recorders. Drake kept his promise, and most of the songs were recorded in two days' time, on June 30 and July 1. (Prior to Ringo's arrival in Nashville, Drake had prerecorded Presley's favorite backup singers, The Jordanaires, for several tracks he thought Ringo would like.)

"It was all over by eight o'clock at night," Ringo said. "I'd written one called 'Coochy Coochy.' I wanted to play guitar because Pete [Drake] had bought George and me guitars as gifts. So I was playing this incredible Harmony guitar and I went to this band of Nashville professionals and said, 'I've written this song and it's in E.' Only E—it didn't go anywhere." The only unpleasant moments for Ringo during his Nashville stay were the gawkers who came by the studio to "meet the 'Fab Ringo.' . . . That kind of thing was a drag then."

Beacoups of Blues turned out to be a total musical about-face from *Sentimental Journey*—a full-on country album, giving Ringo the chance to indulge his love for the genre with some of the best backing musicians in the business. The album was released in late September and included twelve songs, including the title track, "Woman of the Night," "Without Her," and "Wine, Women and Loud Happy Songs." It failed to chart in the UK and did just okay in America, where it crept to Number Sixty-Five on the country charts and received a condescending review in *Rolling Stone*:

Make no mistake about it, though, this record is a real winner. . . . Fortunately, the only reason Ringo can carry a tune is that the composers of the tunes were singing along with him on most of the songs, just out of mike range. No matter how morose the material gets, Ringo's easy-going baritone assures us that he has little idea of what's going on, anyway. . . . If *Beaucoups of Blues* reminds one of any record it's *Nashville Skyline*, only instead of being lovable, spaced-out Bobby Dylan in front of those luxurious Nashville backups, it's lovable Richard Starkey who is crooning his heart out. . . . Ringo plays the part, and it sounds as though he hardly did any rehearsing. All he had to do was act naturally. Natural Ringo Starr may not exactly be New Horizons in Pop Music, but, hell. He's really pretty good after all.

John Lennon told the magazine he thought "it was a good record"—but that he wasn't going to buy it.

There were kinder assessments of the album, thankfully. A music critic for the *New York Times* wrote:

What is remarkable is not simply the fact of Ringo Starr singing country music, but that he does it so well. . . . There surely is something ironic about the fact that the performer who was so often described as the extra wheel of The Beatles, as a mediocre drummer who happened to fall into a good thing, should now start to come into his own. Comfortably ensconced in a relaxed Nashville setting, Ringo Starr has shown what he can do, and created a recording that accurately certifies his self-chosen last name.

Time magazine's reviewer thought the idea of Ringo in Nashville "seems as logical as Mick Jagger at Glyndebourne," but was effusive in his praise of the album:

In truth, Ringo poses no immediate threat to such country greats as Eddy Arnold or Johnny Cash. Yet his straightforward, unadorned singing style—customarily sure death in the quasi-Baroque world of rock—turns out to be just the thing for the classic country songs devoted to simple words, gentle irony and love gone haywire. . . . His baritone is occasionally too beery. But his cornhusky mastery of the album's title song . . . more than makes up for his failings.

Ringo's "Coochy Coochy" and "Nashville Jam," on which he played the drums, were not included on the original release of *Beaucoups of Blues*. They were included as "bonus" tracks when the album was re-released in 1995 to capitalize on the resurgence of The Beatles, thanks to *The Beatles Anthology*, a television documentary that premiered that year.)

By the end of 1970, Ringo had two solo albums on his résumé. *Sentimental Journey* and *Beaucoups of Blues* were not hits by any stretch—the former effort, in fact, generated outright derision in some circles—but the music gave Ringo the extra push he needed to find some sense of professional purpose other than being known as "Ex-Beatle Ringo Starr."

He spent most of 1971 focusing on his movie career, and welcoming Harry Nilsson, Keith Moon, and flamboyant T. Rex front man Marc Bolan into his inner circle. Nilsson, Moon, and Bolan would influence Ringo's career at least in the short-term. Nilsson, especially, would spend the next decade as one of Ringo's closest friends and his constant drinking and drugging partner. Ringo and Harry would carouse their way through the 1970s in a blur of jet-setting rock-star hedonism for which they paid a dear price. Keith Moon paid with his life.

In early March 1970, with Harrison as producer behind the console, Ringo re-recorded the song, now called "It Don't Come Easy," at Trident Studios. He was complemented by Harrison on guitar, backing vocals from Badfinger members Pete Ham and Tom Evans, Stephen Stills on piano, Klaus Voormann on bass, and Ron Cattermole on sax and trumpet. Ringo sang the song's catchy lyrics with exuberance and played an interesting drum pattern in his signature straight-ahead style.

The theme of the song finds Ringo—in his familiar flat baritone—noting that one must experience life's hard knocks in order to sing the blues.

Apple waited until April 9, 1971, to release "It Don't Come Easy" as Ringo's first single in the UK (it was backed with "Early 1970," also written by Ringo). "It Don't Come Easy," released a week later in the U.S., climbed to Number Four in both countries, giving Ringo his first breakout solo success.

Ringo appeared on the BBC's *Top of the Pops* (twice) and on Cilla Black's television show, *Cilla*, to promote the song that spring and summer. As a Beatle, he was never one for rivalries, and that didn't change once the band broke up. It's interesting to note, however, that McCartney, Lennon, and Harrison also had competing singles out around the same time: "Another Day" (Mc-Cartney, released in February), "Power to the People" (Lennon, released in March) and "Bangla Desh" (Harrison, released in July). "It Don't Come Easy" outsold them all.

Score one for the little guy.

In August, Ringo flew to New York City from Spain—where he was acting in his next movie, *Blindman*—to perform at The Concert for Bangladesh. The epic event (two shows in one day, one at three p.m. and one at eight p.m.) was organized by George Harrison and Ravi Shankar to aid refugees following a civil war in Bangladesh that left a trail of starvation and atrocities in its wake.

The concert was staged at Madison Square Garden; the usually reticent Harrison not only emceed but also performed along with Eric Clapton, Bob Dylan, Badfinger, Billy Preston, and Leon Russell, among others. Paul McCartney was asked to appear but refused the invitation outright, thinking people would assume that The Beatles were getting back together. John Lennon accepted the invitation, then refused to show up when he realized it was for him only—and not Yoko.

Ringo's appearance generated a huge roar from the Garden crowd as he walked onstage and sat behind his drum kit, dressed completely in black and sporting long hair and the bushy beard he'd grown for *Blindman*. Ringo, Eric Clapton, Leon Russell, and George launched into Harrison's "Wah-Wah" and then into a performance of "Something" from the *Abbey Road* album, which George was performing in public for the first time.

Ringo then sang a sloppy rendition of "It Don't Come Easy" with Harrison on guitar and a second drummer, Jim Keltner, playing the more intricate fills. No one seemed to care that Ringo forgot some of the lyrics or that he let Keltner do most of the heavy lifting; it was enough for the twenty-thousand people packed into Madison Square Garden to see two bearded ex-Beatles sharing a stage again—and actually having fun.

"I enjoyed playing immensely," Ringo said afterward. "It was a bit weird because it was the first time I had been on stage for about three years. I was crazy with nerves beforehand. But if you have done your job, it's okay. You soon relax. It was nice, anyway, because we had a lot of good pals around."

"Performing some of the hit songs they had never played before a live audience, George Harrison and Ringo Starr thrilled more than 20,000 cheering, well-behaved fans," noted a *New York Times* reporter. Although John Lennon did not show up, Harrison surprised everyone by introducing Bob Dylan, who was making his first live appearance since a concert on the Isle of Wight in 1969. It was the first time Dylan shared a stage with any of the now-ex-Beatles, and while Ringo didn't play drums, he banged a tambourine on a few of Dylan's tunes, including "Blowin' in the Wind" and "Just Like a Woman." The scenes were repeated at both the afternoon and evening shows.

Playing with George again gave Ringo a huge emotional boost and, in September, with Harrison once again in the booth producing, Ringo cut his next single at the Apple studio in London. It was a catchy song called "Back Off Boogaloo" and, like "It Don't Come Easy," Ringo collaborated on the song with George (who neither took nor wanted a co-writing credit).

According to Ringo, the song's title was inspired by Marc Bolan, the lead singer of British glam rockers T. Rex, who'd had a Number One hit in the UK with "Get It On" from the group's 1971 album, *Electric Warrior.* (The song was retitled "Get It On [Bang a Gong]" in the States, where it reached Number Ten on the charts.) There was some chatter that Bolan had a hand in writing "Back Off Boogaloo," although there's no evidence to support this. Ringo recalled:

> Marc was a dear friend who used to come into the office when I was running Apple Movies, a big office in town, and the hang-out for myself, Harry Nilsson, and Keith Moon. We'd go on to various venues, but we'd always start down in the office and Marc was so much fun, he'd tell us how many he was gonna sell, and what chart position he'd have. We were only thirty, then, but we were looking at him like he was some crazy kid.
>
> We became friends, we had a holiday together. I took one of his album covers for him, that was just on the roof of Apple, actually. He came over to dinner one night and he had this infectious laugh, and "Back off," [said] in a friendly way, was one of his lines. "Back off, Boogaloo!" I was in bed later and in that twilight zone the whole song just came. . . . I just jumped out of bed, I got a song going.

Ringo rushed to get the song on tape, but discovered that his tape recorder's batteries were dead, so he raided one of the kids' toys. He took the song to Harrison, because, as he explained modestly, "I'm a limited guitar player, I can only play three chords. I'd got the melody down with my three chords and took it over to George's: 'Would you put in a few more chords?' It makes me sound like a genius."

"Back Off Boogaloo" opened with Ringo's military-style snare drumming. He was backed by Harrison playing guitar (slide and acoustic), Gary Wright on piano, and Klaus Voormann on bass and saxophone. For the single's B-side, Ringo wrote and recorded "Blindman," which was originally intended to be the title song on the soundtrack of the movie he'd just wrapped in Spain. The song, which featured Badfinger guitarist Pete Ham and, once again, Voormann on bass, was rejected by the movie's producers—along with the notion that Ringo would (or could) write the movie's entire soundtrack.

"Back Off Boogaloo" was released in March 1972 and was Ringo's second consecutive hit, reaching Number Two in the UK and climbing to Number Nine on the U.S. charts, surprising everyone who wrote off Ringo's musical career after the breakup of The Beatles. "A Number One hit could easily be in store for the maestro of rock drums," wrote *Melody Maker* critic Chris Welch. "There's a touch of the Marc Bolan in this highly playable rhythmic excursion. . . . It's hypnotic and effective, ideal for jukeboxes and liable to send us all mad by the end of the week."

There was speculation at the time that some of the lyrics in "Back Off Boogaloo" were aimed at Paul McCartney, who was battling his ex-band mates in London's High Court over corporate matters (both over The Beatles and Apple business affairs). Critics looking for clues to support their "Back Off Boogaloo" suspicions vis-à-vis McCartney pointed to comments Ringo made in a *Melody Maker* interview July 1971, when commenting on Paul's two solo efforts. "He disappoints me on his albums," Ringo said. "I don't think there's one [good] tune on the last one. . . . It's like he's not admitting that he can write great tunes."

It's easy to see how some of the lines in "Back Off Boogaloo" could be construed as attacks on McCartney. "*Wake up Meathead/Don't pretend that you are dead*" was construed as Ringo's allusion to the "Paul is dead" rumors that abounded in 1969. The line about "sure sounds wasted" was allegedly aimed at McCartney's mediocre solo output and at his prolific marijuana habit. Ringo attributed those lines to English football announcer Jimmy Hill, whom he was watching one Sunday afternoon and heard him describe the skills of one player as especially "tasty."

Ringo denied that "Back Off Boogaloo" had anything to do with McCartney, and it would have been completely out of character for the amiable, unthreatening drummer to target McCartney in a song. But Ringo's relationship with Paul was somewhat strained at the time, and one has to take into account the influence of George Harrison—who, though uncredited as the song's co-writer, had a more acidic relationship with Paul.

So, too, did John Lennon. McCartney and Lennon were going at it full-throttle around this time, with McCartney chiding Lennon on his song "Too Many People" (from his solo album, *Ram*) and Lennon firing back at McCartney with "How Do You Sleep?" on his 1971 album, *Imagine*.

Whatever the case, Ringo's relationship with Paul couldn't have been that damaged: in May 1971, Ringo, Maureen, Paul, and Linda chartered a plane and flew to St. Tropez for Mick Jagger's wedding to Bianca Macias.

And, notwithstanding the bad feelings at the time, it's hard to fathom that Ringo, whose contributions to The Beatles' songwriting catalogue was virtually non-existent, would have the *chutzpah* to scold one of the greatest tunesmiths in pop-music history.

Ringo failed to cash in on the momentum generated by "Back Off Boogaloo" by not supporting his second consecutive hit single with an album. He wanted to focus on his movie career following the relative success of *The Magic Christian*, but *Blindman* would prove to be a poor choice.

He spent the summer of 1971 in Almeria, Spain, filming his role in this violent, bloody shoot-'em-up. The movie, directed by Ferdinando Baldi and produced by Allen Klein (which explained Ringo's involvement), was co-written by Spaghetti Western veteran Tony Anthony, who also starred as the movie's titular character—a tough, blind gunfighter whose task of delivering fifty mail-order brides (scantily clad and often topless) to a bunch of horny mine workers in Texas is short-circuited when an associate double-crosses him, selling the women to a gang in Mexico.

Ringo, sporting a bushy beard and long hair, played a Mexican bandit named Candy(!), the brother of Domingo, the gang's leader. He affected a laughably bad Spanish accent and didn't make much of an impression when *Blindman* opened in 1972. The *New York Times* called it "one of those Spanish Westerns in English" which "bats out in almost every department except sadistic slaughter. See it, if you must, after you eat. . . . By the last reel, the picture . . . lets fly with some murderous stalking. There's mangy Tony Anthony, droning away in a monotone as a sightless killer. There's hairy Ringo Starr, snarling away and still looking like a parrot trying to thread a needle. Lloyd Batista, as another killer, does the only acting in the film. . . ."

There seemed to be something about rock drummers and movies that drew the two disparate elements together. Ringo's good friend Keith Moon, The Who's manic, gifted, wild man drummer, was also eyeing a movie career and, like Ringo, would never quite harness his potential.

Moon tore through his short life with the same ferocity with which he attacked his drums. Ringo first met Keith, who was six years his junior, in the mid-'60s, when The Beatles were at their peak and The Who were just starting to make some noise, both onstage and on the charts. Ringo was with John, Paul, and George at the Scotch of St. James, a club in London and a known Beatles hangout, when Moon approached the Fab Four. "Do you mind if I join you?" Moon asked. "Pull up a chair," one of The Beatles said. "No, do you mind if I *join* you?" Moon said emphatically. "We've already got a drummer, thanks," Ringo answered him—and a lifelong friendship was born.

Moon was one of the chosen few allowed into the studio in 1967 to sing along with The Beatles on *All You Need is Love* during the *Our World* telecast. Several years later, he bought a house near Ringo, often stopping by the Starkey homestead to shower attention on Zak and Jason.

"We really liked him because he was this guy who would come round and play with us—the kids—whereas all our parents' other friends used to just hang out with them and not take notice of us," Zak said. "He was completely different in that respect. We all loved Keith." When Zak turned twelve, Keith gave him one of his huge white drum kits as a birthday present.

One Christmas day, Zak, Jason, and Lee were surprised at Tittenhurst by a pony and sleigh bearing gifts—courtesy of "Uncle Keith," who then failed to pay the bill, which Ringo took care of.

Glyn Johns, the talented engineer and producer who'd worked on the *Let It Be* album, went to a 1970 New Year's Eve party thrown by Ringo and Maureen. "My overriding memory of that evening is hearing the sound of drums being played in another room in the house," he wrote. "I went to investigate and found Keith Moon giving Ringo's four-year-old son, Zak, a lesson. Zak idolized Keith, who was his godfather."

"Keith used to be a kind of musical godfather to him," Moon's Who band mate Pete Townshend said. "He gave him his first drum kit, which I think is rather strange. Ringo may have actually given him his first drum kit, but I think Keith gave him the first drum kit that he really wanted. It had nude women on it."

Several years later, Keith called Ringo and told him to look out the window of his room at the Sunset Plaza in Los Angeles; Keith had hired a skywriter to fly over the hotel and spell out "Happy Birthday Ringo" in white smoke. Ringo paid for that, too, when Keith couldn't come up with the money. "In the end I had to stop Keith buying me presents," Ringo said. "I'd always get the bill."

They were two of The World's Most Famous Drummers, and their *simpatico* relationship crossed over to a 1972 London Symphony Orchestra recording of *Tommy*, The Who's classic rock-opera album. Ringo played the part of Uncle Ernie, the role originated by Keith three years before on the original LP (and which he reprised in Ken Russell's 1975 big-screen movie).

"His interaction with Ringo was incredibly intimate," Ringo's future love, Nancy Andrews, said of Moon. "I've noticed over the years that drummers have a shorthand language and they don't need to complete sentences to convey their thoughts. Ringo and Keith could say two or three words to each other and there would be an instant understanding."

In mid-1971, Ringo and Keith joined the cast of the movie *200 Motels*, the brainchild of innovative rock musician/producer/composer Frank Zappa, known for his ever-changing band, the Mothers of Invention, and his musical experimentation.

The loosely structured plotline of *200 Motels* recounted life on the road for the Mothers of Invention, who slowly lose their minds while in the small town of Centerville. Zappa wanted Ringo to play him—Zappa—in the movie, a typically surreal Zappa touch. Besides, Zappa was directing the movie and wouldn't have time to play himself. He went to see Ringo at Round Hill.

"So he came and laid out a huge music score," Ringo said. "I can't read music. There was no script, just the music score. So I said, 'Sure! I've got to do it now!'" *200 Motels* was funded by United Artists, which invested $630,000 into the project—paltry by Hollywood standards, but Zappa's name carried a lot of weight. Ringo loved the idea, as did Keith Moon, who was always looking for a fun time and signed onto the project. The Mothers of Invention also had roles in the movie, as did Theodore Bikel, who was the only professional actor in the cast.

Zappa hired the Royal Philharmonic Orchestra to perform *200 Motels*; two of its trumpet players resigned after the first rehearsal, disgusted by the movie's preponderance of sex, drugs, and rock 'n' roll. Bikel also threatened to quit; he didn't want to say the word "penis" and was put off by the profanity in the script, but he toughed it out for the entire seven-day shoot (preceded by six days of rehearsals).

The atmosphere on the *200 Motels* set at Pinewood Studios was, to no one's surprise, chaotic. Moon's presence meant that no one slept; although he was in only one scene (dressed as a nun), he stayed with the cast and crew at the Kensington Palace Hotel for the thirteen-day production. The drinking and drugging was prodigious.

"Ringo helped too, but it took Keith to loosen up Ringo—because Ringo was still a Beatle, and still held in reverence even though he was very nice and loose," recalled Mothers of Invention band member Howard Kaylan. "But once Moonie got into the room and they started getting crazy and crude, then everything started loosening up, and everyone got into the spirit that Keith brought to the thing."

Mothers of Invention bassist Jeff Simmons quit during the production, and Zappa declared that whoever walked through the door next would get his part. That honor went to Ringo's chauffeur, Martin Lickert, making his first and last movie appearance.

Ringo, wearing the trademark Zappa soul patch, actually looked like his alter-ego, although that didn't really matter. "Frank was such a nice man," he said. "Because of the image he put out, people were a bit afraid of him—this weird Frank Zappa—but he was just a very nice guy and loved his music. The whole joke of the movie was that I would record the band members talking—I was like the devil guy—and put it to music and force them to play it. So the premise was a lot of fun and it's always good hanging out with musicians."

200 Motels opened to mixed reviews in November 1971. "At its heart, *200 Motels* is a subjective *A Hard Day's Night* in desperate need of the early Beatles," wrote one critic.

Ringo had more success behind the camera directing *Born to Boogie*, a concert film/documentary about Marc Bolan, the twenty-five-year-old T. Rex lead singer and guitarist. Bolan, one of Ringo's friends, was at the forefront of the "glam rock" movement of the early '70s, along with David Bowie and David Essex. T. Rex had several big hits by that time, including "Ride a White Swan," "Hot Love," "Jeepster," and "Get It On."

The idea of the movie, which was an Apple Films production (overseen by Ringo) was to capture what the British press was calling "T. Rextasy." The movie was threaded around a T. Rex concert at London's Wembley Empire Pool (now called the Wembley Arena) in March 1972. In addition to directing the movie, Ringo was credited as one of the cameramen. Keith Moon had a cameo role.

"Most days and all nights, I'd be sitting around the table in my office, with Harry Nilsson, Keith Moon and myself discussing 'world politics,'" Ringo said, explaining how *Born to Boogie* came to pass. "And Marc [Bolan] came in one day—I don't know how he got in but he got in—and he said, 'I came in the charts at Number Ten. Next week I'll be Number One.'" I said to him, 'I want this to be the way of Apple Films.' If you had a great idea we'd supply the cameras and the money and you'd bring the product back. But most people forgot to bring anything back; they just ran away with the cameras. And with him I said, 'You put yourself up, I'll put everything else up.' That's how I wanted to work and we did that with him. He loved the idea."

In addition to the Wembley concert, *Born to Boogie* incorporated in-studio footage, shot at John Lennon's Ascot Sound Studios, of Bolan and T. Rex accompanied by Ringo (on a second set of drums) and Elton John (on piano) jamming on "Tutti Frutti," "Children of the Revolution," and "The Slider" (the former wasn't included in the finished film). "My theory about filming concerts is that you cannot create the atmosphere that was in the hall," Ringo said. "So I needed to do more. We got him to write a few things and set up a couple more days shooting."

There were also several fantasy sequences reminiscent of *Magical Mystery Tour*: Bolan seated in a convertible car with weird costumed characters, and interacting with Ringo with nonsensical dialogue, and a "tea party" scene filmed outdoors at Lennon's home in Tittenhurst. This scene featured a trio of violinists, a butler cooking hamburgers on an outdoor barbecue, and Bolan serenading a trio of nuns (and Ringo, among others) with acoustic versions of "Jeepster" and "Get It On."

"As Ringo and I became more involved in the making of *Born to Boogie*, we decided to add several more scenes—bringing in 'accident' humor and also to shoot from recorded music," Bolan said at the time. "In some of the scenes outside of the concert we let our imaginations take their course and, with the aid of props and a dwarf, let whichever happened, happen."

Born to Boogie opened in December 1972, and the reviews were fair to middling. "The incidental humor is drawn from the nursery surrealist world of *The Magical Mystery Tour*, but lacks that famous disaster's pretensions," noted *The Observer*, while the *Morning Star* called *Born to Boogie* "the best teeny-bopper entertainment since The Beatles succumbed to insecticide."

13

"BETTER YOU THAN SOMEONE WE DON'T KNOW"

As the calendar turned to 1973, Ringo remained on good terms with all three of his former Beatles band mates. The *Back Off Boogaloo* kerfuffle with McCartney, real or imagined, didn't impact their relationship. And Paul was on to bigger and better things. He had a new band, Wings, into which he incorporated his wife, Linda. Wings released two albums in 1973, *Red Rose Speedway* and *Band on the Run*, both of which topped the U.S. charts. (The latter album entered the charts at Number One in the UK.) Paul would also contribute to Ringo's next solo album, recorded that same year.

Ringo also stayed in touch with John and Yoko and was close with George Harrison. Ringo and Maureen invited George and his wife, Pattie, over to the house for dinner on occasion. Ringo had George to thank, in large part, for the success of "It Don't Come Easy" and "Back Off Boogaloo," and he returned the favor by playing drums on Harrison's 1973 album, *Living in the Material World.*

By this time George and Pattie were having marital problems; Pattie was miserable and, according to Peter Brown, George was "cheating on Pattie a great deal by then, and it wouldn't be incorrect to say that he had reverted to his old Don Juan ways." Making matters even worse was that fact that one of George's best friends, Eric Clapton, was in love with Pattie—who didn't exactly shun his advances.

After nearly four years at Round Hill, Ringo and Maureen decided to move again. They, too, were seeing some cracks forming in their marriage and they decided they needed a change of pace. After more than ten years together, eight of them as a married couple, their arguments were growing more frequent. Ringo's drinking was more pronounced and wasn't helped by the company he was keeping: Keith Moon, Marc Bolan, and Harry Nilsson, all prodigious boozers. Perhaps a new house would give Ringo and Maureen a clean slate and a fresh start.

"One thing that we always forget is how young they were," said Chris

O'Dell, who worked at the Apple offices and grew close to both Ringo and Maureen. "I mean, they got married when they were very young, she was very young, and they went through a lot. Very few people survive through a huge amount of success and fame. They were exceedingly famous and I think their marriage began to disintegrate around the time that The Beatles and Apple and everything else was disintegrating. I think it was a normal time for them to be going, 'Well, what do we do now?'"

In September, Ringo bought Tittenhurst Park from John Lennon, who moved to America with Yoko Ono in 1971 and no longer needed the twenty-six-room Georgian mansion. The house was situated on over seventy acres of rolling hills in Sunninghill, Berkshire, about thirty miles outside of London. (There were reports that Ringo's purchase of Tittenhurst was part of an out-of-court settlement related to Lennon's unpaid loans with Allen Klein.)

Lennon and Yoko Ono had only lived at Tittenhurst for two years. John bought the three-hundred-year-old estate in 1969—The Beatles' final photo shoot, for the *Hey Jude* album cover, took place on the grounds there—but he pumped a lot of money into renovations, installing an artificial lake, a swimming pool, and a sauna. He also built the Ascot Sound recording studio, which Ringo used in *Born to Boogie*.

When Ringo took ownership of Tittenhurst, he renamed the recording facility Startling Studios and used it for himself. He also rented it out to his industry friends and associates. "I've talked to Ringo a lot recently because he's just moved into my house at Ascot, which is nice because I've always got a bedroom there," Lennon deadpanned. (According to one account, builders hired by Ringo to work on Tittenhurst Park found clothes, notes, and personal belongings left behind by Lennon—and Ringo ordered them to "put them in the ground and burn them.")

But Tittenhurst proved to be fatal to Ringo and Maureen's marriage. A short time after they moved in, they invited George and Pattie over for a nice dinner. What happened next was a shocker no one could have predicted. Chris O'Dell, who entered The Beatles' orbit when she worked at Apple in the late '60s, claimed in her 2009 rock 'n' roll memoir, *Miss O'Dell*, that she was at dinner with Ringo, Maureen, George, and Pattie that fateful night.

According to O'Dell, she was staying with George and Pattie at Friar Park when Pattie confided to O'Dell that Maureen "comes over all the time. . . . She and George go into a room and shut the door." The very next night, Maureen called Friar Park and invited O'Dell to come over. Chris figured it would be a good idea to let George and Pattie have some quiet time alone at home, and maybe try to talk about their crumbling marriage. But George volunteered to drive O'Dell over to Ringo and Maureen's—and Pattie, ever-suspicious of George's intentions, tagged along for the ride.

It was O'Dell's first time at Tittenhurst, and she describes all five adults sitting at a long wooden kitchen table, with "Ringo and George on one bench, Pattie and I facing them on the opposite bench" while Maureen "spent the entire evening flitting around like a little bird . . . jumping up to cook an omelet for Ringo, refilling our drinks, bringing plates of food to the table." It was nearing midnight when Maureen opened a drawer and took out a pack of Marlboro cigarettes—"George's brand. Maureen and Ringo both smoked Larks."

> We sat there in silence, and then George turned to Ringo and said, "You know, Ringo, I'm in love with your wife." I think all five hearts in that kitchen stopped beating for a few seconds. The room was completely still, no sudden gasps, no deep breaths, no fingers tapping or throats clearing. Absolute silence. . . . Maureen retreated to the far side of the room and stood by the sink, frozen, staring at the kitchen counter. Ringo looked down at the table. He flicked his cigarette ash in the ashtray. His jaw clenched, and a muscle by his mouth twitched. Finally, he looked at George. "Better you than someone we don't know," he said in a steady voice.

Despite his outward sense of calm, Ringo was horrified by the revelation. Out of his three Beatle "brothers," it was George, more than Paul or John, who was the most instrumental in recruiting him into the group in 1962. It was George who threw Ringo a professional and emotional lifeline after the bitter Beatles breakup, co-writing and producing Ringo's two hit singles. How could he do this?

But it only got worse.

A few weeks later, according to Peter Brown, Pattie returned home to the Harrisons' mansion, Friar Park, only to find George in bed with Maureen. No one ever denied the story; Pattie would only say "I don't want to get anybody in trouble," while George, asked why he'd hit on Ringo's wife, "shrugged his shoulders and said, 'Incest.'"

Pattie, meanwhile, avenged George's betrayal by returning to her modeling career—something George had always forbidden—and having her first affair, choosing Ronnie Wood, the guitarist for The Faces (who later joined The Rolling Stones).

Maureen claimed her brief affair with George was emotional—not physical—and always referred to it, even years later, as "the situation." And if Pattie Harrison exacted her revenge on George by having an affair with Ronnie Wood, Ringo got even with Maureen in his own way.

In February 1974, depressed about the state of his marriage and Maureen's "situation" with George, Ringo flew to Los Angeles to "clear his head." For The World's Most Famous Drummer, clearing his head meant carousing around town with drinking buddies Harry Nilsson, Keith Moon, and John Lennon, who was in L.A. with his lover May Pang.

Lennon was going through his own personal crisis. He and Yoko Ono had hit a rough patch in their marriage, and Yoko had kicked him out of the couple's New York City apartment, sending him on his way with Pang, her personal assistant, to keep John company (at Yoko's suggestion). John rented a white stucco beach house in Santa Monica from actor Peter Lawford. It was the same beach house that was allegedly used a decade before by Lawford's brother-in-law, President John F. Kennedy, for his secret trysts with Marilyn Monroe.

Ringo arrived in California on Valentine's Day and, shortly thereafter, was ensconced in John's beach house with his own room on the second floor. Shortly after his arrival in L.A., Ringo looked up Chris O'Dell, who was alerted to his arrival by Maureen—calling long-distance and asking Chris to "look after" Ringo and make sure he was okay. After a bit of flirtation, Ringo and Chris embarked on a months-long affair, with many of their private moments unfolding in Ringo's room at the Lennon beach house or in his suite at the Beverly Wilshire Hotel.

They kept the affair hidden from Maureen, or tried to. But when Ringo returned to Tittenhurst for a month, Maureen sensed something was amiss. Ringo didn't admit to anything, but was giving off a weird vibe. Shortly after he flew back to L.A., Maureen called the Santa Monica beach house and asked Chris O'Dell if Ringo was "seeing someone over there." O'Dell lied and said she had no idea, but the situation came to a head about a week later.

A suspicious Maureen flew to L.A. and checked into Ringo's suite at the Beverly Hills Hotel. One afternoon, when O'Dell was there, and with Ringo staring out of the window, Maureen asked Chris point-blank if she was sleeping with her husband. As O'Dell recounted in her book, *Miss O'Dell*: "I took a deep breath and answered her question. 'Yes,' I said. 'Well,' Maureen said, looking

over at Ringo but speaking directly to me, 'at least you were honest with me.'"
Ringo's marriage to Maureen, for all intents and purposes, was over. They divorced a year later.

All of this was going down at a time when Ringo Starr should have been cel-
ebrating his continued success as a musician. From March through July 1973
he'd recorded his third solo album, called, simply, *Ringo*. Produced by Richard
Perry, who contributed to Ringo's first solo album (*Sentimental Journey*), *Ringo*
was the drummer's finest work as a solo artist. *Ringo* also marked the first time
since their 1970 breakup that all four Beatles appeared on the same album, in
one form or another—a situation that only good-guy Ringo, everyone's friend,
could have pulled off. Ringo recalled,

> I worked with Harry Nilsson in London on his album [*Son of Schm-
> ilsson*] with producer Richard Perry. So Harry and I were invited to
> do the Grammy awards, and Richard was saying, "Remember you
> were talking to me in the club one night, you know . . . you'd like to
> do something? After the Grammys, why don't you come down to L.A.
> for a week?" And we went in. It worked so well, in ten days we had
> eight tracks, you see. Once we started we couldn't stop. And then I
> got John to write me something, and I got Paul, I got George. You
> know . . . dragged in all me friends, 'cause I'm lucky—I got a lot of
> people who'll work for me. I'll work for them, but I always feel very
> lucky that people will come out for me.

For his newest album, Ringo corralled a stable of A-list musicians to record
with him, including Marc Bolan, Harry Nilsson, drummer Jim Keltner, Klaus
Voormann, Nicky Hopkins, Billy Preston, and The Band. Ringo played drums
and sang lead vocals on each of the album's ten songs.

George Harrison, always ready and available to lend a hand to Ringo, came
through once again. The two old friends had made amends after George's dal-
liance with Maureen. Harrison and Ringo co-wrote a beautiful love song called
"Photograph," with George playing guitar (and this time taking a songwriting credit). John Lennon contributed an autobiographical tune called "I'm the
Greatest," on which he played piano and sang backing vocals (with George on
guitar—almost a Beatles reunion!).

Lennon supposedly wrote "I'm the Greatest" for himself in 1970—after
watching The Beatles cavort in *A Hard Day's Night* on television—but decided

against recording it. He'd forgotten about the song until Ringo asked him to contribute something to the *Ringo* LP. Lennon re-tailored some of the lyrics to fit Ringo, throwing in allusions to Ringo's *Sgt. Pepper* alter-ego, Billy Shears, and to *Back Off Boogaloo.*

Paul McCartney contributed what was billed as a "kazoo"—but was, in reality, McCartney's own voice imitating a kazoo—to one of the album's biggest hits, "You're Sixteen," on which Harry Nilsson sang backup. McCartney was more involved on "Six O'Clock," writing the song and playing piano and synthesizer, with Linda McCartney on backup vocals. Harrison added "Sunshine Life for Me (Sail Away Raymond)," on which he played guitar, and even former Beatles roadie Mal Evans got into the act, co-writing "You and Me (Babe)" with Harrison.

Tellingly, McCartney did not appear on any of the same tracks as Lennon and Harrison. Such was the rancor between them at the time. Even Ringo couldn't pull that one off.

The first single spawned by *Ringo* was "Photograph," which was released in late September 1973 in the U.S. and several weeks later in the UK. Ringo filmed a promotional spot for the single at home in Tittenhurst, which was screened on the BBC's popular *Top of the Pops* television show. "Photograph" was almost universally praised for its lush composition, orchestral arrangements, and Ringo's plaintive singing. "We all know already that "Photograph" has got to be a No. 1 single this month, right?" wrote the music critic for *Billboard*, praising *Ringo* as "the best Ringo album ever."

"Photograph" shot to Number One in the U.S. and climbed to the Number Eight spot on the UK charts. The album's second single, "You're Sixteen," followed in December in the States and was released in February in the UK, around the time Ringo was embarking on his affair with Chris O'Dell. "You're Sixteen," backed by "Devil Woman," also went to Number One in America and spent a week in the top spot in late January 1974.

The third *Ringo* single, "Oh My My," hit Number Five in the U.S. following its release in February 1974. It didn't make its debut as a single in the UK until 1976, when Ringo was promoting his *Blast from Your Past* album and "Oh My My" was released as a single, backed by "No No Song."

Apple Records released the *Ringo* album in early November 1973 in both the U.S. and the UK. It climbed to Number Two on the American charts—just behind Elton John's *Goodbye Yellow Brick Road*—and hit Number Seven in the UK. It was Ringo's biggest solo album yet. Lennon sent him a kidding telegram after hearing the good news: "How dare you? Why don't you write me a hit song?"

Some of the reviews for Ringo were downright ecstatic. The *New York Times*: "*Ringo* . . . is an instant knockout, chock full of terrific songs and sensational production effects. . . . Producer Richard Perry has worked so hard to achieve a masterpiece that it's on the verge of being overdone. Luckily Ringo's sense of humor saves it from crossing over the line. Probably one of the reasons this album is so filled with musical ideas is that Ringo got a little help from his friends—like John Lennon, George Harrison, and Paul McCartney (who each contributed songs) as well as the Band."

Ringo and George Harrison, meanwhile, were in talks to launch a nationwide tour of the U.S. in the fall of 1974, consisting of twenty-five concerts "covering twelve to fifteen major cities." Sources "close to the tour" confirmed to the *New York Times* that the tour would feature Eric Clapton, Ravi Shankar, and a twenty-five piece band, a repeat, of sorts, of the 1971 Concert for Bangladesh (*sans* Bob Dylan and Leon Russell). "Word of the tour comes at a time in which rumors of impending Beatles reunions—on a more or less formal, more or less temporary basis—have reached a new intensity," the report breathlessly noted.

The tour never came to fruition.

The dissolution of his marriage to Maureen and his slow march toward alcoholism was taking its toll on Richard Starkey. But to the outside world, Ringo Starr was at the top of his game. The goodwill he'd built up over the years, both in the press and through his public persona, was paying handsome dividends.

He was a successful, chart-topping recording artist with several hit singles and a hit album to his credit. He was on good terms with John, Paul, and George, a claim Lennon, McCartney, and Harrison could not make about one another. He was living a glamorous rock-star life, jet-setting around the globe with his pick of female companionship.

He'd also hired a business manager.

Hilary Gerrard was an eccentric, forty-year-old British financial guru who would manage Ringo's money and his career and would represent him on the Apple board. Gerrard's father adopted the family surname after immigrating to London and "finding himself on Gerrard Street" in the city's Chinatown district. Gerrard was described as a shadowy presence who shunned being photographed and was "charming or abrupt as the occasion requires" with the "attitude of an East End cabbie." He wore a ponytail and a stud earring to mark himself as a rebel. As Ringo's voice in financial and business matters, he was fiercely protective of his client—Ringo's alter-ego "bad cop." They made a good team.

"Hilary is someone who doesn't want to be known," is the way in which his close friend, Chris O'Dell, described Gerrard. "He wants to be in the background. He was with Ringo all the time. I would say he was probably Ringo's best friend during many of those years [in the mid-to-late '70s]. . . . He is an incredibly intelligent man who found himself, in some ways, miscast in rock 'n' roll and yet he seemed to have his own place in it, because of his eccentricity. Back then, he would wear the same pants, the same silk shirt and the same spats-type shoes, but they were never the same shoes or clothes. Everything he owned in his closet looked alike."

Hilary "is so tall and so thin," adds Ringo's friend, Texas-born musician/actor Keith Allison. "He always reminded me of Rasputin for some reason. Hilary doesn't look like Rasputin, but he wore his hair pulled straight back, with rubber bands or little ties holding a little ponytail. And he wore a black velvet coat. He taught me how to travel light. I mean, the guy could get on an airplane with a paper bag. He carried a couple of black slacks, a pair of shoes, a couple of white tux shirts and a black velvet jacket. He flew all over the world like that. He never checked a thing. He just rotated the shirts and the pants."

Although Keith Allison and Ringo came from different backgrounds, they had similar personalities, and quickly bonded when they really got to know each other in the mid-1970s. "I didn't grow up as poor as he did in Liverpool and it wasn't tough on me," Keith said of Ringo. "I didn't have to run to school with older kids kicking the shit out of me everyday like he did. I didn't live in that tough of a neighborhood, growing up in a middle-class little town in Texas. But we had a lot of common experiences from music and starting out and doing this. We would share stories like that all the time."

Ringo also rebounded from the disappointment of *Blindman* with his next big-screen role in *That'll Be the Day*, written by British journalist Ray Connolly, who was friendly with all four ex-Beatles and knew the rock scene. The movie, produced by David Puttnam and based, in part, on the Harry Nilsson song "1941," was shot on the Isle of Wight and focused on the evolution of a wannabe pop star named Jim MacLaine in late 1950s England.

That'll Be the Day is considered to be Ringo's strongest performance on film, which was no surprise considering its subject matter—part of the movie is set at a Butlin's-type holiday camp where Ringo's character, Mike Menarry, is employed as a waiter and fairground operator. One of the movie's lateral characters, Stormy Tempest, was said to be modeled after Rory Storm. Ringo also looked forward to working with his drinking buddy and *200 Motels* co-star, Keith Moon, who had a small role in *That'll Be the Day*. Claude Whatham, known primarily for working on documentaries for Granada Television and the BBC, was hired to direct the movie.

For the part of Jim MacLaine, Puttnam and Connolly chose David Essex, a onetime drummer who'd recently starred as Jesus in the London production of *Godspell*. Unlike his *That'll Be the Day* alter-ego, Essex would become a big star with a string of hits, including "Rock On" and "Gonna Make You a Star" but, at the time, was largely an unknown. Keith Moon, who was interested in further-ing his acting career, was gunning for the role of Mike Menarry, but accepted the smaller role of camp drummer J. D. Clover when Ringo entered the picture. "He was very helpful in persuading Ringo to take the part," Puttnam said.

"I had written this movie, but none of us had been to Butlin's," Connolly said. "So we said, 'Who's been to Butlin's?' Well, Ringo went with Rory Storm, so we thought we would approach him. We had a sandwich with Ringo, Derek Taylor, and Neil Aspinall, who had also been to Butlin's at some point. Ringo and Neil sat there, very amusing, and we were going to offer Ringo a tiny part, the part of Stormy Tempest that Billy Fury had in the film. On the way out I said, 'Why don't we offer Ringo the role of Mike?' Ringo grabbed it and was great."

Although Ringo was thirty-two, and Mike was at least a decade younger, it didn't seem to matter. Ringo made the transformation, dying his hair darker and growing his sideburns into Teddy Boy muttonchops to make himself look more like a guy in his early twenties.

"I knew Ringo could act, but I wasn't sure how well he could act because it wasn't sort of the zany, madcap films that The Beatles had made," Essex re-called. "But pretty soon I saw that he was a natural and truthful actor. We had almost too much fun; the problem we both had was to stop laughing. It was a really happy time. The Isle of Wight, like so many of our seaside towns, had a '50s feel to it and we were filming in the '70s about working-class boys in the '50s so, you know, it was a good location."

That'll Be the Day was shot throughout October and November 1972. The timing was coincidental, but ironic and touching nonetheless: in late Septem-ber, just before shooting began, Rory Storm was found dead in his Liverpool home at the age of thirty-four. The body of his mother, Violet Caldwell, was found beside him. It was believed she took an overdose of sleeping pills after discovering Rory's corpse.

The Hurricanes had long since disbanded and Rory was working as a disc jockey in the Liverpool area when he was diagnosed with a chest infection, for which he was taking sleeping pills to help get him through the night. Although sleeping pills and alcohol were discovered in his system, his death was ruled accidental. Ringo did not attend the funeral. "I wasn't there when he was born either," he said when asked why he didn't show up.

With Rory's death fresh in his mind, and the memories of his days with The Hurricanes flooding back, Ringo began shooting his scenes for *That'll Be the Day*. He had about twenty-five minutes of screen time, and was so convincing as Mike that Connolly wrote an extra scene for him into the movie.

"He was just terrific and he brought his own clothes and he was smashing," Connolly said. "We got on really well. We discovered that we had an extra half-day with Ringo and we thought it would be a real shame not to use that half-day doing something else. Over the weekend I wrote an extra scene in the pool hall, where Ringo and David Essex [as Mike and Jim] are playing pool and talking about Mike's background. And that was an afterthought because he had been so good. We had all been surprised. We didn't think he was going to be so good."

But Ringo only agreed to shoot the extra scene if he was finished by a certain time, so he could catch the ferry from the Isle of Wight back to the mainland. "And he meant it," Connolly said. "He wasn't prepared to stay on another day to finish it. I thought that told me a bit about him, because most actors would have said, 'Okay, I'll stay another half day.' But he was a star. A big star. I think he could have been a good character actor. But he didn't become one."

In its review of *That'll Be the Day*, *Time* magazine opined that Ringo played Mike "with wit and affection" and called the movie "an intelligent, rueful attempt to get at the roots of pop culture by dramatizing the shaky beginnings of one musician's career."

Ringo declined to reprise his role as Mike in the movie's 1974 sequel, *Stardust*, which was written by Connolly, produced by Puttnam and directed by Michael Apted. Adam Faith replaced Ringo, while Essex returned as Jim MacLaine, and Keith Moon was back as J. D. Clover. "David [Puttnam] said Ringo thought that it was too close to the story of The Beatles," Connolly said. "But it wasn't really. And I wondered whether he had found it onerous being in a film, and in *Stardust* he'd have to commit to eight weeks of filming, where he did *That'll Be the Day* in about ten days. I'm not really bothered about this, because he was such a huge star anyway." Connolly ended up winning a BAFTA

Award for his *Stardust* screenplay. Ringo's explanation for passing up the offer: "I couldn't face Beatlemania again."

Back in Los Angeles, Ringo was entering a phase of his life defined by drinking, partying, womanizing, and bad career choices—aided and abetted, in large part, by his friendship with songwriter Harry Nilsson.

14

"WE WERE JUNKIES DABBLING IN MUSIC"

Harry Nilsson first entered Ringo Starr's orbit in 1968, but their bond grew closer once Ringo moved to Los Angeles in 1974. They shared a lot in common, despite growing up on different continents.

Harry, born in Brooklyn, New York, in June 1941, was less than a year younger than Ringo. They were both three years old when their fathers, Richard and Edward, respectively, abandoned their families, never to return (a fact Nilsson alluded to in his song "1941," on which *That'll Be The Day* was based).

They both enjoyed alcohol and practical jokes and were garrulous in nature, at least early in their relationship. Neither man had completed any semblance of an education. Ringo left school at the age of fifteen; Nilsson, who was extremely bright, dropped out of school in the ninth grade.

"They became really, really close friends, and a lot of it was based on how much alike they were," said Chris O'Dell. "They shared a sense of humor. You can never underestimate Ringo's sense of humor. It's there, it's a huge part of who he is. Harry was also like that. He kind of lived in this bouncy little world of his own. It was the '70s and everybody was partying, but I think they respected each other's musical talents. They were like brothers."

"Harry had a big ego. He wasn't intimidated by Ringo or anybody else," said Nilsson's first cousin, Doug Hoefer, who had a close relationship with Harry despite their age difference (around ten years) and who later played on a few of Harry's albums. Doug (to whom Ringo referred as "Cousin Dougie") also hung around with Harry and Ringo and spent a lot of nights partying with them.

"Harry and Ringo were very close," he confirms. "They would fight about shit and hang up on each other. Then time would go by and one of them would call the other back and they would pick up where they'd left off. I'm not really sure exactly how they pissed each other off, but they would . . . because Harry had a very strong personality as well."

Unlike Ringo, Nilsson was a gifted singer and songwriter, which is what first brought him to the attention of The Beatles. In 1967, while still working his day job dealing with the prehistoric computers at a Los Angeles bank, Nilsson cut his first album, *Pandemonium Shadow Show*, which was released that December by RCA. The LP included Nilsson's reworked version of Lennon and McCartney's 1964 B-side single "You Can't Do That." Nilsson's version was slower, and he included references throughout the song to twenty Beatles tunes (including "I'm Down," "A Hard Day's Night," "Drive My Car," "Good Day Sunshine," "Day Tripper," "Yesterday," and "Paperback Writer").

Lennon and McCartney loved Nilsson's treatment of their song, as did George Harrison, who invited Harry to a party in the Hollywood Hills and took a bunch of Nilsson's recordings back to England to play for his Beatles band mates.

One night, in April 1968, Nilsson was stunned when Lennon called him out of the blue, saying, "This is John. Man, you're too fucking much, you're just great. We've got to get together and do something." McCartney called a few nights later with similar sentiments. Ringo didn't call. When Lennon and McCartney came to America in May of 1968 to publicize Apple, they were asked about their favorite American musician and their favorite American band. They both answered, "Nilsson." Harry was on his way.

The Beatles invited Nilsson to sit in on some sessions at Abbey Road, and he flew to London shortly thereafter. Ringo sent his driver to pick him up at the airport.

It was the beginning of a long, beautiful friendship.

By the time 1974 rolled around, Ringo and Harry had worked together on several projects, including *200 Motels* and the *Ringo* album (Nilsson sang backing vocals on "You're Sixteen"). Ringo (credited as "Richie Snare") played drums on Nilsson's 1972 album *Son of Schmilsson* (on five of the eleven tracks) and narrated the home video release of Harry's animated feature, *The Point*, which had aired on ABC television in early 1971. (Dustin Hoffman was the original narrator, but, for contractual reasons, the role was subsequently re-recorded by Alan Barzman, Alan Thicke, and Ringo.)

"The only reason Harry wasn't more famous was because he didn't want to be," said Chris O'Dell. "He wouldn't tour, he wouldn't do what it took to be that famous. He just wouldn't. He was well-respected by other musicians and, to him, that was a high mark."

When Nilsson decided to buy a place in London in the early '70s, settling on a two-bedroom, top-floor apartment in an eighteenth-century house in Mayfair, he asked Ringo and Robin Cruikshank, who were still going strong with ROR, to help design and furnish the interior.

"As a little gift, Ringo and Robin had made these special mirrors for the two-sinked bathroom," Nilsson said. "They were done in etched glass. One was a picture of an oak tree. But on the other, there was etched a hangman's noose." The noose was Cruikshank's idea, but it bothered Nilsson. "So I called Ringo and told him and he didn't like it either. The next day, it was replaced by an apple tree."

Ringo and Harry also collaborated and starred in a campy musical horror movie called *Son of Dracula*, originally titled *Count Downe*, which Ringo co-produced under the Apple Films banner—dumping $800,000 of his own money into the questionable project. The movie was directed by Freddie Francis, a veteran of Hammer Films, Britain's assembly-line producer of horror flicks. Suzanna Leigh, Dennis Price, Freddie Jones, and Keith Moon had supporting roles.

Ringo claimed not to have known that the cover of Harry's *Son of Schmilsson* album, on which he played drums, showed Harry posing as Dracula, "so it seemed right" to make a vampire/rock/horror genre movie.

"I just think that if Dracula were around today he would be into rock," Ringo said, trying to justify the movie's existence. "We've got the whole family in this one—Frankenstein, the Mummy, Dracula, the Wolf Man and me as Merlin. . . . I went through everything—casting, meetings with actors electricians, the lot. I wanted to make the film in England because it's easier to learn at home."

Son of Dracula wasn't worth the effort. Harry starred as Dracula's son, Count Downe, who embarks on a love affair with a girl named Amber (Leigh). Ringo played Merlin, the Magician. "Drac takes the cure and marries the girl," said Ringo. The movie wasn't released until 1974, since "no one would take it," Ringo said, and it took a financial bloodbath and a critical drubbing (by those brave enough to sit through it).

Ringo's pal, *Monty Python* trouper Graham Chapman, and his writing partner Bernard McKenna, tried to save *Son of Dracula* by completely rewriting the script—with the new lines of dialogue dubbed over the already recorded dialogue—but the idea was scrapped.

Hearing Ringo's memories of life on the *Son of Dracula* set, it's no surprise that the movie was a stinker. Ringo later recalled: "I remember I did a movie with Harry Nilsson. He had all these players in the band, John Bonham, Keith Moon, Jim Price, and it was costing me just union rate, only about 30 quid a day.

But it was costing £1000 for booze!. They were all gone by noon. It was funny. It was fun times; we were just out there playing and making stuff. Someone said, 'We weren't musicians dabbling in drugs and alcohol; now we were junkies dabbling in music.'"

Ringo also complained about the sound men and camera crew being "such a headache. Everyone shouts at you. I didn't know that if you didn't get the crew home and in their beds by midnight, you couldn't work them the next day."

Son of Dracula spawned a Nilsson album of the same name; that, too, was quickly forgotten. The movie did have one benefit for Nilsson: in exchange for working for free, Ringo paid to have his friend's teeth fixed.

"We had the premiere in Atlanta, the first movie since *Gone with the Wind* to open there, and we had twelve thousand kids screaming, we had bands . . . but we left town the next day, and so did everyone else," Ringo said. "In America, the movie only played in towns that had one cinema, because if it had two, no matter what was on down the road, they'd all go there! It's a bit of a shambles now—we went into a studio with Graham Chapman and re-voiced a lot of it, so it makes even less sense now."

With Ringo's marriage in freefall, he was spending most of his time in L.A.—which meant more time blazing a hedonistic trail with Harry, John Lennon and Keith Moon. Keith Allison, who'd known Ringo since 1965, was also included in the drunken revelry when he was visiting L.A.

"All of them were going through divorces at the same time—Keith Moon, John had split up with Yoko," he said. "We were all going through the same thing and so we were just a bunch of crazy kids turned loose in the city. A lot of partying. A lot of late nights."

The partying wasn't limited to California, however; the traveling circus also took its act on the road, often to London, where Marc Bolan and Graham Chapman joined the party. Chapman and his friend Douglas Adams tried to lend Ringo a helping professional hand by writing an outline for a sitcom in which he would star.

"It was to be a science fiction comedy," Adams said. "It involved a bloke called Ringo Starr who worked in an office as a walking chauffeur—he carried the bosses around on his back—until one day a flying saucer landed, bearing a robot which gave Ringo the power to travel through time and space, do flower arranging and destroy the universe by waving his hand. That's as far as we got."

Nilsson was blessed with a soulful singing voice, and his version of Fred Neil's 1966 song "Everybody's Talkin'" was used on the soundtrack of 1969's

Oscar-winning movie *Midnight Cowboy*. He received a further celebrity boost with his 1971 chart-topper "Without You," written by Badfinger members Pete Ham and Tom Evans. Ringo reveled in his friend's success.

"Ringo and I spent a thousand hours laughing," Nilsson said. "All the things we'd do . . . some were friend-like, some Laurel and Hardy–like." In London, the group—usually Ringo, Harry, Keith, Marc Bolan—would meet for an afternoon brandy, each member arriving with the catchphrase, "I hope I'm not interrupting anything?" During one drunken evening, Ringo, Keith, and Harry, who were carousing in London, took Alice Cooper to a T. Rex recording session, resulting in a boozed-up all-star jam session. (The tapes have never surfaced.)

"We would drink until nine p.m.," Nilsson said. "That's six hours of brandy. Then between nine and ten, we would usually end up at Tramp, the most uproarious, exclusive disco-restaurant in the world. Royalty, movie stars, world champions all frequented the place. It was a ride, meeting luminaries and having blow-outs every night."

Somehow, through all the drinking and hard partying, Ringo managed to record his fourth solo album, *Goodnight Vienna*, in the summer of 1974. The album was recorded in L.A., at Sunset Sound and Producers Workshop Studios. (*Goodnight Vienna* refers not to the city, but to Liverpool slang for "Let's get out of here.")

Ringo was still riding high from the success of the *Ringo* album and didn't want to mess with a good thing. So he assembled virtually the same team for *Goodnight Vienna*, including producer Richard Perry and musicians Klaus Voormann (on bass) and drummer Jim Keltner.

Harry Nilsson was included, of course—singing backing vocals on "No No Song" and "Only You (And You Alone)" and contributing a song called "Easy for Me." John Lennon, who was in L.A. and in the process of recording his next LP, *Walls and Bridges*, wrote the album's titular song and played guitar on two tracks, "All by Myself" and "Only You (And You Alone)." Elton John played piano on "Snookeroo," which he and longtime songwriting partner Bernie Taupin wrote especially for Ringo. Guitarist Steve Cropper and members of The Band also contributed to several tracks.

Noticeably absent from the lineup were George Harrison and Paul McCartney, for no other reason than they were busy with their own projects—McCartney with his new group, Wings, and Harrison recording his next solo album, *Dark Horse*.

To illustrate the *Goodnight Vienna* album cover, Ringo used a scene from the 1951 sci-fi movie *The Day the Earth Stood Still*, superimposing his head on the body of the character Klaatu, played in the film by Michael Rennie. Two years later, a Canadian band called Klaatu released an eponymous album, igniting a rumor that the band was, in fact, The Beatles—recording under the pseudonym borrowed from the *Goodnight Vienna* album. It was wishful thinking but terrific marketing on Klaatu's behalf, and it helped the band sell over one million copies of its album.

Klaatu had more success with their knockoff than did Ringo with *Goodnight Vienna*, at least in his native country. The album, released in November 1974, reached a mediocre Number Thirty on the UK charts—the last of Ringo's albums to chart in the UK for another twenty-five years. *Goodnight Vienna* fared much better in the U.S., where it was certified gold and reached Number Eight on the *Billboard* chart, while "No No Song" (backed by "Snookeroo") reached Number Three on the singles charts.

Ringo and John Lennon shot a television commercial on the rooftop of Capitol Records in L.A. to promote the release of *Goodnight Vienna*, with Ringo dressed in the spacesuit he wore on the album cover. Ringo and Harry Nilsson, on the same rooftop, also shot a promo for "Only You (And You Alone)," which was later shown on the BBC's *Top of the Pops*.

Cavorting around town with Harry Nilsson, Keith Moon, and company was a blast for Ringo, but it was starting to take a toll on his health—and on his career choices. For a short time in 1974, Keith moved into Harry's flat in London's Mayfair district. Translation: more partying around the city's West End for Ringo and his pals.

During the production of *Stardust*, the follow-up to *That'll Be the Day*—in which he wasn't appearing—Ringo joined Keith, Dave Edmunds, and actor Karl Howman in a night of drinking that took them from the nightclub Tramp to the nearby Playboy Club, where they were all tossed out for "general misbehavior"—particularly from Keith, who was stabbing Playboy bunnies in their rears with a fork. The Playboy Club promptly withdrew Ringo and Keith's memberships "because damage by Mr. Starr and Mr. Moon came to an amount totaling £30."

"I was sliding down, I wasn't taking enough interest," Ringo said later. "I was more interested in boogeying, just going out to parties and not doing what I did."

The madness of those times also fueled *Harry and Ringo's Night Out*, which got underway in the spring of 1974. The idea of the so-called "documentary," which Ringo co-financed with Pride Records president Michael Viner, was for cameras to follow Harry, Ringo, and Keith Moon as they prowled the L.A. night-life scene, capturing all the supposed fun and chaos they left in their wake.

The movie was budgeted at $1.5 million, with the intention of mixing the live action with animated scenes. Viner told *Billboard* that "Harry and Ringo's Night Out" would also include a companion soundtrack album. Neither proj-ect was finished. According to Harry Nilsson biographer Alyn Shipton, Viner scheduled an industry screening of the initial footage, in hopes of raising ad-ditional funding. He was unsuccessful, and the movie was never completed or released.

One project that was finished around this time was Nilsson's next album, *Pussy Cats*, which John Lennon produced at the Record Plant in L.A. The album featured Ringo, Keith, and Jim Keltner on drums—all three of them playing together (on separate drum kits) on the album's final track, "Rock Around the Clock."

Pussy Cats was recorded during Lennon's "lost weekend," his eighteen-month separation from Yoko Ono during a turbulent time in their marriage (she remained in their New York City apartment in the Dakota). Lennon's low point during the "lost weekend" era in L.A. came the night he and Harry were kicked out of the Troubadour club for drunkenly heckling The Smothers Brothers. Their sheepish mugs were caught on camera as they were being escorted out of the venue like skid-row bums.

While he was producing the *Pussy Cats* album, Lennon thought it would be a great idea for everyone to live together in his rented beach house in Santa Monica to promote a sense of musical harmony. Ringo already had his own room (the site of his trysts with Chris O'Dell), and a delighted Keith Moon soon moved in. He was joined by Nilsson, Klaus Voormann and his girlfriend, Ringo's manager/advisor Hilary Gerrard, and an assortment of hangers-on.

"We had the wildest assemblage of that part of history in that house," Nils-son said. "It makes the round table look like a toadstool."

The arrangement lasted around three weeks, with predictable results. "It was like the Dirty Dozen, or the Four Horsemen," Howard Kaylan said. "'Where are they going tonight? Let's not be there.' It was a traveling road show thing they had going, and wherever they went they caused havoc."

One night, Ringo and Keith Moon, who were both dead drunk, paid a visit to Flo and Eddie (the pop-music alter egos of Kaylan and Howard Volman), who were hosting a radio show on KROQ, a small FM station in Pasadena. The duo attempted to interview Ringo at the end of their show; he said the word "fuck" nearly fifteen times within ninety seconds, according to Kaylan—who, along with Volman and their producer, was fired from the station after the incident.

Nilsson ruptured a vocal chord while recording *Pussy Cats* but didn't tell anyone. He continued to record the album, irreparably damaging his voice. Paul McCartney and Stevie Wonder dropped by during a session and recorded a few tracks, which were later released on a bootleg album.

Ringo, meanwhile, was also wearing out his welcome with the once-friendly press, which was marking the tenth anniversary of The Beatles storming America with retrospectives—and descriptions of Ringo that were unflattering and, often, downright nasty. The "cuddly Beatle" wasn't so cuddly anymore: many observers considered him more of a drunken fool than a musical icon.

"Of those four revolutionary rock musicians, The Beatles, one was generally regarded as an appealingly homely, vulnerably funny and totally uninspired member of the troupe," *People* magazine opined. "He still hasn't shaken the buffoon image, and in fact seems compulsively to cultivate it, mugging for photographers and traveling in a satin jacket patterned with portraits of Marilyn Monroe." Two years later, the magazine described him as "the drummer who clubbed artlessly behind the group's three stars."

Ringo's marriage to Maureen never recovered from her affair with George and they were living apart, notwithstanding Ringo's occasional return visits to London. Ringo's main squeeze now was an American model and photographer named Nancy Andrews, and the gossip columns took notice. It was still big news for an ex-Beatle on the verge of a marital breakup to be squiring around someone who was not his wife.

"At parties in Los Angeles, which has lately become his natural habitat, Ringo Starr whimsically introduces his lady as 'Debbie Idono' or 'Al Schwartz,'" noted a gossip item in *People* magazine. "She is not Maureen, mother of his three kids, but model Nancy Andrews. A divorce for Ringo is apparently near."

He was free to play the scene, and there were plenty of women willing to go to bed with an ex-Beatle. After his breakup with Chris O'Dell and during several rough patches with Nancy Andrews, Ringo was linked to several women, including pixie singer Lynsey de Paul, who had several hits in the '70s ("Sugar Me" and "Won't Somebody Dance with Me?").

De Paul's romantic résumé included affairs with James Coburn, Dudley Moore, and Sean Connery. She hooked up with Ringo after her affair with Coburn ended. Ringo was back in England, putting in his required ninety days as a British tax exile during a cooling-off period from Andrews. De Paul was a pleasant diversion.

They met while de Paul was producing an album for singer Vera Lynn, "The Forces' Sweetheart" whose renditions of "We'll Meet Again" and "The White Cliffs of Dover" helped nurse England through the devastation of World War II. Ringo arrived at the studio one day during a photo shoot for Lynn's album, de Paul stuck a tambourine in his hand, and Ringo ended up shaking the tambourine on a track called "Don't You Remember When?" written by de Paul and Barry Blue.

Ringo's affair with de Paul was short-lived, but momentous. In their weeks together, she accompanied him to the London premiere of *The Man Who Would Be King* (co-starring Lynsey's future lover, Sean Connery), where they were photographed together entering the theater. She also managed to record with Ringo and George Harrison in Ringo's Startling Studios at Tittenhurst.

"For a girl new to the industry, it was something astonishing as I had bought The Beatles records when in school," she said. Ringo, though, was "not technologically minded at the time, insofar as he could not even turn on the equipment. . . . Ringo played drums, George the guitar, and I played piano."

Her romance with Ringo also inspired her single, "If I Don't Get You the Next One Will." As she explained, "We had arranged to go to dinner, and instead he slept through the evening in his offices, so the song relates to revenge."

Actresses Shelly Duvall, Viviane Ventura, and Debralee Scott (the latter of whom was starring on Norman Lear's television soap opera parody *Mary Hartman, Mary Hartman*), were also linked to Ringo in the gossip columns. "He may never get it together again with The Beatles, but every time he's in L.A. Ringo Starr has a reunion with Debralee Scott," one wag coyly noted.

Ringo's prolonged stay in Los Angeles necessitated his having a place of his own, since he didn't want to wear out his welcome at Lennon's beach house. He and girlfriend Nancy Andrews lived for a while in a suite at the Beverly Wilshire Hotel, but they wanted a place of their own that had a kitchen (and some privacy). In late 1974, Ringo and Nancy were invited to a dinner party at a private home on Haslam Terrace, located in the Hollywood Hills just off Sunset Plaza Drive. They both loved the view from the dining room, which overlooked the sparkling lights of L.A., and were thrilled to hear that the house, owned by L.A. restaurateur Nicky Blair, was available to be rented within two weeks. They moved in shortly thereafter.

The three-thousand-square-foot house, designed by famed L.A.-based architect Robert Byrd—who'd designed the house on Cielo Drive where the 1969 Sharon Tate murders took place—had four bedrooms, four bathrooms, "high vaulted ceilings, skylights and an amazing kitchen," Andrews recalled. The yard boasted a small lemon grove and the requisite Hollywood swimming pool.

Led Zeppelin drummer John Bonham, who'd worked with Ringo on *Son of Dracula*, was a frequent visitor to the house on Haslam Terrace. Like Keith Moon, Bonham was a carouser, a prodigious drinker, and a lover of practical jokes—the more outlandish the better.

"There was a party every night," Ringo said. "John Bonham would always get a bee in his bonnet. Whenever he was in L.A., he would drive up to my house, grab me and throw me in the pool. Day or night—he didn't care."

15

"YOU CAN'T *TRY* AND BE MARRIED"

The year 1975 would prove to be momentous in the life of Ringo Starr.

On January 9, a High Court in London legally dissolved The Beatles, five years after John, Paul, George, and Ringo stopped recording together as a band. The ruling, for which Paul McCartney fought the hardest, infused some much-needed cash into Ringo's coffers. (Millions were being held in escrow for all four ex-Beatles until the band's legal dissolution was finalized.) "Ringo Starr . . . the last to join The Beatles and the one generally judged the least exceptional in terms of talent, has done very well on his own," the *New York Times* noted after the legal dissolution was finalized.

The British government was taking 83 three percent of his earnings, and Ringo was in full-blown tax-exile status. His financial advisor/manager, Hilary Gerrard, steered Ringo and his money toward Monte Carlo, located in Monaco on the French Riviera. Once he established residency there, Ringo would not have to pay income tax.

He bought a luxurious, three-bedroom condominium apartment on the thirty-third floor of a building overlooking the Mediterranean Sea and enjoyed gambling at the Loews Casino, recommended to him by Peter Sellers. He also bought a place in Amsterdam and still had his rented house in L.A. He had the best of several worlds, since he could also travel freely to America without fearing the taxman.

As a legal "nonresident" of the U.S., he was entitled to spend as much as half the year in L.A. without being taxed by the IRS on his international earnings. He was earning enough from his Beatles royalties to live comfortably and to afford his jet-setting lifestyle, and Hilary Gerrard had invested Ringo's money wisely.

Ringo's long-percolating divorce from Maureen, which he likened to "the breakup of The Beatles," was reaching its conclusion by the middle of the year. They still loved each other, and always would, but the price of fame, combined with their marital indiscretions, was just too much for them to surmount, despite several attempts at reconciliation. Ringo, who was turning thirty-five, pushed for the divorce and owned up to his role in the breakup of his marriage.

> At one time we used to change together, then we started changing separately in different directions. There's no, like, "Well, she cut my throat so we have to have a divorce." There's no one snap thing that did it. It spread out over a year 'til you found yourself at the end of that year saying, "What are we doing here? This isn't a marriage anymore." And I had a fine marriage for eight-and-a-half years. I really had a fine marriage—which I worked for, and she worked for it too. And it just started slipping away. And then it slipped to the end, and I had to end things. We went through the trial getting back together period. And in a marriage you can't TRY and be married. You're married or you're not married . . . as far as I'm concerned. . . . And so I wanted it ended.

Ringo cited his adultery with Nancy Andrews in the divorce papers, going against Maureen's wishes that he cite his affair with Chris O'Dell as the proverbial straw that broke the camel's back. "That way the whole affair would have stayed in the family, in a sense . . . not a sordid external affair with a beautiful stranger who didn't know Maureen and thus could not understand her deepest feelings," O'Dell said.

Ringo and Maureen were officially divorced on July 17, 1975, after ten-and-a-half years of marriage. Maureen remained in England with custody of Zak, Jason, and Lee, the youngest of whom was not yet five years old.

"The poor girl was devastated," Peter Brown said of Maureen. "Even if it were true that she had gone to bed with George, even if she had strayed, Maureen still loved her 'Richie' with as much passion and dedication as any northern girl could muster. . . . She turned her head when he started to fool around with other women, but she couldn't hold him."

According to Cynthia Lennon, Maureen was so upset by the end of her marriage that she attempted suicide by driving a motorcycle into a brick wall, severely injuring herself and requiring plastic surgery on her face (the results of which pleased her). "She had been in love with [Ringo] since she was fifteen and his public appearances with his new girlfriend, American actress Nancy Andrews, had devastated her."

Maureen got £500,000 cash in the divorce settlement for both herself and the children, with the provision that she could increase that amount in the future, if necessary. Ringo bought Maureen and the kids a £250,000 house in the London neighborhood of Little Venice, in Maida Vale, and signed over Tittenhurst Park, valued at $1.7 million, to his children for tax purposes. He was able to see Zak, Jason, and Lee whenever he wanted to and would sometimes pick them up from school if he was in England. They spent weekends with Ringo and Nancy in Monaco when their schedules permitted.

"The main brain damage of divorce has been the kids," Ringo said later. "They freaked out at first, but they got over it quicker than I did."

It was George Harrison who first met the woman Ringo planned to make his second wife—but John Lennon who facilitated the romance. *With a little help from my friends* . . .

Nancy Andrews was a Ford fashion model from Jersey City, New Jersey, who'd spent her teen years in Alabama. She was in her mid-twenties when she began dating Carl Radle, a noted bass player who played on two of George Harrison's albums—*All Things Must Pass* and *The Concert for Bangladesh*—and was Eric Clapton's regular bass player for most of the 1970s. He also played with Leon Russell and many other A-list artists.

In the fall of 1973, Andrews's boss, Lou Adler, rented his Beverly Hills house to John and May Pang, who were in L.A. during Lennon's "lost weekend" period while he was recording his *Rock 'n' Roll* album. Nancy and May bonded instantly; it was Andrews's entrée into Lennon's world and, when Lennon rented the infamous beach house in Santa Monica and producing Harry Nilsson's *Pussycats* album Andrews was a frequent guest there.

One night in late May 1974, at a birthday party for ex-Beatles roadie Mal Evans, she found herself plunked down next to Ringo Starr at a poker table. "He was so charming, playful, witty and cute as hell," Andrews said. "He might have had sad eyes, but they were twinkling at me that day. We flirted, oh how we flirted." Ringo was "entangled with" one of Andrews's friends, so he and Andrews parted platonically that night.

Three months later, in early August, when Lennon and May were back in town, they invited Andrews over for dinner in their suite at the Beverly Wilshire Hotel, and she was surprised when Ringo answered the door. "Oh, hello. I remember you," Ringo said to her. "You're my poker partner." She joined Ringo,

John, and May that day when they headed over to Sunset Sound Studios, where Ringo was recording his *Goodnight Vienna* album.

"John, May and I spent hours encouraging Ringo as he laid down vocals," Andrews said. "When he finished we ventured to The Fiddler, a favorite hangout on Sunset and LaBrea that stayed open late and served delicious fried fish and chips. It had an old Wurlitzer jukebox loaded with an eclectic mix of songs. The two boys drank, dropped quarters in the jukebox, singing and discussing women, wives and life while May and I chatted, watching them."

Ringo's marriage to Maureen was disintegrating, and he "turned more melancholy" while caressing Andrews's face before he "weaved his way to the jukebox" and punched in Charlie Rich's "The Most Beautiful Girl in the World," which he listened to repeatedly—at one point getting down on his knees and resting his head on the jukebox. "Nancy, he's a good lad," Lennon told Andrews. "Give him a chance."

Shortly thereafter, Ringo and Nancy began dating and, before too long, they were inseparable, moving first into the Beverly Wilshire Hotel and then into the house on Haslam Terrace. "She flashed her eyes once," Ringo said, "and I've been in love with her ever since."

Ringo, "a man without a country or a home . . . always attracted to life in the fast lane," traveled everywhere with Nancy—to Monte Carlo, Amsterdam, England or wherever his flights of fancy took him. She already knew John and George, and soon met Paul and Linda McCartney, Harry Nilsson, Keith Moon, Eric Clapton, John Bonham, and everyone else in Ringo's hard-partying orbit.

"Our world was fast and on the move all over the world," she said. "Between the recording studios, movie premieres, promotion tours, traveling nine months a year and juggling the children, friends and family we were gypsies—elegant gypsies."

Their life in Monte Carlo was one of "reading, writing music, drives along the coast, cooking and fine dining." A few nights each week, Ringo and Nancy would walk to their favorite restaurant, Costa Rica, and "when we felt like dressing up and going out" they walked to the Loews Casino. "We'd dance the night away at Regines, a classic 1970s disco," Andrews wrote. In 1977, George Harrison came to Monte Carlo for the annual Formula One Monaco Grand Prix. Nancy and Ringo hung out with George and his friend, championship race car driver Jackie Stewart, who was announcing the race for ABC's *Wide World of Sports*.

They traveled around the world on flights of fancy. In the spring of 1977,

Ringo, Nancy, Hilary Gerrard, and Nancy's friend, Susin Fair, took a trip to the Yucatan for some sun, sightseeing (Mayan ruins and Chitzen Itza), and relaxation. Ringo grew bored after a week and wanted to leave; Nancy booked a single-engine plane to the Yucatan's capital, Merida, and their plane took off during a brewing tropical storm.

The plane, groaning under the weight of the foursome's luggage, was flying through the jungle and brushing the tops of the trees, throwing everyone into a panic and thinking they were going to crash and die—except Ringo. "Don't worry, it's not my time to go, so we'll all be fine," he told them.

Nancy was also exposed to Ringo's dark side: his heavy drinking, drugging, and dark mood swings, which he attributed to manic-depression. "So I became a clown and wouldn't let him stay that way too long," she said. "It took him a long time to come out of it"—but she noted that Ringo was still "moody and supersensitive."

She did her best to stave off the women who flocked to Ringo like flies to honey. Once a Beatle, always a Beatle. The passage of time made no difference to fans who still bought in to the circa-1964 frenzy. "They would just elbow me out of the way like I was a curtain in the way," Nancy said. "I just became a little ninja and pushed back. Ringo loved that I was overt like that."

Ringo even posed for the cover of *People* magazine, which devoted four pages to the happy couple. "Most nights Starr stays home, with Nancy as the cook of the house," it noted unconvincingly. "'We just curl up on the couch and watch TV or read—I'm into really cheap Gothic novels and Richard reads sci-fi,'" Nancy told the magazine. Ringo, noting that "my divorce had been happening for years. . . . I overreacted to the responsibility of marriage and kids for a long time," said he'd "like to have children with Nancy" since he'd now adjusted to the role of being a father.

Ringo encouraged Nancy's interest in photography, and she had a front-row seat to some of the world's best-known rock stars, who didn't mind having their picture taken (among them George Harrison, Eric Clapton, Keith Moon, Bob Dylan, and Gregg Allman). Over thirty years later, she published many of those photos in *A Dose of Rock 'n' Roll*, a book documenting her years with Ringo through photographs and accompanying text.

"The camera was a huge part of our lives," she said. "We were both posers and loved to give it up for the camera. He loved the way I saw things and encouraged me to shoot." At the very least, Ringo saved the cost of a photographer to shoot the cover images for his albums *Ringo the 4th* and *Bad Boy*, both of which were photographed by Nancy. She also shot other promotional photos for various Ringo-related projects, including an NBC television special.

There were bumps in the romantic road—Ringo's aforementioned tryst with Lynsey de Paul chief among them—but, for the most part, the Ringo-Nancy relationship was on solid footing. They were engaged shortly after moving in together, with Nancy's ticket punched to become Ringo's second wife after he proposed to her in a jewelry store on Rodeo Drive in Beverly Hills.

"He comes over and he says, 'Look at this . . .' There was a black tray and there was, like, five rings in it. He said, 'Which one do you like?' and I said, 'The one that looks like the Chrysler Building.' He said, 'Here, let me see it on you . . . and he puts the ring on my finger . . . and all of a sudden he's on his knees . . . and he goes, 'Darling, I'm asking you to marry me.' Behind him I saw the whole shop kind of stopped . . . I said, 'Yes.' Everyone, there's like fifteen people in the store, cheers and he kisses me. He's so romantic and he would always get me."

Ringo's relationship with Nancy also seemed to renew his creative juices. He was still partying with Harry, Keith Moon, John Lennon, et al., but he was also recording again, and trying to take control of his destiny in the studio and, by extension, of his financial future. The divorce from Maureen hit him hard in his pocketbook, and he was dropping a lot of money in the casinos at Monte Carlo, not to mention on the booze, nightclubbing, jet-setting travel, and the houses in Monaco, L.A., Amsterdam, and England.

The whispers that Ringo was broke grew louder when, in 1976, dueling promoters Sid Bernstein and Bill Sargent offered John, Paul, George, and Ringo $230 million and $50 million, respectively, to reunite for a one-off charity concert. The ex-Beatles all rebuffed the offer. "There might be three of us thinking 'You know, it might not be a bad idea'—but the other one would go, 'Nah, I don't think so' and sort of veto it," McCartney said. "Let's put it this way, there was never a time when all four of us wanted to do it."

Saturday Night Live executive producer Lorne Michaels spoofed the reunion offers on an episode of the NBC television show in April 1976, waving around a "certified check" for $3,000. "You can divide it any way you want," Michaels said. "If you want to give Ringo less, that's up to you." (Ringo hosted *Saturday Night Live* in 1984 and poked fun at himself in several skits.)

Ringo fired back at the rumors that he was hard up for cash and would have accepted Bernstein or Sargent's offers had the others been on board. "I'm no billionaire—Rockefeller, he's *really* loaded—but if you think the Beatles didn't save any money, you're insane," Ringo said. "Broke is relative. I'm just the biggest spender. I'm thirty companies, you know, multinational. We're in everything from dentist chairs to vending machines, but I don't talk about it." But his business managers confiscated his credit cards "because I use them like water. I used to spend them on jewelry, cars and my toys."

Still, a hit album couldn't hurt. The London High Court's decision to legally dissolve The Beatles freed Ringo from his ties to EMI and Apple, but it also severed his ties to both of those companies. He was a man without a record label.

Two years had passed since his last bona fide solo album, *Goodnight Vienna*. His last release on Apple was the *Blast from Your Past* compilation LP, which hit the U.S. in November 1975—where it only reached Number Thirty on the charts. It failed to chart altogether in UK when it was released there a month later. Whatever time Ringo was spending in the recording studio these days was limited to contributing to other people's albums, including George Harrison's *Dark Horse* LP, on which he played drums on two tracks, "So Sad" and "Ding Dong, Ding Dong."

In the spring of 1975, Ringo formed his own record label, Ring O' Records, and signed a deal with Polydor Records in the UK and with Atlantic Records in the U.S. The deal called for Ringo to release seven albums within five years, with the first album slated to hit stores in June 1976. In addition to his own albums, he signed several artists to his Ring O' Records stable (none of whom went on to record anything of significance in the label's three-year history).

The new album was called *Ringo's Rotogravure*, with Ringo borrowing the title from one of Irving Berlin's lyrics in the 1948 movie *Easter Parade*. Arif Mardin, the in-house producer for Atlantic Records, was behind the glass this time around, and Ringo hewed closely to his proven formula of recruiting old friends and associates to contribute material for the album, including Eric Clapton, Dr. John, Melissa Manchester, Peter Frampton, and Harry Nilsson.

Once again Klaus Voormann played bass and Jim Keltner played drums on several tracks. Nilsson sang backing vocals on "Lady Gaye," and Ringo and Nancy co-wrote "Las Brisas," inspired by a romantic Acapulco hotel in which they stayed. Ringo claimed he found Los Galleros, the mariachi band featured on the song, in a Mexican restaurant in L.A. after prowling the city looking for the right sound. (Ringo was apparently fond of mariachi music. In October 1974, he tried to hire a mariachi band in New York to serenade John Lennon on his birthday outside the Dakota. The plan backfired when the band's leader was mugged the night before and no one showed up at the appointed hour.)

And, as he'd done on the *Ringo* LP, Ringo corralled John Lennon, Paul Mc-Cartney, and George Harrison, each of whom contributed in varying degrees to *Ringo's Rotogravure*.

As he explained it, "Well, Paul asked to write a song. I asked John and . . . eventually he came up with "You Got Me Cooking" (sic). . . . I also asked George to write one, but there was an old one of his that was never released by anybody that I always loved, . . . I asked him if instead of writing one, could I have that old one? He said fine; it saved him a job. It's called 'I Still Love You,' a big bally thing."

Recording got under way at Sunset Studios in L.A. in April 1976 before the entire production moved to Cherokee Studios in June. Lennon wrote and played piano on "Cookin' (In the Kitchen of Love)" and played piano on "A Dose of Rock 'n' Roll," while Paul and Linda McCartney recorded the backing track for *Pure Gold*, onto which Ringo's lead vocal was dubbed.

Harrison's contribution was a little stickier. He gave Ringo his blessing to use his tune "When Every Song Is Sung," which began its life as "Whenever." Ringo played drums on the song several years earlier, when it was first recorded by Cilla Black and again for *Ringo's Rotogravure* when it morphed into "I'll Still Love You." But George was unhappy with Ringo's version of the song and threatened legal action. They eventually settled out of court and, over a decade later, joked about the kerfuffle during an interview on British television (when Ringo broached the subject).

Yet despite its superstar lineup, *Ringo's Rotogravure* barely moved the needle upon its release in September. It failed to chart in the UK—another solo strikeout for Ringo in his home country—and quickly disappeared from the American charts. "From *Goodnight Vienna* it started going downhill," Ringo admitted. To others, it was obvious that Ringo wasn't putting a whole lot of effort into his albums.

"Ringo just seemed content to let the producer lay down some backing tracks for him and then he would pop in from Monte Carlo and just stick on his vocals," noted Tony Barrow. Barrow, who was now a senior executive at Polydor, also complained that Ringo just didn't seem interested in working that hard. "We had many offers for TV specials and whatever for him but he was always totally unavailable to do them," he said.

Ringo didn't deny these assertions. "For a lot of those albums, I was just in a hurry to get home—or, more often, someone else's home," he said. "The other thing is that—unless you're interviewing Paul or George—you're talking to a guy who's been in the business longer than most. When you're around this long, you're going to have ups and downs."

On August 12, 1976, Ringo found time to be Harry Nilsson's best man when Harry married his third wife, Una O'Keeffe, at the Airport Marriott Hotel in L.A. Chris O'Dell handled the catering chores with her business partner, Tina Firestone. (Ringo came up with the name for their company: Brains Unlimited.) The day before the wedding, Ringo fulfilled his duties as best man by walking into Tiffany's in Beverly Hills and asking to see a handful of rings," which he took with him after charming the salesman, telling him he'd return the rest of the rings the following day.

On his wedding day, Nilsson, who was feeling sweaty and nervous, snorted some coke as he was getting dressed (which didn't do much to calm his nerves). "The limousine arrived, he recalled. "Ringo gave me a toot for luck and the limo driver gave me a gram for luck. I was obliged to do some more with him, and even the priest. By now I was shaking so much I could barely stand. Ringo reached in his pocket and displayed eight or ten rings. Within two attempts he found the right sizes." Shaking, Nilsson placed the two rings on Una's fingers. "Ringo observed, 'Look he's shaking.' He must have thought it was nerves, and helped me to steady my hands and slip on the ring."

In October 1976, at the tail end of a European promotional push for *Ringo's Rotogravure*, Ringo, Nancy, and Hilary Gerrard flew from Rome to Tokyo. Ringo had been hired to shoot four television commercials hawking leisure suits for a Japanese clothing company called Simple Life. Harry Nilsson wrote the jingles for the campaign, which featured Ringo singing a ditty called "I Love My Suit." Nilsson and ex-Monkeys lead singer Davy Jones sang backing vocals.

In one ad, a flying saucer lands in the middle of a city park. Ringo pokes his head out of the top: "Hello . . . to all Japanese people. I came here to talk about . . . the Simple Life." In another ad, Ringo strolls through a field, singing the "I Love My Suit" song while accompanied by several people (and a pony); a third ad featured Ringo cavorting on a beach with three young people and building some sort of contraption (how this relates to Simple Life clothing is anyone's guess).

———

The failure of *Ringo's Rotogravure* didn't help its namesake's emotional state, nor did the rough patch he was going through with Nancy. "You wonder about getting up, and there is nothing special to do, so you delay it," he said about this time in his life. "Finally, you do get out of bed and you just try to fill the day." He couldn't escape his designation as "ex-Beatle Ringo Starr" and, try as he might to "fill the day" by jet-setting around the world—flying to South Africa on a moment's notice to watch a tennis match or to New York to buy a pair of shoes—it didn't fill the void.

He was looking for some meaning to his life and not enjoying the view, dulled as it was by drinking and drugging. Paul McCartney was racking up hits with Wings, and George Harrison was writing and producing critically acclaimed albums. John Lennon, meanwhile, turned his back on his music career for a contented life in New York as a stay-at-home dad to his new son, Sean, while Yoko ran his business empire.

The public might have been ignoring Ringo's albums, but they couldn't ignore his new look. In the summer of 1976 he completely shaved his head and his eyebrows, and also shaved off the beard and mustache he'd worn for years. What was this? A cry for attention? Just something to do? The first signs of a nervous breakdown? No one knew for sure. (He re-grew the beard and mustache shortly thereafter.)

Ringo joked that he wanted "to see what it [his head] looked like and to make sure I didn't have boils or anything on my scalp," then attributed his disturbing new look to the stifling heat of Monte Carlo: "It got so hot here that I merely walked into a barbershop and said, 'Take it all off' . . . the only hair I had left on my face when he finished was my eyelashes."

In a revealing interview in *People* magazine, he later admitted to more disturbing reasons for the head-shaving incident—attributing his bizarre behavior to "feeling vaguely insane and drinking some new drink. . . . It was a time when you either cut your wrists or your hair, and I'm a coward."

It didn't help that Led Zeppelin drummer John Bonham, already a disruptive presence in Ringo's life back in L.A., was also in Monte Carlo. It's been rumored that it was Bonham, in fact, who shaved Ringo's head and eyebrows. "I went mad and spent a lot of time—it seems like years now—hanging out with John Bonham, who spent a year there," Ringo said.

The nonstop traveling in search of something—*anything*—followed Ringo in his travels; in 1976, during a trip to Denmark, he jammed with Cat Stevens, who was recording his *Izitso* album at Sweet Silence Studios. "And he wiped me off!" Ringo said. "I mean, I can't blame him because around those years, I was losing control. . . . God knows what I played for him." (According to Beatles biographer Kristofer Engelhardt, Ringo and Stevens recorded cover versions of "Blue Monday" and "I Just Want to Make Love to You," with Ringo on drums and Stevens on guitar.)

Barry Sinkow was managing the Loews Casino in Monte Carlo, Ringo's favorite haunt, when he first met a bald-headed man who sauntered over to the bar, introduced himself as "Richard" and offered to buy him a drink. They struck up a conversation; Sinkow, who was living in Puerto Rico during the initial rush of Beatlemania, was out of the pop-culture loop and didn't recognize that the friendly guy with the shaved head was Ringo Starr. They tossed a few back and became friendly.

When Ringo was in Monte Carlo, he often ate dinner at one of his favorite restaurants, Pinocchio's, with Sinkow, sometimes accompanied by Nancy Andrews, Hilary Gerrard, or both. The restaurant was adjacent to Prince Rainier and Princess Grace's palace. Sinkow always made sure the check was "taken care of."

"One night, when I wasn't in the casino, Ringo got stone-assed drunk," Sinkow said. "Somebody kept feeding him booze. And he had a scene with one of the nicest guys in the casino. It almost came to fisticuffs. They were pushing each other. You can get thrown out of Monaco for something like that. Meanwhile, they dragged Ringo out of the casino. I get a phone call in the morning. They said that they banned Ringo. I said, 'No shit? Are you kidding me?' Ringo was so upset. He came to me, we met and he said, 'I am so sorry. I would never do something like that. I was out of hand.'" Sinkow told Ringo he needed to apologize to his (Sinkow's) boss, Mr. Lorenzi, and to Rinaldo Gianni, the casino worker with whom he'd tussled. Ringo did as he was told and the incident was swept under the rug.

"He was the sassiest, most humorous person I've ever met in my life," Sinkow said of Ringo. "He had a sense of humor. He was the funniest guy that you wanted to sit and be with. But he was a mean individual if he did not know you. He did not like to be accosted or people coming up to him. I said, 'Rich, that's your fault. You made money in the business and they're excited to see you, so relax.' So he started to calm down a little bit, but he didn't like people to just walk over to [his] table. If we were sitting at a bar and he looked up and somebody was coming toward him, he would say, 'Uh oh.' And he would give them one of his stares. Once in a while he would sign an autograph, but he didn't like it."

"People notice him and point him out, but they don't go rushing up to him for autographs like they used to," noted Loews manager Paul Maser. "Let's face it; he's hardly a sexy young pop star anymore, is he."

"I got involved with a lot of different medications and you can listen to my records go downhill as the amount of medication went up," Ringo said by way of explanation. "When I really, really got wrecked, I couldn't play," he said. "For years, I just went downhill. We never made records totally derelict. You got derelict and then you made the records. Occasionally we'd have a . . . late night, and we'd make music and the next day you'd think, 'What a load of crap.'"

His so-called movie career, which showed so much promise in the post-Beatles era (*That'll Be the Day*), was also in a tailspin. The drinking and drugging was impairing his decision-making. Ray Connolly, who wrote *That'll Be the Day*, said frankly: "I felt he threw some of his career away by doing silly things like *Caveman*. He had these lovely soulful eyes. I always thought that. And he could tell you an awful lot with his eyes, which he did very well in *A Hard Day's Night*. Maybe he couldn't read a good script.

"He liked films, but I think he just liked being in a Hollywood movie sort of world but he didn't stop to say, 'Hang on, I'm Ringo Starr. I have to choose carefully.' He just did [the movies] because it was good fun. Having a little laugh, you know? You get doomed for that, forever. People remember them."

It was good news for Ringo, then, that his next movie, *Lisztomania*, opened and closed quickly and is remembered today chiefly by diehard movie buffs. Written and directed by Ken Russell in his trademark surreal, overblown style, *Lisztomania* featured The Who's lead singer Roger Daltrey—who'd starred in Russell's movie version of *Tommy*—in the title role of classical composer Franz Liszt, transformed here into the genre's first pop star.

One fantasy sequence involved Daltrey's Liszt and a gigantic erect (plastic) penis; Ringo played The Pope in several scenes. *Lisztomania* was skewered by most critics upon its release in 1975, with Russell taking most of the heat.

The *New York Times* called Ringo's portrayal of The Pope in *Lisztomania* "the one charmingly low-keyed performance in the film." It was a rare positive note for a once-universally beloved man who was quickly wearing out his welcome.

The cuddly, teddy bear Beatles-era Ringo Starr was now transformed into a completely bald, often surly celebrity, known less for his music and acting than for his globetrotting and high-living lifestyle. He was a man without a home whose self-imposed exile from England and bacchanalian lifestyle did not go unnoticed by his ex-band mates.

John, Paul, and George were all settling into their mid-thirties with a veneer of self-respect and purpose in life; Ringo, who turned thirty-seven in July 1977, just seemed lost, confused, and tortured by self-doubt. "Paul was telling me how pleased he was to see that Ringo was doing okay, but I think at that time they were all worried about him," said Ray Connolly. "He was drinking all the time. It's a shame."

"After the band broke up, I wasn't working," Ringo admitted. "I wasn't doing what I love, which is playing drums and performing. I ended up as just some fucking celebrity. Someone in England put it so cruelly: They said, 'If there's an opening of an envelope, *he'll* be there.' That hit me. I thought, 'Shit, yeah, this is what I'm doing now.' I'd be at movie premieres in London with my bow tie on and a bottle of cognac in my pocket mixed with some Coca-Cola, so people would think it was just soda. It got really sad."

To Keith Allison, Ringo's friendship with his drinking buddy Keith Moon—two of The World's Most Famous Drummers from two of The World's Most Famous Bands—was cemented by a common bond: insecurity. Moon "was totally envious of Ringo—who was feeling exactly the same way," Allison said. "I thought, 'How ironic, because these guys are both very talented,' but they were looking down the road, and it looked scary. Because it does to anyone, when you've been that hot, when you've been as huge as they were."

It was more pathetic than funny when Ringo and Keith—both drunk and seated in front of a fireplace in Keith's Malibu beach house—were filmed by Jeff Stein for his documentary on The Who called *The Kids Are Alright*. The two drummers talked about their "medicine" (alcohol) and made little sense.

"It's probably that we're drunk," Ringo says to the camera.

"It could be that," Keith answers.

"Not drunk, teenyboppers," Ringo says, . . . "Keith and me had a lot of medicine, you know, just a lot of medicine 'cause we're getting on now, we need our medicine."

That interview was filmed in August 1977; Moon died in London a year later, in Harry Nilsson's apartment—decorated by Ringo's ROR design firm—after ingesting thirty-two tablets of Heminevrin to help combat his alcohol withdrawal. He was thirty-two. Ringo's friend and collaborator Marc Bolan, the subject of *Born to Boogie*, died in September 1977 in a London car crash at the age of twenty-nine.

Ringo, meanwhile, was still talking wistfully about a possible Beatles reunion, which was never going to happen; his ex-band mates were all doing their own thing (and Lennon was out of the business completely). Still, he clung to the hope that John, Paul, and George would come around to the idea. "We did talk about it, but there's no interest now," Ringo said in early 1977. "If anything, we'd do an album first, then prepare for a tour for six months, and we don't have that kind of time. And we wouldn't do it for the money. We were never into that."

When asked point-blank, later that year—after several more career disappointments—if he would be open to a Beatles reunion, Ringo was more definitive. "As a straight answer—yes. But you see, that can't be the answer. No, you can't lay it all on me," he said. "It can't be the answer. There's too much involved to get together—to make it possible. I would love for the four of us to play . . . don't know if it'll work. I don't see why it shouldn't because . . . I mean, I'm just going from the *Ringo* album. It was John, George and I. It was the closest we ever got to a reunion. And it was fine. I mean, I would dig that."

If that was ever going to happen, Ringo needed to get his own recording career back on track. He still owed several more albums to Polydor and Atlantic, one of which, a children's LP called *Scouse the Mouse*, featured Ringo as the lead character, a mouse who travels from Liverpool to America. He also sang eight songs for the album, which was written and directed by actor Donald Pleasence. *Scouse the Mouse* did well enough in the UK to warrant interest from British television network ITV, which eventually scrapped its plans to turn it into a cartoon series.

Of more significance to Ringo was his next solo album, which he began recording in the spring of 1977, hoping to avoid the dismal fate of *Ringo's Rotogravure*. He called the new LP *Ringo the 4th*, even though it was, in reality, his sixth solo album. According to Nancy Andrews, the idea for the album's title came to Ringo while they were stuck at the Plaza Hotel in New York City during a January snowstorm. "The idea really made sense, him being from England and their royal history," she said. "Then he said, 'I want to go medieval.'"

Ringo and Nancy went to a nearby prop house and procured a scepter; back at the Plaza, Nancy photographed Ringo in a black-velvet jacket as he sat in a walk-in closet on top of a wastepaper basket topped by a pillow. He held the scepter with Nancy's friend Rita Wolf (who was in town for a visit) sitting on his shoulders, her bare thighs sandwiching his head. The photo graced the cover of *Ringo the 4th*. Nancy also shot Ringo and Rita Wolf from the back; that photo was used on the back cover of the album.

The photo shoot, unfortunately, was the only memorable element of the album, which Ringo recorded from February through June, both in New York (at Atlantic Studios) and in L.A. (at Cherokee Studios, with Arif Mardin once again producing). This time around, there were no ex-Beatles contributing material. Ringo collaborated with Vini Poncia on six of the ten tracks and shared drumming duties with Steve Gadd; Bette Midler and Melissa Manchester contributed backing vocals on the album. It's unclear whether the album's disco-flavored feel—it was the height of the disc era, after all—was Ringo's idea or someone else's higher up on the Atlantic Records food chain.

In the end, it didn't really matter. *Ringo the 4th* was pilloried upon its release in September, and followed the now-common trend of Ringo's solo albums failing to chart in the UK. It entered the U.S. charts at an atrocious Number 162 before quickly vanishing. Sales were abysmal; critical reaction, even worse.

"Less than three months after its release, the Ringo fan in me dutifully played this for a third and last time," wrote esteemed music journalist Robert Christgau. "Whereupon the journalist began to wonder how many people were buying such dreary music just because it was by a Beatle. And was both saddened and pleased to learn that the answer, for all practical purposes, was no one."

In 1978, Ringo moved from his rented house on Haslam Terrace in L.A. to a nearby five-bedroom, five-bathroom New England–style house on 7708 Woodrow Wilson Drive in Laurel Canyon. "Nancy wasn't a permanent fixture anymore," said Keith Allison, who was a frequent guest in the new digs and used one of the spare bedrooms upstairs when he stayed over. Ringo's *200 Motels* director, Frank Zappa, had a house nearby. A live-in manservant named Charles—a student at nearby UCLA who was from Nassau in the Bahamas—was hired to look after Ringo's new place. He did the grocery shopping and, occasionally, some light cooking. "He cooked a really good English breakfast," Allison recalled, "and went down to Greenblatt's (on Sunset Boulevard) to pick up wine for us."

According to Harry Nilsson's cousin Doug Hoefer, it was Harry who bought the house on Woodrow Wilson Drive for Ringo. "Ringo was always renting houses when he came to L.A., so Harry bought him a house. He just bought Ringo a house. He said, 'Stop renting houses. Here, I bought you one,'" Hoefer recalled. "He said, 'I'm going to buy you this house so no matter what happens to us, you always have a home.'"

The new place was gated and was set back from the street on an acre of land. It was once owned by actress Natalie Wood. If his movie career was going to wither and die on the vine, at least it would happen in L.A. "Well, I can't get an acting job," he said. "I've turned a lot down, because I was getting offered such small parts."

Despite the dearth of what Ringo considered to be worthy big-screen acting jobs, he accepted another supporting role in his next movie, *Sextette*, which starred legendary big-screen sexpot Mae West—long past her prime and in her late eighties when filming began at Paramount Studios.

West was cast as Hollywood sex symbol Marlo Manners, who's on her London honeymoon with her sixth husband, Sir Michael Barrington (played by future James Bond star Timothy Dalton). West was hard-of-hearing and wore an earpiece under her blond wig, through which she was fed her lines by director Ken Hughes. Ringo was cast as temperamental Hungarian film director Laslo Karolny, one of Marlo's ex-husbands and one of the many characters constantly interrupting Marlo and Michael's attempts to have sex in their hotel room.

Keith Moon played a flamboyant dress designer; the cast also included George Raft (who co-starred with West in 1932's *Night After Night*), Tony Curtis, Walter Pidgeon, George Hamilton, and Dom DeLuise. Ringo's pals Alice Cooper and Keith Allison played waiters. Allison recalled:

> Keith Moon got the last good part in the movie. I had gone by Ringo's house and the producers were there and they said, "We're casting for this movie with Mae West" and I said I wanted to be in it. "What have you got?" Ringo said, "Keith just left, he was here," so he got the last part. They gave me the part of a bellhop. It was one day's work, really. Ringo had shot his scenes the week before and I was over there on the set with him, just hanging out at Paramount. Mae West didn't arrive until ten o'clock in the morning; they would open up the big doors—she had this old limousine, and this muscle builder would get out and open the door and we all stood around and had to applaud. We didn't have to, but we did.
>
> She would be wearing a babushka and a scarf over her head and sunglasses and a big old fur coat and then she would go into her dressing room and about an hour and a half later, Mae West would come out of there. This ninety-year-old woman would hobble in there, and then Mae West would come out. It was like a time warp.

Despite the presence of his close friends, Ringo regretted his decision to appear in *Sextette* after only one day on the set, and reportedly (and unsuccess-fully) tried to buy out his contract.

"Mae is still sexy after all these years," Ringo said diplomatically. "I thought it would be fantastic to play with Mae, just to see what the legend was really like, but on the very first day of shooting I got uptight. Everybody was saying 'Mae this' and 'Mae that' and I felt completely left out of things. But by the end of the second day I would have stayed for as long as she wanted me. She's old enough to be my grandmum, so it's sort of embarrassing to say, but she's bloody attractive—and Mae's no Garbo. Mae doesn't want to be left alone."

In an interview with the *New York Times*—which described him as "the pic-ture of haggard youth as he attended to a horrendous hangover with delicate sips of beer . . . blinking his bloodshot eyes, yawning, burping . . ."—Ringo did his promotional best to pump up *Sextette*. "If Alice Cooper or Keith Moon or George Raft or *any* of us is remembered from *Sextette*, I'll be surprised," he said. "Mae is so fan-bloody-fantastic that she just wipes us out . . . I think a lot of people will go to see Mae the way they go see *King Kong*. They'll want to see how the new Mae stacks up against the old Mae."

He was wrong. The public reaction to *Sextette*, and to Mae West, was one of disgust at watching the eighty-seven-year-old icon, obviously infirm, drop-ping double entendres and trying to turn the clock back forty years. *Sextette* was savaged by the critics, and bombed at the box office. The *New York Times* called it "a disorienting freak show" and referred to West as looking "like a plump sheep that's been stood on its hind legs, dressed in a drag-queen's idea of chic, bewigged and then smeared with pink plaster."

Ringo was anointed one of the movie's "decent actors," along with Curtis, Hamilton, and DeLuise. *Variety* labeled *Sextette* "a cruel, unnecessary and mostly unfunny musical comedy" and said that Ringo, along with Curtis, Dal-ton, and Hamilton, "hardly enhance their reputations."

Ringo's already tarnished reputation in the recording industry wasn't en-hanced, either, when he folded Ring O' Records in 1978 after three years and little to show for his efforts as a wannabe music mogul. The label signed eleven artists and released fifteen singles and five albums in its short lifespan, with four singles and three albums still in the can when the company was dissolved.

Ringo took another hit to the musical gut when he was dropped by Atlantic Records in America after *Ringo the 4th*. His seventh solo album, *Bad Boy*, would be released in the U.S. by his new label, Portrait Records, a sister label of Epic Records.

Bad Boy was recorded over a ten-day stretch in the fall of 1977, with Ringo bouncing between studios in the Bahamas and Vancouver (for tax purposes). In an encouraging sign for the album, NBC committed to airing a prime-time special in which Ringo would star. It was called *Ringo* and was slated to air in April 1978 in conjunction with the release of *Bad Boy*, hopefully giving the LP a promotional push.

This time around in the recording studio, Ringo eschewed the "help from celebrity friends" approach and wrote two of the album's ten tracks with Vini Poncia, who also produced the LP. Ringo played drums and was backed by anonymous musicians "Push-a-Tone" on lead guitar, "Git-tar" on rhythm guitar and "Diesel" on bass—later identified as Lon Van Eaton, Jimmy Webb, and Elton John's bassist, Dee Murray.

The *Ringo* television special was sold to NBC by D. I. R. Broadcasting, whose two principal players, Bob Meyrowitz and Peter Kauff, had a longstanding friendship with Ringo dating back to his Beatle days.

"They were primarily radio syndicators but they wanted to do some TV things, and they had a relationship with Ringo," said *Ringo* producer Ken Ehrlich. The star himself was adamant that he wanted the NBC special to be a top-flight production. He needed some positive vibes in the wake of his disappearing recording and movie careers, and he needed to prove he was still viable as a musician and an actor.

Ringo incorporated both elements in a groundbreaking format described by its co-writer, Neal Israel, as "a jukebox musical" in which Ringo would both act and sing. Maybe television was the answer. "He wanted this show," said Jeff Margolis, who directed the special. "He didn't know if he was ever going to do another. He said, 'This might be my only shot a my own network prime-time television special, so I want it to be perfect.'"

Israel and Pat Proft were hired to write the script, in which Ringo would play himself and his alter-ego, Ognir Rrats (Ringo Starr spelled backwards) in a modern-day twist on Mark Twain's *The Prince and the Pauper*.

"It was an idea that I'd had maybe a year before, but I quickly changed it for Ringo, and also I'd had experience in the theater," Israel said. "I worked for George Abbott and I knew a lot about musicals, so it was very easy for me . . . and we were doing basically a jukebox musical. No one had even done a jukebox musical before on television."

An all-star cast was assembled for the special: Art Carney, the Oscar winner (for 1974's *Harry and Tonto*) and Jackie Gleason's legendary co-star of *The Hon-*

eymooners; Angie Dickinson; Vincent Price; *Star Wars* lead Carrie Fisher; and John Ritter, who was enjoying his first flush of success on the ABC sitcom *Three's Company*. Ritter played Ringo's agent, the hip, medallion-wearing Marty Flesh.

"Everybody wanted to be there for Ringo," Margolis said. "John Ritter was his number one fan, and John was a friend of mine, so when I called him and told him what I was doing, and before I finished explaining anything to him, he said, 'Yes! I'll change my schedule, I'll do whatever I can do.'" (Ritter's character on *Three's Company*, Jack Tripper, took his last name from The Beatles' song "Day Tripper.")

"Carrie Fisher was a big fan of Ringo's and she couldn't wait to do it," Margolis said. "Everybody came prepared and everybody worked really hard, especially Ringo. Everything was memorized—there were no cue cards. We shot it like a movie; I really wanted it to have that feel, so I only used two cameras and sometimes only one camera. It was very different, for that time, for shooting a television special outside of a studio.

"For a guy who's not an actor, for a guy who is a drummer, Ringo really put himself into that character of Ognir Rrats because he wanted it to be totally different than Ringo Starr," Margolis said. "When Ringo liked something a lot, he would just say to me, 'The puppies are in the freezer,' and if he didn't like something he'd say, 'The puppies are in the oven.' I have no idea what the fuck that means, but we had our own code."

Nancy Andrews, who was on the *Ringo* set to shoot publicity stills for NBC, remembered a lot of fun interplay between Art Carney and Ringo, since Carney stayed in character as Ognir Rrats's grouchy father.

Ringo corralled George Harrison, who agreed to narrate the special, and who flew in to L.A. from Hawaii for a few days, despite injuring himself on a mountain in Maui several days before. "He'd fallen on his face but he still came because that was what he was like," Ringo said.

Margolis got the shock of his life when he arrived at Ringo's house on Woodrow Wilson Drive for a prearranged meeting to talk about the project. "I went to the gate and somebody said, 'Who is it?' and they buzzed me in. Ringo was expecting me. And I went up to the front door, and knocked on the door, and his house man answered the door and said, 'Have a seat, Mr. Margolis. I'll tell Mr. Starkey you're here.' Ringo came out, and I got a big hug and a kiss, and he said, 'Come on into the music room, I'd like you to meet some friends of mine.' And I walked in, and there was George, and Paul and John. I almost shit myself. I almost died."

Ringo also tried to get Lennon involved in the special, but to no avail. "Ringo let me be on the extension when he called John," recalled Neal Israel. "And John said, 'I've got to throw the I Ching. I'll call you back.' He called back and said, 'Well, I've got number fifty-three, the well. Sorry, I can't come.' But Ringo said to me, 'I'm the only one who can talk to everybody.'"

The plot of *Ringo* revolved around two babies born in Britain at the same time, to different parents, "who look exactly alike." Ringo Starr remains in Britain and becomes a famous rock icon; Ognir Rrats moves to America, where he's a put-upon schlemiel reduced to selling maps of the stars' homes in Hollywood. Ringo and Ognir eventually meet and swap identities, are both propelled into farcical situations—Ognir, as Ringo, destroys the set of *The Mike Douglas Show*—and the special ends with Ringo performing several songs from *Bad Boy* ("Heart on My Sleeve," "Hard Times," "A Man Like Me") and offering Ognir a job as his road manager.

"The misadventures that follow are mildly amusing in a rather self-consciously juvenile way that anyone over the age of ten or so may find a bit patronizing," one critic noted, "while at the same time lacking the manic energy of a schoolyard at recess."

"Ringo was very natural and he had a friend of his who's a terrific actor named Seymour Casell, who was kind of Ringo's coach," Israel said. "Because he was playing two parts, which was a challenge. He was really terrific. I thought he did a great job. He did such a good job that maybe six or seven years later, I was doing a pilot at Universal called *The Flip Side*, and Ringo committed to starring in it. And about six weeks before we were going to shoot, Hilary Gerrard called and he pulled out of the project and we shot it with another actor and the pilot didn't go."

Bad Boy was released in the UK on April 21, five days before NBC's *Ringo* special hit the airwaves. Its U.S. release was held until mid-June. *Ringo*, meanwhile, failed to make much of an impact, finishing fifty-third out of sixty-five prime-time shows the week it aired—dulling any hoped-for promotional push for *Bad Boy*.

Perhaps a harbinger of *Ringo*'s poor viewership—and, by extension, the failure of *Bad Boy*—was *The Rutles: All You Need Is Cash*, a clever parody of The Beatles saga which aired on NBC in March, a month before *Ringo*.

Co-created and co-written by former Bonzo Dog Band member Neil Innes and *Monty Python* trouper Eric Idle, *All You Need Is Cash* transformed John Lennon, Paul McCartney, George Harrison, and Ringo Starr into Ron Nasty, Dirk McQuickly, Stig O'Hara, and Barry Wom. (Barry, played by rock drummer John

Strange brew: Ringo as frisky Mexican gardener Emmanuel in *Candy* (1968), with star Ewa Aulin; Sugar Ray Robinson tends bar in the background. (Cinema Releasing Corp./Photofest)

Youngman Grand (Ringo) consults with his adoptive father, Sir Guy Grand (Peter Sellers), in a scene from *The Magic Christian* (1969). All four Beatles idolized Sellers from his *Goon Show* days. (Photo by Stanley Bielecki Movie Collection/Getty Images)

1972: Elton John (left), Marc Bolan, and Ringo hit the town to promote *Born to Boogie* (1972), which marked Ringo's directorial debut. (Photo by Michael Putland/Getty Images)

ABOVE LEFT: Ringo garnered critical acclaim as Mike Menary in *That'll Be the Day* (1974). He declined to appear in its sequel, *Stardust*, because he thought the storyline hit too close to home vis-à-vis The Beatles. (Brian Moody/Rex USA)

ABOVE RIGHT: Ringo, wearing his ever-present shades, carouses with '70s party pals Harry Nilsson (center) and Keith Moon, who died in 1978 at the age of thirty-two. (Photo by Frank Edwards/Fotos International/Getty Images)

As Laslo Karolny in the disastrous *Sextette* (1978) opposite eighty-five-year-old Mae West in her final movie: "Like a plump sheep that's been stood on its hind legs . . . bewigged and then smeared with pink plaster." (Crown International/Photofest)

Nearing the end: Ringo and Maureen in 1975; they divorced that same year. (© Bettmann/CORBIS)

Ringo sports his newly shaved head in Monaco, July 1976: "It was a time when you either cut your wrists or your hair." (AP Photo)

January 1978: With Nancy Andrews at Mr. Chow's in Beverly Hills. (Photo by Ron Galella/WireImage)

The look of love: Ringo and Barbara Bach in a scene from *Caveman* (1981). (United Artists/Photofest)

"I played Washington with The Beach Boys—or so they tell me." Ringo with Bruce Johnston (left) and Mike Love, July 1984. (AP Photo)

Ringo and Barbara leave the Dakota after comforting Yoko Ono, one day after John Lennon's assassination in December 1980. George Harrison and Paul McCartney stayed in England. (©Bettman/Corbis/AP Images)

Ringo and Barbara tied the knot on April 27, 1981. The happy couple with George and Olivia Harrison (left); Paul and Linda McCartney (holding their son, James); and Barbara's son, Gianni Gregorini. (Photo by Terry O'Neill/Getty Images)

As Mr. Conductor in *Thomas the Tank Engine & Friends*, which was a hit in the UK and in the U.S., where it morphed into *Shining Time Station*. His ongoing role in this children's television program exposed Ringo to a new generation of fans. (Tony Nutley/Rex USA)

Ringo with the first All-Starr Band lineup in 1989: Clarence Clemons (left), Nils Lofgren, Billy Preston, Joe Walsh, and Rick Danko. (Photo by Ron Galella/WireImage)

Two of us: Ringo and Paul McCartney marked the fiftieth anniversary of their debut on *The Ed Sullivan Show* in an all-star CBS special, *The Night That Changed America: A Grammy Salute to The Beatles*. (Photo by Kevin Winter/Getty Images)

Peace and love: Ringo and Barbara in 2014, still together after nearly thirty-five years of marriage. (Photo by Michael Tran/FilmMagic)

Halsey, was described by the *New York Times* as "a troglodytic Ringo Starr"). The Rutles movies were all there—*A Hard Day's Rut, Ouch!* and *Let It Rot*—as was manager Leggy Mountbatten's best-selling memoir, *A Cellar Full of Goys* and Ron's marriage to avant-garde artist Chastity. George Harrison, wearing a gray wig and mustache, made a cameo appearance as a television interviewer.

All You Need Is Cash aired on March 28, 1978, and finished dead-last in the ratings that week. It had a carryover effect on *Ringo* which, in turn, dulled the impact of *Bad Boy*, the album it was supposed to promote. *Bad Boy* failed to chart in the UK—Ringo's fourth consecutive solo album to achieve that dubious claim—and charted at Number 129 in the U.S. It would be three years before Ringo released another album.

Keith Moon's death in September 1978 did little to curb the partying ways of Ringo and Harry Nilsson. They were together in Ringo's suite at the Beverly Wilshire Hotel, along with Derek Taylor and some others, when they learned about Moon's death.

Both men were saddened, of course; Moon was one of Ringo's closest friends and the godfather to Zak Starkey, who was now thirteen and, like his dad and "Uncle Keith," showing a prodigious talent behind the drum kit. Zak, like his brother and sister, wasn't put off by Keith's antics. A scene from the 1979 documentary on The Who, *The Kids Are Alright*—in which Keith tramples through sand castles built by Zak and his brother Jason—was cut from the movie "possibly because it showed Keith in a bad light."

Everyone was surprised, but not totally shocked, by Keith's death. It was a miracle his body held out as long as it did. Ringo did not attend Keith's funeral. Maureen, however, made an appearance, along with Eric Clapton and Rolling Stones members Charlie Watts and Bill Wyman.

With Keith's death, Harry Nilsson not only lost a dear friend but now had to deal with the fact that his Curzon Place apartment was the site of two celebrity deaths within four years of each other (the first was Cass Elliot, "Mama Cass" of The Mamas & the Papas, who died at the age of thirty-two from a heart attack, in July 1974). He couldn't bear to return there after Keith died and eventually sold the apartment to Keith's band mate, The Who's Pete Townshend.

Harry had spent time with Ringo the previous February on the set of

Ringo's NBC special, and he was a regular visitor to Ringo and Nancy's house on Woodrow Wilson Drive in L.A. Although his recording career was winding down, he still had clout in the industry; Nilsson was hired to write the music for Robert Altman's 1980 movie, *Popeye*.

That, indirectly, led to one of Ringo and Harry's wild adventures in 1979— and Ringo's fling with nineteen-year-old Stephanie La Motta.

Ringo and Nancy had been together for five years by this time. They'd talked about marriage, and even having children, but neither of those life-changing events had come to pass. Their jet-setting lifestyle—a different city or country, sometimes several of each in the same week—caused some tensions every now and then, and they had broken up and gotten back together at least once already, spawning Ringo's short-lived fling with Lynsey de Paul and, reportedly, a fling with Samantha Juste, the ex-wife of Mickey Dolenz, who was photographed with Ringo at an L.A. nightclub in January 1979.

"We loved to go to the discos in Monte Carlo and Regine's was our favorite," Nancy said. "The DJ knew that we loved "I Heard It Through The Grapevine" by Marvin Gaye and would play it at least twice while we were there. Ringo would jump up and pull me to the dance floor. He had moves that were so simple but looked so good. Also we loved to go to Tramp in London . . . they had the best bangers and mash (sausage and mashed potatoes). We would gobble it down around two a.m. before we went home. If other women wanted to dance with Ringo they didn't ask—they knew I would scratch their eyes out."

Stephanie La Motta didn't have to worry about having her eyes scratched out by Nancy, since she was minding her own business when Ringo approached her in Tramp during a whirlwind trip that began in London. "Once Harry Nilsson and I ended up in Australia looking for Johann Strauss," Ringo said. "We met Robert Altman instead and finished up in a hotel in Denmark and I believe we had a heated discussion halfway through dinner . . . and the end result was I ended up in Greece with somebody, in Athens!"

That "somebody" was Stephanie, the daughter of middleweight boxing champ Jake La Motta, memorably played by Robert De Niro in Martin Scorsese's 1980 Oscar-winning movie *Raging Bull*. In 1979, Stephanie was in London, chasing a musical career, when she was sitting at the bar in Tramp. Ringo was there, starting his transatlantic jaunt and intending to meet up with Harry in Vienna.

Ringo asked the owner of Tramp to ask Stephanie if she wanted to have a drink with him. "I said if he wants to have a drink with me, he can come over and ask me himself," she recalled. "And then he came over and he kind of apologized and said, 'Would you like to have a drink with me?' and I said 'Okay.' We started talking and having a nice conversation. He is a very nice, cordial, well-mannered person."

With Tramp closing its doors for the night, Ringo invited Stephanie to go dancing with him at a club called Annabel's, which was also about to close for the night until Ringo persuaded the owner to keep the place open for another hour, a courtesy for which he paid. "His ex-wife Maureen was there, Klaus Voormann was there and a couple of other people were there," Stephanie said. "We went back into Annabel's and he bought me an hour's worth of dancing."

Almost as soon as they met at Tramp, Ringo was asking Stephanie if she wanted to go to Vienna with him the following day. She was supposed to return to New York, but put the trip off (Ringo was persuasive), returned to her apartment to pack a bag, and then spent the night with Ringo in his suite at the Dorchester Hotel.

"The thing I liked most about him was that first night we were together at the Dorchester, there were two big beds in the room and he said, 'This is your bed and this is my bed, only if you want it to be.' I said, 'Yes, I want it to be.' And then another night, when we got to the Bristol Hotel in Vienna, we were in bed, lying down, and he turned away on his side and he said to me, 'Oh, I'm sorry. That's so rude.' I mean, who would ever think to say that? Even if he was drunk he was very conscious about things like that."

They left for Vienna early in the morning and checked into the Bristol Hotel. Stephanie was awakened from a nap by the sound of someone knocking on their door—"this huge guy with dark sunglasses and a big black raincoat and a black hat on." It was Harry Nilsson. "He said, 'I'm Harry' and he goes searching all over the place and I'm screaming for Ringo, who comes out and hugs Harry because he loved Harry. They had a special bond. It was unbelievable this bond I saw between them. He loved Harry as much as Harry loved him. I had no clue at the time who Harry was."

Harry was in Vienna because Robert Altman was hosting a screening of *Popeye*, which featured Harry's music. "Because I was stupid I had no idea who Robert Altman was, either," Stephanie said. "Harry flew in from Malta. The first night of the film festival Ringo fell asleep on my shoulder and he's snoring. Harry, who was sitting to my right, said, 'Poke him! You have to make him stop! It's very offensive to Bob Altman.' So I kept nudging him and he woke up and sure enough *I* fell asleep.'"

Ringo, Stephanie, and Harry stayed in Vienna for the next week and a half.

Ringo told Stephanie they could go anywhere she wanted to go next. She wanted to visit Egypt, but Ringo couldn't get a visa quickly enough. "He said, 'Could we just stay in the neighborhood?' I thought that was funny. He said, 'Can you think of anyplace that's a little closer?' and I said I'd like to go to Greece. I said my mom was born in Greece and I'd love to see it. I'd never been there." So he said, 'Let's go to Greece.'"

During their trip to Vienna, Stephanie started to feel unwell, experiencing problems with her vision and balance. "I was in the middle of recording an album in London before I left and my hands weren't working—and I played lead guitar," she said. "Everybody in the band thought I was drunk but I was extremely sober. I told Ringo my hands were acting funny, and I didn't know why, and he said, 'You probably just need a vacation. Maybe you're working too much.' Which made sense."

It was the beginning of Stephanie's long battle with multiple sclerosis, which continues to this day. At the time, though, she chalked it up to Ringo's diagnosis of overwork and stress, and they continued their trip on to Greece. Harry was going to Paris, and thought Ringo and Stephanie would be joining him there; Ringo didn't have the heart to tell him he was going to Greece with Stephanie.

"Ringo said, 'I want you to tell Harry in a cryptic way that we're going to Greece,' so I wrote down 'kalamata' and we put it in his box in the hotel," Stephanie recalled. "And then we left. We got on a plane and went to Greece. Harry told us when we got back that he'd searched all of Paris looking for the Kalamata Hotel and couldn't find us." They spent about a week in Athens, touring the sites, going to dinner and clubbing in and around the city.

"He kept telling me he was 'in like' with me," Stephanie said. "Which I thought was cute, you know? I mean, I was just a kid. It was one big drunken blur. I was keeping up with him." Their tryst ended when Ringo, the tax exile, had to return to Monaco. Stephanie, who was feeling very ill by that time, was flying back to New York via London, where she saw Ringo, Harry, and Hilary Gerrard in Tramp.

"Ringo said, 'What are you doing here? You're supposed to be in New York.' We had a little bit of an altercation, a little conflict." Harry stepped in and offered to fly back to New York with Stephanie, upgrading her to first class with Robert Altman's gold credit card. Stephanie and Ringo talked by phone a few times thereafter—Ringo wanted to know how she was feeling and asked about her diagnosis—and they saw each other one last time in Tramp around a year later.

16

"CAN'T STOP LIGHTNING"

In the ten years since he'd checked into London's Middlesex Hospital with an "intestinal blockage," Ringo's health had held up remarkably well, considering the punishment he'd inflicted on his small body in his mid-'70s period of drinking and drugging with Harry, Keith, John Lennon, Alice Cooper, John Bonham, et al.

He was rarely seen in public now without dark sunglasses—the better to hide his bloodshot eyes—but he remained wiry and thin as he neared his fortieth birthday. (Unlike Keith Moon, who was bloated and puffy when he died.)

His hair had grown back after the bizarre head-shaving incident—it was, for a time, permed into tight curls in the disco-era style of that time—and along with his longer locks the gray streak in his hair reappeared (it was dyed during his Beatles days).

Ringo offset his notorious dislike of onions and spicy foods—he was the Beatle who brought baked beans with him to Rishikesh in 1968—with an everyman diet. "I'm easy to please," he said of his palate. "Fish, meat, nothin' fancy. I don't need your curries and chop sueys. Garlic and onions kill me. I prefer cognac."

But his history of intestinal troubles caught up to him in April 1979 while he was in Monte Carlo. On April 28, he developed severe stomach pain and was rushed to Princess Grace Hospital; the problems stemmed from the nearly deadly peritonitis he'd suffered as a seven-year-old boy in Liverpool.

"My intestines closed down and I was in a lot of pain," Ringo said. "I got to the hospital finally and they gave me a shot of pain killer. Then, when I felt some relief I said, 'Oh. I can go now.' And Professor Chatalin, the doctor who was taking care of me, said, 'Yes, you can go. And you can die!' So I said, 'Well, maybe we should have the operation.'"

Doctors removed five feet of Ringo's intestines and he remained in intensive care for five days, followed by a week in the hospital's recovery ward. "And then I conned my way out a couple of days later to go and live in the Hotel de

Paris because I hate hospitals—I spent two years in them when I was a boy," he said. "I used to sit in the bar at the Hotel de Paris. I couldn't drink because my intestines were healing but I could hang out with people so it helped get over that low passage." He'd given up cigarettes, but found himself lighting them up for other people "because it gave me a buzz"—and within a week he was up to a sixty-a-day cigarette habit.

Ringo recovered enough from his near-death experience in Monte Carlo to attend a wedding reception in May for Eric Clapton's marriage to George's ex-wife, Pattie (they officially tied the knot in late March). The fete was held in Clapton's garden where George wrote "Here Comes the Sun." George and Paul McCartney were there; along with Ringo, it was the closest thing to a Beatles reunion anyone was going to get. (John Lennon was not invited, according to Pattie, because of his immigration issues).

"Zak and Jim Capaldi were playing drums because Eric had a band set up on stage," Ringo recalled. "I have fond memories of that day." Those "fond memories" included a jam session with Ringo, George, and Paul joined on a makeshift stage by ex-Cream members Clapton, Ginger Baker and Jack Bruce; Mick Jagger and Charlie Watts from The Rolling Stones; Elton John; David Bowie; Wings guitarist Denny Laine; and the onetime "King of Skiffle" Lonnie Donegan, who'd influenced almost every musician there. It was reported, but never confirmed, that one of the songs played on stage that day was "Sgt. Pepper's Lonely Hearts Club Band."

John Lennon might not have been at Eric Clapton's wedding reception, but he continued to stay in touch with Ringo while raising his son Sean, who was now almost four years old. Lennon was about to return to the recording studio after his self-imposed five-year hiatus, and was aware that Ringo's solo career, and his life in general, was on the rocks.

In May of 1979, around ten days before Clapton's wedding reception, John sent Ringo a postcard from New York, which read, in part: "Blondie's 'Heart of Glass' is the type of stuff y'all should do." Ringo included the missive in his 2004 book, *Postcards from the Boys*. "This is John telling me what sort of things to record—he used to say, 'Do this sort of track.' 'Do it in disco style!' In 1979 my career was heading for hell anyway. . . . I was more interested in just being out of my head. The point of the card is, it didn't matter what people's perceptions of us were. . . . The relationship never went away."

Lennon addressed his postcard to "Richard Starrkey" (sic) and sent it to Ringo at 7708 Woodrow Wilson Drive.

On November 28, 1979, a cold, gray day in Los Angeles, Ringo was entertaining his lawyer, Bruce Grakal, and Hilary Gerrard at the Woodrow Wilson Drive house when he smelled smoke. Sparks from the fireplace had ignited a fire on the second floor, which spread to the attic before firemen arrived. The fire, fanned by the Laurel Canyon breeze, erupted into a six-alarm blaze that belched grayish smoke from the roof of the house and took firefighters a half hour to extinguish.

Ringo and his guests escaped unhurt, but he could only watch helplessly as the fire ravaged the house—and, with it, his collection of Beatles memorabilia stored on the second floor.

A local television station sent its "Action News" van to the scene to interview Ringo, who was identified in a graphic as "Ringo Starr, Fire Victim." Someone thought it was a good idea to accompany footage of the house aflame with "It Don't Come Easy" playing in the background. "The house went on fire," Ringo told a reporter. "That's exactly what happened. That's all we have to say, look at it! That's all, guys." Comedian Chevy Chase, one of Ringo's neighbors, can be seen in the footage shaking his head as he walked away from the scene.

Damage to the house was estimated at $135,000, and with the second story totally destroyed by the fire, Ringo was forced to move elsewhere. He rented a big Spanish mansion located high above Sunset Boulevard, on Miller Drive.

"It was a huge pink old mansion with rooms we didn't even go into or use," recalled frequent guest Keith Allison. "It had a huge library and a master suite with a huge balcony that overlooked L.A." Ringo's manservant, Charles, was installed in the chauffeur's quarters over the garage; there was a 1920s-era gas pump on the driveway (which didn't work but looked really cool).

The Miller Drive house was a place to live for the next few months, while Ringo prepared for his next project, a movie comedy called *Caveman*, which was scheduled to begin filming in Durango, Mexico, in February 1980.

Caveman had finally gotten the green light after bouncing around in development hell at United Artists since 1977. Ringo was the movie's nominal star in an ensemble cast, including future *Cheers* co-star Shelley Long, Dennis Quaid, ex-NFL star John Matuszak, veteran character actor Jack Gilford, and Barbara Bach, a beautiful blond model-turned-actress who'd made a splash as Russian spy Anya Amasova opposite Roger Moore's James Bond in the 1977 movie *The Spy Who Loved Me.*

Bach posed for *Playboy* that same year and narrowly missed out on replacing Kate Jackson on ABC's *Charlie's Angels* (the role went to Shelley Hack). Born Barbara Goldbach in Queens, New York, in 1947, she was among the fifty-five-thousand fans who packed Shea Stadium to see The Beatles in August 1965, though her sister, Marjorie, was more of a Beatles fan (Barbara favored The Rolling Stones). Now she was working with Ringo Starr.

Carl Gottlieb, who wrote the screenplay for Steven Spielberg's 1975 box-office bonanza *Jaws*, co-wrote *Caveman* with Rudy De Luca and also directed the movie. Set in prehistoric times, *Caveman* and its simple plot revolve around a mild-mannered caveman named Atouk, played by Ringo, who has eyes for Lana (Bach), the main squeeze of hulking tribal chief Tonda (Matuszak). In an effort to impress Lana, Atouk becomes the leader of his own tribe, aided by his sidekick Lar (Quaid).

The movie's dialogue consists mostly of grunts and monosyllabic words and phrases invented for the movie: "allunda" for "love," "bobo" for "friend," etc. (When *Caveman* opened the following year, audiences were given a list of English translations of "caveman words.") The movie's producer, David Foster, had high hopes for Ringo's starring role. "Ringo is potentially a comic genius," he said. "In the past he never really attacked an acting career seriously enough, perhaps. But now he's determined to do just that."

Ringo, too, was optimistic about *Caveman*, his first movie since *Sextette* hit the skids two years earlier. "To my mind I've already proved I can act," he told a reporter on the *Caveman* set. "The trouble was that I used to approach acting like a rock 'n' roller. I was getting parts simply because of who I was. Geezers would say what a great idea it was to have a Beatle in their movie. And the fact that I wanted to act, that I felt I could act, wasn't really the issue. But no one is going to offer Ringo Starr a top role these days just because I used to be one of The Beatles. I've got to be able to do the job. . . . Maybe *Caveman* is the dawn of a new era for me."

"When we wrote the movie it required a clever but small person, not someone with an imposing stature," Gottlieb said. "We wrote it without an actor in mind, and then, when the screenplay was finished, we were looking at Dudley Moore or Ringo to play Atouk. Those were the choices. Dudley was unavailable and we went with Ringo because we met with him and found out that he was interested in doing it. He had been kind of exploited in *Candy* and a couple of other films and had made some odd choices. I told him this was not like anything he'd done before. It didn't depend on his being a Beatle or a famous person—it's actually an odd, funny little acting part."

Gottlieb and his wife threw a party for the cast and crew at their house in L.A. before everyone left for Durango to begin shooting *Caveman*. "Their eyes met," he said of Ringo and Barbara. "You could sense there was some chemistry there, which was good because they were going to be our leading man and leading lady, so that was nice." Keith Allison, who was set to accompany Ringo to Durango for the *Caveman* shoot, was also at the party, and remembers that he and Ringo took Barbara out for a drink that night.

When filming began Ringo was still with Nancy. In 1978, Barbara divorced her first husband, Italian businessman Augusto Gregorini, after ten years of marriage and two children (Francesca was born in 1968, and Gianni followed four years later) and was involved with cinematographer Roberto Quezada.

She'd followed *The Spy Who Loved Me* with *Force 10 from Navarone*—co-starring Robert Shaw and Harrison Ford—and then acted in a string of schlocky movies (*Screamers*, *The Humanoid*, *Up the Academy*) before landing the role of Lana in *Caveman*. "Somehow, I sensed that the problem was not whether I could act but whether I could be fluffy enough," she said.

"We were casting the picture and we needed a 'va-va-va-voom' kind of girl," Gottlieb said. "Shelley Long was very funny and very alive . . . one of those rarities in comedy, especially in those days—a really good-looking woman who could do comedy, who understood the jokes. Barbara came in with a strategy for the auditions. There is a thing that beautiful girls do for auditions. They come in looking artfully unmade-up, like 'I just came from the gym' wearing sweats with their hair tucked up under a baseball cap. My wife saw through it in a moment but I was taken, as were the other males in the room."

Ringo, who was drinking heavily, asked Keith Allison to accompany him to Durango for the *Caveman* shoot to keep an eye on him and keep him out of trouble. "We all drank heavily back then, you know?" Allison said. "Not when we worked but when it was over, we hit the bar. I went down to Durango only to help Ringo and to be his minder—which is kind of like the blind leading the blind. They wanted someone who he knew and trusted to go, and I told him I'd go with him. So I went with him and they put me on the payroll as a personal assistant. We had a suite in the hotel at the end of the hall with two bedrooms—he was in one bedroom on one side and I was in the other."

The cast and crew left for Durango in February, and the flight to Mexico was uneventful until their plane landed in Guadalajara. The Mexican *Federales* were paying special attention to the American movie crew entering their country.

The previous month, Paul McCartney had been busted for marijuana possession in Japan at Tokyo's Narita International Airport and spent ten days in jail before being deported back to England. Now his hard-partying ex-Beatles band mate was going south of the border. The *Federales* wanted to be sure that no laws were being broken.

"They kept telling the producers 'Make sure there are no drugs!' and I said 'There won't be any goddamn drugs! We're not stupid!'" Allison said. "We landed in Guadalajara and had about a two-hour layover before taking another plane to Durango." Ringo and Keith arrived in Mexico with several cases each, including a "road case" holding a four-track tape recorder and a guitar "in case we wrote something." The *Federales* were suspicious, and approached Ringo and Keith as they sat in an upper-level coffee shop. Ringo sat with his back turned so no one could see his face. He was the first Beatle to ever visit Mexico; if word got out that he was there, he knew he'd attract a crowd. Allison recalled:

> I saw four guys in suits in the doorway and they're looking around the room and they spot Ringo and me and they make a beeline right to us. They ask for our passports so we pull them out and then they say, "Will you come with us please?" I said "What for?" I was polite, but belligerent. So they take us down to a private room that had a table in it and a couple of chairs. They had us take off our coats, they checked the buttons, they took my boots off, they checked the heels, they thought for sure we were smuggling. They got wind that one of The Beatles is coming into Mexico and some guy says, "I don't want to be lieutenant anymore. I want to be captain, and double my salary if I bust a Beatle. So that's what they were trying to do.

The *Federales* put a piece of black marble on the table and tapped all of Ringo and Keith's cash "to see if any residue came off, like coke or something" before being informed that they'd made a mistake. "They started apologizing and they went and opened the door and there must have been three hundred people out there shrieking and screaming. Word had gotten out that one of the Beatles was in there," Allison said. When Ringo and Keith finally arrived in Durango, they sent McCartney a telegram: "Thanks a lot."

The *Federales* didn't disappear after the Guadalajara airport incident. They were a constant presence on the *Caveman* set, but kept their distance and didn't interfere with filming. Nancy Andrews, who visited Ringo shortly after shooting began, wrote that "armed *Federales* surrounded the set for the duration of the location shoot," an assistant director telling her they were there to protect the cast and crew "from rebel soldiers who in the past had pillaged food, animals, equipment and had even kidnapped women."

Nancy was in Durango as a substitute "Ringo minder" because Keith Allison had to return to L.A. to record some songs for a television pilot. "I arranged for Nancy Andrews to fly in and take my place, to look after him," Allison said. "They were broken up by then. She just did it because she knew him well and she knew his idiosyncrasies and could put up with him. So she came down and I flew back to Durango two-and-a-half weeks later, arriving on Easter Sunday."

It's unclear whether Nancy, who knew Barbara from her days as a model, suspected that Ringo and Barbara were falling in love. She claimed later to have been blindsided by the affair, but it was obvious to everyone else that Ringo and Barbara had eyes only for each other. On-set romances are par for the course in Hollywood, particularly between the stars, so it wasn't so surprising.

"After Durango we went to Puerto Vallarta for a week where we kind of relaxed. We had only three-and-a-half days of work and we were there for five days, so everybody could chill," said *Caveman* writer/director Carl Gottlieb. "And then we went to Mexico City to finish shooting the interiors on the sound-stages there."

One of the key comedy scenes in *Caveman* involved Ringo's Atouk trying to seduce Barbara's Lana, while the beefy Tonda, played by the 310-pound Matuszak, is asleep next to her.

"In order to get a rehearsal for physical comedy, we had to work that out after the shooting day was over," Gottlieb said. "So me and Matuszak and Ringo and Barbara went to Barbara's room at the Holiday Inn. She had a king-sized bed, and we worked on the physical thing of rolling over, basically working out the blocking for that scene. By that time it was midnight or one a.m. and we had like a five, six or seven a.m. call in the morning so we wrapped it up. Ringo was the last to leave and the next morning he and Barbara literally came to the set holding hands. They were glowing. And Doris Grau, who at the time was the script supervisor, a real old-timer, she looked up from her desk and she was like, 'Oh! Look who's in love!' And from that moment on they were inseparable."

"I was never that much of a Beatles fan, which made it easier," Barbara said. "I just treated him like anyone else. As time went on, however, I was touched by his generosity. He is so patient and understanding. Let me give you an example. Richy can't swim, but there's a scene where he has to rescue me from a river. Carl said they could use a stunt man, but it'd be better if Richy jumped in. So he jumps. By the time he reaches me, he's headed for the bottom. And when we get to the rock I'm literally pushing him up."

In Ringo's narrative of events, it wasn't until ten days before *Caveman* wrapped production "that we said hello for the first time properly. Five days later—it's in me book, it was a Sunday afternoon—I was in love with the woman."

Ringo, who referred to Barbara as "Doris," said he "was first attracted to her by photographs in *Playboy* magazine, which left little to the imagination. Then, during breaks in the filming, I told her a lot about the South of France. I explained about the Monaco Grand Prix and asked Doris to come with me. I said I'd be upset if she didn't and I'd miss her very much."

The press didn't pay much attention to Ringo's blossoming romance with Barbara Bach. All they wanted to know was when The Beatles were going to reunite, a query which irritated Ringo to no end. Throughout the three-and-a-half-month *Caveman* shoot, he was plagued by reporters asking that same question over and over again. Carl Gottlieb remembered, "A lot of journalists came to see him and he would always begin every press conference with, 'I'm not here to talk about The Beatles. Please don't ask me if we are ever going to get together again.' And the first question would be, 'We hear the band is getting together.' He was stuck with that."

"He had been out of The Beatles longer than he was even in them, and still that's all they wanted to talk about," Keith Allison recalled. "Not about the movie, not about a new album, but 'When are The Beatles getting back together?' That was sort of ironic, I thought."

Ringo's distaste about being asked about The Beatles, and his unwillingness to answer yet another question about his former band, carried over into *Caveman*, which featured a campfire scene in which Ringo's character joins in a group song.

"He said 'Don't ask me to shake my head, I'm not going to do that,' you know, that characteristic Beatle move from *The Ed Sullivan Show*," Gottlieb said. "I said, 'I don't want you to do that. As a matter of fact, if you don't have drumsticks in that scene, I'm happy. You don't have to play the drums. We know you do that.' He was very wary about being exploited for being an ex-Beatle and not being Richard Starkey, an actor. That was a concern of his. Everybody else had just tried to exploit him. I said, 'I'm not going to be going, oh, look, I've got a Beatle in my movie.' That's not the intent.'"

By all accounts the *Caveman* set was a happy and professional place during the two-month shoot. Ringo's kids came to Mexico for a visit and Ringo got along well with everyone, spending many off-hours carousing with co-stars Dennis Quaid and John Matuszak. Carl Gottlieb recalled:

> Durango was a movie-making town and Ringo would fully participate in whatever diversions there were. One night, Jimmy Halty, who was the stunt man who doubled for Ringo, was working on some action where Matuszak, as Tonda, threw him across the room into some rafters. And Jimmy said, "That's great. Do it again." So it became a drinking game. They got a bottle of tequila and a case of beer, piled up all the mattresses in the corner of this big room, and Matuszak would take turns throwing anybody who wanted to be thrown. It was dwarf-tossing, only with everyone participating. Matuszak would throw Ringo, and the producers and insurance staff threw their hands in the air going, "Make them stop!" And Ringo would get tossed with the rest of them.

Ringo and Dennis Quaid, wrote Nancy Andrews, "acted like juvenile brothers. . . . The cast was fun and loose, which was a positive."

Gottlieb, who spent a lot of time with Ringo, also discovered he "was a bit of a provocateur. . . . He would kind of push you to see what your limits were in terms of your sense of humor or what you would accept regarding his behavior." Ringo, Gottlieb noted, enjoyed getting other people to give him personal items, like a sports coat or a jacket. "He talked several people out of items of clothing. He would keep them. He wouldn't give them back and say, 'I was just kidding.' He would get them to literally part with some favorite item, a well-broken-in hat or a comfortable jacket. He would work on them until they gave in. I guess he was a little reckless."

Caveman wrapped in late March and, shortly thereafter, Ringo broke the news to Nancy that their six-year relationship was over. "I didn't hear from Ringo for two weeks. He and co-star Barbara Bach had fallen in love on the set," she wrote. "'I'm with Barbara now,'" Ringo told me when he got back to Los Angeles." Nancy said she went to visit Ringo and Barbara at the Beverly Wilshire Hotel to bring them a box of pictures she'd taken of them on the *Caveman* set.

"It was strange visiting the man I had lived with just a month earlier and was betrothed to marry sitting with another woman, acting like a couple in love. As I waited for the elevator I looked down the long hallway thinking of all the times through the years we had stayed in this hotel, possibly in that very same suite."

Andrews wrote those words in her photo book, *A Dose of Rock 'n' Roll*, which was published nearly thirty years after the end of her romance with Ringo. At the time of the breakup, she wasn't so philosophical or forgiving.

"I was furious at being abruptly dropped by Ringo for Barbara," she said. "He had already proposed to me and I wanted to settle down with him and raise a family. I was very hurt and angry at the way he treated me. He did not behave at all like a gentleman. I had been his 'wife' for the best part of a decade and he suddenly dropped me without warning. It was like being slapped in the face. I considered Barbara a close friend and I felt humiliated that their love affair had started behind my back."

In April 1981, a year after the breakup—and just weeks before Ringo married Barbara Bach—Andrews filed a palimony suit against Ringo. Her pit-bull celebrity divorce lawyer, Marvin Mitchelson, was famous for coining the term "palimony" when he represented Michelle Triola Marvin in her case against her live-in companion, actor Lee Marvin. She lost, but the case established the right in California of unmarried partners to sue for the division of property after a breakup.

Nancy filed her lawsuit in Los Angeles County Superior Court, suing Ringo for $5 million and for half of their common property, which amounted to $2.5 million. She alleged in the suit that Ringo had promised to provide for her for the rest of her life if she gave up her career to take care of him—and that she acted as Ringo's "homemaker, companion, cook and confidante" throughout their relationship. She also alleged the Ringo repeatedly promised to marry her.

"He took good care of Nancy very well when they broke up," Keith Allison said. "He bought her a brand-new Mercedes and paid a year's rent to give her time to get back on her feet. She sold the Mercedes and bought a used BMW. I asked her why she was suing Ringo and she said she was doing it to protect him, that she was afraid it looked like he was going to marry Barbara. Nancy thought he was being 'taken' and that she was trying to run up a red flag."

Ringo and Barbara were inseparable once shooting wrapped on *Caveman*. Before leaving for Durango in February, Ringo packed up the house on Miller Drive (with a little help from Keith Allison) and moved his belongings into storage, leaving him "homeless" in L.A. for the time being. When they returned to L.A. after the *Caveman* shoot, Ringo and Barbara stayed in Ringo's suite at the Beverly Wilshire Hotel and eventually rented a palatial estate on Bedford Drive in Beverly Hills. The house was built by Greta Garbo and counted Gene Kelly, Rex Harrison, and Barbra Streisand as onetime occupants.

The happy couple flew to England in May, posing for the paparazzi, their love in full bloom and on full display. Ringo, who loved to drive, was eager to show off his native country to Barbara. They did a lot of sightseeing with Ringo behind the wheel of his white Mercedes 350SL.

On Monday, May 19, Ringo and Barbara were driving south of London near Kingston, Surrey, on their way to a party. It had been raining, and the road was slick; the Mercedes skidded off the road and slammed into two lampposts before rolling over and ending up on the opposite side of the highway. Ringo was thrown clear of the car; dazed, but with only a slight leg injury, he ran back and pulled Barbara out of the wreckage. She, too, was mostly uninjured, save for some cuts, bruises, and a wrenched back, which were all treated at nearby Roehampton Hospital. She walked on her own power to the waiting ambulance.

"We had a crash. It's cool," Ringo told a reporter on the scene. Ringo and Barbara decided that night they never wanted to be separated from each other. "It was a miracle that we both got out alive and that Barbara's beauty wasn't scarred," he said. "As soon as I could, I went and played the drums to see if I could still play. I'm still the best."

Ringo eventually had the wrecked Mercedes crushed into a cube, which he kept on his living room table as a bizarre centerpiece. He also had tiny shards of the shattered windshield set into lockets, which he and Barbara wore around their necks as reminders of their commitment to each other.

"Until I met Ringo, my stability in my crazy kind of job lay in my children," Barbara said. "If an actress doesn't have some kind of responsibility she can very easily go off the deep end. Ringo is part of my stability now. He has given me even more than I already had and that's what I want for our future. We have no intention of losing each other."

Both Maureen and Nancy Andrews *had* lost Ringo, and they dealt with the situation differently. Andrews sought legal recompense from Ringo with her 1981 palimony suit. His ex-wife Maureen, the mother of his three children, told friends in the first years following their 1975 divorce that she hoped the couple would eventually reconcile.

In 1976, Maureen met Isaac Tigrett, the co-founder of London's Hard Rock Café, who was born in Tennessee but had spent years in London as a successful businessman. In 1987, Maureen and Tigrett had a daughter, Augusta Tigrett, and were married two years later. Once Ringo hooked up with Barbara, his relationship with Maureen, always rocky in the post-divorce years, took a turn for the better. "The two of us can talk together again," Ringo said. "We've become sort of friends and I can go into the house in London to see the kids without feeling odd."

Zak Starkey, who'd shown prodigious talent behind the drum kit (even as a young child being tutored by "Uncle Keith" Moon), was approaching his fifteenth birthday and was starting to make noise about becoming a professional musician. The idea of any of his children entering show business once horrified Ringo, but he accepted Zak's zeal and admired his blossoming talent.

"Zak plays drums in a heavy metal rock group and already he wants to leave school and do it full time," he said. "I'm having to play the heavy father and say, 'No, you'll stay at school until you're older or else daddy will have to go to jail.'" Ringo and Maureen's younger son, thirteen-year-old Jason, also played the drums. Once Isaac Tigrett entered the picture he became a big part of his children's lives.

Ringo, by his own admission, had been an absentee father. His relationship with Zak, who had inherited his father's passion for drumming, could be rocky at times. "To be perfectly honest, being Ringo's son is the biggest drag in my life," Zak said as a teenager. "I'm always written about as Ringo's son, always classed in with him in every single thing I do. . . . And if I do get successful, I don't want to live like my old man, on a big estate and all that.

"My old man was never there," he said. "During my puberty, Moonie was always there with me while my old man was far away in Monte Carlo or somewhere. My old man's a good timekeeper, one of the best, but I've never thought of him as a great drummer, not really. . . . Ringo gave me one lesson, just one, when I was young. Then he told me to listen to records and play along with them."

In the coming years, Zak would hone his drumming skills with several bands and would also get into trouble. On one occasion, "drunk and abusive," he was banned from his local pub "after swearing at the landlord for playing a tape of Beatles hits."

By June 1980 Ringo and Barbara were talking marriage. Like her romantic predecessor, Nancy Andrews, Barbara also sparked Ringo's creative juices, and in July he started work on his next album, tentatively called "Can't Stop Lightning," for the Boardwalk label in the U.S. and RCA in the UK. The working title came from a phrase Ringo used to describe his feelings for Barbara. (Nancy Andrews says he also used the line on her, when they parted for good at the Beverly Wilshire several months before, to explain his relationship with Barbara.)

Ringo and Barbara had bumped into Paul and Linda McCartney at the

Cannes Film Festival in May (right before the car accident), and Paul agreed to produce "Can't Stop Lightning" and also to play on the album. John Lennon, who was back in the recording studio after a five-year hiatus, working with Yoko on their *Double Fantasy* album, contributed the song "Life Begins at 40," which he wrote specifically for Ringo. Both men were reaching their big milestone fortieth birthdays: Ringo on July 7 and Lennon on October 9. The timing was right.

Ringo played drums on the new album, and once again assembled a talented roster of backing musicians, including drummer Jim Keltner, sax player Howie Casey, bassist Herbie Flowers, and Al Kooper (one of five keyboard players used on the LP). As recording progressed over the next four months, George Harrison and Ringo covered the '50s-era love song "You Belong to Me"—with George playing guitar and producing—and also recorded George's "All Those Years Ago," which Ringo didn't like and didn't include on the album. George wrote and played guitar on "Wrack My Brain." Stephen Stills, Ronnie Wood, and Harry Nilsson would also contribute to the "Can't Fight Lightning" project.

Recording got underway on July 11 at Super Bear Studios in France, with Ringo and Paul recording four songs, two of which, "Private Property" and "Attention," were written by McCartney. They also recorded a cover version of Carl Perkins's "Sure to Fall" and Ringo's "Can't Fight Lightning." After a short hiatus, Ringo and company switched venues to Devonshire Sound Studio in Hollywood—where Ringo recorded "You've Got a Nice Way," written and produced by Stephen Stills—before the production moved again, this time to Cherokee Studios, where Ringo recorded Ronnie Wood's "Dead Giveaway," which they co-produced. Nilsson wrote and produced "Drumming Is My Madness"; he and Ringo co-wrote "Stop and Take the Time to Smell the Roses," which Nilsson produced.

Ringo flew to New York in November, where he met with John Lennon at the Dakota. They agreed to record a song John had written for Ringo called "Nobody Told Me." John already recorded his own version of the song, ostensibly for the *Double Fantasy* album, but thought it was perfect for Ringo. John also gave Ringo the demo for "Life Begins at 40." They booked some studio time in New York for mid-January to record the songs, both of which John would produce for Ringo's new album.

"He and Yoko came over to our hotel, and we had a great time saying 'hello' again," Ringo recalled. "His head was together. His album was done, and we worked it all out that come January, we were going into the studio together. Even though he was always treated in the press as a cynical put-down artist,

John had the biggest heart of all of us. He was so up, so happy then—he blew me away, he was so happy."

With a recharged Lennon on board, Ringo flew back to England and, on December 5, he and Barbara left for a vacation in the Bahamas. On December 8, the phone rang. It was Barbara's daughter, Francesca, calling to tell them the horrible news: John Lennon was dead. He'd been shot and killed outside the Dakota after returning with Yoko from a recording session. Earlier that day, John had autographed a copy of *Double Fantasy* for the crazed fan who was now in custody for his murder.

Stunned, Ringo called Maureen in London to tell her the news. John's ex-wife, Cynthia, had arrived that day for a visit with Maureen and the kids. She needed to sign some legal papers and was going to stay with her old friend for the night. She was asleep in the spare room when she was awakened by screaming. It was Maureen, who threw the receiver down and burst into Cynthia's room.

"Cyn, John's been shot. Ringo's on the phone—he wants to talk to you." In her memoir, *John*, Cynthia wrote, "I don't remember getting out of bed and going down the stairs to the phone. But Ringo's words, the sound of his tearful voice crackling over the transatlantic line, was crystal clear: 'Cyn, I'm so sorry, John's dead.'"

Paul McCartney, upon hearing the news, went to work in a fog and put in a full day in the recording studio on Oxford Street in London. As he was leaving the studio, chewing on a piece of gum, a reporter stuck a microphone in his face and asked him about his reaction to John's murder. "I'm very shocked. It's terrible news . . . drag, isn't it?" McCartney said. He later attributed what was perceived as his flippancy to shock: "I meant 'drag' in the heaviest sense of the word."

As he related in *The Beatles Anthology*, George Harrison said he received a phone call telling him that John was dead—and, in his sleepy stupor, promptly fell back to sleep. When he woke again, he realized the enormity of the news.

Ringo's reaction was different from his other two "brothers." His first and only thought after hearing about John's murder was to charter a plane and fly, with Barbara, to New York (via Miami) so he could comfort Yoko Ono, who was holed up in the Dakota after witnessing her husband's killing.

"We rented a plane as early as we could and we flew up to New York, not that you can do anything, but you just have to go and say hello. . . . There's nothing you can do," he said later, "but say, 'We're here and you know, if you want some ice cream or whatever,' 'cause you know, your brain is adult at the time. But I said [to Yoko], 'You know I know how you feel.' And the woman straight as a die, in all honesty, said, 'No, you don't.' Because no matter how close I was to him, I was not half as close as she was to him. And that blew me away, more than anything."

Ringo's arrival at the Dakota, with Barbara on his arm, was covered by a phalanx of television cameras and the reporters who'd converged on the scene as soon as news broke of John's murder. When they were ushered into the Lennons' apartment, Yoko only wanted to talk to Ringo; Barbara, she said, should remain in another room.

"I told her, 'Look, it was you who started all this. We're both coming in,'" Ringo said. "Barbara and I do everything together." After talking with Yoko for a while, Ringo played with five-year-old Sean, too young to process his father's death.

"I was given two bodyguards, and there were two of Yoko's [bodyguards] supposed to be looking after me, but in that huge block, we lost all the bodyguards," Ringo recalled. "I ended up getting lost and walking out into the street by the wrong door on my own."

He was annoyed at the hundreds of fans who camped outside the Dakota, shouting for Yoko or even for Sean to come to the window while they blasted Beatles music. "It would have been better if they left her alone," he said. "Because they're not going to bring him back, and it didn't help her by having this whole crowd outside playing his music, which is, you know, fine, if they want to do that. And then we came out, I didn't need to hear people telling me how much they loved The Beatles or any of that, when we just lost John, because I wasn't there to see a Beatle, I was there to see my friend."

Shortly thereafter, Ringo and Barbara returned to L.A. Ringo was having a tough time processing the grief he felt over John Lennon's senseless death, and he turned to Barbara and to close friends like Harry Nilsson and Ken Mansfield for support.

"We went to see *Popeye* right after John got killed because Ringo had gone to see Yoko in New York and then he came back and he just wanted to get away from it all," Mansfield said. "So Harry set up a private screening of *Popeye* and we had dinner at Mr. Chow's that night in a private dining room and went over to the studio and watched *Popeye* together. Ringo was kind of melting down. There was a threat on his life on the return flight to L.A. I think he just wanted to come home and get away from it."

Ringo did, in fact, admit to having "several threats" made to his life, and was forced to hire bodyguards to protect he and Barbara. "I hate it," he said. "I always felt safe in America until John was shot. But you can't go on living in fear. If the President himself can't stay properly protected, what chance do other people have? They even got the Pope," he said, alluding to the attempted 1981 assassination attempt on Pope John Paul II.

Upon their return to L.A., Ringo and Barbara agreed to be interviewed by ABC's Barbara Walters for her annual Oscar night special, both to promote *Caveman*, opening in mid-April, and for Ringo to talk about his reaction to John Lennon's death.

Walters, who was notorious for bringing celebrities to tears, worked her mojo on Ringo. When the interview aired in March, viewers saw him break down sobbing when Walters inevitably raised the subject of John's assassination. "Do you want to stop that now?" he asked Walters, pointing to the camera. "'Cause it doesn't help, you know, but it always gets me upset."

Keith Allison visited Ringo the day of the Barbara Walters interview. "I called and said, 'I'm coming over' and he said, 'Yeah, just come over,'" Allison recalled. "We didn't talk on the phone. I said, 'I'll talk to you when I get there.' So I drove over, wheeled into his driveway real fast and pulled in. Before I could get out of the car, there were detectives swarming all over with guns out and so forth. There had been death threats on all of them—Ringo, George and Paul. Every nut in town came out of the woodwork. They were on me like white on rice. I threw up my hands and said, 'I'm a friend!' I sat with Ringo for a long time. He was ashen. As we all were. He said, 'Barbara Walters is coming over with a film crew in about thirty minutes.' He didn't want me or anybody else there. He had a tough time with it."

(In 1981, George Harrison re-worked "All Those Years Ago" as a tribute to John Lennon and recorded the lead vocal himself, leaving Ringo's original drum track. Paul McCartney sang backing vocals. It was the first time Ringo, George, and Paul had recorded together since working on "I Me Mine" for the *Let It Be* album. "The track was originally written for me so we did the backing track, we did four tracks, but only used two and George kept that one and changed the words," Ringo said. "Then Paul came to visit and did some backing vocals. But we didn't go out to do a tribute record. I don't really consider it a tribute record, it's a record that the three of us are all on. Sounds like publicity to me.")

Ringo still had to finish recording "Can't Fight Lightning." The New York recording sessions were canceled in the wake of Lennon's death. Ringo didn't have the heart to record John's "Nobody Told Me," and his "Life Begins at 40," which Ringo did record, was not used on the album. On January 14, Ringo returned to Cherokee Studios in L.A., where he recorded with Ronnie Wood, visiting the studio one final time, on January 20. The album's title was changed to *Stop and Smell the Roses* and, in February, it was mixed for a fall release date.

During his interview with Barbara Walters, which aired March 31, Ringo casually dropped the news that he and Barbara were going to get married. "We never actually said that before. We're getting married this year. And, so, that's the end of that, of, like, we'll never get married again."

He was true to his word. On April 27, 1981, Ringo and Barbara were married in a small ceremony at the Marleybone Registry office in London. Joseph Jevons, who'd officiated at Paul and Linda McCartney's wedding twelve years earlier, performed the honors for Ringo and Barbara in front of witnesses Hilary Gerrard and Ringo's longtime friend Roger Shine. George Harrison and his wife, Olivia, were there, as were Ringo's mother, Elsie, and his "stepladder" Harry Graves. Ringo's ten-year-old daughter, Lee, and Barbara's daughter, Francesca, twelve, were the bridesmaids.

They tried to keep the wedding hush-hush but someone tipped off the press, and there were hundreds of fans waiting outside as Ringo and Barbara emerged from the building, Ringo wore a black suit, black bow tie, and sunglasses, and Barbara was in a cream-colored wedding dress trimmed with roses.

A reception was held at Rags, a club in Mayfair, for seventy or so guests. Paul and Linda McCartney were there, along with George and Olivia Harrison, Elsie and Harry, and guests from Barbara's side of the family, including her daughter Francesca, her brother Peter, and her parents, Marjorie and Howard Goldbach. Ringo asked his old friend Terry O'Neill, the first photographer to capture The Beatles for a national newspaper back in 1962, to document the reception. (O'Neill was reportedly paid more than twenty-thousand dollars for his services.)

"I [was] married [to] Faye Dunaway for a while and I lived in Wharton Place and Ringo's office was just down the street about fifty yards away from where I lived, so I saw quite a bit of him during that time," O'Neill said. During the reception, Ringo, Paul, and George got up to play a few tunes. It was first time they'd shared a stage since that cold January day in 1969 on the Apple rooftop. "They had a jam session. It was great," O'Neill recalled. "Paul played the piano, Ringo and Ray [Cooper] were on the spoons and all that type of thing. It was a fab time."

From UK reporter Danny McGrory:

> With just a little help from his friends, Ringo Starr turns his wedding reception into a Beatles reception. It's back in the old routine for Ringo, George Harrison and Paul McCartney, together again for the first time in twelve years. George on guitar, Paul on piano and Ringo on drums, or rather champagne bucket, were back in the Mersey Beat accompanied by percussionist, Ray Cooper . . . Ringo's bride, American actress Barbara Bach, screamed with delight at the impromptu singsong. Silver spoons in hand, Ringo and Ray beat out that old rhythm and booze.

According to the report, the "band" played "Whole Lotta Shakin'," "Lawdy Miss Clawdy," and Barbara's favorite, "She'll Be Coming Round the Mountain"—ending the impromptu jam session with "I Saw Her Standing There" and "Twist and Shout."

During the wedding, Paul and Ringo found themselves in the men's room, alone. "He happened to say that there were two times in his life when I had done him in," McCartney said. "Then he said that he had done himself in three times. I happened to be spitting something out and by chance, the spit fell on his jacket. I said, 'There you go, now I've done you three times. Now we're equal.' I laughed it all off. It was all affectionate. It wasn't a row. It wasn't slagging off. He just suddenly said it and we moved on. But now, I keep thinking all the time, what are the other two times that Ringo thinks I put him down?"

McCartney, not one to waste a public-relations opportunity, used the day of Ringo's wedding to officially announce that he was disbanding his '70s rock group, Wings.

Caveman opened in mid-April 1981 and Ringo earned some of his best movie reviews in years. "Among the players, Mr. Starr is better here than he's been in anything since the Beatles films, abandoning his former deadpan quality for something more active and engaging," wrote *New York Times* critic Janet Maslin. She also singled out the movie's claymation dinosaur for praise. "Mr. Starr . . . is very nearly as charming as his animated friend."

"Ringo is splendid leading his tribe in man's first jam session, and the rest of the cast is fully up to the demands of the script," *Time* magazine noted.

Ringo and Barbara spent the early summer promoting *Caveman* on American television (*Good Morning America*, *PM Magazine*) and in a slew of magazine and newspaper interviews. In mid-June, London's *Daily Mirror* reported that "ex-Beatle Ringo Starr is believed to be planning to leave America and settling in Britain because of the death threats he and his bride, actress Barbara Bach, have received."

"Since John was killed, we've all received death threats," Ringo said. "It's like there were people out there who decided they wanted to get their own Beatle. It's something, like, that makes you want to become a recluse—it frightens you, but you can't let a terrible thing by one man dictate the rest of your life."

The report also noted that Ringo was weary of paying bodyguards to hover around him and Barbara. And there was news that his onetime fling, Stephanie La Motta, was planning on turning their short-lived affair into a movie she was calling "Goodnight Vienna." The movie, which La Motta said would document her "wild time" with Ringo and Harry Nilsson—as well as her battle with the onset of multiple sclerosis—never came to fruition.

The new album, *Stop and Smell the Roses*, was released in late October in America. The following month, in the UK, Ringo signed a new, multi-album deal with RCA (he had left Portrait Records in the spring following a dispute), which released *Stop and Smell the Roses* on its U.S. subsidiary label, Boardwalk (the LP was on the RCA label in the UK).

The new label, and whatever nostalgic goodwill and/or empathy Ringo might have earned in the wake of John Lennon's death, didn't carry over to the new album. Paul McCartney's "Private Property" and George Harrison's "Wrack My Brain," both released as singles, didn't fare much better. *Stop and Smell the Roses* failed to chart in the UK—another Ringo Starr flop in his native country—and only reached Number Thirty-Eight in America before slipping away.

Ringo and Paul collaborated on a short featurette called *The Cooler* to help promote the album. The eleven-minute video featured the three songs from *Stop and Smell the Roses* that McCartney wrote and/or produced: "Private Property," "Attention," and "Sure to Fall."

The video, shot in London in January 1982 and directed by Kevin Godley and Lol Crème, was built around a futuristic prison run entirely by women; Ringo played a convict who habitually escaped, Paul essayed three different parts, and Barbara and Linda McCartney had small roles (Linda played a prison guard; Barbara, the prison warden). *The Cooler* came and went and made no impact whatsoever.

"Mr. Starr's new album has its ups and downs," wrote *New York Times* critic John Rockwell. "At its worst, it's a monument to the self-indulgence of superstars, with Mr. McCartney and Mr. Harrison contributing particularly disappointing lyrics and Mr. Nilsson providing a novelty tune, "Drumming Is My Madness," that's positively moronic. Mr. Starr deserves better material. When he gets it, from Carl Perkins and from his collaboration with Ron Wood, he produces pop that's infectious and charming. And since he's Ringo, one doesn't have to plumb it for profundity in order to enjoy it."

People magazine was kinder—but just slightly: "Nobody ever accused Ringo of singing. He never seems to take himself seriously either and comes across here as affably atonal as ever. . . . This is less a musical enterprise, though, than a friendly note from an old friend to let you know he's still around."

Ringo's heavy drinking continued, and the cracks were beginning to show—even in public.

In the summer of 1981, during their promotional tour to publicize *Caveman*, Ringo, Barbara, and John Matuszak were guests on *The John Davidson Show*, a syndicated television talk show hosted by the affable singer/actor (hired by the show's producer, Westinghouse, to replace veteran talk show host Mike Douglas, who was thought to be past his prime). Ringo, dressed in black and wearing his ever-present dark sunglasses, came out alone (Barbara and Matuszak joined him later) and appeared to be drunk. He slurred his words, took Polaroid selfies with Davidson's other guests (actress Karen Grassle and Andy Gibb) and gave nonsensical, childish answers to Davidson's earnest questions about his childhood and post-Beatles career.

It was embarrassing, and Davidson wasn't amused, eventually stalking off the set when he couldn't rein Ringo in. (He returned later to re-shoot his introductions.) "While they were convincing him to come back, I was in my dressing room having a few more cognacs," Ringo said of the appearance.

"I got angry," Davidson said. "I'm not interested in doing a nonsense show."

And now Barbara was joining the party. Less than a year into their marriage there were already rumors of fights and public arguments that threatened to spiral out of control. In March of 1982, the syndicated gossip columnist, Suzy, reported: "Bottles and punches were thrown during a violent argument between Ringo and Barbara . . . their marriage could crash anytime. Their rows take place in public as well as at home. Ringo and Barbara had one of their biggest fights during a recent holiday on the Caribbean island of Antigua. Bottles flew through the air and slaps were administered. So far they have managed to kiss and make up but for how long?"

"Barbara fell into the trap because of me," Ringo admitted later. "She was an actress who used to go to bed at ten at night and get up at eight in the morning. Till we met. Then her career went the same way as mine. I did two records, a few shows. But working two days a year is not having a career." He said that Elsie and Harry, now both in their eighties and still living in Liverpool, worried about their son, who was a continent away and seemingly adrift. And, although Barbara joined in the drinking, she, too, was aware of how out of control it could be. "Every couple of months she'd try and straighten us out, but then we'd fall right back into the trap," Ringo said.

As the opportunities began to dry up, Ringo's drinking kicked into high gear. If he wasn't drinking with Barbara, then he was knocking back a few with Harry Nilsson, whose career had taken a similar nosedive. Alcohol had already killed their pal and drinking buddy, Led Zeppelin drummer John Bonham, who literally drank himself to death in September 1980 during rehearsals for the band's first tour in three years. He was thirty-two.

"I lived that ridiculous myth: to be creative you have to have your brain twisted in some way," Ringo said. It was all relative, since "creative," as it related to Ringo Starr during this period of his life, was an adjective used generously. He wasn't completely stagnant, but the professional projects on which he chose to become involved came and went, barely registering a blip on the pop-culture radar screen.

In 1982, he appeared on Paul McCartney's first post-Wings album, *Tug of War*. McCartney reunited with producer George Martin and Ringo played drums (along with Steve Gadd) on "Take It Away," which was released as a single and reached Number Ten on the U.S. charts and Number Fifteen in the UK. Ringo also appeared (with a full beard and a head of curly hair) in the music video for "Take It Away" along with George Martin, actor John Hurt, and Linda McCartney.

That same year, Paul asked Ringo to play himself in a movie McCartney had written called *Give My Regards to Broad Street*, a comedy about Paul's search for the master tapes to his next album, which are thought to have been stolen. Barbara would play the part of a journalist.

"Ringo and I are good friends," McCartney said in explaining Ringo's involvement in the movie. "After all The Beatles' years, and all the troubles of the break-up, we find it easy to get along. I saw him one night socially and I was very excited. I said, 'I'm gonna do this film and I'm gonna get you involved. Will you do it with me?' For some reason, he got the idea it was like a Beatles film. Well, we'd had a few drinks."

The movie, released in 1984, didn't do much at the box office, although Ringo, through his haze, was praised for his acting "and with his droll wit, steals most of the scenes he's in." McCartney said later that Ringo refused to play drums on some old Beatles songs Paul intended to include in the movie: "So we scrapped the idea of doing them. Peter Webb, the director, really wanted to do, 'Hey Jude,' and I was quite up for it, but Ringo said, 'No, I've already done that one.' He felt the records we'd made of some songs were the definitive performances of those songs."

Ringo and Barbara walked through their small roles as a social-climbing, bisexual married couple in *Princess Daisy*, an adaptation of a Judith Krantz novel that aired on NBC in 1983. "We loved doing *Daisy* because they paid us for four days and we only had to work three," Ringo explained. "I'm ready for more TV parts, though not necessarily guest shots on *Love Boat* or *Fantasy Island*. . . . That doesn't mean I'm not a musician anymore, but you have to put your energies in one direction and we're putting our energy into our acting careers right now."

Ringo and Barbara moved back to England, and to Tittenhurst, after John Lennon's murder, and lived there when they weren't cavorting in Monte Carlo or elsewhere around the globe. Ringo had cameras installed on the front gates at Tittenhurst: a brutal reminder of the price of fame.

He also decided to record his next album, *Old Wave*, at his Startling Studios on the grounds at Tittenhurst. He asked ex-Eagles guitarist (and his future brother-in-law) Joe Walsh to produce the LP, since Ringo and Joe had known each other from the '70s-era L.A. music scene. This time around, Ringo would need to be creative with the distribution of his latest solo album. RCA had canceled his contract after *Stop and Smell the Roses*—following the death of Boardwalk president Neil Bogart—and he was considered industry poison. No one wanted to touch a Ringo Starr solo album.

Still, Walsh and Ringo co-wrote the bulk of *Old Wave* and managed to assemble an impressive lineup of musicians, including Eric Clapton, Who bassist John Entwistle, guitarist Waddy Wachtel, and drummer Russ Kunkel. Ringo's name still meant something to *them*.

Most of the album was recorded at Startling Studios from February through July 1982 but Ringo could not persuade a U.S. or UK label to release his music.

RCA Canada and Bellephon, a small label in Germany, were the only outlets to release *Old Wave*, which flopped and quickly disappeared upon its release in June 1983.

"I was furious," Ringo said. "I go round saying it's now very big in Afghanistan or wherever, oh yeah, Canada, I keep forgetting, but I was very disappointed. I liked the album. I thought it was the best I'd done. I called it *Old Wave* as a joke, as opposed to 'New Wave.' I suppose I am the old generation now." He said "a bloke in L.A." was interested in releasing the album in the States, "but he canceled when his Mum fell ill."

Ringo didn't help his cause by refusing to tour in support of his albums. Unlike Paul McCartney and George Harrison, he couldn't rely on his name alone to sell records (and even Paul and George weren't guaranteed breakout success, both suffering setbacks in their solo careers). It was obvious even to Ringo that he needed to get up off his ass and get the word out about his music if he wanted anyone to pay attention. But the drinking took over. He claimed to have been "entirely straight" while recording *Old Wave*—"You have breaks from that; you're not totally deranged every day of your life. You straighten up for a bit, but you can't hold onto it"—but alcohol would, like a nightmare, return once again to consume his life after brief respites of sobriety.

"Drunks are great talkers," he said. "We'd sit around for nights on end and talk about what we were going to do. And of course I'd get so bleedin' drunk, I couldn't move. The result of being drunk was that nothing happened. It got progressively worse, and the blackouts got worse, and I didn't know where I'd been, what I'd done. I knew I had the problem for years. But it plays tricks with your head. Very cunning and baffling is alcohol.

"I've got photographs of me playing all over the world but I've absolutely no memory of it. I played Washington with the Beach Boys—or so they tell me. But there's only a photo to prove it."

That would have been on July 4, 1984, when Ringo joined The Beach Boys onstage at the Mall in Washington, D.C., one year after the group was banned from appearing there by then-Interior Secretary James Watt (who cited "rock bands attracting the wrong element"). Something else Ringo didn't remember was that he also joined The Beach Boys onstage that night when they played a concert at South Beach in Miami to an estimated crowd of two hundred and fifty thousand people.

In December, he hosted *Saturday Night Live*, eight years after being mocked by NBC's late-night show. The opening sketch was a Beatles memorabilia auction (Martin Short played the auctioneer) where no one offers any money for the actual Ringo Starr; some people in the auction audience get up to leave when a bearded Ringo, his hair dyed black and wearing a circa-1964 Beatles mohair suit, is wheeled in on a hand truck. There are, however, generous bids for a guitar pick used by John Lennon and Paul McCartney's old toothbrush. Ringo could still laugh at himself during those dark days.

17

"GETTING OUT OF BED'S A PROBLEM THESE DAYS"

In late 1983, Ringo pulled himself together enough to sign a deal with English television writer/producer Britt Allcroft to narrate a series of five-minute television episodes based on Rev. Wilbert Awdry's series of children's books, *The Railway Series*.

Awdry's collection of short stories about the British rail system was set on the fictional island of Sodor and featured lifelike steam-engine characters (with eyes and mouths) including Henry the Green Engine, Thomas the Tank Engine, Annie and Clarabel, Percy the Small Engine, and Toby the Tram Engine.

Awdry's first book was published in 1945; Allcroft met him while she was producing a 1979 documentary about British steam trains. She and her husband, Angus Wright, formed Britt Allcroft Railway Productions and, four years later, had finally raised enough money to produce a children's television show based on *The Railway Series* that they called *Thomas the Tank Engine*; it was later changed to *Thomas & Friends*. They sold the show to British television network ITV, but they needed a narrator.

"One Saturday night, the family were in the sitting-room watching *The Michael Parkinson Show* on television," Allcroft said. "I was not; I was pacing up and down wondering who I was going to find to be my storyteller. I was just passing the sitting-room door when I heard a voice, and I thought, *that* is the voice of *Thomas the Tank Engine*'s storyteller. I put my head round the door and asked who it was—it was Ringo Starr."

Allcroft said she was attracted to the "warmth and originality" of Ringo's "railway voice," which she thought would appeal to children (and their parents, many of whom were, no doubt, Beatles fans).

Allcroft met with Ringo at Tittenhurst in the fall of 1983 and he initially rebuffed her offer to narrate the show, telling Allcroft he thought kids were more interested in "dinosaurs with lasers" than in trains. But he had a change of heart after reading a few of Awdry's books and signed on to narrate twenty-six five-minute episodes of *Thomas & Friends*. He also cut himself in for a percentage of the profits, which turned out to be a smart move.

When the deal was announced in the press, one reporter wondered if the Rev. Awdry "purists" would approve of Ringo's "rich Liverpudlian street drawl." Angus Wright (who also played the drums), defended his wife's choice of narrator, saying, "The idea that you could take this rather untutored Liverpool voice, which actually has a beautiful dark brown quality, and put it onto this middle-class niche story for little children was an astonishing one. You've got this extraordinary voice and suddenly a little five-minute program for children is getting full-page coverage in the tabloids."

Ringo played all the parts in *Thomas & Friends*, though he admitted his portrayal of the Fat Controller was "too big and bossy. We had him so mean to the engines that you thought he'd go and pull their wheels off; then we realized he was quite kind, really a sort of father figure."

Allcroft called her hiring of Ringo a "bonus," but she must have foreseen the publicity that his name would generate for the project. It was big enough news that the *Mail on Sunday* sent a reporter to accompany Ringo and Barbara on a visit to Rev. Awdry, who lived in the town of Stroud, in the Cotswolds.

Ringo, wearing a blue-satin jacket, went upstairs with Awdry (Barbara stayed downstairs). Awdry, who was seventy-three, showed Ringo his trains ("Tell me when you're bored," he said to Ringo, who answered, "Not yet"). The two of them then took a stroll in Awdry's back yard, during which Ringo offered Rev. Awdry "a ciggy" and made the mistake of referring to Thomas as "Tommy."

"*Thomas*," Awdry reminded him. "*Never* Tommy."

The first series of *Thomas & Friends* episodes were shot using live-action models in two London studios, Clearwater and Shepperton. The show, with Ringo's narration and voiceovers, premiered on ITV on October 9, 1984, on what would have been John Lennon's forty-fourth birthday. That morning, Ringo and Rev. Awdry appeared together on ITV's *Good Morning Britain* to promote *Thomas & Friends*, with Awdry dressed in his clerical garb, and Ringo wearing dark sunglasses to hide his bloodshot eyes.

"I always sort of felt I got on with kids. I like kids. I used to be one," Ringo deadpanned. He was asked if he was looking for new challenges. "Getting out of bed's a problem these days," he answered—an honest assessment, if only for those who were aware of his alcoholism. He also claimed never to have lacked self-confidence, but copped to being nervous when he first signed on to narrate *Thomas & Friends*. He said it took him eight days to record all of the episodes.

Ringo flew under the pop-culture radar for much of the next three years. The drinking continued and, if possible, grew more pronounced. There were fights with Barbara, which were always patched up with effusive apologies. The blackouts, too, were even more alarming. One morning he awoke to discover his house was trashed, only to be told that he'd done it himself the night before.

"I was hiding because of all those pressures," he said of those days. "You just sit around the house like everyone else does. You go into London, or you go shopping or to the movies or watch the telly. I didn't work or do anything. I wouldn't go out, because you'd have to be in the car for forty minutes without a drink."

He turned forty-five in July 1985 and, two months later, he became a grandfather when Zak's wife, Sarah Menekides, gave birth to Tatiana Jayne Starkey, whom proud granddad Ringo dubbed "a little beauty." Zak and Sarah, a hairdresser, had married the previous January in a ceremony in Bracknell, a suburb about thirty miles outside of London. Zak was only twenty; Sarah was five years older. The marriage was witnessed by only three people and Ringo was told about it after the fact, when Zak called him in his office and said he had a "surprise" for him.

"I thought it must be some sort of recording deal," Ringo said. "When I got home, it turned out that he'd got married that morning. We've known the girl, Sarah, for some time. We didn't expect them to get married, not just then, but I was quite glad he'd done it secretly, with no fuss. I couldn't be more pleased."

Zak, who'd been critical of his father in previous years, was now living with Sarah and the baby in a cottage on the grounds of Tittenhurst. Maureen, who was living with Isaac Tigrett in New York, flew in to see her new granddaughter. "We all sleep, but when she wakes up, so do we," Ringo said of Tatiana.

Ringo's mother, Elsie, lived long enough to see her first great-grandchild. She died in 1986 at the age of seventy-two, leaving behind her devoted husband, Harry, and a family who loved her. She'd always believed in her Richy and stayed involved in his life as much as she could, even after he became famous as Ringo Starr.

After Elsie died, Ringo returned to Liverpool to clear out her belongings, and was astonished to find a treasure trove of memorabilia she'd kept through the years, dating back to Richy's early childhood: baby pictures, report cards, photos of Richy in the hospital when he was fourteen, assessments on his abilities from Henry Hunt and Son, letters to Ringo from Rory Storm and, of course, Beatles memorabilia.

Years later, Ringo published some of the photos Elsie saved in an e-book called *Photograph*. "That woman loved every second of my life and remembered every second of it," he said.

Throughout that time there were the occasional one-off projects and reunions with his fellow ex-Beatles. Ringo had a small role as the Mock Turtle in a two-part adaptation of *Alice's Adventures in Wonderland*, which aired on CBS in December 1985. Earlier that fall, Ringo and George Harrison played together on a televised tribute to their hero, guitarist Carl Perkins. *Carl Perkins & Friends* aired on Channel 4 in the UK and on Cinemax in America and featured, among many others, Eric Clapton and Dave Edmunds. Ringo wore his now-customary dark sunglasses, which seemed to be glued to his face for public appearances. In addition to the assembled talent, the special, also called *Blue Suede Shoes: A Rockabilly Session*, was notable for being Harrison's first public performance in over ten years.

In 1987, Ringo chipped in on George's critically acclaimed comeback album, *Cloud Nine*, which included "Got My Mind Set on You." That single went to Number One in the U.S., Harrison's first hit in over a decade. Ringo played on several tracks on *Cloud Nine* and also appeared in the music video for the LP's second single, "When We Was Fab."

Ringo also became the first ex-Beatle to sign an endorsement deal, inking a seven-figure contract in 1986 to film a series of television and radio commercials and appear in print ads for Sun Country Classic Wine Coolers, owned by Canandaigua Wine Company, based in upstate New York. "He fits the image of the product: he's a classic with a dry and humorous sense that matches the dry, clear, happy taste of our new cooler," Canandaigua's president said in a statement. Little did he know that Canandaigua was employing an alcoholic to promote alcohol. Classic. Ringo filmed the Sun Country ads in the Bahamas, but was spared the indignity of appearing in a polar bear suit—a fate that befell actor Vincent Price when he endorsed the same product. (Ringo interacted with the polar bear only at the end of the commercials.)

But the Ringo Starr name, already diluted as a solo recording artist, didn't help his career as a corporate spokesman, and the ad campaign backfired. "Canandaigua . . . made the mistake of hiring Ringo Starr to appear in its ad campaign," the *New York Times* noted the following October. "The aging rocker failed to appeal to the younger cooler drinker, and the company, which had booked months of air time, had to come up quickly with another ad campaign, which also flopped."

There was better news in the extended Starkey family when Maureen became a mother for the fourth time, giving birth to Augusta King Tigrett in January 1987. The baby was the first child for Isaac Tigrett—who often referred to Maureen as "my most authentic piece of rock and roll memorabilia"—but they would not marry until over two years later (in Monaco).

In the meantime, Maureen went to court in London that November, claiming that Ringo wasn't giving her enough money and calling him "a sodding great Andy Capp." According to court records, Ringo was still paying Maureen £70,000 a year. She claimed it wasn't enough. She didn't attack Ringo directly, however; the suit was brought against her former lawyers for not getting her enough cash in the original divorce settlement twelve years earlier.

Maureen lost her case two weeks later, when the court ruled in her ex-lawyer's favor and ordered Maureen to pay £200,000 in legal bills. "Maureen brought no money to the marriage and did nothing to contribute to Ringo's wealth," the judge, Mr. Justice Bush, said. "When she went to see her lawyer . . . he found her 'unworldly' about finances. She could spend and enjoyed it but she could not budget. . . . Ringo was and no doubt is, a generous man."

Ringo's spokesman was asked if he would help pay Maureen's legal bills. "Unless or until she asks him, I doubt very much he'll consider it," he said.

Ringo tried to rip a page out of Isaac Tigrett's entrepreneurial playbook by investing in The London Brasserie, a restaurant located in Atlanta's Peachtree Center. It was the flagship eatery for British Restaurants, Inc., which had also enlisted Rolling Stones bassist Bill Wyman and legendary country singer Willie Nelson as investors.

Ringo and Barbara attended the restaurant's grand opening that September, a lavish affair, which included an impromptu jam session featuring Ringo, Jerry Lee Lewis, Isaac Hayes, and Jermaine Jackson. But the goodwill didn't last too long—the restaurant folded within two years. Isaac Tigrett, by comparison, sold his interest in his Hard Rock Café and House of Blues chains to the Rank Organisation for an eight-figure sum.

It was hard to compete with that, even for Ringo Starr.

In late 1986, while Ringo and Barbara were on a vacation in the Bahamas—likely the same trip on which Ringo filmed his Sun Country Classic Wine Cooler commercials—Ringo met record producer, guitarist, and songwriter Lincoln Wayne "Chips" Moman.

In a career spanning nearly thirty years, Moman had worked with a galaxy of stars, including Wilson Pickett, Elvis Presley, Petula Clark, Bobby Womack, and Aretha Franklin. He and Ringo struck up a friendship, and they made plans to record together in Memphis—perhaps up to three albums—with Chips producing and Ringo singing (but not playing drums). Moman had relocated to Memphis from Nashville to run 3 Alarm Studios, a new recording facility built specifically for him in an old firehouse in an effort to attract more music production to the city. Getting Ringo to record there would be a feather in his cap.

Ringo, Barbara, Hilary Gerrard, and Ringo's "minder," Alan Pariser, arrived in Memphis in early February. Their presence in town was kept quiet because, according to several insiders interviewed for this book, Ringo didn't have the proper work visa; he would eventually leave Memphis for a bit to procure his visa before returning to resume recording the album.

The sessions got underway shortly after the star's arrival. Ringo and Moman agreed that he would only sing on the tracks he and Chips selected, and Moman hired Keith Seppanen as his engineer. He also assembled a top-flight roster of session musicians, including bassist Sam Shoup, drummers Steve Mergen and Gene Chrisman, singer Reba Russell, and guitarist J. R. Cobb.

Ringo was drinking heavily, along with everyone else assembled at 3 Alarm Studios. "We would send out for wine or else there would be tequila there or cognac or whatever anybody else felt like drinking," he recalled later. "There was always plenty of alcohol on the premises. Certain nights we were all under the influence."

As Ringo later said of the doomed project, "We should have noticed something from the first day. I went down to the studio, hanging out and just doing that hello-ing day before we started. And I came back that night and said to Barbara, 'We gotta get out of here. I don't understand a word he's saying!' And that was like the hidden clue. I found out later that he'd gone back to his wife and said, 'I don't know if I can do this, I don't understand a word he's saying!' But anyway we went on not understanding one another for several weeks. . . . We'd done it with a lot of Tequila and several unrecognizable substances."

On the surface, the early recording sessions seemed to run smoothly. "We started with a couple of old rock 'n' rollers, including "Ain't That a Shame," Ringo said shortly after recording began, explaining his method of getting to know the musicians with whom he was working for the first time. "I'm singing real well. Chips is pulling things out of me."

Toni Wine, Moman's wife, worked with Ringo on his vocals, he said, "because that's the one area where I do get nervous. My game is drumming. I tend to croon. Toni's great because she's an old rock 'n' roller. She gets me out of crooning."

Wine returned the compliment :"I've never seen a harder worker in my life than him. I mean, fourteen to fifteen hours straight."

Videographer Marius Penczner was hired to document the Memphis sessions, as Ringo was expecting several special guests in the studio, including Carl Perkins, Dave Edmunds, and Bob Dylan. He also planned to record a few tracks at the legendary Sun Studios.

"Alan Pariser called up the studio and said Ringo is going to come in and do this album with Chips, and Ringo wants to document it and he wants to have a record of it because this was going to be a special moment in his career," Penczner recalled. "He was going to be recording over in Sun Studios, which he really wanted to do. They were in the process of thinking about tearing the studio down at the time, so he wanted to help be part of saving that and he wanted to work with Chips.

"They would record a block of it in February and then come back and do a block of it in April and finish out the album. I had a Betacam at the time and was there the entire time, from the beginning, when Ringo landed, and covered the whole thing. We kept a continual record of everything that he did while he was in the studio."

In early March, Memphis *Commercial Appeal* columnist Rheta Grimsley Johnson wrote a screed about Ringo's presence in the city. "The other three Beatles were not just better looking; they were accomplished musicians," she sniffed. "Ringo's songs were comic relief . . . an aging Beatle is yesterday's news . . . it's hard to believe a real, live Beatle was walking the streets of Memphis and the town wasn't even in an uproar."

Moman, who was working hard to draw major talent to his new studio, was outraged. He blasted the article as "total sabotage of what we're trying to do" and subsequently threw two *Commercial Appeal* reporters out of the studio. He also staged a protest in front of the newspaper's offices. "Chips got really mad at the newspaper and so we all had to go down and picket," bassist Sam Shoup recalled. "I mean, they didn't make us do it, but you had the feeling that if you wanted to continue working there, you'd better show up."

Moman's protest worked. Later that day, Memphis television stations reported that the city council would honor Ringo with a special resolution. Ringo, for his part, claimed not to have ever read the offending column. "I mean all we heard about was it took a page to say I wasn't worth mentioning," he said.

The recording sessions continued, along with the heavy drinking. "He was the kindest man I ever met," Shoup said of Ringo. "I'm thirty-three years old and Chips calls me and goes, 'Do do you want to come down and play with one of the Beatles?' I walked in and Ringo was just the nicest. He immediately put me at ease. He was a totally nice, just wonderful man. Ringo just wanted to sing. He didn't want to play the drums, but he did play drums when we were clowning around and stuff like that."

One of the tracks recorded by Ringo was called "Whiskey and Soda"—apropos for the atmosphere in the studio.

"We had a great time, so there was never an issue there," engineer Keith Seppanen recalled. "There was no animosity toward anybody anywhere along the line. And it wasn't that the music was crap. The music itself was good; the other part of it . . . wasn't there because somebody wasn't there, themselves. Everything was affected. Chips was indulging, too, and that's going to affect someone's judgment. Ringo had a couple of moments when he went off, but let's put it this way—he wasn't in his own mind, if you know what I mean."

Reba Russell, one of the backup singers hired by Moman, recalled:

> The main thing I remember was how fun it was. I didn't see any of the bad stuff. If there was bad stuff that happened during the sessions, I was not privy to any of that. Every time Ringo was there and we were there, it was a joyful atmosphere. Now, granted, there were a couple of days that we got to be there while he was tracking vocals and they were doing tracks. Ringo would be unhappy with either the song or the fact that Chips wasn't satisfied with the vocal and would become frustrated. There were some days where he was frustrated. . . . And there was drinking.
>
> But I've never been to a major session, and I've been on hundreds of sessions, where there wasn't drinking. People were not walking around drunk. That was not the case. It was very professional every time I was in there. Ringo was happy and telling stories and he and Chips got along famously.

"My impression of Ringo when he went into the session was he was hoping for the best," videographer Marius Penczner recalled. "He is generally an optimistic guy. And I think he was used to a different workflow than Chips had. I think he wanted everything to be kind of set in place and he would drop in and do his part, and then let them do the music and everything. But the entire kind of creative process was foreign to him and it wasn't really working and he was drinking heavily. I want to say he would go through two bottles of vodka a night. When I was there, I said to my assistant, 'I just don't know how somebody can drink that much and not be on the floor and still be relatively coherent.'"

What began as a fun endeavor eventually devolved into what Penczner described as "a train wreck," particularly in regard to some of the songs Moman wanted Ringo to record:

> They cut a song that Johnny Nash did called "I Can See Clearly Now." They were trying to get Ringo to sing this thing. And Ringo has about a six-note range. So he's out there in the studio singing and Toni Wine is singing in his ear, trying to keep him on pitch. And they get through that. And after it's over, he walks into a lounge in the back of the building where the soda machine is. And there's a couch back there. And he's sitting on the couch with his head in his hands. So I walk back there and I say, "Man, are you okay?" And he said, "This guy doesn't get it. John and George got it. This guy doesn't get it. Don't try to make me a great singer. Give me great songs to sing." And I thought, that's the most profound thing I'd ever heard.
>
> They were trying to get him to sing these parts that were really well beyond his ability to sing and . . . your pitch ain't the best when you've been drinking pretty heavily. It's not a pitch augmenter. So the engineers were trying all sorts of tricks to make adjustments. Ringo's not a bad singer.

By late April, the sessions were over. As a parting gift to the people of Memphis and to the talent with whom he'd worked at 3 Alarm Studio, Ringo threw a big celebration aboard the *Island Queen* riverboat. Over two hundred and fifty guests munched on barbecue and enjoyed the scenery along the Mississippi River. Ringo even jumped behind a drum set and sat in with Reba Russell's band, bashing out a few tunes.

———————————

Ringo closed a fifteen-year chapter in his personal history when he sold Tittenhurst in January 1988. The move surprised many of his friends, as he and Barbara enjoyed their time in the mansion, which was their primary residence in England when they flew in from Monte Carlo so Ringo could fulfill his status as a British tax exile. Zak, who was still living in a cottage on the property, was forced to find new digs.

Ringo earned a terrific return on his original 1973 investment in Tittenhurst, selling the twenty-six-room mansion for a reported £5 million to Sheik Zayed bin Sultan Al Nahyan, president of the United Arab Emirates and the ruler of Abu Dhabi. "It's been sold, but I don't know exactly why Ringo and Barbara are going," a friend told the *London Sun*. "Ringo and Barbara have not found a new home yet. There has been talk of them finding a home on the West Coast of America."

On January 20, The Beatles were among the artists inducted into the third class of the Rock and Roll Hall of Fame in Cleveland, Ohio. Only Ringo and George showed up for the star-studded ceremony. Paul McCartney refused to join his ex-band mates, informing the event organizers he "was keen to go and pick up my award, but after twenty years, The Beatles still have some business differences, which I hoped would be settled by now. Unfortunately, they haven't been, so I would feel a complete hypocrite waving and smiling with them at a fake reunion." McCartney's statement surprised Ringo and George, especially since they'd put The Beatles' years-long legal bickering on the back burner.

Ringo and George didn't let McCartney's snub get in the way of a good time. They accepted their award gracefully from Mick Jagger and both said a few words—Ringo, naturally, wearing his sunglasses—and were joined on stage by Yoko Ono and John's sons, Julian and Sean. Later, Ringo and George were among a galaxy of rockers—including Billy Joel, Bruce Springsteen, Bob Dylan, Jagger, Dave Edmunds, Elton John, and even guitar legend Les Paul—who jammed to "I Saw Her Standing There" (vocals by Joel and Springsteen) and to Dylan's "All Along the Watchtower."

Several weeks later, it was reported in the press that Ringo was teaming with *Miami Vice* star Don Johnson for a television sitcom called "The Flip Side," written by his *Caveman* director Carl Gottlieb. In the show, which would be produced by Johnson's production company, and was being offered to NBC,

Ringo would play "an aging pop star forced to quit the concert circuit to care for his children when his former wife dies." *Taxi* co-star Jeff Conaway, who auditioned for the role of Ringo's roadie, said one of the writers explained the show to him: "Just think of it as a kind of 'Keith Richards Knows Best.'" The project never came to fruition.

That summer, a familiar old friend reentered Ringo Starr's life. In the four years since *Thomas & Friends* premiered on ITV, the children's show had grown exponentially and was a proven and durable hit on British television. Ringo left the series in 1986 and was replaced, in 1991, by actor Michael Angelis, a fellow Liverpudlian. Angelis remained on the show as its narrator for another twenty-one years.

New York–based television producer Rick Siggelkow fondly remembered Ringo's brief run on *Thomas & Friends*, and was convinced that the show could be adapted to American television, which offered up a steady diet of cartoons for children and a dearth of live-action shows (*Sesame Street, Mister Rogers' Neighborhood*, and *The Electric Company*).

Thomas & Friends creator Britt Allcroft had the same idea as Siggelkow, and had given a cassette copy of *Thomas & Friends* to John Iselin, the president of WNET, New York's public television station. Iselin, in turn, approached his top producer, Siggelkow, and asked if he thought *Thomas & Friends* could be adapted for an American television audience.

"A lot of people at the time said, 'No kids are going to want to watch this. It's too slow,'" Siggelkow recalled. "'Kids don't want trains—they want exploding robots.' But I took *Shining Time Station* around and showed it to a number of kids and realized the so-called 'experts' were wrong. The kids said the pacing was right and the way it was shot was right—the close-ups on the engines' faces—and what appealed to me was Ringo's voice and his narration. It was lulling, like a bedtime story."

The children to whom Siggelkow showed *Shining Time Station* focused mostly on Ringo's voice. "They understood it, but they thought it was strange," he said "For a lot of kids that age, it was probably the first time they heard an English accent." Siggelkow thought that, if the show was going to work for an American audience, it needed more than just Ringo's narration. "I said, 'Okay, he's strange.' We really ought to put him in a character that is, by definition, strange. In other words, if he is already kind of offbeat or magical, he would be more palpable to the kids in the audience."

Siggelkow contacted Britt Allcroft, who flew to New York for a meeting.

They both agreed that, if Ringo was going to be involved in the show, he needed to be on-camera, and not just a disembodied voice. "The goal became to develop a half-hour show that Thomas could live in but that would also have Ringo on the air," Siggelkow said. "It just seemed absolutely critical to get him on. . . . And then we had the idea that he would play this little conductor character."

Allcroft began negotiating a deal with Hilary Gerrard for Ringo to star in the revamped show, which would be called *Shining Time Station*. The show would be produced by WNET to air nationally on Public Broadcasting Service (PBS) stations. Ringo would be shrunken down, via special effects, to an eighteen-inch-high character named Mr. Conductor, who would interact with a cast of kids (and one adult, played by actress Didi Conn).

Shining Time Station would retain most of Ringo's original narration from *Thomas & Friends*, save for some dialogue he re-recorded in an effort to "Americanize" the show for his new audience.

WNET, for its part, was nervous about the show, and about Ringo. Were they getting an out-of-control rock star to host a show aimed at kids? Children's television pioneer Joan Ganz Cooney, who was on the board of WNET, called Siggelkow up to her office "to make sure this show . . . wasn't some crazy thing that was going to reflect badly on PBS or, God forbid, *Sesame Street*," he said.

"I think they didn't quite know what to make of it," Siggelkow said. "And it was frustrating. I ended up convincing them to have Ringo cut a bunch of spots for fundraising. It hadn't even occurred to them. And my feeling was, you have this incredible thing, you've got a Beatle for God's sakes. You got a new show. There is no other kid's show out there like this. You should be doing everything in the world you can to support it. And you should be jumping up and down. The show really ended up kind of having to make its way . . . without a lot of support."

Ringo and Barbara flew to New York in the summer of 1988. *Shining Time Station* was being shot in a television studio in Harlem, as WNET lacked the special effects equipment Siggelkow needed for the new show.

"My first impression was that I felt kind of sorry for him in his conductor's outfit," Siggelkow said of Ringo. "Barbara was there and she was clearly the icebreaker for him. She was a very friendly woman, a wonderful person. She introduced herself and came up to talk to me and Ringo just looked around and I just felt like he felt very lost, kind of 'What have I gotten myself into?' He looked vulnerable."

But Ringo relaxed once Siggelkow explained how the shoot would work via "green-screen" technology, which was basically a plain green screen onto which Ringo's Mr. Conductor character would be projected. "He began to see that maybe he could have some fun with this," Siggelkow said.

Very early in the shoot, the producer heard Beatles music playing in one of the dressing rooms. "So I went to find the source of the music," he said, "and it was Ringo, listening to all the early Beatles stuff. All by himself. I just sat down and talked about the music and I told him a little bit about what it meant to me. We kind of made a connection there, and then I realized that basically, we'd all been kind of pussyfooting around him. He is one of the most famous people in the world.

"I think the real breakthrough with Ringo came when there was a prizefight on HBO, and a lot of people didn't get it, but of course the TV guys knew how to pirate it," Siggelkow said. So they had a tape. And we all got together to watch the fight, and Ringo came in. And he was like the life of the party around this prizefight with all the techies—not the writers, but the tape guys and the grips. I guess you would say the 'working class' guys. And they were all cheering and hooting and stuff like that, and Ringo was into it. And from that point on the crew loved him. He had a connection with them and that was great."

He also got along famously with the kids in the cast, who had a little club-house in an alcove on the set of *Shining Time Station* and made Ringo an honorary member of their club. "They really didn't know who he was, and they felt no inhibition around him . . . and the way they presented Ringo his honorary membership was such a big deal and it obviously meant so much to these kids," Siggelkow said. "And he really responded to that, and by the time we did our first press conference the kids were climbing all over him. They were hanging on his arms, running around him. He had clearly made a real connection with them."

Ringo held his drinking in check while shooting his scenes as Mr. Conductor. It was a different story once the cameras were off. "Ringo was drinking then," Siggelkow confirms. "I'm thirty years old, maybe [at that time], and we're going to the Russian Tea Room and all these very fancy places. When you are with somebody who drinks a lot, you tend to drink more. And when you're with somebody who is famous and drinking a lot, you really drink a lot. So I definitely tied on some pretty drunken nights."

Siggelkow got so blotto one night while drinking with Ringo and several others at the Russian Tea Room that he stood up and promptly fell back on the table behind him. "And seated at that table was David Rockefeller. And I looked up, and there he was, looking down at me. And I looked up and I said, 'Oh, shit, I just spilled soup all over this guy.' And Ringo turned around and came over and David Rockefeller looked up and said 'Ringo Starr.' And it was like all was forgiven. It was like, yeah, I spilled soup on Rockefeller's lap, but Ringo trumped all that."

Ringo had such a good time shooting *Shining Time Station* that he asked Siggelkow if there was any way to work Harry Nilsson into the show. "I went and looked at *The Point*, which Harry Nilsson had done, but I could never quite figure out a way to get him into the show that made sense," he said. "That was probably the only real request Ringo made."

18

"WE NEED HELP"

It was an early October morning in 1988 when Ringo and Barbara finally hit rock bottom. They'd been drinking around the clock for several days—a disturbing pattern that never ended well. "I came to one Friday afternoon," Ringo recalled of a particular drinking bout, "and was told by the staff that I had trashed the house so badly they thought there had been burglars, and I'd trashed Barbara so badly they thought she was dead."

And their drinking was now becoming more public—and people were taking notice. *The People*, a British newspaper, reported that earlier in the year, "Ringo and Barbara had a typical public punch-up in front of guests at a Jamaican hotel. They watched in amazement as the angry pair stood twenty feet apart lobbing bottles at each other then swooped and started slapping each other."

It was a "moment of clarity," Ringo said, that made the couple realize the extent of their self-destruction. "I had a real bad alcohol problem. Very few people in the public—no one in the public—knew my problem. We could hide it from them. We could go out and put the bow tie on, and we could wave to the cameras and they'd say, 'There he goes, good old Ringo.' But we'd be maintaining at those moments. We'd be dashing home right after it." Barbara "decided to have a taste too and got gripped in the madness.

"Of course, there was one moment of clarity. It was a Friday around three o'clock in the afternoon. Barbara had been talking about rehab. This was just the end of the line for me. I'd had enough and I'd caused a lot of damage. I had come out of a huge blackout. I said, 'You've got to get us into one of the places. We need help.' And she did."

Within hours they were on a plane headed for the Sierra Tucson Rehab Center, located in the Arizona desert near the Santa Catalina Mountains. "We went into rehab because we needed desperately [to make] a change," Barbara said. "I got used to living at the bottom. But you get to a point where you realize, 'This isn't living.'"

Ringo's alcohol addiction was so strong that he drank himself into oblivion on the flight to Arizona. "I landed drunk as a skunk at the clinic," he said. "I drank all the way and got off the plane completely demented. I thought I was going to a lunatic asylum. I thought I'd gone too far and they were going to put me away in a little cell and forget about me. Instead of that, they put their arms around me and loved me and told me it [would] get better. 'Give us a chance,' they said. With God's help a day at a time it certainly has."

The five-week course of treatment reportedly cost $35,000 per person. Upon their arrival at Sierra Tucson, Ringo and Barbara were put in separate rooms with no televisions or phones. "Eight days in, I decided, 'I'm here to get help because I know I'm sick,'" Ringo said. "And I just did whatever they asked me and, thank God, it pulled me through."

About halfway through their stay, word about Sierra Tucson's newest celebrity residents began to leak out. On November 7, former Beatles spokesman Derek Taylor, who was himself a recovering alcoholic, was summoned to make a public statement in London. He refused to confirm where Ringo and Barbara were being treated, but admitted they were indeed being treated for alcoholism. (Several years later, Ringo and Barbara repaid Taylor's support by writing the foreword to his book, *Getting Sober . . . and Loving It!*)

Ringo and Barbara were given no preferential treatment. They worked at assigned menial jobs, did their laundry, cleaned ashtrays, and were in bed early. They also attended group therapy sessions and counseling sessions.

"Until I got to the clinic I didn't realize I was from a dysfunctional family," Ringo said later. "We had parties, everyone gets drunk and passed out, and that's part of life. My mother always told me that when I was nine, I was on my knees crawling drunk. A friend of mine's father had all the booze ready for Christmas, and we decided to try all of it. I don't remember too much. That was my first blackout.

"You always think you're witty on alcohol and cocaine," he said. "You think you're so witty that you decide to tell the same story over and over and over and over and over again. To the same person. I meet people now . . . and I think, 'God, was I like that?' And a little voice inside says, 'Yes, you were.'"

According to *The People*, doctors at Sierra Tucson warned Ringo that his liver was enlarged from all his drinking and that his heart was damaged because of his drug use. Barbara was told that her liver, too, was damaged from alcohol abuse.

Ringo and Barbara's close friends were "astonished" at the couple's visit to rehab, but Linda McCartney said she and Paul "knew about Ringo's addiction to the bottle for years but were afraid to say anything. . . . We were only too aware that Ringo and Barbara were wrecking their lives, but we dreaded what would happen to the friendship we so cherished if either tried to intervene. There was nothing we could do about it."

Others were less charitable, including British journalist Ellie Buchanan, who wrote a snarky column once the news about Ringo's stint in rehab was made public.

> Since Ringo's announcement that he has a drink[ing] problem, some of his fair-weather friends have begun to show their true colors. Sly jokes about *Thomas The Tanked-Up Engine* have found their way into conversations and some commentators have decided the reason for his drink[ing] problem is that he suddenly realized he was a useless drummer, a passenger in The Beatles with no real musical ability.

Ringo fired back in an interview with British reporter Chris Anderson, telling him he believed "my beloved Britain turned against me when Barbara and I checked into the drying out clinic. I got terrible coverage in England. They were all supportive in America but in England they thought I was only doing it for the publicity. They thought I had some sort of madness."

Ringo and Barbara left Sierra Tucson in early December, on the road to recovery and resolute in their determination to stay sober—yet nervous about retaining their sobriety in the rock 'n' roll jet-setting world they inhabited.

"You get very safe in the clinic," Ringo said. "I didn't want to leave. I didn't know if I could handle it. If any of my friends can't deal with me being sober, then I just don't bother with them. Because for me to live is more important than a friend getting uptight because I won't have a drink. If we go to a party now, Barbara and I usually leave around about eleven thirty, when everyone else starts getting rocky. Your life is changed completely around."

As the calendar turned to 1989, his words would ring true.

———

The year began on a bright note for the newly clean and sober Ringo Starr. He went on a round of interviews to promote *Shining Train Station*. When asked about his stay in rehab, he talked openly about the experience: "I'm still the happy-go-lucky Beatle. All I do is not drink, you know. All that is in the past. My darkest hour was too dark but everything is fine . . . now. I used to sink a bottle of brandy in five hefty shots, then pick up another."

He was excited about the premiere of his new show—or professed to be. "*Shining Time Station* is meant to be a children's series, but it's going to become a big hit with mums and dads, too," he said. "I've always got on with kids. Kids and mothers were my crowd. John had the intellectuals; Paul had the teenies; and George, the mystics. I always got the mothers and babies."

Shining Time Station producer Rick Siggelkow accompanied Ringo, Barbara, and Hilary Gerrard on the national tour to promote the show, which Ringo later plugged on his first visit to *Late Night with David Letterman.*

"A lot of things were starting to feel good in his life," Siggelkow said. "We flew to Chicago, and this radio reporter stood up and said, 'Well, how do you think being a drunk on a kid's show, what kind of impression do you think that is giving to kids?' It was a horrible question. Ringo got angry. We all got angry. There was like a collective groan in the room and the wife or mother of one of the kids on the show, who was from The Bronx, said, 'I ought to kick your ass.' Ringo was clearly angry, but then he sort of collected himself and said, 'Look, the real point is, what does this question have to do with this press conference?' I mean, he turned it around on the guy. That was really the only sour note."

From Chicago, the group traveled to New York by rail in a special train provided by Amtrak. (Ringo filmed some short promotional spots aboard the train for *Shining Time Station,* which were sent to local PBS stations.) The group played charades and generally had a very nice (non-alcoholic) time.

"My wife was pregnant at the time, and she and Ringo really hit it off," Siggelkow said. "She was very good at charades and at one point he turned to her and said, 'Don't you think it's time to go to bed now?' And another time he said, 'You know, there's too much smoke in this car. Maybe you shouldn't be in this car' because she was pregnant and we were all smoking like chimneys. So he was very sweet to her. We were all just laughing, on a train, riding across the country, and it was probably the most down-to-earth that we got for that period of time. Ringo was just this funny guy from Liverpool who liked to play charades and sort of looked at us as one big family."

Shining Time Station premiered on January 29th, and it was quickly apparent that WNET, and PBS in general, had a hit show on its hands. Ringo's Mr. Conductor struck a chord with young viewers, and the show garnered national attention for its innovative use of green-screen special effects and for Ringo's appeal to the under-seven set.

The *New York Times*: "The setting is an old-fashioned railroad station, the more prominent features of which include a jukebox with musical puppets and, rising to only eighteen inches, an amiable Mr. Conductor, played by Ringo Starr, formerly of The Beatles. He introduces the animated *Thomas the Tank Engine* segments. . . . Each half hour has a song, a few laughs and clever little lessons to encourage social and creative development. At least in the first couple of episodes, the results are quite charming and most welcome."

Later that spring, Ringo was nominated for a Daytime Emmy Award as Outstanding Performer in a Children's Series for his work on *Shining Time Station*. He didn't win—the award went to Jim Varney for a CBS series called *Hey, Vern, It's Ernest*—but he did present an award at the ceremonies.

The initial success of *Shining Time Station* thrust Ringo back into the spotlight, this time in a more positive light. There were some sneers that the World's Most Famous Drummer was now reduced to playing an eighteen-inch-high character in a children's television show—and not even on a major network, no less—but if he was bothered by the barbs, Ringo didn't let on. He and Barbara were focused on staying clean and sober and hoping to put a decade's worth of decadence behind them.

Their new outlook on life, supported by Alcoholics Anonymous meetings, had a carryover effect into Ringo's professional career, which was rumbling back to life after lying dormant for so long.

He hadn't released a solo album in six years, since the disastrous *Old Wave* LP back in 1983. *Starr Struck: Ringo's Best*, was released in February 1989, but it was a compilation album (like its predecessor, *Blast from Your Past*). And while it was sold only in America it did, at the very least, remind the music industry that Ringo Starr had once sold a lot of albums. It also didn't hurt that three of the songs included on the LP—"Cookin' (In the Kitchen of Love)," "Private Property," and "Wrack My Brain"—were written, respectively, by John Lennon, Paul McCartney, and George Harrison.

In March, Ringo co-starred on the video for Tom Petty's new single, "I Won't Back Down," along with George Harrison and ELO founder Jeff Lynne. Drummer Phil Jones, and not Ringo, played on the actual recording (which featured Harrison's acoustic guitar and backing vocals).

Later that month, Ringo and country music legend Buck Owens went into Abbey Road to record a new version of Owens's "Act Naturally," one of Ringo's signature numbers with The Beatles (which he sang on *The Ed Sullivan Show* in 1964). They sang a duet on "Act Naturally," and later shot a video for the single in which they joked around on the back lot of a Hollywood movie set (a dusty Western, naturally)—Ringo was wearing a beard and his dark sunglasses. The single and the video were released in the States in July.

By that time, Ringo Starr's world was completely turned around by a young entrepreneur, agent, and promoter all rolled into one—whose visionary concept for The World's Most Famous Drummer saved his professional life and propelled him on a course that still resounds in his life twenty-five years later.

———————————————

David Fishof was only thirty-three years old in 1989, but was no stranger to show business, having represented singer/actor Herschel Bernardi and sports figures including Lou Piniella and Phil Simms. In 1984, Fishof organized the first "nostalgia" package tour of '60s pop groups (The Association, The Turtles, Gary Puckett, and Spanky and Our Gang) and, in 1986, organized a twentieth-anniversary tour for The Monkees. Fishof followed that with several other successful music tours, including a sold-out stage revue based on the 1987 movie *Dirty Dancing*, which was sponsored by Pepsi.

In early 1989, he set his sights on Ringo.

"I was always putting packages together and coming up with original ideas and I had this idea of putting an all-star band together around Ringo," Fishof recalled. "The folks at Pepsi were so happy with the sponsorship I gave them for the *Dirty Dancing* tour that they came to me with Alan Pottasch, who created the 'Pepsi Generation' [advertising] campaign. It was the twenty-third anniversary [of the campaign] and Alan said to me, 'We want you to produce a show for us like you did with *Dirty Dancing*, can you come up with some ideas?'"

Ringo was out of rehab and re-emerging onto the music scene, and Fishof thought the timing was right to pitch him the all-star band idea. He wrote Ringo a letter, offering him $1 million to tour. If Ringo agreed, it would be his first time touring since The Beatles broke up almost twenty years earlier.

"I waited a few months until I got an answer back," Fishof said. "I got a call: 'Come over to England. Ringo wants to meet you.' So I went off to England and I prepared a commercial and a print ad of what I thought the concept would look like. I flew over there on a Monday and, Friday morning, I got my ten o'clock appointment with Ringo in his office in London. I showed up there and I think he had a ponytail and Barbara was there. I'm usually calm but, you know, he's a Beatle. But he was very sweet and very nice and warm and so it was a good meeting."

After hearing Fishof's pitch, Ringo turned to him and said, "I was thinking the same thing," and they talked about possible musicians for the backing band. "I had chosen Billy Preston because he played keyboards with The Beatles, and I knew Ringo had a relationship with Nils Lofgren," Fishof said. "And then he came up with Levon Helm and Joe Walsh and said, 'I gotta do this thing with Jim Keltner. I would feel secure if Jim was there.' So we went over a list of musicians. A few days later I got a call from his lawyer and he said, 'He wants to do it.' So that was exciting."

Ringo was the star of the show, of course, but the concerts would not be comprised totally of his Beatles songs and his later solo output. Each of the members chosen for the band would have the chance to sing a few of their own songs, and Ringo wouldn't even be onstage for all the sets (though he would introduce each song).

"I still love to play," he said happily. "I go down the front and sing 'Photograph' or whatever, then I get to go back to the drums and play with all these other musicians. It's a win-win situation. I get the chance to be both the entertainer and the musician. Everyone's a star, but I'm the big star. The band gets to play twelve numbers between them and I do twelve numbers."

Fishof flew to L.A. to meet with the CAA talent agency, who'd booked his previous tours. Bobby Brooks, who was Eric Clapton's agent, came into the meeting. "Bobby said to me, 'Okay, Fishof, I bet you got us the drum roadie of The Beatles and you want to call [the tour] The Beatles.' And I said, 'No, I got Ringo.' So I gave him my idea and they liked it and we started putting it together."

Bruce Springsteen's production manager, George Travis, was hired to organize the tour, which would be sponsored by Pepsi. Dr. John, Rick Danko from The Band, and Clarence Clemmons, Springsteen's sax player, were added to the lineup of supporting musicians.

And it now had a name: Ringo Starr & His All-Starr Band.

"The great thing about these guys is that they are all stars in their own right so they don't spend all their time feeling they have to prove something," Ringo said when the group members' names were announced. "It makes for a happy group." He also made a sly allusion to Paul McCartney and George Harrison. "I have also sent our tour details to a couple of other guys I used to play with and they are welcome to drop by at any time and sit in."

"The deal I made with Pepsi was that they would get $1 million and I would get the next $1 million," Fishof said. "Ringo got the first $1 million." The All-Starr Band tour would be heavily promoted, with full-page newspaper advertisements in major cities, a coast-to-coast poster campaign, and T-shirts and jackets thrown into the promotional mix.

"You go right from rehab and all of a sudden you're going out to face the world," Fishof said of Ringo. "You had to give him credit because he went . . . back into the limelight. So I think the timing was great for me to have approached him."

On June 20, Ringo held a press conference at the Palladium in New York City to announce the tour, which would begin July 23 in Dallas, Texas, and end in L.A. on September 3, encompassing thirty cities in forty-three days. The tour sold out within minutes.

That night, wearing a ponytail and dark sunglasses, Ringo paid a visit to NBC's *Late Night with David Letterman* to promote the All-Starr Band, mentioning Fishof by name in explaining how the idea originated. "I've been thinking about it for like ten years—I'm a real slow guy," he told Letterman. "I didn't want to go [on tour] with just me in the front with the band behind you and up all the time. I wanted to have fun. So I just called a few friends up and they were all enthusiastic and here we are."

Letterman asked Ringo if the tour would support an album. "There's no album right now, but the album would be if we record it live. That would be the album," he said. The next morning, he got up early and stopped by ABC's *Good Morning, America* to once again talk about the All-Starr Band.

Ringo turned forty-nine in early July, and rehearsals for the first tour began shortly thereafter in Dallas. David Fishof joined him there.

"We did the first rehearsal and then we did the first couple of shows and I was planning to go home," Fishof recalled. "I said to him, 'I'm going to head home and I'll see you in two weeks in Chicago,' and he said, 'Wait a minute. Didn't you tell me you were going to be with me when I was going to tour?' And I said, 'Yeah, but I never go on the road. I have my family back home and I'm just not a road person.' And he said, 'Well, you promised to be here with me. Please don't leave.' So I was on the road for the next eight weeks."

The All-Starr Band spent two weeks rehearsing, learning one another's songs, and working out musical arrangements. Ringo was optimistic, and was recharged—though a bit nervous—to once again be playing in a band.

"I feel good," he told a journalist visiting one of the band's practice sessions.

"It's been hard work but I really feel great about getting back to it. More important, I feel really good about myself and I know that if I had not done what I did last year, I wouldn't be able to do any of this."

Ringo Starr & His All-Starr Band officially opened for business on July 23, 1989, before a sold-out audience at the Park Central Amphitheater in Dallas. Ringo opened the first show with the apropos "It Don't Come Easy," followed by "The No No Song." He also sang "Photograph," "Back Off Boogaloo," "Act Naturally," "Yellow Submarine," "Honey Don't," "Boys," and "With a Little Help from My Friends."

"I was nervous before I went on," Ringo said. "I kept thinking, 'What's it like? What do you do? All those madnesses go through your brain. But once you're out there, you see that people haven't come to see you get nervous. They've come to have a good time. And we're having a good time, too."

The audience at the Park Central Amphitheater—many of them Baby Boomers over forty, accompanied by their kids (who got in for free)—lapped it up. The tour was off to a flying start. "It's great being down front," Ringo said. "I've never done that before. I've always been behind the kit. After the first show, I read some stuff about my voice. But I'm not Pavarotti. People know who I am, and I'm giving them my best shot on my songs. And when the other guys are doing their numbers, I get back on the kit, and we play. It's fabulous."

More importantly, Ringo stayed sober during the tour, though he admitted he was sometimes tempted to start partying again.

"After each gig it was really tough because I didn't know what to do with myself, because my whole body and head went into, 'Lets' party!' you know, 'Let's get crazy, let's get messed up.' But there's one little seed of reality in there saying, 'But we don't do that anymore.' And we didn't. But it was hard. Just the first week. To do anything again, the first week you have to really learn to do it again. And that's all it takes. I had some fears that sobering up I wouldn't be humorous and I wouldn't be able to play. But they were just fears. They weren't true."

Ringo had, in fact, argued against David Fishof hiring former Cream bassist Jack Bruce, a heavy drinker, as part of that first backing band "because at the time he was very concerned . . . he wanted to surround himself with people who were not alcoholics," Fishof said. "Even though the irony is that, at the end of that first tour, five out of the nine people went to rehab."

Dr. John was one of them. "I got inspired to actually get myself clean off of drugs," he told the author. "Touring with Ringo . . . all little weird things happened when I made a decision toward [getting clean]. And that was a big thing for me. Ringo really did inspire me to get clean. So December 17 of that year, that's the day I got clean. That's the day I celebrate my birthday now."

There were other highlights of that first tour. Zak Starkey, now twenty-four and a much-sought-after professional drummer—considered by many to be on par with his idol, Keith Moon—sat in with the All-Starr Band on several shows, as did Max Weinberg, the drummer for Bruce Springsteen's E Street Band. When the tour stopped at the Garden State Arts Center in Holmdel, New Jersey, in early August, comedian John Candy jumped onstage with a tambourine for the final number.

The *New York Times*: "It's the better kind of nostalgia tour—one that doesn't take itself too seriously and promises nothing more or less than familiar songs, cheerfully played so the crowd can sing along. With his sunglasses on and his hair pulled back in a tight ponytail, Mr. Starr stepped out front tonight to begin and end the show, strutting like a by-the-numbers rock star and trying not to sing out of key. . . .When he's not singing, Mr. Starr plays drums while the other band members each lead the group."

"A lot of celebrities came to the shows," Fishof recalled. "I'll never forget one night my phone rang—a lot of calls were coming in to Ringo and he would go under an alias—but somehow I got one of his calls one night and it was Elton John, calling to congratulate him. It was amazing. What was also amazing to me was how many people were trying to get hold of Ringo, to see him.

"We did about ten thousand people a night and played all the amphitheaters," Fishof said. "We really had the best crew. We had a private plane that took us from city to city and Barbara was traveling with Ringo. I think the most exciting thing was sitting back and hearing all the stories shared by the musicians.

"As the tour got longer, Ringo started getting into a groove and I think he really enjoyed it," Fishof said. "He was getting more and more used to the crowd. It was exciting for him because no one had ever done something like that before. All the musicians had respect for Ringo. I think they all wanted to be there. The big thing was he didn't want to talk about The Beatles. He wanted to talk about the All-Starr Band. His goal was to promote everybody by themselves. And I thought that was quite interesting."

He also helped to promote Oldsmobile cars for General Motors. Earlier that year, Ringo signed on to appear in the company's "New Generation of Olds" advertising campaign, which featured such celebrities as William Shatner, Peter Graves, astronaut Scott Carpenter —and even Albert Einstein's great-grandson—in humorous situations with their lesser-known children or relatives. (The tagline for the campaign: "This is not your father's Oldsmobile.")

Ringo shot a television commercial with his eighteen-year-old daughter, Lee, in which he's mobbed by adoring fans—and is saved by Lee, who drives up in a four-door Oldsmobile Cutlass Supreme (which she refers to as "a fab four-door"). The commercial was shot in L.A., which made it easy for both Ringo and Lee. Ringo's daughter was living in the city and was a co-owner of Planet Alice, a "psychedelic boutique" specializing in '60s-era clothing—"'90s interpretations of '60s styles," Lee said—that was started in London by Christian Paris. In 1991, Lee convinced Paris to open a branch of Planet Alice in L.A. on Melrose Avenue. She designed much of the clothing sold in the store. "I didn't consciously do this because it's what the Beatles wore in their heyday, but it must have had something to do with it," she said.

Ringo was happy to see Lee try something on her own—and even happier that she didn't ask him to financially invest in the store. He was glad, he said, that she "finally found something to put herself into. She tried acting school and decided she didn't like that. She got her diploma from makeup school and wasn't really enthusiastic about that."

Lee and Paris, who described their relationship as "platonic," lived in Beverly Hills with Maureen, Isaac, and Lee's half-sister, Augusta, until they found places of their own. Lee moved back to England a year later when the store folded.

Ringo's summer of goodwill was interrupted in late July when a blast from his past showed up in the form of Chips Moman. With Ringo back in the spotlight, Moman, through his record company, CRS Records, was pushing to release the songs Ringo recorded two years earlier at 3 Alarm Studio in Memphis. Moman claimed he'd bankrolled the sessions himself (which was true) and wanted a return on his investment (reportedly $150 per hour for studio time).

Ringo pushed back. The album, he claimed in a deposition in August, was unreleasable; he'd been drinking at the time and wasn't up to the task. Moman claimed the album could earn as much as $3.5 million with Ringo now back in form.

"He wanted to put it on hold," Moman said of Ringo's reluctance to release the album. "That didn't seem fair because I'd been working for months on this album and put a lot of my money into it. I'm not as rich as Ringo. It went on for months. Finally I said, 'Ringo, I'm gonna put this album out. It's taken me a year to get you on the phone. Send me your picture. If not, I'll just have an artist draw one."

In November, he flew to Atlanta to testify against Moman, stating that "he and other musicians were under the influence of drink and drugs when they recorded the album" and that his reputation in the music business would be harmed if Moman released the fourteen songs, which included "Whiskey and Soda."

Moman fired back, saying "he was just trying to help out a fading star" and that he'd spent $146,000 of his own money to record the album. "Mr. Starr conceded that he had not had a hit record in recent years," the *New York Times* reported, "but denied that he was desperate when he and Mr. Moman made their arrangement. In any case, the world may never know just how bad the record is. The court granted a permanent injunction blocking its release."

In January 1990, Moman was forced to surrender the master tapes to Ringo, who agreed to fork over nearly $75,000 in recording expenses on top of 7 percent interest. The *Sunday Mirror*: "Though Ringo claimed he owed nothing for the recording, his lawyer said he was happy with the court's £46,000 ruling. Moman, who had demanded more than £90,000 from the ex-Beatle, may now appeal."

In June 1991 Moman did appeal, returning to the Georgia court in an attempt to squeeze Ringo for more money. He was unsuccessful.

The first All-Starr Band tour wrapped in L.A. in early September, and Ringo and Barbara flew back to Monaco for a few weeks of rest and relaxation before the tour resumed in Japan—Ringo's first time performing there since he was a Beatle back in 1966.

The success of the first All-Starr Band re-awakened a long-dormant public interest in Ringo Starr. Suddenly, he was hot again, and David Fishof began planning the second All-Starr Band tour.

But the renewed spotlight created a double-edged sword; with Ringo's revitalized career and his willingness to sit for press interviews to promote the band—and to talk about the addictions that sent his life spiraling toward his 1988 stay in rehab—came the inevitable questions about The Beatles.

Even now, twenty years after the breakup—and ten years after John Lennon's death—he was asked about The Beatles, and if a "reunion" with Paul McCartney and George Harrison was possible. He'd answered those questions, often with a prickly response, hundreds of times since the band's breakup in 1970. Now, as he turned fifty, The World's Most Famous Drummer was more philosophical about the group and his legacy.

"Sure, there have been times when I felt weighed down by it," he told one interviewer. "I'm still weighed down by it. Everybody wants to talk about those days, and sometimes it gets heavy for me. Right now that waitress is not looking at me as Richard Starkey. It's Mr. Starr to her. It's the Beatle, not even the former Beatle.

"When I am the oldest man on the planet, and I'm wheeled onto *This Is Your Life*, it will be as Beatle Ringo Starr. This will never end. But that's cool, I suppose. Never get this wrong—I'm totally, honestly proud of the music that we made and the friendships. It was the best band that I've ever been in."

The public adulation he experienced with The All-Starr Band—the sold-out crowds chanting his name ("Ringo! Ringo! Ringo!"), the rocking arenas —also re-ignited his thirst to perform and to get back into the studio. He opted out of *Shining Time Station* after only one season (of twenty episodes) and was replaced, in 1991, by comedian George Carlin, who assumed the role of Mr. Conductor.

But Ringo's success as a live act failed to translate into excitement over his recording career. The hoped-for live All-Starr Band album was released in October 1990 (by EMI in the UK and by Rykodisc in the U.S.). *Ringo Starr and His All-Starr Band* failed to chart, but Ringo charged ahead with plans for his first studio album in nearly ten years.

In March 1991 he signed a new recording deal with a small label, Private Music, and shortly thereafter entered the studio to begin recording his next solo album. This time around he hedged his bets—a bad flashback to Chips Moman in Memphis?—and hired four producers (Don Was, Jeff Lynne, Peter Asher, and Phil Ramone) to work on *Time Takes Time*, which he recorded over the next eleven months.

"This is the first time since the *Ringo* album that I put this much energy into making an album," he said later.

Ringo played drums on *Time Takes Time*, which boasted guitar work from Lynne and Waddy Wachtel and several keyboard players, including Benmont Tench from Tom Petty's band, the Heartbreakers. Backup vocalists included Doug Fieger and Berton Averre from The Knack, former Beach Boy Brian Wilson, and even Harry Nilsson on one track ("Runaways").

Time Takes Time was completed in February 1992 and was released in time for the second All-Starr Band tour, which launched in early June. The new lineup included Todd Rundgren, Dave Edmunds, and Timothy B. Schmidt from The Eagles. Zak Starkey also played on a few gigs. ("He's a hell of a fine drummer. Must run in the family," Ringo joked.)

Despite the good vibes, *Time Takes Time* flopped and failed to chart, either in the U.S. or in the UK. Nevertheless, *Rolling Stone* wrote glowingly about the album in a lengthy interview with Ringo, calling it "far and away" his best album since 1973's *Ringo*, while another critic called it "an album that's so sunny and good-spirited you'll be tempted to pinch it."

The *New York Times* hailed it as "Starr's best: more consistently pleasing than *Ringo*, it shows him as an assured performer and songwriter."

But it didn't make a difference. Ringo took it all in stride. He thought the album was "brilliant. But people didn't seem to want to go for it. It was on Private Music. Which was so private . . . you had to be a member to hear it. Ha ha! No, I could make excuses, but you put your record out and you hope for the best."

"I was disappointed," he said candidly. "I thought, 'This is great. We'll be off again in the charts.' I was really proud of that album, and I kept saying, 'This is going to be No. 1.' But I'm afraid they didn't want it out there, and that's what happens. They may want the next one. That's why we keep on going." It would be another six years before Ringo released another album.

But while he talked about how proud he was of *Time Takes Time*, he wasn't going out of his way to promote the LP during his second All-Starr Band, which traveled to England this time around for a concert at the Hammersmith Odeon.

"His album received pretty short shrift," wrote a reporter for *The Telegraph*. "Indeed, as the show progressed, it became clear that Ringo was here in little more than name, and that most of the hard work was being done by the other troubadours."

"They should really be called 'Eight Men and a Baby,'" wrote a correspondent for the *Evening-Standard* (referencing a title of a 1987 film, *3 Men and a Baby*). "The All-Starr format wasn't so bad if you were prepared to put critical faculty, taste and embarrassment on ice, though a fairly strong stomach was necessary to endure the sight of so many old codgers forcing the jollity buttons for His Ringoness."

19

"PEACE AND LOVE"

The mid-1990s were, for Ringo Starr, a time of loss and redemption, a time of emotional lows and professional highs.

The bad news arrived quickly at the beginning of 1994 with the death of Harry Nilsson, who passed away on January 15 at the age of fifty-two, the victim of a bad heart and years of abusing his body with drugs and alcohol. He'd suffered a heart attack the previous February and seemed to realize his time was short, starting work on his memoirs and pushing for RCA to release a retrospective of his recordings.

In his final years Harry didn't go out much; he made his final appearance as a performer, fittingly enough, in 1992 with Ringo's All-Starr Band in Las Vegas. Harry sang his hit "Without You" and, when the song ended, went over to Ringo for a loving embrace between two old friends who'd lived a life few could ever imagine.

They didn't see each other much in the early '90s, but their emotional bond remained strong: when, toward the end of his life, Harry fell on hard times and lost most of his money—and his large house—Ringo bought him a small place in Agoura, California. He also loaned Harry twenty-five-thousand dollars.

For reasons of his own, Ringo did not attend Harry's funeral, which was held on January 17, a day that was rocked by aftershocks from an earthquake in nearby Northridge. He claimed to be too grief-stricken, and Barbara went in his place. Jeff Lynne was there. Jim Keltner was there. George Harrison was there.

"Ringo wouldn't even show up," recalled Harry's cousin, Doug Hoefer, who'd palled around with Harry and Ringo in the '70s and '80s. "To me, that was just plain wrong. George Harrison flew in from Hawaii and stood up in the back room because there was no place left to sit. I mean, Barbara came and I was talking to her. I said, 'I guess Ringo took it pretty hard' and she said, 'Yeah, well, we all did.' But I just thought that was wrong. Ringo's ego is so big, maybe he thought the crowds would get too big at the funeral if he came."

Three months later, in April, Maureen collapsed at home on the same day that her husband, Isaac Tigrett, was opening the L.A. branch of his House of Blues theme restaurant. Doctors initially thought Maureen might be anemic, but when her blood tests came back two weeks later the diagnosis was grim: a form of leukemia called myelodysplasia.

In October, Maureen was moved to the Fred Hutchinson Cancer Research Center in Seattle, where she underwent a bone-marrow transplant. The marrow had been donated by her son Zak, whose blood type closely matched his mother's. When that didn't work, Zak donated blood platelets and, finally, his white blood cells.

But Maureen developed a fungal infection that proved fatal. As she hovered near death, Ringo flew to Seattle to stand vigil by her bedside along with their children (Zak, Jason, and Lee), Isaac and Augusta Tigrett (only seven years old) and Maureen's mother, Florence Cox. Maureen died on December 30, 1994, at the age of forty-eight. Three years later, Paul McCartney immortalized her with "Little Willow," a song he wrote for the Starkey children, which he included on his *Flaming Pie* LP.

"There is no one that knew her better than me than perhaps Ringo," Tigrett told the author. "She was by my side for nineteen years and we shared the raising of her children by Ringo since 1976 and had a lovely child together, Augusta. [Maureen] was the kindest creature I have ever been blessed to share time with . . . kind and gracious to all."

There was more bad news the following August. Ringo's stepfather, Harry Graves, died on August 27 at the age of eighty-seven. Ringo and Barbara attended his funeral in England. After Elsie passed away, Ringo had remained close to the man he considered his real father.

In July 1992, Ringo returned to Liverpool with his All-Starr Band to play the Empire Theatre—a journey documented by the Disney Channel for an April 1993 television special called *Ringo Starr: Going Home*, which was co-produced by David Fishof and Hilary Gerrard. Harry, wearing a suit and tie, joined Ringo and his son Jason as they toured Ringo's old haunts (including St. Silas, Admiral Grove, Madryn Street, and Royal Liverpool Children's Hospital), with Ringo sharing his memories for the cameras.

Also in August, Ringo's twenty-four-year-old daughter, Lee, collapsed in London and was rushed to the hospital, where she was diagnosed with a rare type of brain tumor called an ependymoma. Ringo and Zak, who were on the road with the third All-Starr Band, canceled the rest of tour to be with Lee.

She was flown to Boston where, in late September, doctors at Brigham and Women's Hospital removed the tumor during a four-hour operation, calling Lee's condition "potentially curable." Ringo, Barbara, Jason, and Zak were there with Lee for her surgery and recovery, which included radiation treatments. By December, she was well enough to return to England.

Lee Starkey's recovery from her brain tumor sent the year out on a better note for Ringo. He had further reason to smile when, in late-November 1995, *The Beatles Anthology* aired on British and American television.

The ten-hour documentary was literally twenty-five years in the making and featured the participation of all three surviving Beatles. They'd been interviewed extensively on-camera, alone and together, starting in 1992, with audio and video of John Lennon added from archival footage. Neil Aspinall, Derek Taylor, and George Martin were the only non-Beatles interviewed for the documentary, which aired in the U.S. on ABC (November 19, 22, and 23) and in the UK on ITV.

ABC reportedly paid $20 million for the rights to air *The Beatles Anthology*, while ITV coughed up £5 million for a six-part version—with Paul, George, and Ringo demanding the network not be allowed to seek sponsorship "from anyone involved in selling alcohol, tobacco or meat."

"It was great therapy for the three of us," Ringo said. "We went over things that we thought were really big at the time, and they aren't that big at all—those little arguments that form up in your mind. It just brought back what a great time it was, and how close we all were. We tend to forget that. We did live in a box, and saved each others' lives."

The project also gave Paul McCartney, George Harrison, and Ringo Starr the impetus to—finally!—reunite, as they went into the studio to record and release two of John Lennon's unfinished songs, "Free as a Bird" and "Real Love." EMI would also release three double-CD sets of rare Beatles material as an audio adjunct to *The Beatles Anthology* television documentary.

The project dated back to 1970, when Neil Aspinall began amassing audio and video footage of The Beatles for a ninety-minute documentary of the band called *The Long and Winding Road*. (None of The Beatles were involved.) It was completed in 1971 but sat dormant for years, until John Lennon mentioned it in a lawsuit against the producers of the *Beatlemania* stage show, claiming that he, Paul, George, and Ringo were planning to film a live concert as an updated ending to the 1971 documentary, which would air as a television special.

The Long and Winding Road went no further after Lennon's murder until

1992, when the project was resurrected, this time with Paul, George, and Ringo agreeing to participate. By 1994, when Capitol Records released *Live at the BBC*—and the CD featuring rare Beatles recordings from their '60s visits to "The Beeb" sold eight million copies worldwide—the project was well on its way. Details were kept under wraps, though dribs and drabs leaked out from time to time, including some details Ringo revealed in a 1992 interview in *Rolling Stone*.

"I just did an interview about the early days with Neil Aspinall, who runs Apple Records, in England," he said, "for a series of videos that we're calling *The Long and Winding Road*. We're all doing it, too. We do the early years, the later years, our visits to *The Ed Sullivan Show*, and the making of *Sgt. Pepper*, because it's been twenty-five years. In that way you could say that we're really getting together.

"While we're cleaning out the files, the things I'd like to get out are the BBC tapes—all the stuff we played live on the BBC in our early days," he said. "It's been a problem, because they can't find the good tapes. We have a second-generation tape, which would still be cool by me because of what it is."

Ringo also dismissed rumors that he, Paul, and George had met with director Steven Spielberg about making a documentary about The Beatles.

"I never met him. Basically, we did the film five years ago," he said. "Neil Aspinall put it together from what we had in the archives, and then we sent copies to several directors. And a lot of them got uptight, because we actually sent it to somebody else. So it sort of faded into the blue. But that won't happen now, because we're breaking it up into the videos. It's not going to be the life. It's going to be the life in periods. In the original cut there's a lot of airplanes, a lot of landings and takings off, because that's where the crowds were."

The name of the project was eventually changed to *The Beatles Anthology*, the new title meant to keep George and Ringo (and Yoko Ono) happy with a neutral title—and not one lifted from a Paul McCartney song. In January 1994, McCartney, always with an eye toward publicity, announced that he, George, and Ringo—now dubbed "The Threetles"—would go into the studio to record. There were no further details released.

"There are reports that Lennon may be electronically resurrected," the *New York Times* noted. "When Mr. McCartney was in New York to induct Lennon into the Rock and Roll Hall of Fame, the story goes, Yoko Ono handed him master tapes of 'Boys and Girls' and 'Free as a Bird,' two songs left unfinished when Lennon was shot in 1980 . . . and could easily benefit from those open

McCartney-Harrison harmonies and a Ringo Starr backbeat." McCartney "has spoken in terms of a song or two. And Mr. Harrison says that if the chemistry is right, they might record a whole album."

Not everyone was happy to hear about the reunion. The *Sunday Times* editorialized in January:

> The sad truth is that the strokes of individual genius and miracles of group chemistry that once touched these fiftysomethings with greatness went missing long ago. Their individual CVs are now starting to look decidedly dog-eared. George Harrison and Ringo Starr have been, for the past decade, only part-time musicians. . . . For most of the Eighties, Starr was an alcoholic without a recording contract, best known for his unseen role as the Scouse voice of the children's television series *Thomas the Tank Engine and Friends*. . . . The nature of Starr's involvement in this project is best illustrated by his recent unavailability for a recording session penciled in for January 11. After deciding to extend his skiing holiday, Ringo phoned to say he would be unable to attend.

In March, there was further news: "Paul McCartney, George Harrison and Ringo Starr, the surviving former Beatles, have spent much of the last month recording new music in England," both at McCartney's home studio, the Mill, and at Harrison's Friar Park studio. Journalists were barred from the sessions—too much pressure, it was said—and everyone involved in the recording sessions was sworn to secrecy.

Ringo told the Beatles journal *Beatlefan* that the sessions went "much better than expected," and were extended to a month rather than only lasting a week, as originally planned. An unnamed EMI executive also "said he understood" that Paul, George and Ringo did some recording at Abbey Road. "And if they are not satisfied, then the recordings will never see the light of day," he said.

Still, Paul, George, and Ringo had a long history together, and some of the old resentments and bad feelings flared up during their recording sessions for *The Beatles Anthology*. Insiders said it was often tense between Paul and George—much like it had been during the *Let It Be* sessions in 1969—and Ringo admitted as much. "There have been lots of bad feelings," he said. "We've been in and out of favor with each other for the last twenty years. But this project brought us together. Once we get the bullshit behind us, we all end up doing what we do best, which is making music. The crap went out the window and we had a lot of fun."

Ringo launched his third All-Starr Band road show in June, and was inevitably asked about *The Beatles Anthology* while promoting the new tour. "So we began talking about how we could bring John into the project, and I think it was Paul who thought of asking Yoko if she had any tapes," he said. "She sent us three tracks. One of them, 'Free as a Bird,' wasn't even finished, but we took it because it was really beautiful. We had to write a lot of new words, and turn it into a track. Quite a lot of work went into it. But it saved us."

Ringo confirmed that "The Threetles" had finished a second song, "Real Love," and that a third, untitled track was not completed. In the spirit of his All-Starr Band, he was asked if there was any talk of a "Threetles" tour once *The Beatles Anthology* was completed.

"It would be easy," he said. "If we wanted to look at it, it would be real easy for the three of us to go on tour. Paul has his band, and all his Beatle numbers and Paul numbers. George actually rehearsed forty songs for his tour. I've got my numbers. If you want to be real, it would take two weeks of rehearsal, that's all. Why don't we? It's because of people thinking 'It's the Beatles.' Now we could go out tomorrow as Paul, George and Ringo. But we don't want to do that; we don't seem to want to do that. But it would be easy."

The Beatles Anthology, which was heavily hyped by ABC (calling itself "A-Beatles-C" for the occasion), wasn't the blockbuster the network was expecting when it premiered on November 19, 1995.

Although Part 1 premiered to an estimated forty-two million viewers in seventeen million homes—solid numbers—it failed to topple NBC's Thursday-night sitcom lineup and finished sixth for the week behind *ER*, *Seinfeld*, *Friends*, *Caroline in the City*, and *Single Guy*. Part 2 finished thirteenth for the week, and Part 3, which aired on Thanksgiving, finished thirty-sixth for the week (on a traditionally low-rated night of television). ABC estimated that twenty million people, on average, watched all three parts of the documentary.

The documentary didn't fare much better on ITV, at least critically. "To call the first film dull would be to do dull a disservice," Pete Clark wrote in the *Evening Standard*. "*The Beatles Anthology* is the perfect example of alchemy in reverse, gold transmuted into base metal." Part 1 did, however, attract an estimated audience of over fourteen million viewers on ITV, solid numbers for British prime-time television.

The accompanying two-CD set, *Anthology 1*, was released on November 21 in the U.S. and sold an estimated 1.2 million copies in its first week and 450,000 copies the first day—a new record for first-day sales. It entered the charts at Number One, putting The Beatles back on top twenty-five years and one death after their bitter breakup.

The two singles from *The Beatles Anthology*, "Free as a Bird" and "Real Love," also propelled The Beatles back on the charts.

"Free as a Bird," which received mixed reviews upon its release, sold 120,000 copies in its first week in the UK and climbed to Number Two on the charts. It reached Number Six in America—the thirty-fourth time The Beatles had a Top Ten single in the U.S. It went on to win a 1997 Grammy Award for Best Pop Performance by a Duo or Group with Vocal.

"It really sounds like a Beatles track," Ringo said of "Free as a Bird." "I think you could say they could have made this in 1967. It was weird for me, and I'm on it! When I was listening to it, it was like a light going on in my head—'It's them!'"

"Real Love" reached Number Four on the UK charts and Number Eleven in America. "Recording the new songs didn't feel contrived at all, it felt very natural and it was a lot of fun, but emotional too at times," Ringo said. "But it's the end of the line, really. There's nothing more we can do as The Beatles."

In 2000, Chronicle Books published *The Beatles Anthology*, a massive, 366-page coffee table book written "By The Beatles" that charted the band's history, year by year, via John, Paul, George, and Ringo's narration (plus memories from Neil Aspinall, Derek Taylor, and George Martin).

The book, priced at sixty dollars, also included mini-biographies of each band member (told in their own words). It was, in essence, a published record of its 1995 video predecessor, chock-full of rare photos, press releases, bits and pieces of Paul, John, and George's song lyrics, and Beatles memorabilia—including childhood photos of all four Beatles. (As in the television special, John's quotes were culled from archival sources.)

Shortly after the book appeared in print, Ringo popped up in a television commercial for Charles Schwab, the investment company. In the thirty-second spot (which aired during the Super Bowl), Ringo tried to help musicians come up with words to rhyme with "elation," including "dividend reinvestment participation" and "asset allocation." A spokesman for the ad agency that created the commercial called it "a happy coincidence" that it aired right after *The Beatles Anthology* book was released. In January 2001, the book hit the *New York Times* best sellers list.

Pete Best and Stuart Sutcliffe were remembered, too, in all The Beatles nostalgia. Best's appearance on several pre-Ringo Beatles recordings were included on the *Anthology1* CD; the resulting seven-figure royalties earned him enough money to retire from his job and become a full-time musician in Liverpool.

"For me, the poignant tracks are those that I was involved in," he said. "Frankly, I'm bloody proud and believe they stand the test of time." Back in the spotlight, if even briefly, Pete appeared in a Heineken beer commercial for which he was paid £10,000—and which aired on ITV during Part 2 of *The Beatles Anthology.*

Sutcliffe's bass playing, or lack thereof, was also heard on the *Anthology 1* tracks on "Hallelujah, I Love Her So," "You'll Be Mine," and "Cayenne."

As Ringo neared the age of sixty, he seemed to be at peace with himself and with his legacy. He and Barbara lived a healthy and sober lifestyle—Ringo became a vegetarian—and he continued touring with his All-Starr Band, and its ever-changing lineup, every two-to-three years.

"It was just a matter of timing, of getting the right band together," said All-Starr Band creator David Fishof. "I think the other thing that came out of the tours was that Ringo must have saved a bunch of musicians' lives over the years. We would insure the musicians, and I remember we insured Dave Edmunds and we sent him out for a medical exam [for insurance purposes] and it turns out he didn't realize how sick he was. And he basically thanked Ringo for saving his life. Ringo really helped straighten out and cleaned up a lot of musicians."

Barbara pushed her acting career into the background and became involved in charity work. In 1989, she teamed with George's wife, Olivia Harrison, in the "Parents for Safe Food Campaign," which was supported by other celebrities, including Twiggy and comedienne Pamela Stephenson. In 1991, she set up a free clinic for addicts in London called SHARP (Self Help Addiction Recovery Program) with the help of George Harrison, Eric Clapton, and George's first wife, Pattie Boyd. She also went back to school and, in 1993, earned a master's degree in psychology, from UCLA.

There were more live All-Starr Band albums, none of which charted or engendered too much excitement. In March and April of 1997, Ringo went back into the studio to record his first solo album in six years, this time for a major label (Mercury). The LP, called *Vertical Man*, featured songs co-written by Ringo with contributions from Paul McCartney (bass, vocals) and George Harrison (guitar on "King of Broken Hearts" and "I'll Be Fine Anywhere"). It also included a remake of The Beatles' "Love Me Do."

"Originally we backed off the John Lennon harmonica line, because I thought that might be pushing it," Ringo said of his "Love Me Do" remake. "So Steven [Tyler] did some sort of scat version, then the next day I said, 'No, c'mon, it's so silly we're hiding from this.' So we did the harmonica again."

The album's title, Ringo said, came from a saying he found while leafing through a decade-old book of quotes that Barbara's daughter, Francesca, had brought home from school.

> And it says, "Let's hear it for the vertical man, so much praise is given to the horizontal one." And you think, "Sure, let's hear it for what's happening now, I don't wanna hear it when I'm horizontal."
>
> For a while there I was heading for horizontal-dom. Substance abuse and alcohol was getting in my way. And the end result for many people is you're horizontal and they're all saying "What a guy." You think of all the musicians we've lost, the horizontal ones. Well, let's hear it for the vertical ones, who did have a problem but have come through. . . . So now it's either: Are you vertical? Or are you horizontal? Doesn't matter what the day is. It's like I'm living in this vertical/horizontal world. It's a vertical breakfast or it's a horizontal breakfast.

Vertical Man was released in 1998 to mediocre reviews and disappointing sales. It was followed several months later by a live album, released by Mercury, which Ringo recorded for an episode of VH1's *Storytellers* series—in which he appeared before a small live audience and reminisced about his life and the stories behind his songs. He also performed live versions of over ten tunes (including "With a Little Help from My Friends," "Back off Boogaloo," "Photograph," "Octopus's Garden," and "It Don't Come Easy").

The next year, Ringo released a holiday album, *I Wanna Be Santa Claus*, and then left Mercury Records because he felt they didn't do enough to promote the LP (which tanked).

In 1997, George Harrison, a heavy smoker, was treated for throat cancer and underwent radiation treatments. Then, in late December 1999, he was attacked in his Friar Park mansion by a deranged, thirty-three-year-old man from Liverpool who stabbed him forty times before Geoge's wife, Olivia, clubbed the intruder into submission with a fireplace poker and a lamp.

George suffered a punctured lung and head wounds and was reportedly near death. Olivia was also treated for cuts and bruises. "Both Barbara and I are deeply shocked that this has occurred," Ringo said in a statement at the time. "We send George and Olivia all our love and wish George a speedy recovery."

George eventually recovered from the attack, but in May 2001 he had a cancerous growth removed from his lung; by the summer, the cancer had spread to his brain. He died on November 29 in Los Angeles.

"We will miss George for his sense of love, his sense of music and his sense of laughter," Ringo said in a statement.

In the 2011 documentary about George's life, *Living in the Material World*, Ringo gave a tearful interview in which he recalled his last visit with his ailing "brother."

"The last weeks of George's life he was in Switzerland, and I went to see him," Ringo said. "He was very ill, and he could only lay down. And while he was being ill, and I had come to see him. . . . I was going to Boston, 'cause my daughter had a brain tumor. And I said, 'Well, I gotta go to Boston,' and he goes—they're the last words I heard him say, actually—and he said, 'Do you want me to come with ya?' So that's the incredible side of George."

After leaving George's bedside, Ringo and Barbara flew to Boston to care for Lee Starkey. Six years after her first brain tumor was treated, tests showed that another tumor in her brain had developed, and she returned to Brigham and Women's Hospital for treatment. "The news will have devastated Starr, whose family seems to have faced countless health problems," the *Daily Mail* reported. Lee pulled through with flying colors, began dating guitarist Jay Mehler and, in 2009, gave birth to triplets Ruby, Jakamo, and Smokey.

In 2004, David Fishof decided he'd had enough of life on the road and handed the All-Starr Band off to Dave Hart, who'd been booking arenas for the shows since Day One.

"I definitely learned so much about life being around Ringo, and one of the things I really admired most about him is his marriage and his relationship with Barbara," Fishof said. "To me, it was total eye-opener to see his respect for her. When it was Barbara's birthday, he told me, 'It's Barbara's birthday and I don't want to tour that week. I'm going to go to Aspen to be with her.' And when it came time and I was dating someone and decided to get married,

I sat down with him and he was very positive. He really encouraged me to get married again."

On November 29, 2002, the first anniversary of George Harrison's death, Ringo appeared at the *Concert for George,* an all-star tribute held in London's Royal Albert Hall and organized by George's wife, Olivia, and his son, Dhani. Eric Clapton and Jeff Lynne provided the musical direction. Paul McCartney was there, along with rock luminaries, including Tom Petty, and several members of *Monty Python's Flying Circus,* who performed a few classic Python routines.

"I loved George and George loved me," Ringo told the cheering crowd before launching into "Photograph" and "Honey Don't." He also accompanied McCartney on drums on George's "For You Blue," "Something," and "All Things Must Pass." Ringo and Paul joined the other musicians on stage for a rousing rendition of George's "Wah Wah."

The following year, Ringo released his twelfth solo album, *Ringo Rama* (on an independent label, Koch) and this time heavily promoted the LP on television, appearing on *Late Night with Conan O'Brien; Good Morning, America; The Tonight Show with Jay Leno;* and MTV's *Total Request Live. Ringo Rama* was critically well received but failed to move the sales needle, though it did crack the Billboard 200, settling in at Number 113.

"Ringo should probably have skipped the hard-rocking numbers on his twelfth solo album," *People* magazine's critic noted. "But his more characteristic easygoing numbers, which have the folksy affability of the Traveling Wilburys' tunes, are nice little nostalgia nuggets packed with sly references to more than a dozen classic songs ('Yesterday,' 'Here Comes the Sun'). The highlight is a sweet tribute to George Harrison, "Never Without You," decorated by Eric Clapton, who contributes some guitar licks that cleverly mimic the style of his departed friend."

As the decade rolled on, Ringo continued touring with various iterations of his All-Starr Band. "Lean and boisterous in tight pants, T-shirt, sneakers and funky sunglasses, he could be mistaken for a fifty-something in the first throes of an affair with a younger woman," was the way a reporter for *Time* magazine described Ringo in a two-page article published on the eve of his 2008 album, *Liverpool 8.* There was talk of Ringo collaborating with Dave Stewart on a show called *The Hole in the Fence,* about his childhood in Liverpool, but the project never came to fruition.

In addition to his requisite dark sunglasses and closely cropped beard and mustache, Ringo added other elements to his unique arsenal. He began constantly flashing the peace sign during public appearances, and that was usually accompanied by his mantra-like proclamation of "Peace and Love," which became his Lennon-like slogan.

"He's always got two fingers in the air and is repeating 'love' all the time," Stewart said. "But that's because he's been through so much." He even used the "Peace and Love" excuse in 2008, when he posted an odd video on his website in which he basically told off his fans (while flashing numerous peace signs, of course):

> This is a serious message to everyone watching my update right now. Peace and love, peace and love. I want to tell you, please, after the twentieth of October, do not send fan mail to any address that you have. Nothing will be signed after the twentieth of October. If that has a date on the envelope it's gonna be tossed. I'm warning you with peace and love. I have too much to do. So no more fan mail. Thank you, thank you, and no objects to be signed. Nothing. Anyway, peace and love, peace and love.

An unnamed record executive said he counted "twenty obsessive repetitions" of Ringo's "Peace and Love" message during a one-hour meeting.

The message angered a lot of fans—and left others perplexed. The strange behavior continued in January of 2008 when Ringo was a guest on the BBC One television show *Friday Night with Jonathan Ross* to promote his new album, *Liverpool 8*, and his appearance with the All-Starr Band in Liverpool.

When asked by Ross if there was anything he missed about Liverpool, Ringo smiled and said, "Er . . . no," though he did say he loved the city in which he grew up and still had family. Whether he was kidding is debatable—Ringo claimed he was joking—but his comment nonetheless angered some people back in Liverpool.

"I played the Echo Arena and everything was great," Ringo said. "Then I did *The Jonathan Ross Show* and he said, 'Is there anything you miss about Liverpool?' I said, 'No.' I was being flippant. It was funny. I thought the whole of Liverpool would laugh. My auntie and my relations laughed at what I said to Jonathan."

But many people in Liverpool weren't amused. There were complaints to the BBC, and, in April, a topiary sculpture of Ringo at Liverpool South Parkway train station—created by Italian sculptor Franco Covill—was beheaded by vandals, who left the sculptures of John, George, and Paul unscathed. Message delivered.

"I apologize to those people [who were offended], as long as they live in Liverpool, not outside," Ringo said. "No real Scouser took offense, only, I believe, people from the outside."

Later that month, Ringo was scheduled to appear on the syndicated morning talk show *Live with Regis and Kelly*, hosted by Regis Philbin and Kelly Ripa, to promote *Liverpool 8*. But when he was told he would have to shorten the song he was going to perform (also called "Liverpool 8") by two-and-a-half-minutes, in order to adhere to the show's time constraints, he balked—and walked off the show less than an hour before he was scheduled to go on.

"We offered to cut back our chat time and asked them to fade or go to commercial," his publicist said. "They were not willing to do that and Ringo was not willing to cut it further, so without a compromise we were not able to stay. Ringo left saying, 'God bless and goodbye. We still love Regis.'"

A *Live with Regis and Kelly* spokeswoman told the Associated Press that Ringo had been booked since November—and that the show's producers tried to work something out with him, as he'd been told "numerous times" how long the song needed to be to fit the show's format.

The old saying "There's no such thing as bad publicity" didn't apply in this case: *Liverpool 8* sank like a stone, selling a little over seven-thousand copies in its first week of release in America.

"I'm doing okay, but it's hard to get the [radio] play you want," a disappointed Ringo told one journalist shortly thereafter. "It's just how it is. If you're over twenty-one, it's difficult. I don't think it's only [difficult] for me. I think it's most people who've been around for a while. There's still artists coming through from the same era, so there's a lot of us still out there, and it's difficult—and there's a lot of new people. There's only so much room."

The city elders of Liverpool, meanwhile, weren't showing much "peace and love" to Ringo when they announced plans to bulldoze all the houses on Madryn Street, including Number 9, where Ringo was born, as part of a plan to regenerate the area. All the houses on the street were eventually vacated and boarded up, with Number 9 covered in spray-painted Ringo- and Beatles-related graffiti.

The house at 9 Madryn Street had plummeted in value, from £60,000 to just £525, when it was purchased by the Liverpool City Council and a local housing association. "To paraphrase John Lennon talking about Ringo, this isn't the best house in the world," said Jonathan Brown from SAVE Britain's Heritage. "It's not even the best house in Liverpool, but it does draw thousands of tourists from all around the world." By comparison, John Lennon's childhood home sold for a little less than half a million pounds, and both Lennon's Menlove Avenue home and Paul McCartney's family home in Speke belong to Britain's National Trust.

Ringo said he thought his house should be saved "because of the impact the Beatles had on Liverpool, that people come to see—and they should see—where we came from. The only thing I want, if they save my house 9 Madryn Street, is that it stays where it is because there was a rumor that they were going to knock it down and put it up somewhere else, which I thought doesn't really mean anything. Deep down I think it should stay."

In 2012, the Liverpool Housing Minister, Grant Shapps, announced that, due to "a tide of community support," 9 Madryn Street would be saved, along with fifteen other houses on the street, which would all be refurbished and put back on the market to be sold. "Ringo Starr's home is a significant beacon of Beatlemania," Shapps said. "But it's also a lot more than that—a real example of communities having the power and voice to step in and save the places they treasure most. Its future will now be in the hands of local residents. If they can make a success of this street then many more similar houses and streets could be saved."

Ringo turned seventy years old on July 7, 2010. Earlier that year he released his fifteenth solo album, *Y Not*, on the Hip-O label. Paul McCartney played bass on one song ("Peace Dream") and contributed vocals on "Walk with You."

Ringo used the occasion of his eighth decade to reference his boyhood friends Davey Patterson and Brian Briscoe on the *Y Not* track:

It was you and Brian Briscoe/Got me through my early teens alright.

Roy Trafford, Richy Starkey's friend at Henry Hunt and Sons, was also remembered in the song:

It was you and me on the factory floor/When rock and roll had just begun, oh yeah.

"I brought my family to Ringo's seventieth birthday concert with the All-Starrs," said Max Weinberg, the longtime drummer for Bruce Springsteen's E Street Band. "So they go off and it looks like they're going to play 'With a Little

Help from My Friends.' And they come back on, and the bass player is gone, and I can see one of the tech guys bringing out a Hofner bass.

"It was a complete surprise to Ringo that Paul showed up to sing 'Birthday' to him. Ringo didn't know. I've seen Ringo play fifteen times with the All-Starr Band and I've played with him. And with Paul playing bass on 'Birthday,' Ringo's drumming went back to 1964. He was playing like he did on *The Ed Sullivan Show*. Suddenly he's up there with Paul and you have The Beatles' rhythm section and Paul singing his song. It just raises everybody's game. With Ringo playing with Paul, he naturally went back to how he played and psychologically went to a place where suddenly it's The Beatles again."

Nostalgia for The Beatles continued unabated—and, with it, a growing appreciation of Ringo Starr's role in the band.

In 2009, Ringo and Paul McCartney reunited for a few songs at "Change Begins Within," a concert at Radio City Music Hall in New York City to benefit the David Lynch Foundation. After McCartney finished his set of songs, including some Beatles tunes, he told the crowd: "At this point we would like to introduce somebody to you who you know, you've heard his name. He's going to come out here and play you a little song this joyful night. Ladies and gentlemen: Billy Shears!"

Ringo came out onstage and together he and Paul sang "With a Little Help from My Friends," sharing a microphone and an embrace at the song's conclusion. Ringo also performed "Yellow Submarine" and "Boys" with his All-Starr Band.

The year 2010 also marked the release of Beatles music on Apple's iTunes after protracted legal wrangling over the use of the Apple name. Ringo got his own star on the Hollywood Walk of Fame and, that fall, yet another Beatles tribute show, *Rain*, opened on Broadway. It was very similar in tone and presentation to its late-'70s Broadway cousin *Beatlemania*, featuring four musicians portraying John, Paul, George, and Ringo in pitch-perfect recreations of Beatles songs, whereas *Rain* took its audience through all the phases of the band's history.

In 2011, Ringo and Barbara celebrated their thirtieth wedding anniversary, and the readers of *Rolling Stone* magazine voted Ringo Starr the fifth-greatest drummer of all time. He was sandwiched between Nirvana's Dave Grohl and—in a moral victory of sorts—ahead of Buddy Rich, who had always been so critical of Ringo's drumming. (Ringo's '70s party pals, John Bonham and Keith Moon, were voted Number One and Number Two, respectively.)

There was a best-selling video music game, *The Beatles: Rock Band* and a popular Cirque du Soleil show in Las Vegas called *Love*—which used interpretations of Beatles music and was co-produced by George Martin and his son, Giles. And plans were already afoot for televised celebrations to mark the fiftieth anniversary of The Beatles on *The Ed Sullivan Show*—still considered one of the seminal pop-culture moments in American history.

Paul McCartney was now Sir Paul McCartney—he'd been knighted in 1997—and some wondered if Ringo Starr, the other surviving Beatle, would ever be so honored. McCartney himself seemed to support that possibility, and was asked in an interview with Absolute Radio why he thought Ringo had not been knighted—and if he could personally ask the Queen if she would add Ringo to the annual honors list.

"Yeah, well, don't look at me," he joked. "The last time I went by she was out. Otherwise I would have popped in and said 'Look, love, Sir Richard Starkey.' Because I do think it's about time, but she probably was a bit busy with Sir Brucie." (McCartney was alluding to British comedian Bruce Forsyth, who was knighted in 2011—and added that nobody would have ever thought that Forsyth would be knighted before Ringo.)

"Well, that's up to them," Ringo said of the knighthood snub. "It doesn't grate with me. It doesn't alter my life. People have tried campaigns, but it never goes anywhere."

That same year, an editorial in *The Guardian* took up the Knighthood-for-Ringo cause:

> No matter that Ringo's stalwart percussion rarely interrupted Beatles recordings in the way his bandmates' mistakes did; and no matter, either, that drumming techniques like the matched grip are belatedly being traced back to him. It was Ringo's psychology as much as his drumming which cast a sorely needed steadying beat. A grounded personality was required to keep bossy Paul and angry John together—and transcendental George, who ended in the Natural Law party, was hardly the man. Later on, children lapped up Ringo's warmth as the voice of *Thomas the Tank Engine*. Now he is writing a story, *Octopus's Garden*, for them, while also publishing a trove of personal photos for his older fan base. All generations can agree he is bang on.

In 2013, Ringo *was* honored—by the French government, which made him a Commander of France's Order of Arts and Letters in a ceremony in Monaco. He joined Sean Connery and David Bowie, among others, in that rarefied club.

Ringo also added painting to his repertoire. Monaco's Oceanographic Museum, featured an exhibition of his artwork, as well as works by Paul McCartney and Bob Dylan. "I'm a drummer, but I can do other things," Ringo told the press, his new medal hanging around his neck, "like painting, living, breathing."

In May, Ringo published *Photograph*, an e-book collection made available on iTunes which included 140 rare photos he discovered while cleaning out Elsie's things after she died. That was followed in October by the thirty-two-page children's book *Octopus's Garden*, written by Ringo, with illustrations by Ben Cort.

Proceeds from the *Photograph* e-book went toward the Lotus Foundation, the London- and L.A.-based charitable organization founded by Ringo and Barbara. The foundation's aim is to "fund, support, participate in and promote charitable projects aimed at advancing social welfare in diverse areas included, but not limited to: substance abuse, cerebral palsy, brain tumors, cancer, battered women and their children, homelessness and animals in need."

Some of the historical memorabilia Ringo found in Elsie's attic also became part of *Ringo: Peace & Love*, a retrospective of his life and career that opened in June 2013 at the Grammy Museum in Los Angeles. (The museum's executive director, Robert Santelli, called Ringo "the most significant drummer in the history of rock 'n' roll.")

The exhibit included the drum kit Ringo used on *The Ed Sullivan Show*, a "Ringo for President" sticker, letters to Ringo from Rory Storm, the sequined suit Ringo wore on the cover of the *Sgt. Pepper's Lonely Hearts Club Band* album, and a painting which George Harrison gave to Ringo in 1974 as a birthday present.

"It was in several places on the planet and we pulled it all together," he said of the exhibit, adding that he was "shocked" that he still had a lot of the memorabilia. "It was in basements, it was in storage facilities. It was put in places of safety mainly by two of my assistants through the years in England," he said.

"I'd like to say I was the one [who found the memorabilia], but no, I was pretty careless, myself. But we found it, which was great. For a piece of the exhibition, we have to thank my mother. When she died in '86, we took a couple of boxes from the house, and we found the Rory Storm letter that's there, which I love, because I didn't know I had anything like that. There's also letters from Brian Epstein about an important gig: 'Dress smart.' I was blown away by some of the stuff I found."

There were more honors to come.

On January 20, 2014, Ringo was given the David Lynch Foundation's "Lifetime of Peace and Love Award" in a star-studded concert at the El Rey Theater in L.A. The foundation had been started ten years earlier by the noted movie and television director (*Blue Velvet, Twin Peaks*) to teach Transcendental Meditation to at-risk students, veterans with Post Traumatic Stress Disorder (PTSD), abused women, and homeless and incarcerated individuals. Ringo, it was noted, had practiced TM since traveling to Rishikesh with John, Paul, and George in 1968.

Tickets for the evening were priced at $1,000 to $100,000 and the attendees were treated to a Ringo Starr tribute concert, featuring Ben Folds, Brendan Benson, Ben Harper, Bettye LaVette, Dave Stewart, and Ringo's frequent collaborator and brother-in-law, Joe Walsh (Walsh married Barbara's sister, Marjorie, in 2008). Don Was served as the musical director.

Each musician performed one song from Ringo's years with The Beatles and from his solo work. "I truly believe in the David Lynch foundation," Ringo said. "They started to bring meditation into inner-city schools and now it's a fact that in those schools and neighborhoods violence has gone down," Ringo said. "Meditation brings people back to being human again."

The evening also included video greetings from Paul McCartney and Yoko Ono. George's widow, Olivia Harrison, was in the theater, as were Jeff Lynne, Jim Keltner—Ringo's favorite drummer—and Edgar Winter. "It's weird to be here this evening," Ringo said as he joined Lynch onstage. "All this praise is overwhelming."

After receiving his award from Lynch—and a citation from Los Angeles Mayor Eric Garcetti—Ringo did a fifteen-minute set, singing "Photograph," "Boys," and, naturally, "With a Little Help from My Friends." Cameras were there to capture the occasion for a television special, *Ringo Starr: A Lifetime of Peace and Love*, which aired the following July on AXS TV.

Less than a week after the David Lynch Foundation gala, Ringo reunited with Paul McCartney at the Grammy Awards in L.A. McCartney was nominated for two Grammys (he won for "Cut Me Some Slack," a song he performed with the surviving members of Nirvana). Ringo was honored with the 2014 Recording Academy Lifetime Achievement Award.

The awards ceremony aired live on CBS, and viewers watched as Ringo sang "Photograph" and later, on the drums, backed McCartney on a song called "Queenie Eye" from Paul's 2013 album, *New*. It was all a precursor to a

CBS prime-time special which aired February 9—fifty years to the day that The Beatles appeared on *The Ed Sullivan Show.*

The Beatles: The Night That Changed America: A Grammy Salute, was taped the night after the Grammys in L.A. during a four-hour concert that was edited down to a more manageable two-hour telecast. It featured a vibrant Ringo jumping around the stage and singing "Yellow Submarine," "Matchbox" and "Boys," and, with McCartney, performing "With A Little Help from My Friends." Ringo got behind the drums to back Paul on "Hey Jude," during which the two surviving Beatles gave a shout-out to their late "brothers," John Lennon and George Harrison.

There were interpretations of Beatles songs from, among others, Annie Lennox and Dave Stewart ("The Fool on the Hill"), Ed Sheeran ("In My Life"), Imagine Dragon ("Revolution"), Katy Perry ("Yesterday"), and Alicia Keys and John Legend ("Let It Be"). Interspersed throughout the telecast were glorious black-and-white clips from The Beatles' live appearance on *The Ed Sullivan Show* on February 9, 1964—reminding everyone of the magic woven that night by John, Paul, George, and Ringo.

Ringo celebrated his seventy-fourth birthday on July 7, 2014, by announcing his partnership with clothing designer John Varvatos to publicize a media campaign called #PeaceRocks, intended to help raise money for Ringo's Peace and Love Foundation. Ringo was in good company; he was one of the many musicians featured in Varvatos publicity campaigns, including Willie Nelson, Paul Weller, The Roots, Cheap Trick, Alice Cooper, Joe Perry, Jimmy Page, and Slash.

Ringo made the Varvatos announcement at his annual "Peace and Love" birthday celebration, which was always open to photographers (the better to publicize whatever project he had going at the time). This birthday bash took place at Capitol Records in L.A. Ringo, wearing Varvatos-designed duds, was joined by several current All-Starr Band members, including Todd Rundgren and Joe Walsh, and Ringo's new mentor, David Lynch.

Ringo explained that every time someone used the hashtag #PeaceRocks on social media, Varvatos would donate one dollar to the Ringo Starr Peace and Love Fund, an offshoot of the David Lynch Foundation in its quest to introduce Transcendental Meditation to at-risk students, veterans, abused women, etc.

"I've waited a long time to become a male model," Ringo joked, "and what a great way to do it. All for a good cause. I want to thank John for this campaign and all he has done. What a nice guy, inside and out. So remember, #PeaceRocks and Love Rolls! Peace & Love."

He also appeared in a two-and-a-half-minute, black-and-white promotional film for the campaign, which was shot in the back yard of an L.A. mansion. A drum set, its bass drum covered by a peace symbol, was placed just a few feet away from a sun-dappled swimming pool. While Ringo reminisced about his life, celebrity pals, including Steven Tyler, Jim Keltner, and ABC's late-night ABC talk show host Jimmy Kimmel took a few thwacks on the drum set.

"My dream, which I had at thirteen, to play drums came true," Ringo told the camera. "I remember it so well. I would walk around Liverpool looking in music stores just at the drums. My stepdad bought me the first kit which was like $20, £12 pounds in England, and I just starting hitting them.

"I had no lessons," he continued. "I loved the sound of them, the depth of them, what they give me . . . it's just my instrument, just what I wanna play."

That was followed, in October 2014, when Ringo was hired by the footwear company, Skechers, as the new face of its "Relaxed Fit Footwear" ad campaign. Previous spokesmen included NFL greats Joe Montana and Joe Namath and billionaire entrepreneur Mark Cuban.

"Ringo possesses the charm, cool charisma and instant global recognition that will elevate awareness for our popular Relaxed Fit footwear collection," the company said in a press release. "Ringo is not only a music icon, but also a style icon and is the perfect ambassador to illustrate how our footwear helps keep you relaxed in any situation."

It was all relative, of course. Ringo personal wealth was estimated to be in the £200 million range and, in the fall of 2014, he announced he was selling his two-hundred-acre Rydinghurst Estate in Surrey for £20 million.

He paid £2 million for the six-bedroom, seventeenth century mansion in 1999, when he purchased the house and property from Count George Bardeau. It was his and Barbara's primary residence whenever they were in England, and included two music rooms, a movie theatre, a cottage and a coach house—which had its own cottage and staff quarters. The property, surrounded by a lake, also included a helipad, a block of stables, and an indoor riding school.

"We have spent fifteen years at Rydinghurst and will always have wonderful memories of our time there," the couple told the *Sunday Times*. "It is a beautiful home with some very special features, but we are, reluctantly, unable to spend as much time there as we would wish. With commitments in America and our family in all England, we will continue to divide our time between Los Angeles and London."

They still had one home in England, located in West London off the King's Road in Chelsea—but it was clear that America currently took precedence in Ringo's life.

"L.A. is the right place for us to be now," he said. "It's not that sad, because it's time for a change. And the weather is better over there. I'm really into the healthy lifestyle that they have out in L.A. I do yoga every day and eat healthy. I'm obsessed with broccoli—I eat it every day with absolutely everything. No matter what, I always add broccoli. It's become a running joke—my wife makes fun of me for it."

In December 2014, the Rock and Roll Hall of Fame announced it would award Ringo its Award for Musical Excellence. Ringo learned the news from Paul McCartney, who phoned to tell him the news. "This means recognition to me," Ringo said. "And it means, finally, the four of us are in the Rock and Roll Hall of Fame even though we were the biggest pop group in the land."

In the late 1960s, when the pop-culture world seemed to orbit around The Beatles, the band's diminutive, sad-eyed drummer was asked how he would like to be remembered.

"It'll be nice to be part of history, some sort of history anyway," he said. "What I'd like to be is in school history books and be read by kids."

Mission accomplished.

Epilogue

In the course of researching this book, I interviewed four well-known, universally respected rock and roll drummers about one topic: Ringo Starr.

Phil Collins, John Densmore, Max Weinberg, and Kenny Aronoff are considered the crème de la crème of rock drumming. They're also big Ringo Starr fans, and each of them credits Ringo with influencing the world of drumming as a groundbreaking percussionist.

Phil Collins was born in Chiswick, England, in 1951 and took up the drums at the age of five. He would eventually join the progressive rock group Genesis and followed that with an incredibly successful solo career with hits including "In the Air Tonight," "Misunderstanding," "Easy Lover," and "Against All Odds (Take a Look at Me Now)." He is only one of three artists—Paul McCartney and Michael Jackson are the other two—who has sold over 100 million albums worldwide, both as member of a band and as a solo artist.

John Densmore, born in 1944 in Los Angeles, began playing the drums in high school. He provided the backbeat for 1960s rock icons The Doors ("Light My Fire," "Break on Through," "The End," "Riders on the Storm") for all eight years of the band's existence. He wrote the best-selling autobiography *Riders on the Storm*, is in the Rock and Roll Hall of Fame (as a member of The Doors), and has acted in movies and in television.

Max Weinberg was born in 1951 in Newark, New Jersey. He started his life as a drummer after watching D. J. Fontana back Elvis Presley on *The Milton Berle Show* in 1956. Weinberg has been the drummer for Bruce Springsteen's E Street Band since 1974 and, for seventeen years, was the drummer and musical director for NBC's *Late Night with Conan O'Brien* and *The Tonight Show with Conan O'Brien*. He's sat in with Ringo's All-Starr Band on several occasions and also plays jazz with The Max Weinberg Quintet.

Kenny Aronoff, who was born in 1953, is considered one of rock's elite studio drummers. He has toured with John Mellencamp, John Fogerty, The Red

Hot Chili Peppers, Melissa Etheridge, Johnny Cash, and dozens of others. In 2014, he backed Ringo and Paul McCartney on drums as they performed together on the Grammy Awards.

First Impressions of Ringo and The Beatles

Max Weinberg: In November 1963, it was the day before Thanksgiving and we were still reeling from the Kennedy assassination. I had a good friend who returned from England with her family—I was in the seventh grade—and she'd come back with *Meet the Beatles*. My big hero at the time was D. J. Fontana, who played with Elvis Presley, and when I heard that Beatles record, it was just so full of life . . . and sounded so fresh. I had no idea at the time who they were. I was twelve years old. . . . The anticipation waiting for The Beatles to be on *The Ed Sullivan Show* was incredible. I still didn't have any of their records; when I wanted to hear The Beatles, I had to go to my friend's house and listen to the record. From the first downbeat on *The Ed Sullivan Show* you could tell Ringo was having the time of his life. It looked like he was having fun, like it was the greatest thing you could ever do. From that moment on, my future was split between being a drummer in a rock and roll band and a placekicker for the New York Giants. They were about equal.

Kenny Aronoff: I was jealous of Ringo because I thought, "Man! I should be in The Beatles," and because I was into jazz, I didn't understand how amazing Ringo was—how great of a musician he was. He might not have played jazz, but he grew up in that time when it was all over the place. Ringo has that swing thing, because he grew up in that time. Every drummer is unique, and Ringo had an even more unique feel because of who he is. And he also was the left-handed guy playing right-handed and he came up with different little fills. He is an artist. His beats were simple, but they were so spot on. I can't say that I would have come up with those clever beats the way he did. . . . The Beatles on TV . . . was like taking heroin or something, in the positive sense. I was addicted to it, and I had to have it full-time, to be in a famous rock and roll band. So I lived that dream. Seeing Ringo when I was ten years old and years later, me playing with Ringo and Paul at the tribute to them, honoring them for that night on *The Ed Sullivan Show*, is amazing. There [are] only a few of us in the world that can say they did that.

Phil Collins: I was playing since I was five, so Ringo wasn't the reason for me to start playing the drums. There were really no drum heroes to speak of for me. I just took to it for some reason. But of course when "Please Please Me" and Ringo came along, that kind of changed everything, certainly. It was a reason to play every day and to be enthusiastic about it. I mean, it was life-changing, as anybody that grew up in the '60s will tell you.

The Ringo Style

John Densmore: I love Ringo's drumming. The thing with drummers is the feel. The groove, the pulse. And when you kind of play on the front of the beat, it comes out sort of military. If you play on the back of the beat—in other words, you wait until the last second to finish that beat—it's sort of like the blues. And then there is everything in-between. And those minute little increments are what makes the feel for a drummer. And Ringo's feel is heaven! Jim Keltner is a great studio drummer who's played on everything. We talked about Ringo's feel. It's sort of like his personality. It's just so full of life, you love it. . . . Drummers usually count the band off when they're playing live for each song. And whenever I can't think of exactly what the tempo should be, it's really important, I ask whoever, "Give me the first key bars of the melody or the words or something." If I hear just a couple of bars of that, a cappella by another band member, that tells me what the tempo is. I just know immediately, and that's what Ringo's got. That sense of musicality, the tempo that is appropriate for "Hey Jude," or whatever. Intuitively, he's perfect.

As far as technique, I say to young musicians, "You need to have enough technique to find your own uniqueness and say what your soul needs to say." On the other end of the spectrum, there are a lot of musicians that are so technically proficient, they miss their uniqueness. I would say I'm not the fastest drummer in the world, nor is Ringo. But I think we found whatever is in us that is kind of unique to our approach to rhythm. . . . I know I've heard that there are a few songs that Ringo wasn't on [on *The White Album*], when The Beatles were fighting. Paul sort of took over. . . . I don't know the specifics of about that, but Ringo was the soul of that band.

Kenny Aronoff: Technically he's not Buddy Rich, but to play like Ringo does is literally just as hard. It really is. I used to put down the "simple drummers." And then I became famous for that simple drumming style. I became famous for the kind of drummer I used to make fun of. That's the irony—that's a great lesson in life.

Max Weinberg: Ringo's drumming was very different. Prior to that you never heard such splashy drumming. That was Ringo's style, playing on the hi-hat and keeping it loose. That's how he got that sizzle. Drummers were much tighter on rock and pop records before Ringo; if they were playing eighth notes, they were kind of tight, instead of the *sssshhhhh*, the white noise that Ringo got. That was a real revelation, that he could get away with doing that. . . . When Ringo played, what he played at that time was not conceptually very difficult, but just the fact that he did it.

The Beatles were a phenomenal vehicle for his abilities. If another drummer played on all those records it would be completely different. They would not have had the shattering success because the missing element would be Ringo. I've talked to friends in England, and among northern English musicians, even before he joined The Beatles, Ringo was known as the best drummer within 150 miles. It was a major coup for The Beatles to get Ringo into the band.

The way Ringo re-interpreted the drums on the girl-group songs of the early '60s like "Money" . . . it was interesting how he took the rhythmic drumming approach on those records and turned it around and did something completely unique. One of his major influences was country and western music, and if you listen to most of his drumming going on at the time, the Mersey Beat was with a quarter-note bass drum; Ringo played a country beat to those songs and gave them a much different feeling. He turned it around and played a really heavy backbeat with a country/Latin bottom and continued doing that. Suddenly, in my view, the rock beat changed dramatically.

Ringo didn't have jazz chops. He wasn't a jazz drummer. He was a rock drummer who grew out of country and western music and rock rhythms. When the jazz of the 1920s through the 1940s went left to bebop and right to jump blues, that was the precursor to all rock drummers—who were basically swing band drummers. D.J. Fontana was a Big Band drummer. Ringo learned how to play from them; his favorite records were all made by swing drummers. That, in itself, was a big difference.

That trend in 1966 to '67—if you listen to those Beatles records as opposed to the first two years of Beatles records, Ringo's drumming got funkier. It got tighter. He suddenly started clamping down on the hi-hat on *Rubber Soul*. John and Paul wanted him to play like that, to keep the hi-hat open. If you watch *The Ed Sullivan Show*, he's just swinging away on that hi-hat, which is one of his greatest contributions to rock and roll. Suddenly you have this swishing sound, which helps you compete, volume-wise. I don't think I've ever heard Ringo play on a ride cymbal; he just crashed his left hand and sometimes ended up not hitting it very hard.

He was a lefty so he led with his left hand on a righty drum set. I'm not quite sure, exactly, what his influence was regarding that, but it was a little odd. He would hit the crash cymbal on the left side with his left hand. Most people hit it with their right hand off the hi-hat. And nobody ever played the tom-toms like that. It's a classic Ringo thing—*da da da dum dum dum*. His use of staggered tom-tom fills was tantamount to early bebop drummers like Max Roach and Roy Haines, putting the emphasis of the cymbals on top rather than on the bottom.

Phil Collins: I suppose at the time, you flaunted your technique and you showed people that you were as good as you could be, as opposed to Ringo. What he did was perfect. I don't think you could imagine any of those [Beatles] tunes with a different kind of drummer. . . . I mean, that guy Jimmy Nicol, who took over for Ringo when he was sick [in 1964], was obviously probably a more-than-adequate drummer. But one can't imagine him doing the drum fills on "A Day in the Life." I mean, that stuff was unique, and I would raise a glass to Ringo at any point when you talk about that kind of drumming.

The way someone like Buddy Rich would hold the drumsticks is the "traditional" grip, but Ringo didn't have that. He just held the sticks. And for me, it was his swishing of the hi-hat, so songs like "It Won't Be Long" and "All My Loving" . . . that swish sound, mixed with the sound of The Beatles' records— that was totally jaw-dropping for me. I mean, it still is—the technical side of how they managed to get that stuff.

Ringo's Impact

Max Weinberg: The Beatles happening in America was the first fun breath of fresh air after the assassination of President Kennedy. No matter what your politics were, it was shocking. Suddenly, whoosh, The Beatles came along and it was big change for everybody. Ringo happened to be the guy. When Benny Goodman played "Sing, Sing, Sing" at Carnegie Hall in 1939, Gene Krupa was his drummer—he was a great drummer and a good-looking guy and had a cool personality. As a result, he became the biggest star in swing jazz. That was Ringo in rock and roll. Everybody grew their hair long and started to play like Ringo Starr.

The influence Ringo had on the world of drumming, and rock and roll, was almost exactly what Gene Krupa did thirty years earlier. Suddenly you had the attention being drawn to the drummer by virtue of the way Ringo played. Suddenly, everyone had to play like Ringo—it didn't matter what was going on before.

Ringo's Influence on the Industry

Phil Collins: I think if you talk to drummers, as opposed to people who weren't musicians, I don't know how many people picked up sticks because of Ringo. But I do know that amongst the drumming fraternity, Ringo is much appreciated. I've been thinking about what we'd be talking about and certainly he came in for a bit of bashing amongst the so-called "legitimate" drummers at the time, certainly people like Buddy Rich.

I think Keith Moon and Ringo did unorthodox things with both of the bands they were in, to the point where nobody else could really do what they did and it would sound the same. I mean, I've read that people used to call Ringo's drum fills "silly little drum fills," and in *Modern Drummer* magazine he actually once said, "They are not silly little drum fills, they are actually very good drum fills," and I sympathized with him.

Kenny Aronoff: For me, it was that you had the greatest jazz drummers, greatest technicians in the world playing, and all of the sudden The Beatles come in, and they knocked the whole world out. And here's this drummer, and people are going, "What?" And then pretty quickly, in rock and roll, you had drummers with technique and a lot of people were saying, "Oh, Ringo's no good," including me. We were going, "What the fuck? I can play The Beatles." We didn't understand Ringo's feel, his technique, his style—it's all so unique. That's the problem. He wasn't getting any good credit, because his technique wasn't at the level of other people around who had mad technique—and that's how people judge other people. Nobody understood.

Jazz was all about the music. It wasn't as much about style and vibe and branding. Rock and roll became fashion. Look at The Beatle haircut. It became how you dressed and, very quickly, it became the hippie psychedelic thing with people like Hendrix and Cream. Ringo doesn't get credit, because he was surrounded by people with massive technique, and people didn't understand this new movement and all the different factors involved in the English [rock] movement, which was not just about technique. That's why he got nailed.

Max Weinberg: The drumming world generally was not ready for Ringo. He took a lot of heat from jazz drummers and "legitimate" drummers. Jazz drummers actively disliked him. The Beatles were the big kahunas of music and in pop culture. If you can imagine, all those people surfing from Frank Sinatra to Dean Martin to great jazz musicians to great vocalists . . . they all got wiped out by a big wave, and that big wave was The Beatles. There was a certain bitterness that "real" musicians were not being accepted like The Beatles. I think there was a certain amount of jealousy and bitterness that jazz, which was an American phenomenon, was not mainstream at all, that "any gorilla" could play music like The Beatles if they only wanted to make money.

The Ringo Legacy

John Densmore: The drummer's first job is to keep the beat. You gotta get that down. But then maybe that's what helps me and Ringo. If you can play musically—somehow support the guitar solo, the keyboard solo, the chorus or the verse, what's in that beat—you're playing with a musical field that is appropriate to the song. That's Ringo. It's more than just a beat.

Kenny Aronoff: I'd say the thing that stands out for me with Ringo is his unique musical ideas on the drum set, and his feel. Feel first, but they go hand-in-hand. He had a swing and a swagger; it went just exactly like his personality. It was perfect. Ringo as a human being showed up on a drum set. There was no other feel like his, which made The Beatles sound great and his musical drum parts sound great. That was Ringo's specialty. That *is* Ringo's specialty. His feel and his drum fills. That's him in a nutshell. Nobody will ever be like him; nobody can be like him.

Phil Collins: I met Ringo a few times and I've played with him a few times and he is always great. I had given him an award a couple of years ago in London and in fact, I turned up and I had to bail, because I was sick at the event, but Ringo left a message for me saying, "I hope you're feeling better." But he was genuinely flattered that someone who was known to be a pretty good drummer had bothered to come out for him. I mean, for me, it was like without a doubt, but for him it was flattering. I mean, amongst the fraternity of drummers, I think most of us realize that Ringo is a great drummer. But I think he himself has probably taken some of that battering to heart.

It was never an issue for me. There was never one of those moments where you think, "Oh, actually, he is better than I thought he was." Ringo has always been the guy. I mean, the things that he did on the first album, you know, the swing on "All My Loving," some of those things are not easy to play, that kind of "I Saw Her Standing There"–type of rock and roll and make it swing. And, I mean, the guy is great. And that's why The Beatles chose him. And at that point, they were a working band and he was a working drummer. I have nothing but praise for him.

Max Weinberg: Those of us who played drums wanted to be Ringo Starr; we wanted to play with that kind of infectious beat. Technically speaking, Ringo had incredible time, he still does, and he has amazing feel and exceptional taste.

Notes

CHAPTER 1

2 "Your mother would boil the water": Author interview.

2 "Nine times out of ten you had no toilet paper": Author interview.

4 "I was just able to manage": *Life* (September 13, 1968).

4 "My father sort of decided to leave": *Inner-View* (August 29, 1977).

4 "We swapped houses with them": Author interview.

4 "We moved into a great house": *Inner-View*.

5 "The war had finished": Author interview.

5 "I think I gave him his first drum": Author interview.

6 "I remember [Richard] coming back to Liverpool": Author interview.

7 "After that, I think that's when I really started to hate it": *Inner-View*.

7 Despite the fact that Annie's: David Bedford: *Liddypool: Birthplace of The Beatles* (Deerfield, IL: Dalton Watson Fine Books, 2009), 96.

7 "He was so much a part of our family": Hunter Davies, *The Beatles* (New York: W.W. Norton & Company, 1985), 144.

7 "I started teaching him to read": Davies, *The Beatles*, 144.

8 given the nickname "Lazarus": Alan Clayson, *Ringo Starr: Straight Man or Joker?* (London: Sanctuary Publishing Ltd., 1996), 23.

8 "We were always in contests with each other": Author interview.

8 "We would come out of the movies": Author interview.

9 "That was our playground on Madryn Street": Author interview.

9 "His grandfather was a boiler maker": Author interview.

9 "We made our own go-carts, things like that": Author interview.

9 "He always liked drums": Author interview.

10 "We had been on school holiday": Author interview.

10 "As a kid you didn't care": *The Daily Mail* (May 26, 2011).

11 "That was taken at a place": Author interview.

12 dated Richy's widowed aunt: Bob Spitz, *The Beatles: The Biography* (New York: Little, Brown, 2005), 339.

12 "You couldn't help but like Harry": Author interview.

12 "He was great": Davies, 146.

12 "With Harry working": Author interview.

13 "So you'd be an engineer": *Ringo Starr: Going Home*, The Disney Channel, 1993.

13 "I told Richy": Davies, 145.

14 "Richie contracted tuberculosis": Bedford, *Liddypool: Birthplace of The Beatles*, 96.

14 "There used to be balconies": *Going Home*.

14 "They used to push him out": Author interview.

CHAPTER 2

15 Eric Delaney's rendition: David Bedford: *Liddypool: Birthplace of The Beatles* (Deerfield, IL: Dalton Watson Fine Books, 2009), 97.

16 "We used to make general nuisances": Author interview.

16 "she used to give my mum": Author interview.

17 "throwing photographs to the girls": *Ringo Starr: Going Home*, The Disney Channel, 1993.

17 "I went to the railways": *Going Home*.

17 "It wasn't just not getting the uniform": Hunter Davies, *The Beatles* (New York: W.W. Norton & Company, 1985), 146.

18 "One night a week": *Going Home*.

18 "I was on the bike": *Going Home*.

18 "Richy and I were apprentice bench fitters": Author interview.

18 "It was a great gang of people": Bob Spitz, *The Beatles: The Biography* (New York: Little, Brown, 2005), 341.

19 "When I started playing": *Inner-View* (August 29, 1977).

19 "But skiffle was music we could play": Spitz, 44.

20 "Flat tins were cymbals": *Modern Drummer* (January 1982).

20 "It was a sort of mixture": *NME* (August 8, 1963).

21 "He could play anything": David Bedford, *The Fab One Hundred and Four* (Deerfield, IL: Dalton Watson Fine Books, 2013), 352.

21 "I played guitar": Spitz, 341.

22 Trafford claims he even dragged Richy: Spitz, 342.

22 "We used to visit": Bedford, *The Fab One Hundred and Four*, 352.

22 "That's where I met him": Author interview.

23 They would appear: Bill Harry, *triumphpc.com/mersey-beat/archives*.

23 "with his bird's-eye maple Hofner": Spitz, 342.

23 "He was a smashing fellow": *mersey-beat/archives.*

23 "The Eddie Clayton Skiffle Group": Bedford, *The Fab One Hundred and Four,* 352.

23 Trafford claims it was he: Bedford, *The Fab One Hundred and Four,* 352.

23 "If his granddad": Davies, 149.

24 "It was in my soul": Andy Babiuk, *Beatles Gear: All the Fab Four's Instruments from Stage to Studio* (Montclair, New Jersey: Backbeat Books), 69.

24 "We thought we were": Spitz, 343.

25 "Neither of our mums": Bill Harry, *The Ringo Starr Encyclopedia* (London: Virgin Books, 2004), 180.

25 "He and Geraldine were very close": *beatlegirls.net.*

26 "Richy was shy in a way": *beatlegirls.net.*

26 "It was very difficult for a drummer in those days": *Rock Cellar*, December 2, 2013.

26 Years later, Ringo: Bedford, *The Fab One Hundred and Four,* 353.

27 boasted a rare female lead singer: Bedford, *The Fab One Hundred and Four,* 355.

CHAPTER 3

29 "He could walk on water": *Rory Storm and the Hurricanes: A Documentary,* youtube.com.

29 The building once housed: Bill Harry, *The Ringo Starr Encyclopedia* (London: Virgin Books, 2004), 299.

30 Rory thought that Wally: Harry, 300.

31 "I was an apprentice engineer": *The Daily Mail,* May 26, 2011.

31 "We were probably": *Rory Storm* documentary.

32 "We told him of all the women": *triumphpc.com/mersey-beat/archives.com.*

32 "I just felt I wanted to": Hunter Davies, *The Beatles* (New York: W.W. Norton & Company, 1985), 150.

32 "Everyone was doing covers": David Bedford, *The Fab One Hundred and Four* (Deerfield, IL: Dalton Watson Fine Books, 2013), 359.

32 "When you see Rod Stewart today": Author interview.

33 "Each one was a showman": *triumphpc.com/mersey-beat/archives.*

33 "He had a pair of gold lamé shorts": *Rory Storm* documentary, youtube.com.

33 "He was very fit and": *triumphpc.com/mersey-beat/archives.com.*

33 "no sissy! I just happen to like trinkets." *NME,* August 23, 1963.

34 "Ringo Starr always seemed": *triumphpc.com/mersey-beat/archives.com.*

35 "His music always came first": *sentstarr.tripod.com/beatlegirls/gerry.html.*

35 They began their set with: *triumphpc.com/mersey-beat/archives.com*.

36 "It could stand for 'Rory Storm' or 'Ringo Starr'": Andy Babiuk, *Beatles Gear: All the Fab Four's Instruments from Stage to Studio* (Montclair, New Jersey: Backbeat Books), 70.

36 "Ringo was the lazy one": *triumphpc.com/mersey-beat*.

36 "I can't go around the kit": *Modern Drummer*, January 1981.

37 "like the black hole of Calcutta": Davies, 76.

38 "I was trying to knock off": Davies, 79.

39 "The only person": Babiuk, 35.

40 "He had sort of one style": *Modern Drummer*.

40 Due to their ability: *triumph.com/mersey-beat*.

41 "We'd gone on holiday there": Author interview.

41 "We went in Rory's car": Author interview.

41 "Well, I was only sixteen": Author interview.

42 Guests included Gerry & The Pacemakers: Davies, 150.

42 We were making . . . not great money": *Modern Drummer*, January 1981.

42 "He happened to be": Davies, 249.

43 "He was a notch above": *Ottawa Beatles site* (February 16, 2002).

43 "The Beatles were playing": Babiuk, 64.

45 "I got up on stage": Babiuk, 62.

46 "There were different campers every week": Bob Spitz, *The Beatles: The Biography* (New York: Little, Brown, 2005), 327.

CHAPTER 4

49 "Pete had never quite been": Mark Lewisohn, *The Complete Beatles Recording Sessions* (New York: Sterling Publishing, 2013), 6.

49 "Paul was showing Pete": Bob Spitz, *The Beatles: The Biography* (New York: Little, Brown, 2005), 326.

51 where the group was mobbed: Philip Norman, *Shout: The Beatles In Their Generation* (New York: Touchstone, 2003), 170.

51 "Ringo had one end": Spitz, 327.

51 The first part of the show: *triumphpc.com/mersey-beat*.

53 "TV and films were a possibility": Lewisohn, 6.

54 "They had a recording contract": *triumphpc.com/mersey-beat*.

55 "Once I was home": Pete Best and Patrick Doncaster, *Beatle! The Pete Best Story* (Medford, NJ: Plexus Publishing, 1994), 167.

55 "I wouldn't rate Ringo as a better drummer": *triumphpc.com/mersey-beat*.

55 "Technically Ringo was a better drummer": Author interview.

55 "Brian asked me to join": David Bedford, *The Fab One Hundred and Four* (Deerfield, IL: Dalton Watson Fine Books, 2013), 241.

56 "We were cowards when we sacked him": *triumphpc.com/mersey-beat*.

57"There were riots": *Modern Drummer*.

57 "Ringo is a much better drummer": *triumphpc.com/mersey-beat*.

58 "I fancied him then": Tony Barrow, *John, Paul, George, and Me: The Real Beatles Story* (New York: Thunder's Mouth Press, 2005), 245.

58 "You belong to every girl fan": Tony Bramwell, *Magical Mystery Tours: My Life with the Beatles* (New York: Thomas Dunne Books, 2005), 76.

58 "I might have been killed": Hunter Davies, *The Beatles* (New York: W.W. Norton & Company, 1985), 154.

58 Maureen's time alone with Ringo: Bramwell, 75.

59 "fights and rows among the girls": Davies, 154.

59 In February 1963, she hid under the blanket: Bramwell, 155.

CHAPTER 5

61 "He couldn't do a roll": Hunter Davies, *The Beatles* (New York: W.W. Norton & Company, 1985), 163.

61 "I've a feeling that Paul": Mark Lewisohn, *The Complete Beatles Recording Sessions* (New York: Sterling Publishing, 2013), 18.

62 "On all these Lita Roza, Alma Cogan records: Lewisohn, 6.

62 "Andy was the kind of drummer": Davies, 163.

62 "A lot of the time": Author interview.

62 "I was nervous and terrified": Davies, 163.

63 "He had only just joined the group": nj.com (March 11, 2011).

63 "The other bloke": Davies, 163.

63 "I didn't realize": Paul McCartney/George Martin interview, YouTube.com, 2013.

64 "Look at what that bloody drummer": Geoff Emerick and Howard Massey: *Here, There and Everywhere* (New York: Gotham Books), 53.

65 "I didn't think it was all that brilliant": Davies, 164.

65 "too amateurish": Bob Spitz, *The Beatles: The Biography* (New York: Little, Brown, 2005), 356.

65 His screaming awoke his father: Davies, 163.

66 "He wasn't too much of a challenge": Author interview.

66 "I became a drummer": Bill Harry, *The Ringo Starr Encyclopedia* (London: Virgin Books, 2004), 180.

66 "joining a new class": *Melody Maker*, November 1964.

66 "Ringo found his chronic lack": Author interview.

66 "He let his backbeat speak for itself": Tony Barrow, *John, Paul, George, and Me: The Real Beatles Story* (New York: Thunder's Mouth Press, 2005), 59.

67 "I think he worked hard": Barrow, 59.

67 "Ringo wasn't especially moody": Emerick, 102.

67 "He told me, 'Pete was a good drummer. Ringo is a good Beatle.'": Author interview.

68 "The focus was always on John and Paul": Max Weinberg and Robert Santelli, *The Big Beat: Conversations with Rock's Greatest Drummers* (New York: Billboard Books, 1984).

69 And something called "Tip of My Tongue": Lewisohn, 23.

69 "Drummer Ringo Starr had just cause": *triumphpc.com/mersey-beat/archives*.

69 "They all saw this pop thing coming": Author interview.

70 "It's obvious from the first picture": Author interview.

CHAPTER 6

73 "musically and visually the most accomplished group": Philip Norman, *Shout: The Beatles in Their Generation* (New York: Touchstone, 2003), 190.

74 "One reason I think they'll succeed": Martin Creasy, *Beatlemania! The Real Story of the Beatles UK Tours 1963–65* (London: Ominbus Press, Kindle edition, 2011).

74 "They played their hearts out": Bob Spitz, *The Beatles: The Biography* (New York: Little, Brown, 2005), 369.

75 "the audience was waiting for them": Spitz, 370.

75 "It was a big thrill": Hunter Davies, *The Beatles* (New York: W.W. Norton & Company, 1985), 172.

76 "Best of all, there were four young men from Liverpool": Creasy.

76 "Who are these guys The Beatles?": Creasy.

76 "After Number One, where else is there to go?": Davies, 173.

77 "Elsie felt they were taking him away from her": Spitz, 392.

77 "I always thought Richy": *triumphpc/mersey-beat/archives*.

77 "Mum was frightened": *Woman's Own*, December 1969.

77 "chipping bits off the door": Davies, xxxiii.

77 "When we go home": BBC TV interview (August 28, 1963).

78 "During the four or five years": *triumphpc/mersey-beat/archives*.

79 "The Beatles stole top honors": Creasy.

80 "It was complete mayhem": Creasy.

81 "That was his signal": Geoff Emerick and Howard Massey: *Here, There and Everywhere* (New York: Gotham Books), 104.

81 "Ringo was a nice guy": Author interview.

82 "I did quickly realize": George Martin and Jeremy Hornsby, *All You Need Is Ears* (London: St. Martin's Griffin, 1994), 127.

82 "Ringo had a definite talent and style": Emerick, 104.

82 "Ringo's a damn good drummer": *Playboy*, January 1981.

83 "Ringo's got the best backbeat": Elliott J. Huntley, *Mystical One: George Harrison: After the Breakup of The Beatles* (Montreal: Guernica Editions, 2004), 107.

83 "When we first started": *Viva Magazine*, 1978.

83 "We always gave Ringo direction": *Musician*, May 1980.

83 "What kind of solo was that": Mark Lewisohn, *The Complete Beatles Recording Sessions* (New York: Sterling Publishing, 2013), 28.

84 "I remember Ringo was looking": Andy Babiuk, *Beatles Gear: All the Fab Four's Instruments from Stage to Studio* (Montclair, NJ: Backbeat Books, 2009), 86.

84 "He alone took out a piece of stationery": Babiuk, 87.

84 "There were about three or four options": Babiuk, 88.

85 "It was terrible, following Roy": Davies, 174.

85 "They opened with 'Some Other Guy'": Creasy.

87 "My darling, dear, delightful Ringo": *Good Old Freda*, 2013.

87 "Richy came in [the office] one day": Spitz, 410.

87 "He must have thought I was terrible": *Good Old Freda*.

87 "I loved coming here every week": *Good Old Freda*.

88 "I got a raise two weeks later": *Good Old Freda*.

88 When he admitted: *triumphpc/mersey-beat/archives*.

88 "One day a guy called John Foster": *triumphpc/mersey-beat/archives*.

88 Smith also used an electronic device: Emerick, 67.

89 "Scores of hysterical, screaming girls": Emerick, 66.

89 "It would only be for certain numbers": *New Musical Express*, August 28, 1963.

90 "It exploded with a fury": Peter Brown and Steven Gaines, *The Love You Make: An Insider's Story of the Beatles* (New York: Penguin, 2002), 95.

93 "If he couldn't mentally picture [the song]": Spitz, 423.

93 "It was a throwaway": *Rolling Stone*, December 5, 1980.

93 "My first impression of Ringo": Author interview.

95 "There were no riots": Norman, 209.

96 "I don't like talking": Norman, 212.

97 "A quartet of young men": *NBC News* (November 18, 1963).

98 even a candy called a "Ringo Roll": Norman, 232.

98 "made him look like Brecht being smuggled out of Germany": Norman, 229.

98 "They look like Peter Pans": *Time*, November 15, 1963.

99 "In all our handouts": Davies, 187.

100 "I've come to terms": *Melody Maker*, November 1964.

100 He also agreed to foot the bill: Spitz, 440.

100 "There has been adulation before": *New York Times*, December 1, 1963.

CHAPTER 7

102 "We couldn't believe it": *triumphpc/mersey-beat/archives*.

102 "There's twenty-billion kids out there": *Inner-View* (August 28, 1977).

103 "Three thousand teenagers stood four deep": *New York Times*, February 8, 1964.

104 "He sits with his drums": *The Saturday Evening Post*, March 1964.

106 "You know something very nice happened": *The Ed Sullivan Show*, CBS (February 9, 1964).

107 "He was dumb": *Interview Magazine*, May 1973.

107 "Sure enough, at half past twelve": *Movieland Magazine*, June 1964.

108 "Visually, they are a nightmare": *Newsweek*, February 24, 1964.

109 "asexual and homely" and "75 percent publicity, 20 percent haircut and 5 percent lilting lament": Philip Norman, *Shout: The Beatles in Their Generation* (New York: Touchstone, 2003), 251.

109 "I was a kid running around outside": Author interview.

109 "not too good looking either": Marilyn Crescenzo, "Diary of a Beatlemaniac: 50 Years Later," *The Huffington Post*, July 15, 2014.

110 "The impact and memory": Max Weinberg and Robert Santelli, *The Big Beat: Conversations with Rock's Greatest Drummers* (New York: Billboard Books, 1984).

111 "We were absolutely pelted": Bob Spitz, *The Beatles: The Biography* (New York: Little, Brown, 2005), 477.

111 "Ringo, in particular": Albert Goldman, *The Lives of John Lennon* (New York: William Morrow, 1988).

113 "He seemed to be standing": Hunter Davies, *The Beatles* (New York: W.W. Norton & Company, 1985), 198.

113 "The first time I really noticed": Davies, 200.

114 "We were making records": *Billboard*, July 2014.

116 "We didn't know when we went that day": Author interview.

117 Advance orders in Britain: Mark Lewisohn, *The Complete Beatles Recording Sessions* (New York: Sterling Publishing, 2013), 43.

118 "I've always fancied": *The Mersey Sound*, The BBC (August 28, 1963).

118 "I figure it would be a good business move": *New Musical Express*, August 28, 1963.

118 "Elsie wanted to be close enough": *liddypool.com*, 2009.

119 "It was so beautiful": *16 Scoop: Beatles Complete Story from Birth to Now*, 1965.

120 "It really did not surprise my wife": *rocklopedia.com*.

CHAPTER 8

121 "His fame has brought Ringo": *The Saturday Evening Post*, March 1964.

122 "Not good for him": Bob Spitz, *The Beatles: The Biography* (New York: Little, Brown, 2005), 506.

122 "This could only have happened with Ringo": Tony Barrow, *John, Paul, George, and Me: The Real Beatles Story* (New York: Thunder's Mouth Press, 2005), 132.

123 "Didn't think we could miss you so much": *triumphpc/mersey-beat*.

123 "I thought I could drink": Spitz, 506.

124 "It was a madness": Spitz, 509.

124 "His first words were": Beatles press conference, June 16, 1964, *beatlesinterviews.org*.

124 "I was starting to get a little panicky": Beatles press conference (June 16, 1964).

124 "The boys were very kind": *beatlesinterviews.org*.

126 The Beatles watched the movie: Spitz, 511.

126 "In the first place": *New York Times*, August 12, 1964.

126 "He is the only one of The Beatles": *Daily Express*, July 7, 1964.

127 "emerges as a born actor": *The Observer*, July 12, 1964.

127 "I had lots of films offered": Hunter Davies, *The Beatles* (New York: W.W. Norton & Company, 1985), 337.

127 "Friends kept coming down to London": Spitz, 512.

128 "Ann-Margaret? 'Anned' Margaret and, um, you know": *beatlesinterviews.org*.

128 "*A Hard Day's Night* suggests a Beatle career": *New York Post*, August 12, 1964.

128 "America was now very aware": Spitz, 519.

128 "Most of the Beatlemaniacs liked Ringo": Crescenzo.

129 They socialized with fellow Liverpudlians: Tony Bramwell, *Magical Mystery Tours: My Life with The Beatles* (New York: Thomas Dunne Books, 2005), 118.

129 "for as long as we could remember": Barrow, 143.

129 "Although it was publicized": *San Francisco Examiner*, August 20, 1964.

130 "the grandeur of an F. Scott Fitzgerald novel": Larry Kane, *Ticket to Ride: Inside the Beatles' 1964 Tour That Changed the World* (Philadelphia: Running Press, 2003), 41.

132 "By the time Ringo took his place": Peter Brown and Steven Gaines, *The Love You Make: An Insider's Story of the Beatles* (New York: Penguin, 2002), 141.

132 "The funniest bit that no one else knows": *Late Night with David Letterman*, NBC (June 20, 1989).

132 "instantly revealed The Beatles' pecking order": Al Aronowitz, *The Blacklisted Journalist, bobdylanroots.com.*, 1995.

133 "Until the advent of rap": Aronowitz.

133 "Oh well—the Beatles are here": Crescenzo.

134 "There were good nights and bad nights": Davies, 206.

135 "Oh God—they were beautiful": Crescenzo.

136 "It took about two years": *Evening Standard*, March 11, 1966.

136 John, Paul, George, Ringo, and Brian Epstein . . . "several times over": Jack Doyle, *Beatles in America, 1963-1964*, pophistorydig.com, September 20, 2009.

137 "The drumming is basically": Barry Miles, *Paul McCartney: Many Years from Now* (New York: Holt, 1998).

138 "Ringo—My Ringo": Crescenzo.

139 "I wasn't trying to take advantage": Barrow, 245.

CHAPTER 9

141 "Maureen hated the spotlight": Bob Spitz, *The Beatles: The Biography* (New York: Little, Brown, 2005), 552.

141 "I didn't want hundreds": *Photoplay*, June 1965.

141 "We went to the Ad Lib": Spitz, 552.

141 "Like any northern girl": Peter Brown and Steven Gaines, *The Love You Make: An Insider's Story of the Beatles* (New York: Penguin, 2002), 155.

141 "I didn't know till three weeks": *Photoplay*, June 1965.

142 "Eventually I saw the wedding story": Tony Barrow, *John, Paul, George, and Me: The Real Beatles Story* (New York: Thunder's Mouth Press, 2005), 143.

142 "It's 7:00 AM": Crescenzo.

143 "On The Beatles as a whole": *Photoplay*, June 1965.

143 "But then Maureen and I": *Photoplay*, June 1965.

143 "was stocked with the latest electronic inventions": Brown, 155.

144 "It was not one of the better Lennon-McCartney numbers": Mark Lewisohn, *The Complete Beatles Recording Sessions* (New York: Sterling Publishing, 2013), 55.

144 "It's ridiculous to take a wife": *Photoplay*, June 1965.

146 "Paul's contribution was the way Ringo": *Rolling Stone*, January 1981.

146 "John and Paul could be quite rude": Geoff Emerick and Howard Massey, *Here, There and Everywhere* (New York: Gotham Books, 2007), 103.

146 "Sir Stork en route to the Ringo Starrs": Crescenzo.

147 In 1966, when counter-culture: *Call Me Burroughs: A Life* (London: Twelve, Hachette Book Group, 2014), 450.

147 "The thing about being in Weybridge": Ringo Starr, *Postcards from the Boys* (San Francisco: Chronicle Books, 2004), 9.

147 "Ringo spent money on the house": Brown, 179.

148 "When I walk round": Davies, 327.

148 "I mainly saw John": *Postcards*, 10.

148 "When we don't record, I don't play": Clayson, 135.

148 "There are shelves full of trophies": *Evening Standard*, March 11, 1966.

149 "made some excellent and ingenious": Davies, 328.

149 "What I like would be": *Evening Standard*, March 11, 1966.

150 "It seems that the road from rebellion": Spitz, 557.

150 "In the name of all that's sane": Spitz, 557.

150 "Its meaning seems to be worthless." Spitz, 557.

150 "Ringo, how do you feel": *British Calendar News,* June 12, 1965.

151 "Why expect reason in a picture": *New York Times*, August 24, 1965.

153 "We'd get in the car": *Playboy*, February 1965.

155 wrote later how surly John Lennon was: Spitz, 582.

155 "We didn't jam with Elvis": Interview with Bob Santelli at Grammy exhibit, June 2013, collider.com.

156 "inherited the magnificent Ringo nose": *Time*, October 1, 1965.

156 "Ringo was bitterly disappointed": Robert Ross, *Sid James: The Authorized Biography* (London: J. R. Books, Ltd., 2009), 162.

156 "I was frightened at first": *Late Night Line-up*, BBC2 (December 10, 1969).

156 "I used to be terrified": *Evening Standard*, March 11, 1966.

156 "Nothing made him happier": Spitz, 596.

156 "I used to wish that": Barry Miles, *The Beatles: In Their Own Words* (Larchwood & Weir, Kindle edition, 2013).

157 "he had to be coached and nurtured": Emerick, 103.

157 "I would constantly": Emerick, 103.

160 "No one heard us": *Inner-View* (August 28, 1977).

CHAPTER 10

162 "I took one of Ringo's malapropisms": John Lennon, *The Playboy Interviews* (1980), 153.

162 "There's an early picture": Mark Lewisohn, *The Complete Beatles Recording Sessions* (New York: Sterling Publishing, 2013), 72.

163 "The drumming on 'Rain'": *Rolling Stone*, 1984.

163 "I've never played like that since": *Nightline* (February 19, 2010).

163 "I was thinking of it": Barry Miles, *Paul McCartney: Many Years from Now* (New York: Henry Holt, 1997), 287.

163 "It's wrong but it's great": *Many Years from Now*, 287.

163 "The theme of the lesson": Lewisohn, 81.

163 "Many people have interpreted it": Barry Miles, *The Beatles: In Their Own Words* (Larchwood & Weir, Kindle edition, 2013).

166 "was kicked in the ribs": Tony Barrow, *John, Paul, George, and Me: The Real Beatles Story* (New York: Thunder's Mouth Press, 2005), 197.

168 "The awful thing was": Author interview.

169 "We built a lot of very good houses": Hunter Davies, *The Beatles* (New York: W. W. Norton, 1985), 328.

169 "would wait up until Ringo came home": Cynthia Lennon, *A Twist of Lennon* (London: Star Books, 1978), 134.

170 "When he's recording": Davies, 333.

170 "I like answering the letters": Davies, 334.

170 "He didn't seem to have a lot of ego": Author interview.

171 "He was surrounded by rich people": Author interview.

173 "I never really liked *Sgt. Pepper*": *Inner-View* (August 28, 1977).

173 "would take over the drums": Davies, iix.

173 "inches behind the microphone": Geoff Emerick and Howard Massey, *Here, There and Everywhere* (New York: Gotham Books, 2007), 182.

174 "Ringo's got a great sentimental thing": *Rolling Stone*, April 7, 2011.

174 "to be a character in this operetta": *Many Years from Now*, 310.

174 achieved by removing the bottom heads: Emerick, 149.

175 "He would like to correct it": Davies, 250.

175 "I could have gone on": Davies, 251.

175 "I will say this": Davies, 251.

176 "I think I preferred": Davies, 251.

176 "It's all out of this world": Davies, 252.

176 "If I said give us my money tomorrow": *Life*, September 20, 1968.

176 "All governments are the same": *Life*, September 20, 1968.

177 "just uses a card": *Life*, September 20, 1968.

177 He once borrowed Peter Brown's car: Davies, 332.

177 putting sequins on an old lampshade: Davies, 333.

178 "That's how it is": Davies, 333.

178 "I don't think women": Davies, 333.

178 "I own her, of course": *Evening Standard*, March 11, 1966.

178 "If all four of us": *Life*, September 20, 1968.

179 "I'm not the creative one": Davies, 337.

179 "I do sometimes feel out of it": Davies, 337.

180 "People were comfortable with him": Author interview.

180 "a new and golden Renaissance": Philip Norman, *Shout: The Beatles in Their Generation* (New York: Touchstone, 2003), 331.

181 Ringo's live drum roll: Emerick, 205.

181 "He just stood at the back": Lewisohn, 122.

182 "I rang Maureen in hospital": Davies, 231.

182 "appeared close to tears": Emerick, 212.

183 "made foolish jokes": Peter Brown, *The Love You Make: An Insider's Story of the Beatles* (New York: Penguin, 2002), 248.

183 "In the end, the Maharishi told Ringo": Cilla Black, *What's It All About?* (London: Ebury Press, 2003), 153.

183 "We collapsed. I knew that we were in trouble": *Rolling Stone*, 1970.

CHAPTER 11

186 breaking up fights between the fat ladies: Peter Brown and Steven Gaines, *The Love You Make: An Insider's Story of the Beatles* (New York: Penguin, 2002), 253.

186 "They'd blithely expected": Hunter Davies, *The Beatles* (New York: W. W. Norton, 1985), 235.

186 "Paul would come in": Philip Norman, *Shout: The Beatles in Their Generation* (New York: Touchstone, 2003)358.

186 "I didn't photograph all": *Variety*, January 28, 2014.

186 "It didn't do very well in England": *Variety*, January 28, 2014.

187 "I'd read the book": *New Musical Express*, March 23, 1968.

187 "Ringo Starr waits nervously": *Life*, March 8, 1968.

188 "the movie, directed by Christian Marquand": *New York Times*, December 18, 1968.

188 "An incomprehensible mess": Nile Southern, *The Candy Men: The Rollicking Life and Times of the Notorious Novel Candy* (New York: Arcade Publishing, 2004), 318.

188 "a lot better than you might expect": *Chicago Sun-Times*, December 26, 1968.

189 "Mal, my arm's killing me": *Sunday Times*, March 20, 2005.

190 "Ringo wants to leave": *Sunday Times*, March 20, 2005.

190 "We had to leave the others": Ringo Starr, *Postcards from the Boys* (San Francisco: Chronicle Books, 2004), 17.

193 "We decided to play businessmen": *The Tonight Show*, NBC (May 14, 1968), and *beatlesinterviews.org.*

193 "The front of the Apple building": Author interview.

193 boutique was £200,000 in the red: Brown, 282.

194 "Everything about it seemed": Brown, 282.

194 "I mean, we started it": *Late Night Line-up.*

195 "My association with The Beatles": Author interview.

198 "At one time we used to change together": *Inner-View* (August 28, 1977).

198 "I remember being freaked out by Yoko": *Inner-View.*

198 "There's that famous old saying": *Scene and Heard*, BBC Radio (January 21, 1969).

199 "Ringo probably had the hardest job": Mark Lewisohn, *The Complete Beatles Recording Sessions* (New York: Sterling Publishing, 2013), 151.

199 "Ringo was always sitting in the reception area": Lewisohn, 151.

199 "was often virtually ignored": Davies, 346.

200 "Every time I went for a cup of tea": *Postcards*, 25.

201 "It was just a beautiful moment": *Postcards,* 25.

201 "just beat the shit out of the drums": Bob Spitz, *The Beatles: The Biography* (New York: Little, Brown, 2005), 793.

201 "John and Paul weren't writing together": *The Big Beat.*

202 "Yoko came in. And that was fine": *Inner-View.*

203 "When we were on the roof": Author interview.

204 "You'd pull up to the front of Brookfield": Author interview.

205 "Because of the name Ringo as a Beatle": *Late Night Line-up.*

207 "Go a bit faster, Ringo!": thebeatlesrarity.com, March 26, 2012.

207 "It was just a drag coming into town": *Late Night Line-up.*

208 "ROR are undoubtedly a success": *Times of London*, May 18, 1972.

209 "I suppose it's a bit nasty on the fans": Associated Press, March 27, 1969.

211 "Ringo sent his man backstage": Andy Babiuk, *Beatles Gear: All the Fab Four's Instruments from Stage to Studio* (Montclair, NJ: Backbeat Books, 2009), 248.

211 "an unmitigated disaster": *New York Times*, October 5, 1969.

211 "By now everything was tough": *Postcards*, 31.

211 "John was in a good space": *Postcards*, 55.

213 "I remember John talking about Ringo": Author interview.

213 "I was lost for a while": Paul Du Noyer, *Mojo*, 2001.

213 "I called George Martin": Du Noyer.

214 "We had Quincy Jones": Du Noyer.

214 "The great thing": Alan Clayson, *A Starr Is Born!* Mojo, *The Beatles' Final Years* (Special Edition), 117.

214 "*Sentimental Journey* may be horrendous": *Rolling Stone*, May 14, 1970.

214 "a great album . . . really nice": *The Beatles Today*, BBC1 Radio (March 30, 1970).

214 rose to Number Twenty-Two: Bill Harry, *The Ringo Starr Encyclopedia* (London: Virgin Books, 2004), 312.

215 "The thing was": *Postcards*, 35.

215 "Ringo is fine, and Sellers is finer": *New York Times*, February 12, 1970.

215 "just another flagging satire": *Time*, February 23, 1970.

215 "Ringo Starr's effort": *Variety*, December 31, 1968.

216 "I put my album out": *Off the Record 2.*

217 "The gentlest of The Beatles": Spitz, 852.

217 "I was talking to the office": *Off the Record 2.*

CHAPTER 12

219 what the hell he was doing there: Glyn Johns, *Sound Man: A Life Recording Hits with The Rolling Stones, The Who, Led Zeppelin, The Eagles, Eric Clapton, The Faces* (New York: Blue Rider Press, 2014), 160.

220 "I said, 'I love country music.'": Ringo Starr, *Postcards from the Boys* (San Francisco: Chronicle Books, 2004), 58.

220 "He's one of the finest drummers": *Nashville Scene*, July 10, 2008.

221 "He played that backbeat": Max Weinberg and Robert Santelli, *The Big Beat: Conversations with Rock's Greatest Drummers* (New York: Billboard Books, 1984).

221 "It was all over by eight o'clock at night": *Postcards*, 59.

221 "That kind of thing was a drag then": *Postcards*, 59.

222 "Make no mistake about it": *Rolling Stone*, October 29, 1970.

222 "What is remarkable": *New York Times*, November 22, 1970.

222 "In truth, Ringo poses": *Time*, October 26, 1970.

224 "I enjoyed playing immensely": *The Beatles Diary Volume 2: After the Breakup*, Ebook.

224 "Performing some of the hit songs": *New York Times*, August 2, 1971.

225 "Marc was a dear friend": Paul Du Noyer, *Mojo*, 2001.

225 "A Number One hit": Chris Hunt, *NME Originals: Beatles—The Solo Years, 1970–1980* (NME Originals, Ebook, 2005).

226 "He disappoints me": *Melody Maker*, July 11, 1971.

227 "one of those Spanish Westerns": *New York Times*, April 1, 1972.

228 "We've already got a drummer, thanks": Tony Fletcher, *Moon: The Life and Death of a Rock Legend* (New York: Omnibus Press, 1998), 138.

228 "We really liked him": Fletcher, 293.

228 One Christmas day: Fletcher, 389.

228 "I went to investigate": Johns, 159.

228 "Keith used to be": Ira Robbins interview with Pete Townshend, 1996.

229 "In the end": Fletcher, 491.

229 "His interaction with Ringo": Nancy Lee Andrews, *A Dose of Rock 'n' Roll* (Deerfield, IL: Dalton Watson, 2008), 125.

229 "So he came and laid out": *Postcards*, 66.

229 Bikel also threatened to quit: Fletcher, 296.

230 "Ringo helped too": Fletcher, 297.

230 "Frank was such a nice man": *Postcards*, 67.

230 "At its heart, *200 Motels*": *New York Times*, November 11, 1971.

230 "Most days and all nights": *Variety*, January 28, 2014.

231 "So I needed to do more": Bill Harry, *The Ringo Starr Encyclopedia* (London: Virgin Books, 2004), 92.

231 "As Ringo and I": Harry, 92.

CHAPTER 13

233 "cheating on Pattie a great deal": Peter Brown and Steven Gaines, *The Love You Make: An Insider's Story of the Beatles* (New York: Penguin, 2002), 357.

233 "One thing that we always forget": Author interview.

234 There were reports: Peter Doggett, *You Never Give Me Your Money: The Beatles After the Breakup* (New York: Harper, 2010), Ebook.

234 "I've talked to Ringo a lot": *The Beatles After the Breakup*, Ebook.

234 "put them in the ground": BBC News (May 11, 2011).

234 "comes over all the time": Chris O'Dell, *Miss O'Dell: My Hard Days and Long Nights with The Beatles, The Stones . . . and the Women They Loved* (New York: Touchstone, 2009), 262.

235 "Ringo and George on one bench": O'Dell, 263.

235 "We sat there in silence": O'Dell, 263.

235 "I don't want to get anybody": Brown, 359.

235 having her first affair, choosing Ronnie Wood: Brown, 359.

236 Ringo looked up Chris O'Dell: O'Dell, 267.

236 "I took a deep breath": O'Dell, 278.

237 "I worked with Harry Nilsson": *Inner-View* (August 28, 1977).

238 "How dare you?": Brown, 362.

239 "*Ringo* . . . is an instant knockout": *New York Times*, November 25, 1973.

239 "finding himself on Gerrard Street": *The Beatles After the Breakup*, Ebook.

239 "attitude of an East End cabbie": *The Beatles After the Breakup*, Ebook.

240 "Hilary is someone": Author interview.

240 "is so tall and so thin": Author interview.

240 "I didn't grow up as poor": Author interview.

241 "He was very helpful": Tony Fletcher, *Moon: The Life and Death of a Rock Legend* (New York: Omnibus Press, 1998), 344.

241 "I had written this movie": Author interview.

241 "I knew Ringo could act": Author interview.

242 "I wasn't there": *triumphpc/mersey-beat/archives*.

242 "He was just terrific": Author interview.

242 "with wit and affection": *Time*, December 6, 1974.

242 "David [Puttnam] said Ringo": Author interview.

243 "I couldn't face Beatlemania again": *The Beatles After the Breakup*, Ebook.

CHAPTER 14

245 "They became really, really close friends": Author interview.

245 "Harry had a big ego": Author interview.

245 "Harry and Ringo were very close": Author interview.

246 "Man you're too fucking much": Alyn Shipton, *Nilsson: The Life of a Singer-Songwriter* (Oxford University Press, 2013), 75.

246 "The only reason Harry": Author interview.

247 "So I called Ringo": Shipton, 146.

247 "I just think that if Dracula": Bill Harry, *The Ringo Starr Encyclopedia* (London: Virgin Books, 2004), 316.

247 "I remember I did a movie with Harry Nilsson": Paul Du Noyer, *Mojo*, 2001.

248 "such a headache": Shipton, 148.

248 paid to have his friend's teeth fixed: Shipton, 148.

248 "We had the premiere in Atlanta": *Q* magazine, 1998.

248 "All of them were going through": Author interview.

248 "It was to be a science fiction comedy": *The Guardian*, October 6, 1979.

249 "All the things we'd do": Shipton, 145.

249 took Alice Cooper: Tony Fletcher, *Moon: The Life and Death of a Rock Legend* (New York: Omnibus Press, 1998), 348.

249 "We would drink until nine p.m.": Shipton, 145.

249 Noticeably absent from the lineup: Robert Rodriguez, *Fab Four FAQ 2.0: The Beatles' Solo Years 1970–1980* (Backbeat Books, 2010), 36.

250 It helped the band: Harry, 207.

250 stabbing Playboy bunnies in their rears: Fletcher, 396.

250 "because damage by Mr. Starr and Mr. Moon": Keith Badman, *The Beatles Diary Volume 2: After the Breakup* (London: Omnibus, 2009), Kindle edition.

250 "I was sliding down": Du Noyer.

251 The movie was budgeted: *Billboard*, May 4, 1974.

251 He was unsuccessful: Shipton, 177.

251 "We had the wildest assemblage": Shipton, 171.

251 "It was like the Dirty Dozen": Fletcher, 409.

252 "Of those four revolutionary rock musicians": *People*, May 6, 1974.

252 "the drummer who clubbed artlessly": *People*, April 5, 1976.

252 "At parties in Los Angeles": *People*, December 2, 1974.

253 "For a girl new to the industry": *The JC.com*, August 8, 2013.

253 "We had arranged to go to dinner": Harry, 181.

253 "He may never get it together": *People*, June 28, 1976.

254 "high vaulted ceilings": Nancy Lee Andrews, *A Dose of Rock 'n' Roll* (Deerfield, IL: Dalton Watson, 2008), 73.

254 "There was a party every night": Ringo Starr, *Postcards from the Boys* (San Francisco: Chronicle Books, 2004), 74, 75.

CHAPTER 15

255 "Ringo Starr . . . the last to join The Beatles": *New York Times*, February 16, 1975.

256 "At one time we used to change together": *Inner-View* (August 28, 1977).

256 "That way the whole affair": Chris O'Dell, *Miss O'Dell: My Hard Days and Long Nights with The Beatles, The Stones . . . and the Women They Loved* (New York: Touchstone, 2009), 344.

256 "The poor girl was devastated": Peter Brown and Steven Gaines, *The Love You Make: An Insider's Story of the Beatles* (New York: Penguin, 2002), 363.

256 "She had been in love with Ringo": Cynthia Lennon, *John* (New York: Crown, 2005), 6.

257 signed over Tittenhurst Park: Brown, 364.

257 "The main brain damage": *People*, January 19, 1977.

257 "He was so charming, playful, witty": Nancy Lee Andrews, *A Dose of Rock 'n' Roll* (Deerfield, IL: Dalton Watson, 2008), 45.

258 "John, May and I": Andrews, 45.

258 "She flashed her eyes once": *People*, January 19, 1977.

258 "a man without a country or a home": Brown, 364.

258 "Our world was fast and on the move": Nancy Andrews interview, *beatlelinks.net.*

258 "We'd dance the night away at Regines": Andrews, 201.

259 "Don't worry, it's not my time to go": Andrews, 269.

259 "So I became a clown": *People*, January 19, 1977.

259 "I just became a little ninja": *St. Louis Woman*, March 4, 2009.

259 "Most nights Starr stays home": *People*, January 19, 1977.

259 "The camera was a huge part of our lives": *beatlelinks.net.*

260 "He comes over and he says": *Beatles Stories*, 2011.

260 "There might be three of us": *Radio Times*, October 16, 2007.

260 "I'm no billionaire": *People*, January 19, 1977.

261 The plan backfired: Cherry Vanilla, *Lick Me: How I Became Cherry Vanilla* (Chicago Review Press, 2010), 210.

262 "Well, Paul asked to write a song": Robert Rodriguez, *Fab Four FAQ 2.0: The Beatles' Solo Years 1970–1980* (Backbeat Books, 2010), 37.

262 "From *Goodnight Vienna* it started going downhill": Paul Du Noyer, *Mojo*, 2001.

262 "Ringo just seemed content": Alan Clayson, *Ringo Starr: Straight Man or Joker?* (London: Sanctuary Publishing Ltd., 1996), 246.

262 "For a lot of those albums": *Rolling Stone*, July 9, 1992.

263 "The limousine arrived": Alyn Shipton, *Nilsson: The Life of a Singer-Songwriter* (Oxford University Press, 2013), 217.

264 "It got so hot here": *The Reading Eagle*, September 12, 1976.

264 "feeling vaguely insane": *People*, January 19, 1977.

264 "I went mad": *Postcards*, 84.

264 "And he wiped me off!": Ringo Starr, *Postcards from the Boys* (San Francisco: Chronicle Books, 2004), 80.

265 Ringo and Stevens recorded: Kristofer Engelhardt, *Beatles Deeper Undercover, majicat.com.*

265 "taken care of": Barry Sinkow, *The Count in Monte Carlo* (AuthorHouse, 2008), 182.

265 "One night, when I wasn't in the casino": Author interview.

265 "He was the sassiest": Author interview.

265 "People notice him": Clayson, 243.

266 "I got involved": Du Noyer.

266 "When I really, really got wrecked": *Daily Telegraph*, August 9, 1998.

266 "I felt he threw": Author interview.

266 "the one charmingly low-keyed performance": *New York Times*, October 19, 1975.

267 "Paul was telling me": Author interview.

267 "After the band broke up": *Rolling Stone*, October 7, 1992.

267 "was totally envious of Ringo": Tony Fletcher, *Moon: The Life and Death of a Rock Legend* (New York: Omnibus Press, 1998), 510.

267 "It's probably that we're drunk": *The Kids Are Alright*, 1979 documentary on The Who.

268 "We did talk about it": *People*, January 17, 1977.

268 "As a straight answer—yes": *Inner-View*.

268 "The idea really made sense": *St. Louis Woman*, March 9, 2009.

269 "Less than three months": *robertchristgau.com*.

269 "Nancy wasn't a permanent fixture anymore": Author interview.

269 "Ringo was always renting houses": Author interview.

270 "Keith Moon got the last good part": Author interview.

271 reportedly (and unsuccessfully) tried to buy out his contract: Fletcher, 499.

271 "Mae is still sexy": *New York Times*, February 25, 1977.

271 "If Alice Cooper or Keith Moon": *New York Times*, February 25, 1977.

271 "a disorienting freak show": *New York Times*, June 8, 1979.

271 "a cruel, unnecessary and mostly unfunny": *Variety*, December 31, 1977.

271 The label signed eleven artists: Bill Harry, *The Ringo Starr Encyclopedia* (London: Virgin Books, 2004), 280.

272 "They were primarily radio syndicators": Author interview.

272 "a jukebox musical": Author interview.

272 "He wanted this show": Author interview.

272 "It was an idea": Author interview.

273 "Everybody wanted to be there": Author interview.

273 "He'd fallen on his face": *Postcards*, 77.

273 "I went to the gate": Author interview.

273 "Ringo let me be": Author interview.

274 "The misadventures that follow": *New York Times*, April 26, 1978.

274 "Ringo was very natural": Author interview.

275 "possibly because it showed Keith": Fletcher, 517.

276 "We loved to go to the discos": *beatlelinks.net*.

276 "Once Harry Nilsson and I": *Postcards*, 45.

276 "I said if he wants": Author interview.

277 "His ex-wife Maureen was there": Author interview.

277 "The thing I liked most": Author interview.

277 "this huge guy with dark sunglasses": Author interview.

277 "Because I was stupid": Author interview.

278 "He said, 'Could we just stay'": Author interview.

278 "Everybody in the band": Author interview.

278 "I want you to tell Harry": Author interview.

278 "He kept telling me": Author interview.

278 "Ringo said, 'What are you doing here?'": Author interview.

CHAPTER 16

279 "I'm easy to please": *People*, January 19, 1977.

279 "My intestines closed down": Ringo Starr, *Postcards from the Boys* (San Francisco: Chronicle Books, 2004), 84.

279 "And then I conned my way": *Postcards*, 85.

280 "Zak and Jim Capaldi": *Postcards*, 85.

280 "This is John telling me": *Postcards*, 87.

281 "It was a huge pink old mansion": Author interview.

282 "To my mind": Keith Badman, *The Beatles Off the Record* (London: Omnibus, 2009), Kindle edition.

282 "When we wrote the movie": Author interview.

283 "Their eyes met": Author interview.

283 "Somehow, I sensed": *Weekend*, April 24, 1984.

283 "We were casting the picture": Author interview.

283 "We all drank heavily back then": Author interview.

284 "They kept telling the producers": Author interview.

284 "I saw four guys in suits": Author interview.

284 "to see if any residue came off": Author interview.

284 "Armed Federales surrounded the set": Nancy Lee Andrews, *A Dose of Rock 'n' Roll* (Deerfield, IL: Dalton Watson, 2008), 277.

285 "I arranged for Nancy": Author interview.

285 "After Durango we went to Puerto Vallarta": Author interview.

285 "In order to get a rehearsal": Author interview.

286 "that we said hello": *People*, February 23, 1981.

286 "was first attracted to her by photographs": *Off the Record*.

286 "A lot of journalists": Author interview.

286 "He had been out of The Beatles": Author interview.

286 "He said, 'Don't ask me to shake my head . . .'": Author interview.

287 "Durango was a movie-making town": Author interview.

287 "acted like juvenile brothers": Andrews, 277.

287 "was a bit of a provocateur": Author interview.

287 "I didn't hear from Ringo": Andrews, 277.

287 "It was strange visiting": Andrews, 277.

288 "I was furious": *Off the Record.*

288 "He took good care of Nancy": Author interview.

289 "We had a crash. It's cool": UPI, May 19, 1980.

289 "It was a miracle": *Off the Record.*

289 "Until I met Ringo": *Woman Magazine*, October 4, 1980.

289 "The two of us": *Off the Record.*

290 "Zak plays drums": *Off the Record.*

290 "To be perfectly honest": *London Sun*, September 23, 1982.

290 "drunk and abusive": *London Sun*, December 30, 1982.

291 "He and Yoko came over": *People*, February 23, 1981.

292 "Cyn, John's been shot": Cynthia Lennon, *John* (New York: Crown Archetype, 2010), Kindle edition.

292 "I meant 'drag' in the heaviest sense": *Playboy*, December 1984.

292 "We rented a plane": *Barbara Walters' Most Fascinating People*, ABC (March 31, 1981).

293 "I told her, 'Look, it was you'": *People*, February 23, 1981.

293 "I was given two bodyguards": Hunter Davies, *The Beatles* (New York: W. W. Norton, 1985), 351.

293 "It would have been better": Walters.

293 "We went to see *Popeye*": Author interview.

294 "I always felt safe in America": Davies, 350.

294 "Do you want to stop that now?": Walters.

294 "I called and said": Author interview.

294 "The track was originally written": *Good Morning, America*, ABC (May 7, 1981).

295 "We never actually": Walters.

295 O'Neill was reportedly paid: *People*, October 5, 1981.

295 "I [was] married [to] Faye Dunaway": Author interview.

296 "With just a little help": *Off the Record.*

296 "He happened to say": Davies, 373.

296 "Among the players": *New York Times*, April 17, 1981.

297 "Ex-Beatle Ringo Starr": *Off the Record.*

297 "Since John was killed": *Ottawa Citizen*, March 10, 1984.

298 "Mr. Starr's new album": *New York Times*, November 11, 1981.

298 "Nobody ever accused Ringo": *People*, January 25, 1982.

298 "While they were convincing him": *New York Times*, August 2, 1989.

298 "I got angry": *People*, August 25, 1980.

298 "Bottles and punches were thrown": *New York Daily News*, March 30, 1982.

299 "Barbara fell into the trap": *People*, August 28, 1989.

299 "Every couple of months": *People*, August 28, 1989.

299 "I lived that ridiculous myth": *People*, August 28, 1989.

299 "Ringo and I are good friends": *Off the Record*.

300 "So we scrapped the idea": *New York Times*, October 24, 1984.

300 "We loved doing *Daisy*": *Off the Record*.

301 "I was furious": Davies, 355.

301 "You have breaks from that": *New York Times*, August 2, 1989.

301 "Drunks are great talkers": *People*, August 28, 1989.

301 "I've got photographs of me": *The Express*, July 9, 2010.

CHAPTER 17

302 "One Saturday night": Brian Sibley, *The Thomas the Tank Engine Man* (Oxford, England: Heinemann Young Books, 1995).

304 "too big and bossy": Sibley.

304 "I always sort of felt": *Good Morning, Britain*, ITV (October 9, 1984).

305 "I was hiding because": *People*, August 28, 1989.

305 "When I got home": Hunter Davies, *The Beatles* (New York: W. W. Norton, 1985), 358.

305 "We all sleep": *People*, October 14, 1985.

306 "He fits the image": Associated Press, December 12, 1986.

306 "Canandaigua … made the mistake": *New York Times*, October 19, 1987.

307 "Maureen brought no money": *Off the Record*.

307 "Unless or until she asks him": *Off the Record*.

308 "We would send out for wine": Associated Press, August 25, 1989.

308 "We should have noticed": Paul Du Noyer, *Mojo*, 2001.

308 "We started with a couple of": Bill Harry, *The Ringo Starr Encyclopedia* (London: Virgin Books, 2004), 247.

309 "I'm singing real well": Harry, 247.

309 "Alan Pariser called": Author interview.

309 "The other three Beatles": *Memphis Commercial Appeal*, March 7, 1987.

309 "Chips got really mad": Author interview.

310 "I mean all we heard": G. Wayne Dowdy, *On This Day in Memphis History* (The History Press, Amazon Digital Services, 2014), 83.

310 "He was the kindest man": Author interview.

310 "We had a great time": Author interview.

310 "The main thing I remember": Author interview.

311 "My impression of Ringo": Author interview.

311 "They cut a song": Author interview.

312 "It's been sold": *Off the Record.*

312 "an aging pop star": *Off the Record.*

313 "Just think of it": *People*, February 29, 1988.

313 "A lot of people": Author interview.

313 "They understood it": Author interview.

314 "The goal became": Author interview.

314 "to make sure this show": Author interview.

314 "I think they didn't quite know": Author interview.

314 "My first impression": Author interview.

315 "So I went to find": Author interview.

315 "I think the real breakthrough": Author interview.

315 "They really didn't know": Author interview.

315 "Ringo was drinking then": Author interview.

315 "And seated at that table": Author interview.

316 "I went and looked": Author interview.

CHAPTER 18

317 "I came to one Friday afternoon": *The Independent*, October 28, 1995.

317 "Ringo and Barbara had a typical public": Keith Badman, *The Beatles Off the Record* (London: Omnibus, 2009), Kindle edition.

317 "I had a real bad alcohol problem": *Orange Coast Magazine*, June 1992.

317 "We went into rehab": *People*, August 28, 1989.

318 "I landed drunk as a skunk": *People*, August 28, 1989.

318 "I thought I'd gone too far": *Orange Coast Magazine.*

318 "Eight days in": *People*, August 28, 1989.

318 "Until I got to the clinic": *People*, August 28, 1989.

318 "You always think you're witty": *Daily Telegraph*, August 8, 1998.

319 "knew about Ringo's addiction": *Off the Record.*

319 "Since Ringo's announcement": *Off the Record.*

319 "my beloved Britain turned": *Off the Record.*

319 "You get very safe": *People*, August 28, 1989.

319 "I'm still the happy-go-lucky Beatle": *Off the Record.*

320 "I've always got on with kids": *Deseret News*, March 7, 1989.

320 "A lot of things": Author interview.

320 "My wife was pregnant": Author interview.

321 "The setting is an old-fashioned railroad station": *New York Times*, January 28, 1989.

322 "I was always": Author interview.

322 "I waited a few months": Author interview.

323 "I had chosen Billy Preston": Author interview.

323 "I still love to play": *Daily Mail*, May 26, 2011.

323 "Bobby said to me": Author interview.

323 "The great thing": *Off the Record*.

324 "The deal I made with Pepsi": Author interview.

324 "You go right from rehab": Author interview.

324 "I've been thinking about it": *Late Night with David Letterman*, NBC (June 20, 1989).

324 "We did the first rehearsal": Author interview.

324 "I feel good": *Off the Record*.

325 "I was nervous": *New York Times*, August 2, 1989.

325 "After each gig": *Orange Coast Magazine*.

325 "because at the time": Author interview.

325 "I got inspired": Author interview.

326 "It's the better kind": *New York Times*, August 7, 1989.

326 "A lot of celebrities came": Author interview.

327 "I didn't consciously do this": *People*, July 1, 1991.

327 "finally found something": *People*, July 1, 1991.

327 "He wanted to put it on hold": Peter Doggett, *You Never Give Me Your Money: The Beatles After the Breakup* (New York: Harper, 2010), Ebook .

328 "Mr. Starr conceded": *New York Times*, November 19, 1989.

328 "Though Ringo claimed he owed nothing": *Off the Record*.

329 "Sure, there have been times": *Rolling Stone*, July 9, 1992.

329 "This is the first time since": *Rolling Stone*, July 9, 1992.

329 "He's a hell of a fine drummer": *Rolling Stone*, July 9, 1992.

330 "an album that's so sunny and good-spirited": *Entertainment Weekly*, June 5, 1992.

330 "Starr's best: more consistently pleasing": *New York Times*, May 31, 1992.

330 "But people didn't seem to want": Paul Du Noyer, *Mojo*, 2001.

330 "I was disappointed": *New York Times*, July 13, 1995.

330 "His album received": *Off the Record*.

330 "They should really be called": *Off the Record*.

CHAPTER 19

331 He also loaned Harry: Alyn Shipton, *Nilsson: The Life of a Singer-Songwriter* (Oxford University Press, 2013), 277.

331 "Ringo wouldn't even show up": Author interview.

332 "There is no one": Author interview.

333 "from anyone involved": Peter Doggett, *You Never Give Me Your Money: The Beatles After the Breakup* (New York: Harper, 2010), Ebook .

333 "It was great therapy": *Orange County Register*, April 27, 1997.

334 "I just did an interview": *Rolling Stone*, July 9, 1992.

334 "I never met him": *Rolling Stone*, July 9, 1992.

334 "There are reports": *New York Times*, December 30, 1994.

335 "The sad truth is that": *Sunday Times*, January 23, 1994.

335 "Paul McCartney, George Harrison and Ringo Starr: *New York Times*, March 3, 1994.

335 "And if they are not satisfied": *New York Times*, March 3, 1994.

335 "There have been lots of bad feelings": *Record Collector*, July 1995.

336 "So we began talking": *New York Times*, July 13, 1995.

336 "It would be easy": *New York Times*, July 13, 1995.

336 Part 2 finished thirteenth: *Baltimore Sun*, December 3, 1995.

336 ABC estimated that: Associated Press, November 22, 1995.

336 "To call the first film dull": *Evening Standard*, November 26, 1995.

337 sold an estimated 1.2 million copies: Wally Everett, *The Beatles as Musicians: Revolver through the Anthology* (Oxford University Press, 1999).

337 "It really sounds like a Beatles track": *Record Collector*, July 1995.

337 "Recording the new songs": Kenneth Womack, *The Beatles Encyclopedia: Everything Fab Four* (Santa Barbara: Greenwood, 2014).

337 "a happy coincidence": *New York Times*, November 26, 2000.

338 "For me, the poignant tracks": *The Sun*, November 21, 1995.

338 "It was just a matter of timing": Author interview.

339 "Originally we backed off": Paul Du Noyer, *Mojo*, 2001.

339 "And it says": Du Noyer.

340 "The last weeks of George's life": *George Harrison: Living in the Material World* (HBO, 2011).

340 "I definitely learned": Author interview.

341 "Ringo should probably": *People*, April 7, 2003.

341 "Lean and boisterous in tight pants": *Time*, December 12, 2007.

342 "He's always got two fingers in the air": *Time*, December 12, 2007.

342 "twenty obsessive repetitions": Doggett, 334.

342 "I played the Echo Arena": *Daily Mail*, May 26, 2011.

343 "I apologize to those people: *BBC News* (May 25, 2011).

343 "We offered to cut back our chat time": *New York Daily News*, January 22, 2008.

343 he'd been told "numerous times": Associated Press, January 22, 2008.

343 "I'm doing okay": *Prefixmag.com*, July 1, 2008.

344 "To paraphrase John Lennon": *Liverpool Echo*, October 12, 2014.

344 "because of the impact": *BBC News* (May 25, 2011).

344 "Ringo Starr's home": *BBC News* (June 14, 2012).

344 "I brought my family": Author interview.

346 "Yeah, well, don't look at me": *NME.com*, June 17, 2011.

346 "Well, that's up to them": *Daily Mail*, May 26, 2011.

346 "No matter that Ringo's stalwart percussion": *The Guardian*, June 12, 2013.

347 "I'm a drummer": *Daily Mail*, September 23, 2013.

347 "fund, support, participate in": *lotusfoundation.com*.

347 "the most significant drummer": *New York Daily News*, June 12, 2013.

347 "It was in several places": *Rolling Stone*, June 12, 2013.

348 "I truly believe in the David Lynch foundation": *GQ.com*, September 2, 2014.

348 "It's weird to be here": *Los Angeles Times*, January 21, 2014.

349 "I've waited a long time": *Daily Mail*, July 8, 2014.

350 "Ringo possesses the charm, cool charisma": Skechers press release, October 20, 2014.

350 "We have spent fifteen years": *Sunday Times*, September 21, 2014.

351 "L.A. is the right place for us": *Daily Mail*, September 6, 2014.

351 "It'll be nice to be part of history": Hunter Davies, *The Beatles* (New York: W. W. Norton, 1985), 338.

Bibliography

Andrews, Nancy Lee. *A Dose of Rock 'n' Roll*. Deerfield, IL: Dalton Watson, 2008.

Aronowitz, Al. The Blacklisted Journalist, Bobdylanroots.com, 1995.

Associated Press, March 27, 1969; August 25, 1989; November 22, 1995; January 22, 2008.

Babiuk, Andy. *Beatles Gear: All the Fab Four's Instruments from Stage to Studio*. Montclair, NJ: Backbeat Books, 2009.

Badman, Keith. *The Beatles Diary Volume 2: After the Breakup*. London: Omnibus, Kindle edition, 2009.

———. *The Beatles Off the Record*. London: Omnibus Press, Kindle edition, 2009.

Baltimore Sun, December 3, 1995.

Barbara Walters' Most Fascinating People (ABC TV), March 31, 1981.

Barrow, Tony. *John, Paul, George, and Me: The Real Beatles Story*. New York: Thunder's Mouth Press, 2005.

Beatlegirls.net.

Beatlesinterviews.org.

Beatles, The. *The Beatles Anthology*. San Francisco: Chronicle Books, 2000.

Beatles Today, The. BBC Radio, March 30, 1970.

Bedford, David. *Liddypool: Birthplace of the Beatles*. Deerfield, IL: Dalton Watson Fine Books, 2009.

Bedford, David. *The Fab One Hundred and Four*. Deerfield, IL: Dalton Watson Fine Books, 2013.

Best, Pete, and Patrick Doncaster. *Beatle! The Pete Best Story*. London: Plexus Publishing, 1994.

Billboard, May 4, 1974; July 2014.

Black, Cilla. *What's It All About?* London: Ebury Press, 2003.

Bramwell, Tony. *Magical Mystery Tours: My Life with the Beatles*. New York: Thomas Dunne Books, 2005.

British Calendar News, June 12, 1965.

Brown, Peter. *The Love You Make: An Insider's Story of The Beatles.* New York: Penguin, 2002.

Chicago Sun-Times, December 26, 1968.

Clayson, Alan. *Ringo Starr: Straight Man or Joker?* London: Sanctuary Publishing Ltd., 1996.

Creasy, Martin. *Beatlemania! The Real Story of the Beatles UK Tours 1963–65.* London: Omnibus Press, Kindle edition, 2011.

Crescenzo, Marilyn. *Diary of a Beatlemaniac: 50 Years Later. The Huffington Post,* July 15, 2014.

Daily Express, July 7, 1964.

Daily Mail, May 26, 2011.

Daily Telegraph, August 8, 1998; August 9, 1998.

Davies, Hunter. *The Beatles.* New York: W.W. Norton, 1985.

Desert News (Salt Lake City, Utah), March 7, 1989.

Doggett, Peter. *You Never Give Me Your Money: The Beatles After the Breakup.* New York: Harper, 2010.

Doyle, Jack. *Beatles in America, 1963–1964.* pophistorydig.com (September 20, 2009).

Dowdy, G. Wayne: *On This Day in Memphis History.* The History Press, Amazon Digital Services, 2014.

Du Noyer, Paul. "The Ringo Starr Interview." *Mojo,* July 2001.

Ed Sullivan Show, The (CBS TV), February 9, 1964.

Emerick, Geoff, and Howard Massey: *Here, There and Everywhere.* New York: Gotham Books, 2007.

Englehardt, Kristofer. "Beatles Deeper Undercover." majicat.com.

Evening Standard (London), March 11, 1966; November 26, 1995.

Entertainment Weekly, June 5, 1992.

Everett, Wally. *The Beatles as Musicians: Revolver Through the Anthology.* New York: Oxford University Press, 1999.

Express, The, July 9, 2010.

Fletcher, Tony. *Moon: The Life and Death of a Rock Legend.* New York: Omnibus Press, 1998.

Goldman, Albert. *The Lives of John Lennon.* New York: William Morrow, 1988.

Good Morning, America (ABC TV), May 7, 1981.

Good Morning, Britain (ITV), October 9, 1984.

goodolfreda.com, 2013.

GQ.com, September 2, 2014.

Guardian, October 6, 1979; June 12, 2013.

Harry, Bill. *The Ringo Starr Encyclopedia*. London: Virgin Books, 2004.

Hunt, Chris. *NME Originals: Beatles—The Solo Years 1970–1980*. NME Originals, Ebook, 2005.

Huntley, Elliott J. *Mystical One: George Harrison: After the Breakup of The Beatles*. Montreal: Guernica Editions, 2004.

Independent (London), October 28, 1995.

Inner-View (radio show), August 29, 1977.

Interview Magazine, May 1973.

"Interview with Bob Santelli at Grammy Exhibit," Collider.com, June 2013.

Johns, Glyn. *Sound Man: A Life Recording Hits with The Rolling Stones, The Who, Led Zeppelin, The Eagles, Eric Clapton, The Faces*. New York: Blue Rider Press, 2014.

Kane, Larry. *Ticket to Ride: Inside the Beatles' 1964 Tour That Changed the World*. Philadelphia: Running Press, 2003.

Kids Are Alright, The (documentary on The Who), 1979.

Late Night Line-up. BBC2, December 10, 1969.

Late Night with David Letterman (NBC TV), June 20, 1989.

Lennon, Cynthia. *A Twist of Lennon*. London: Star Books, 1978.

———. *John*. New York: Crown, 2005.

Lennon, John, David Sheff, Yoko Ono. *The Playboy Interviews with John Lennon and Yoko Ono*. New York: Berkley Publishing Group, 1981.

Lewisohn, Mark. *The Complete Beatles Recording Sessions*. New York: Sterling Publishing, 2013.

Liddypool.com, 2009.

Life, March 8, 1968; September 13, 1968; September 20, 1968.

London Sun, September 23, 1982; December 30, 1982.

Los Angeles Times, November 7, 1988; January 21, 2014.

Martin, George, and Jeremy Hornsby: *All You Need Is Ears*. London: St. Martin's Griffin, 1994.

Melody Maker, November 1964; July 11, 1971; October 2, 1976.

Memphis Commercial Appeal, March 7, 1987.

Mersey Sound, The (BBC TV interview), August 28, 1963.

Miles, Barry. *John Lennon: In His Own Words*. London: Omnibus Press, 2005.

———. *The Beatles: In Their Own Words*. Larchwood & Weir, Kindle edition, 2013.

———. *Call Me Burroughs: A Life*. London: Twelve, Hachette Book Group, 2014.

———. *Paul McCartney: Many Years from Now*. New York: Henry Holt, 1997.

Movieland Magazine, June 1964.

"Nancy Andrews Interview." Beatlelinks.net.

Newsweek, February 24, 1964.

New York Daily News, March 30, 1982; January 22, 2008; June 12, 2013.

New York Post, August 12, 1964.

New York Times, December 1, 1963; February 8, 1964; August 12, 1964; August 24, 1965; December 18, 1968; October 5, 1969; February 12, 1970; November 22, 1970; August 2, 1971; November 11, 1971; April 1, 1972; November 25, 1973; February 16, 1975; October 19, 1975; September 17, 1976; February 25, 1977; April 26, 1978; June 8, 1979; April 17, 1981; November 11, 1981; October 24, 1984; October 19, 1987; January 28, 1989; August 2, 1989; August 7, 1989; November 14, 1989; May 31, 1992; December 30, 1994; July 13, 1995; November 26, 2000.

NBC News, November 18, 1963.

Nightline (ABC TV), February 19, 2010.

nj.com, March 11, 2012.

NME, August 8, 1963; August 23, 1963; June 17, 2011.

Norman, Philip. *Shout: The Beatles in Their Generation*. New York: Touchstone, 2003.

Observer, The, July 12, 1964.

O'Dell, Chris. *Miss O'Dell: My Hard Days and Long Nights with The Beatles, The Stones . . . and the Women They Loved*. New York: Touchstone, 2009.

Orange Coast Magazine, June 1992.

Orange County Register, April 27, 1997.

Ottawa Beatles Site, February 16, 2002.

Ottawa Citizen, March 10, 1984.

People, May 6, 1974; December 2, 1974; April 5, 1976; June 28, 1976; January 19, 1977; August 28, 1980; February 23, 1981; October 5, 1981; January 25, 1982; October 14, 1985; February 29, 1988; August 28, 1989; July 1, 1991; April 7, 2003.

Playboy, June 1965; January 1981; December 1984.

Q Magazine, September 1998.

Radio Times, October 16, 2007.

Reading Eagle, September 12, 1976.

Record Collector, July 1995.

Ringo Starr: Going Home. The Disney Channel, 1993.

"Ringo Starr Meets The Beatles." *Modern Drummer*, January 1981.

Robertchristgau.com.

Rocklopedia.com.

Rodriguez, Robert. *Fab Four FAQ 2.0: The Beatles' Solo Years 1970–1980*. Montclair, NJ: Backbeat Books, Ebook, 2010.

Rolling Stone, May 14, 1970; October 29, 1970; December 1970; December 5, 1980; January 1981; July 9, 1992; October 7, 1992; July 12, 2013.

Rory Storm and the Hurricanes: A Documentary. YouTube.com.

Ross, Robert: *Sid James: The Authorized Biography*. London: J. R. Books, 2009.

San Francisco Examiner, August 20, 1964.

Saturday Evening Post, March 1964.

Scene and Heard (BBC Radio), January 21, 1969.

Shipton, Alyn: *Nilsson: The Life of a Singer-Songwriter*. New York: Oxford University Press, Ebook, 2013.

Sibley, Brian. *The Thomas the Tank Engine Man*. Oxford, England: Heinemann Young Books, 1995.

Sinkow, Barry. *The Count in Monte Carlo*. Bloomington, IN: AuthorHouse, 2008.

St. Louis Woman, March 4, 2009; March 9, 2009.

Sunday Times (London), January 23, 1994; March 20, 2005; September 21, 2014.

Southern, Nile. *The Candy Men: The Rollicking Life and Times of the Notorious Novel* Candy. New York: Arcade Publishing, 2004.

Spitz, Bob. *The Beatles: The Biography*. New York: Little, Brown, 2005.

Starr, Ringo. *Postcards from the Boys*. San Francisco: Chronicle Books, 2004.

Thebeatlesrarity.com, March 26, 2012.

TheJC.com, August 8, 2013.

Times of London, May 18, 1972; June 6, 2014.

Tonight Show Starring Johnny Carson, The (NBC TV), May 14, 1968.

triumphpc.com/mersey-beat/archives.

Vanilla, Cherry. *Lick Me: How I Became Cherry Vanilla*. Chicago: Chicago Review Press, Ebook, 2010.

Variety, December 31, 1968; December 31, 1977; January 28, 2014.

Viva, 1978.

Weekend (TV show), April 24, 1984.

Weinberg, Max, and Robert Santelli. *The Big Beat: Conversations with Rock's Greatest Drummers*. New York: Billboard Books, 1984.

Womack, Kenneth. *The Beatles Encyclopedia: Everything Fab Four*. Santa Barbara: Greenwood, 2014.

Woman's Own, December 1969.

Index